Sad Riddance

Sad Riddance

THE MILWAUKEE BRAVES' 1965 SEASON AMID A SPORT AND A WORLD IN TURMOIL

• • •

Chuck Hildebrand

ISBN: 1539475719
ISBN 13: 9781539475712

Dedication

To Steve Gorczany, 1956-2012
Promise kept, my friend

Table of Contents

Part One

...

CHAPTER 1
Eve of Dysfunction

• • •

THIS IS THE STORY OF the 13th and last season of the Milwaukee Braves. It is also a story about many other endings that took place beyond the baseball diamond at Milwaukee County Stadium.

For Milwaukee Braves fans of every age, and particularly pre-adolescents and teenagers who had come to regard the Braves as their birthright, 1965 was a year of disillusionment that still reverberated 50 years later. The Braves, after arriving in Milwaukee just before the start of the 1953 season, had never come close to a losing season during their 13 seasons in Wisconsin. By leading the major leagues in attendance in each of their first six years as the Milwaukee Braves, they had changed the fiscal landscape of baseball inalterably and prompted a succession of moves by other franchises - including the transfer of the National League's two New York franchises to the West Coast - over the ensuing decade.

Now, in 1965, the Milwaukee Braves were in the hands of a Chicago-based consortium that was eying a vast and virgin professional sports realm - the American South - and the profits it could accrue in a brand-new, futuristic-looking sports plant. The consortium - known variously in Milwaukee as the Rover Boys and the Carpetbaggers, among other less-flattering names - had announced in October 1964, after two years of accusations and denials about its long-term intentions, that it would be moving the Braves to Atlanta in time for the 1965 season. Milwaukee County then obtained a court order barnacling the team to the final year of its lease at County Stadium. As a result, the 1965 Braves thus became the first and only major league team of the 20th century to begin a season *knowing* that the franchise would be located elsewhere the following season. The ownership even changed the franchise's corporate name at midseason, doing business as the Atlanta Braves while it was still playing in Milwaukee.

The financial losses the Braves incurred during their season in limbo were such that ownership three times offered Milwaukee County a buyout in exchange for waiving the lease terms and allowing the team to move to Atlanta *during the season*. This had happened only twice since the beginning of major league baseball in 1876, and never since 1890, when the Brooklyn Gladiators of the American Association (then considered a major league) moved to Baltimore to complete their season after winning only 26 games and losing 73.

To Milwaukeeans and their city, 1965 was a long, lingering and sometimes loathsome farewell, and not only to the Braves. On a broader scale for a city that was only a 90-minute Milwaukee Road train ride from Chicago, it was a year during which the legitimacy of Milwaukee's claim to "major league city" status - seemingly cemented by the Braves' arrival in Milwaukee in 1953 - began to be doubted, both in perceptual and economic terms. Most of the industrial titans that for generations had fueled Milwaukee's growth and employed its citizens were still thriving, but by 1965, their collective growth had reached a plateau and the enormity of their environmental impact was being widely seen as intolerable. It was a year during which Milwaukee, long described as the most segregated city in America, moved closer to black-white confrontation and bloodshed that would manifest themselves in earnest within the next two years. It was a year during which the idyll of youth in one of America's most tranquil states would be shattered by the escalation of what became America's longest and most divisive foreign war.

Meanwhile, both within and beyond major league baseball's long-cloistered temples of unchallenged power, the turmoil that inundated what had been a flagship franchise was seen as a culmination and a reflection of two decades of inept and benign leadership that had forever compromised baseball's century-old position as "America's Pastime." The Braves' departure from Milwaukee became a continuum of litigation that brought baseball within one judicial vote of losing its long-sacred antitrust exemption, which had not been seriously questioned or challenged in a high-level courtroom since 1922. It also left baseball as a sport grappling, sometimes aimlessly and counterproductively, to remain relevant as an industry, especially with the emergence of professional football as the nation's foremost sports avocation and preoccupation.

All of those sub-subjects have been chronicled extensively and well over the past half-century. This book represents an attempt to intertwine them with the tumult of a vigorous and, at one mortifying flash point, violent National League pennant race - in which the doomed Milwaukee Braves were participants for five months - as the backdrop.

The most acrimonious divorce in major league baseball history came only 12 years after perhaps its most joyous and euphoric wedding.

The Braves' move from Boston to Milwaukee had been announced on March 13, 1953, and thousands of citizens, not caring that they were inheriting a team that in 1952 had finished seventh in the eight-team National League, gathered to greet the team three weeks later when it arrived by train from spring training in Florida. On Monday, April 13, at Crosley Field in Cincinnati, Billy Bruton became the first batter in Milwaukee Braves history when he led off the top of the first inning with a single off Reds starter Bud Podbielan. Bruton subsequently scored on a single by left fielder Sid Gordon, and Max Surkont pitched a three-hit shutout and the Braves won 2-0. Surkont, a heretofore-anonymous 30-year-old right-hander, went 9-1 in his first 13 starts of 1953. After he mentioned in passing during an interview that he loved Milwaukee sausage, dozens of crates containing sausage appeared at his front door within days. The story goes that he ate them all, not wishing to offend, and gained so much weight that his pitching was permanently affected. He won only two more games in 1953 and was traded after the season to Pittsburgh, where he went 9-18 and 7-14 the next two seasons and was out of the majors by the end of the 1957 season.

The next day - Tuesday, April 14 - the Braves played their first home game at County Stadium, before a crowd of 34,357 in a ballpark with only 28,111 permanent seats. (Portable seating to increase the capacity had been hurriedly installed after the announcement of the team's transfer.) Bruton hit a home run in the bottom of the 10th off Gerry Staley as the Braves beat the Cardinals 3-2. "When Bruton won that game, it seemed like V-E Day to me," Johnny Logan, the Braves shortstop that day and the regular at that position through the 1960 season, said many years later. "The fans cheered everything we did in those years. It made you try a little harder. Everywhere you went, people wanted to talk baseball. They gave us free cars, milk, bread, dry cleaning, gas. Cops stopped us to talk baseball, not to give us tickets. Some of the teachers taught the alphabet by using our names."

Logan, who was born and had grown up in New York state but had moved to Milwaukee in 1953, resided in the Milwaukee area for the remainder of his life, and died there in 2013 at the age of 87. He was buried in nearby Brookfield.

"The big year was 1957," Logan said. "When we won the pennant, we had a champagne party that lasted until 3 or 4 a.m. I've never seen more people than after we won the World Series. Bob Hazle (a 26-year-old outfielder who emerged from obscurity to bat .403 in 41 games late that season) could have run for mayor. The next year (when the Braves won the NL pennant again and were up 3 games to 1 on the New York Yankees in the World Series before losing the final three games), the people didn't feel we had let them down, because they had respect for the Yanks. (General manager) John Quinn quit after that. The next year, we tied for the pennant (with the Dodgers) and lost the playoff (largely due to an injury to Logan). Then we lost (manager) Fred Haney. Enthusiasm seemed to fall off some then. Maybe the people didn't like the changes. But it (had been) unbelievable to me that Milwaukee would be without major league baseball.

Milwaukee was the backbone of the National League, and (in 1965 it was still) big league."

In fact, baseball arguably never has been bigger anywhere than it was in Milwaukee in 1957. Buck Herzog, the man-about-town columnist for the *Milwaukee Sentinel*, wrote about a Milwaukee woman during the 1950s who was about to give birth to her first child. "The child was delivered," Herzog wrote, "and when a friend visited the new mother at the hospital and asked, 'What time was the baby born?' the woman responded, 'Right after the seventh inning.'"

Twelve and a half years after that 1953 season opener and 2,215 miles to the southwest of Cincinnati, in a city that in 1953 didn't have a major league team and in 1965 had two, the Milwaukee Braves officially ceased to exist. On Sunday, October 3, 1965, at Los Angeles' Dodger Stadium - a baseball Acropolis that indirectly owed its existence to the Milwaukee Braves - on the final day of the major league regular season, Los Angeles pitcher Nick Willhite got the first two outs in the top of the ninth. Braves third baseman Mike de la Hoz then tapped a grounder to first baseman Wes Parker, who stepped on the bag to notarize a 3-0 Dodger victory. The Braves managed only three hits - the last a single by Woody Woodward to lead off the eighth - against six Dodger pitchers, none of whom worked more than two innings because the Dodgers had clinched the National League pennant the day before, and were resting their starting pitchers and most of their other regulars in preparation for the start of the World Series against the Minnesota Twins three days later. The Braves, who had been in first place as late as August 20 and within 1 1/2 games of the lead as late as September 2, finished in fifth place in the 10-team league, 11 games behind the Dodgers. Their record was 86-76, giving them 13 winning seasons in 13 Milwaukee seasons - an achievement that rang hollow to the constituency it abandoned.

de la Hoz, a utility infielder whose 81 game appearances in 1965 represented his highest single-season total of his nine-year major league career, was one of 168 players to wear a Milwaukee Braves uniform in at least one major league game. Those 168 men wove a tapestry as colorful and vivid as their uniforms, which until 1964 were adorned with a gold-and-red tomahawk on the jersey chests and a maniacal-looking Brave on one sleeve. In 13 seasons, they never won fewer than 83 games, and that 83-win season was in 1961, the last year the National League played a 154-game schedule before the New York Mets and Houston Colt .45s were added to the league in 1962 and the schedule was expanded to 162 games. Their regular-season record as the Milwaukee Braves was 1,146 wins and 890 losses for a .563 winning percentage that only the Yankees and Dodgers exceeded during that span. During their first year in Milwaukee, the Braves drew 1,826,397 to set a National League record that they proceeded to expunge the following year, when they drew 2,131,388 - the first of four successive seasons during which the Braves surpassed the 2 million mark. The euphoria peaked in 1957, the year they won the NL pennant and then their only World Series championship, when the Braves drew 2,215,404.

The Braves' total attendance for their first seven seasons (1953-59) in Milwaukee totaled 13,945,569 and they led the major leagues in that category in each of their first six seasons. They finished second in NL attendance in '59 to the Dodgers, who won the World Series (after beating the Braves in a best-of-three NL playoff) and were playing in the Los Angeles Memorial Coliseum - which, with about 90,000 usable-for-baseball seats, had more than twice the capacity of 43,000-seat Milwaukee County Stadium. During those same seven seasons, the Yankees - who won five pennants and three World Series within that time frame, playing in 70,000-seat Yankee Stadium - drew 10,472,506, almost 3 1/2 million fewer than the Braves. The Dodgers, first in Brooklyn and then in L.A., drew 9,375,960 during that same seven-year span. Only the fans of the Cleveland Indians of 1948-50 numerically embraced their team to the extent that Milwaukee's fans later did, and even that was for a much shorter period. Owned by Bill Veeck (whose first baseball property had been the minor-league Milwaukee Brewers in the early 1940s) and playing in 80,000-seat Cleveland Stadium, the Indians drew a then-major-league record 2,620,627 spectators in 1948 as they earned their most recent (as of 2016) World Series championship by beating the Boston Braves. The Indians' attendance dipped to 2,233,771 in 1949, and Veeck sold the club after that season. In 1950, the Indians drew 1,727,464 - a total they did not surpass again until 1993.

During that final 1965 season, the Braves finished last in the National League and 19th among the 20 major league teams in attendance, with a 555,584 total that was barely one-quarter of what they had drawn in 1957. Milwaukee was left without a primary tenant for its taxpayer-financed ballpark, and scant hopes of ever regaining major league baseball in the aftermath of litigation that was still tangled after the Braves had begun play in Atlanta in 1966. The Braves drew 1,539,801 - fewer than they had attracted in any of their first seven years in Milwaukee - in 1966.

They didn't exceed that total until 1982. In 1967, the Braves' attendance dropped to 1,389,222, good for fourth in the 10-team National League. Their attendance didn't rank higher than fourth in the NL again until 1992.

More than 50 years later, memories of the Milwaukee Braves are fogged and ambivalent. With a few exceptions - most notably Logan and Felix Mantilla, a member of the '57 and '58 championship teams who also moved permanently to Milwaukee after his retirement from baseball - few of the Milwaukee Braves maintained ties with the city after the Braves left. The only permanent monument to the team, aside from various recreational facilities that were named after Hank Aaron in the aftermath of his successful quest to break Babe Ruth's career home-run record, is a stone rendering in the parking lot at Miller Park, completed in 2001 on what had been the County Stadium parking lot.

The Braves were in Milwaukee only 13 years, all under absentee and at times hostile ownership, while their replacements, the Milwaukee Brewers, completed their 47th season in 2016 and throughout their existence have been under ownership committed to keeping the team in Milwaukee. The Brewers, at the end of the 2016 season, had been to only one World Series and four postseasons, and Milwaukee's population shrank from 741,324 in 1960 to 594,642 - much of it impoverished - in 2014. Yet the Brewers in 1983 broke the Braves' 1957 single-season attendance record. They had surpassed 2 million every season except two since moving into Miller Park, and have drawn over 3 million three times (2008, 2009 and 2011). In sum, the Braves generally are seen by the current Milwaukee generation as passers-through - abstract vestiges of the time when their grand-parents toiled in the Menomonee Valley industrial plants by day and danced to Frankie Yankovic and Lawrence Welk by night.

Still, there are many of a certain age who remember the Braves' presence rather than their departure and absence. They remember the team for what it brought to a city starving for national identity, and they remember a team that still was able to bestir them even after it descended into mediocrity and then oblivion.

As kids, those people got to see Warren Spahn, Eddie Mathews, Hank Aaron and Red Schoendienst in their Hall of Fame primes, and, if they were old enough, they had experienced the unbridled ecstacy that enveloped an entire state after Eddie Mathews backhanded Moose Skowron's sharp ground ball and stepped on third base for the force play that sealed Lew Burdette's 5-0 shutout in Game 7 of the 1957 World Series at Yankee Stadium.

Despite injuries that cost them important regulars Billy Bruton and Joe Adcock for most of the season, and buoyed by the acquisition of Red Schoendienst to play second base and fill their final gaping void, the Braves had cruised to the NL pennant, finishing eight games ahead of the second-place St. Louis Cardinals, and 11 games ahead of the remnants of the Brooklyn Dodgers, who bade goodbye to Ebbets Field and moved to Los Angeles after that season. Milwaukee was enraptured by the Braves from the day they pulled into the Chicago & North Western railroad station and readied to begin the 1953 season as the Milwaukee Braves. But national media outlets, almost all of which operated from and for viewers and readers from New York and other major population centers on the Eastern Seaboard, questioned without letup the Braves' credentials as worthy usurpers of the Dodgers and Yankees, who had met in the World Series seven times since 1941. Doubt even seeped into the local fan base and media. The Braves' individual talent was unquestioned, but whether they were better than the sum of their parts, as the Yankees and Dodgers had been for almost two decades, was debated right up to the final pitch of that 1957 World Series.

In September 1957, before the Braves won their only World Series title as the Milwaukee Braves, *Sport* magazine printed what it described as "secret ratings," which it claimed were taken directly from the scouting and personnel files of the eight NL teams, to determine the league's best at each position. Three of the Braves' usual position players - second baseman Schoendienst, right fielder Aaron and third baseman Mathews - were rated the best at their positions. Del Crandall was the third-ranked catcher, Joe Adcock and Johnny Logan were ranked fourth at first base and shortstop respectively, and the Braves' pitching staff was ranked second overall to the that of the Dodgers. However, the accompanying story did not indicate whether the "scouting reports" quoted were put together in 1957 or in 1956, and given the fact it ranked the Braves' bench only sixth, it seems likely that the reports were outdated and/or based on East Coast bias. The Braves were ravaged by injuries in 1957, but unknowns like Mantilla and Bob "Hurricane" Hazle played huge roles as the Braves easily held off the Cardinals and Dodgers down the stretch. The story also was more wishful than factual in that it specified Brooklyn starting pitchers Don Newcombe, Sal Maglie and Sandy Koufax as three of the primary reasons the Dodgers had a better pitching staff than the Braves. This might have been true in 1956, when Newcombe (27-7, 3.06 ERA) won both the Cy Young and MVP awards and strong-armed the Dodgers into the World Series virtually by himself, and Maglie - a waiver-wire acquisition from the Indians after a distinguished stint with the Giants - went 13-5, including a no-hitter. But Newcombe, plagued by arm trouble and alcoholism, flat-lined in '57 (11-12, 3.49) and Maglie, whose career ended in the spring of 1959, went 6-6 before the Dodgers waived him in September 1957. Koufax today is considered a rival to Spahn and Lefty Grove for the distinction as the best left-handed pitcher ever, but he hadn't yet corraled his own stuff and was a non-entity during the Dodgers' final three years in Brooklyn. A "bonus baby" who was locked onto the major league roster in 1955 and 1956 when he should have been honing his skills in the minor leagues, Koufax was 9-10 in his three years as a Brooklyn Dodger.

In that same magazine edition - one that featured the Dodgers' Duke Snider on the cover - a story by Irv Goodman outlined a tableau that had manager Fred Haney struggling to hold his job, players on the verge of rebellion and committed more to individual objectives rather than team goals, and a franchise (and a city) overwrought and undermanned against the Dodger team that had overshadowed the Braves since their arrival in Milwaukee. The overriding theme was that of a nervous manager trying to guide a nervous team amid the shrill demands of a nervous city, even though the Braves had taken over first place for good on August 7 and had never been more than 3 1/2 games out of first place all season. But after August 4, and before the magazine edition appeared, the Braves had won 34 of their final 51 games, and then defeated the Yankees in the World Series.

Those memories intersect with another, half-empty-glass legacy that still is associated with the Braves: That they could have - *should have* - done so much more.

The argument goes that with those four Hall of Famers as the engines and a multi-cylinder lineup and a pitching-rotation threesome - Warren Spahn, Bob Buhl and Lew Burdette - that had been virtually intact since the team arrived, the Braves could have and arguably should have played in four straight World Series, and possibly won all four of them. The Braves went into the final weekend of the 1956 season with a one-game lead over the Dodgers, but couldn't hold it, losing two of three to the St. Louis Cardinals in no small part because of a couple of game-saving catches by an otherwise undistinguished Cardinals outfielder named Bobby Del Greco. In 1958 they won the NL pennant for a second straight year and were ahead 3 games to 1 in the World Series before losing the last three games to the Yankees. The following year, they tied with the Dodgers for the title and then lost the first two games of a best-of-three playoff. So if you add just 12 more wins over those four seasons - two regular-season wins and four World Series wins in '56, one World Series win in '58, and one regular-season and four World Series wins in '59 - you have a Braves team with four straight World Series titles. No franchise other than the Yankees had ever done that, and no team, including the Yankees, had done it again as of 2016. If it had happened, there would be no dispute, contemporary or retrospective, about the Braves' status as one of the best teams of all time.

Alas, the Braves got "only" the one World Series and the two pennants, and there were those, then and much later, who felt the team undermined itself while underachieving. Jackie Robinson, who retired from the Brooklyn Dodgers after the 1956 seasons, flatly said: "The Milwaukee Braves lost the (1956) pennant because two or three key players were night-clubbing until 6:15 a.m. while the Braves were in Pittsburgh."

Robinson never elaborated on that statement, and whether - or to what degree - the Braves' proclivity for "night-clubbing" played in a role in some of their Milwaukee disappointments will never be known. By all accounts, the Braves had a penchant for after-hours merriment, and at least one of their best players exhibited symptoms of acute alcoholism both during and after his career, but that hardly made them unique at a time when many MLB players were military-hardened men who came from rural or industrial backgrounds. It was a work-hard-play-hard mentality that was accepted both within and beyond the industry as a by-product of the mental and physical demands made on major league baseball players. The dominant team of the 1950s and early 1960s was the New York Yankees, whose manager from 1949-60, Casey Stengel, had only one road rule for his team: "The only place that's off-limits is the hotel bar, because that's where *I* drink." And even at the time, Yankees like Billy Martin, Mickey Mantle and Whitey Ford were known to do more than a little loosening up after their games.

What *is* known is that from 1960 through 1964, as the Braves attendance dwindled and they sank into the middle tier of the NL standings, lethargy and underachievement became the lenses through which they were viewed. In 1961, in his baseball-season narrative *Pennant Race*, Cincinnati pitcher Jim Brosnan referred to the Braves thusly:

The sight of the 1961 Milwaukee Braves lineup was enough to make a pitcher's arm ache. Apparently the Braves had a mass of muscled batters, an array of graceful fielders, a staff of veteran pitchers, and enough overweaning confidence to crush any impressionable spirit. The Braves also had a manager (Charlie Dressen) who modestly declaimed that, with a little help from his ballplayers, he ought to be a cinch to win the pennant. Yet at the start of our second series of the season with them, we'd beaten them four straight. That could *have made them mad. "How are we going to pitch to them?" I asked Joey Jay* (a pitcher who had spent seven years with the Braves before being traded to the Reds after the 1960 season). *"Don't worry about 'em," he said. "Pitch a good game, they won't beat you. Sure, they'll beat the hell out of you once in a while. But they don't care enough any more. Not like they did four, five years ago."*

Jay had signed with the Braves in 1953 for a $40,000 bonus, one of the largest ever given up to that time, and because the "bonus-baby" rule then in effect required teams to keep high-priced amateur signees on the major league roster for two years, made his debut with the Braves at age 17. Seven years later, he was still more promise than productivity, and the Braves traded Jay and Juan Pizarro, a highly-regarded 23-year-old lefty who had pitched with sporadic success with the Braves for the previous four years, to the Reds for Roy McMillan. The Braves hoped McMillan, one of the best defensive shortstops of that era, would be both a replacement for and an improvement over Johnny Logan, who'd been a starter since the Braves' arrival in Milwaukee, and had played for the minor-league Brewers before that. McMillan and second baseman Frank Bolling, acquired from Detroit, did congeal the Braves' defense up the middle. But the deals did little to slow the Braves decline;

Pizarro, meanwhile, was promptly traded by the Reds to the Chicago White Sox, for whom he was an American League All-Star in 1963 and 1964. The Jay-Pizarro-McMillan trade, and the Braves' real or perceived lack of motivation, reflected the general image of the Milwaukee Braves of the early 1960s after their decline began.

And in October 1964, when the Chicago-based group led by Bill Bartholomay that had purchased the team after the 1962 season finally went public with the truth about its intention of moving the Braves to Atlanta for the 1965 season, the prevailing sentiment among many Milwaukeeans became: Good riddance. As Furman Bisher, sports editor and columnist of the *Atlanta Constitution* from 1950-2009, put it in his book *Miracle in Atlanta*: "If ever a city lifted its skirts and crooked its finger and winked its eye at a susceptible, fan-rejected, unloved baseball franchise, Milwaukee is the guilty party."

Even during the halcyon years, it was written and said more than occasionally that the euphoria of the first seven years was artificial and unsustainable, especially in a market Milwaukee's size. When the Braves first came to Milwaukee, County Stadium crowds were widely characterized by outsiders as being almost as baseball-ignorant as they were large, and the fans' habit in the honeymoon years of cheering even long foul balls by the Braves was ridiculed. After 1959 and the playoff loss to the Dodgers, the team aged less than gracefully and was never adequately rebuilt, especially after general manager John Quinn, who had begun to build the team even before it left Boston, left after the 1958 season to take over direction of the Philadelphia Phillies. Much of the attendance-built wealth that the franchise and owner Lou

Perini had accrued during the 1950s was wasted on "bonus babies" like Hawk Taylor, John DeMerit, Mel Roach and Dennis Overby - all of whom got six-figure bonuses in the pre-draft, what-the-market-will-bear era, but did little or nothing as major leaguers. Ownership and management, went this line of reasoning, ruined the team with bad trades and amateur signings. Some even saw these moves as an attempt to deliberately de-value the team, thereby creating an artificial hardship situation that left them with no choice but to move to Atlanta. The Braves also hired three highly unpopular martinet-managers after the resignation of Fred Haney after the 1959 season, and those managers - Chuck Dressen, Birdie Tebbetts and Bobby Bragan - did nothing to stop the Braves' reveling ways and did much to belittle and antagonize players and fans alike.

Meanwhile, the Bartholomay group lied for almost three years about its long-term intentions - Bartholomay himself famously said a few months after the sale that the Braves would stay in Milwaukee "this year, next year and as long as we are welcome" - and finally tried to break its lease after the 1964 season before a court ruling forced them to comply with the lease's terms and play a final 1965 season in Milwaukee. Then, with the 1965 regular season and the team's obligation to stay in MIlwaukee legally over, the Milwaukee Braves - who had been selling tickets and advertising as the Atlanta Braves in Georgia for more than a year in preparation for the move, and actually played several in-season exhibition games in Atlanta - packed and shipped the last vestiges of their Milwaukee residency. Roger Angell, who in 1965 was writing periodic baseball pieces for the *New Yorker* and later consolidated that work into transcendent baseball anthologies, wrote at the time:

Two ghosts haunted the 1965 World Series - the Yankees (who had finished sixth in the American League that year after winning 16 of the previous 18 AL pennants) *and the Braves. The Braves became the first modern team to move its franchise when they left Boston for Milwaukee in 1953. In the ensuing six years, they won two pennants, set a major league single-season gate record, and regularly enjoyed attendance in excess of two million per year. This same Milwaukee team is now defunct; it has just moved to Atlanta, leaving behind a mixed residue of indifference, bitterness and lawsuits. At the Series this (1965) fall, at least a dozen Eastern fans, sportswriters, and baseball men separately described to me an identical experience - a sudden doubt, a momentary shivery silence, that they had felt when their plane paused in Milwaukee before carrying them on to Minneapolis and the noisy, unquenchable joys of another Series. I, too, had been chilled by that same cold breath at the Milwaukee airport: Perhaps baseball was not, after all, immortal.*

What was it like for those who were in Milwaukee in 1965 and were enveloped by these cascades of emotion and bewilderment as their beloved Braves, having lost three-quarters of their 1957 constituency, toiled through the only court-ordered season of exile in modern major league baseball?

This book will begin with four of their stories. They represent a cross-section of the emotions that were pervasive in Milwaukee during the 1965 season. All are told by men for whom the 1965 Milwaukee Braves would, indirectly, become a springboard to success on virtually every level of their professional lives. Two of these men were born in 1953, the same year the Braves moved to Milwaukee, and both saw the greatness and the demise of the Milwaukee Braves through pre-adolescent eyes that allowed for no gray, only black and white. One story is told by a man who was still in baseball a half-century later, and has a plaque in the Baseball Hall of Fame in Cooperstown, N.Y. The other is told by the man who in 1965, as a 29-year-old car dealer and minority Braves stockholder, did what he could first to prevent and then mitigate the Braves' departure from Milwaukee. Five years later, in 1970, he brought major league baseball back to Milwaukee, buying the effectively-defunct Seattle Pilots in a bankruptcy court and subsisting with a modest bankroll for almost a decade before general manager Harry Dalton forged a contender and, in 1982, came within one win of duplicating what the 1957 Milwaukee Braves had done. In 1992, he became the commissioner of Major League Baseball, and guided the sport through some of its most profound crises since the Black Sox scandal of 1919. Though his 23-year commissionership included some of the sport's low points, it can be said without equivocation that his efforts ensured that only one city, Montreal, would lose major league baseball as Milwaukee had in 1965.

All four were at the final home game the Milwaukee Braves ever played - a game that was, in a lot of ways, a microcosm of the Milwaukee Braves. On September 22 at County Stadium, the Braves battered Sandy Koufax, who only 13 days earlier had pitched a perfect game (the fourth no-hitter of his career) against the Chicago Cubs. This time, Koufax was out of the game in the third inning after giving up six runs, four on a grand slam by Frank Bolling. But the Dodgers rallied to tie the game 6-6, then won it 7-6 in the 11th.

Tom Barrett, who in 2016 was elected to his third term as Milwaukee's mayor with 70 percent of the vote, previously had represented the Milwaukee area in the U.S. House of Representatives for 10 years, and in both houses of the state Legislature before that. In 1965, he was an 11-year-old boy living three blocks west of Washington Park and a few minutes by car from County Stadium. Like most of his friends and many of the adults he knew, he was an ardent Milwaukee Braves fan even though he was fully aware that they would call Atlanta home in 1966 and subsequently. To a greater degree than many of his contemporaries, he remembered, during an interview in his City Hall office, the last year of the Milwaukee Braves with more fondness than rage.

I don't even remember the first time I went to a game, but I grew up three blocks west of Washington Park, so it took about six minutes to get from my home to the ballpark. Tickets, as I remember, were 50 cents for the right-field (grandstand) *extension, the same price as bleacher tickets. I would bet I went to 30 Braves games that year ... it was a place where my parents could send or allow me to go without worrying about safety. I just loved going to the games. I was at a game, a weeknight game very early in the season, and I think paid attendance was 913. I was with my dad ... I remember I'd gotten into a fight with one of my neighbors and my parents wanted to help me feel better. It was a cold, cold night, but I don't remember the cold as much as I remember how few people were in the ballpark. I also remember the very last game* (on September 22). *My dad was to pick us up after the game, and we got a little carried away with the moment. They allowed people on the field after the game and we were running the bases. I remember how angry my dad was ... he'd been waiting for us for 25 minutes when we finally got back to the car. We still loved baseball* (even after the legal contretemps, and the Braves' continued decline, over the previous three years) *and the Braves were our team. The next four years were hard. The White Sox played here* (in 1968 and 1969), *but I never felt like "we want the White Sox here." It wasn't the same. I think a lot of people were very angry. My recollection was that (Milwaukee County) got a state-court decision and the (Wisconsin Supreme) Court reversed it. I've never looked at the decisions, and I will now that you mention it. What would have been interesting is if (the decision) had gone the other way ... the whole question of baseball's antitrust exemption would have gone before the Supreme Court, and who knows what would have happened?*

When I was still in high school, I got a job right away as a Brewers usher when they came here in 1970. So I saw both the first Brewers game and the last Braves game. But I still had so many memories of the Braves. I loved going there. I remember catching a foul ball that was hit by Bob Aspromonte when he was with Houston. I remember my grandparents coming from California and us going to the park to see Stan Musial (who retired after the 1963 season) *play. My grandparents were Stan Musial fans, and that's the first game I remember, going to County Stadium with my grandparents to see Stan Musial play.*

My parents didn't move to Milwaukee until 1950 or so, and they were here when the Braves moved here. My dad was a fan, but not as much as I was. For me it was a matter of our neighborhood. There were a lot of kids. We never did it and it probably would have taken an hour to do it, but we could have walked to County Stadium from our house. It was so unbelievably convenient ... our parents would drop us off and pick us up, and they'd take us early so we could get autographs. We had always gotten Braves autographs, but one night we decided to get some Cardinals autographs. They had an outfielder named Ted Savage, and I believe this was the day he got called up by the Cardinals. (Savage, a powerfully-built but light-hitting outfielder, played for eight clubs, including the 1970 Brewers, during his nine-year major league career. He was acquired by the Cardinals from Pittsburgh before the 1965 season, and played in only 55 games for St. Louis before being sold to the Cubs in May 1967.) *I got his autograph. The next day it was an afternoon game and we were out there in the right-field stands and he was out there before the game, just throwing the ball around. This was before players wore their names on the backs of their uniforms, so nobody knew who he was. I looked at him and I see that's Ted Savage, who'd given me his autograph the previous day. I yelled at him, 'Hey Ted, can I have a ball?' I'm sure he was shocked. Here he is, just 24 hours in the big leagues and some kid already knows who he is! He smiles, comes over and hands me a ball. I've never forgotten that.*

Who were my favorite players? Without a doubt Aaron and Mathews. I batted left-handed and threw right-handed like Mathews. I'd spend hours trying to practice raising my leg like Warren Spahn did and trying to throw like he did. But I loved all the Braves. I still remember asking my dad - it was probably the night they had that game with so few fans - what was going on. "Why is nobody at the ballpark?" He probably said it was because they were going to move at the end of the season, but it didn't really register. They were the Milwaukee Braves, and I felt that, even much later. In 1993 when I was elected to Congress and when I was meeting some of the congressmen from Georgia, I walk into one of their offices and I see this Braves pennant on the wall. Even after all those years, it was still a jolt, seeing that pennant there.

Before the Braves left, my upbringing was Leave It To Beaver, *very much so. There were dozens and dozens of kids who grew up on the street I lived on, just west of where the expressway was. We'd joke about my family having "only" four kids ... some of the other families we knew had five, seven, even 11 kids. It was a very tight-knit neighborhood, all ages. The biggest day of the year was always a summer block party. Two of the kids down the street were in a band and they'd play at that party. My parents had visitors virtually every night. We had lots of good friends. Everybody knew each other. My mom's best friend was Marge Gillespie* (wife of Earl Gillespie, the voice of the Braves from 1953-64 on radio station WTMJ), *and there were times I'd go to the park with her son John. We'd go up to the booth - just to say hello, but it was like we knew this big celebrity because we knew Earl Gillespie. That last year, he'd left the Braves by then and was at Channel 6. Over the years, the urban myth for us was that Bob Uecker had lived in our neighborhood, near Cherry and Galena, but I never got that confirmed. Spahn had a townhouse just into Tosa* (Wauwatosa, which bordered Milwaukee's northwest side). *But no, we didn't know him.*

(On the Braves' departure) *I think it was more of a sense that* (regardless of sentiment) *that it was going to happen. I don't really remember talking to my friends about it other than probably out of sadness that they were leaving, until the very end. We were still caught up in them. I remember Joe Torre I really liked, No. 15, and another I loved was Rico Carty ... he came up in '64 and batted something like .330. He changed his number later, but I think he was No. 43 when he first came up. Wes Covington might have had that number earlier.*

I don't remember much about that pennant race, though I don't remember them being in the hunt at the end. The image (of their departure) that's still in my mind is me running around the bases after that last game. My dad was livid. He was not a guy who got angry very often, but he thought it was crazy that we wouldn't come out of the ballpark. Maybe that's the closing chapter for me: We wouldn't leave the ballpark. We didn't want to have it end. I had grown up loving baseball the most. I still loved baseball the most growing up. I wasn't good enough to play in high school, but I played Little League and in a league called Stars of Yesterday (a Milwaukee recreation-department league with teams named after former Braves and minor-league Brewers) *and things like that. When I was in Congress, they had a baseball game between Democrats and Republicans at RFK Stadium* (in Washington); *now they play it at Bowie* (in Maryland) *at a very nice minor league stadium.*

I became a Braves fan after their heyday, when they were drawing incredible crowds, but for every kid who loves baseball, that was a great treat, a major league team closer to your home than your high school. Fifty cents was very affordable even for us; you never had an assigned seat, and you tried to get there early in time to catch foul balls and talk to players, and then stay as long as you could to get autographs. It was very personal, and it really hurts for an 11-year-old to lose his team. Again, we were lucky that the Lazarus came back with the Brewers. It's amazing ... it shouldn't be, but the Brewers have been here almost 50 years and the Braves were only here 13. There's a lot more people here now who have fallen in love with the Brewers than fell in love with the Braves. I just happened to be here when the Braves were here.

Which team did I follow after the Braves left? Probably the Braves, quite honestly, at least at first. I had this thought that maybe, OK, they made this mistake and they'll realize it and come back. It wasn't really until the White Sox were here (for nine games in 1968 and another 11 in 1969) *that I started realizing, whoa, this is permanent. The thought that we would never have another team just didn't register, even then. Later after the first court decision in our favor, I was think-ing, 'Oh, they'll come back.' Some of what I thought toward the end was unfair in retrospect. I thought Bobby Bragan was a bad manager and a bad guy, but now looking at it through the eyes of an adult, the only thing you really know for sure was that he managed the team at that time. I also remember John McHale* (the Braves' GM during their last six years in Milwaukee). *You felt like you knew about them even if you didn't know exactly who they were.*

I got the job as Brewers usher (in 1970) *because I had ushered at a couple of Packer games at County Stadium the summer before and I think they just called up all those people when the Brewers came here* (during spring training, only two weeks before the start of the regular season). *I was also a ticket taker. I used to root for the games to be long, because they started the night games at 8 then and we got paid a extra dollar if the game went longer than three hours. That was rare then; today, they all do.*

Overall I think the Braves moving was a sort of loss of innocence, but having said that, as I got older, I thought, well, there was a kid in Boston in 1952 who had lost his team too. Through the eyes of an 11-year-old kid, it was bigger than life. I think that went back all the way to the 1957 World Series and all the comments Casey Stengel made about Milwaukee being Bushville and all that. If I remember anything from that far back, it was those comments about Bushville and Milwaukee proving that it was major league. It wasn't really until 1982 that I was able to completely let it go, when the Brewers won; it was a fabulous experience just having a winner here again. But I think it was redemption when the Brewers came. Bud (Selig) *was instrumental in getting the White Sox to play some games here those two years. and his style to this day is to not take no for an answer. He just kept working and working until we got baseball back here.*

I think the Brewers have provided us with so much happiness, it's allowed us to move beyond the Braves, and I think that's great. We bounced back pretty quickly, which I think shows the resilience of this city, but there will always be that love in an 11-year-old boy's eyes. During one of those early games in '65, one of those cold, cold nights, I went with a friend. We were able to sit in some good seats just because nobody was in them and there were hardly any ushers to stop us. It was so cold we'd run out between innings to go into the men's room just to get warm. One inning, it was so cold that we ran into the women's bathroom by mistake! We got out of there in about a second and a half, of course, but that's how much we wanted to be at the game in those days.

We were spoiled. We had a major league team, our own major league team. And I've never forgotten that.

Michael Curley was 12 during the Braves' final season in Milwaukee. Like Tom Barrett, he lived within a five-minute drive of County Stadium, on 46th Street, and his passion for baseball lasted far longer than the Milwaukee Braves did. While many of his contemporaries swore off major league baseball forever after the Braves left Milwaukee, Curley was imbued forever by the game. He attended several games at County Stadium in 1968 and 1969 when the White Sox played 20 home games in Milwaukee. He also attached his emotions to the emerging Chicago Cubs, albeit on a far diminished scale than had been the case with the Milwaukee Braves, and mourned when they were overtaken by the "Miracle Mets" at the end of the 1969 season. Elated by the return of major league baseball to Milwaukee in 1970, he was at County Stadium on April 7, 1970, when the newly-transplanted Brewers conducted their first Opening Day (losing 12-0 to the California Angels). Through 2016, he had been at 47 of the Brewers' 48 home openers, and has held a 20-game season-ticket package since 1980. Michael graduated from the University of Wisconsin-Milwaukee, and began a successful career in the paper industry. He and his wife Connie have three adult daughters - Catherine, Marisa and Sarah - and live in Delafield.

I started going to Milwaukee Braves games in 1959, when I was 6, with my grandfather, Todd Mahoney, my dad and my brother. My grandfather had season tickets and took me to many, many games from '59 onward. Baseball was a large part of my life; it bonded us not only as a family but as a neighborhood. I was part of a group that our parents (affectionately) called the 46th Street Alley Rats, and all of us were Braves fans ... even in 1965 (with the Braves' departure already finalized), that didn't stop us from going. I vaguely remember them winning the World Series in 1957, but I was really too young to understand what it meant.

My grandfather had come to Milwaukee as a young man and had played high school baseball for Marquette (University High), *and one of his childhood friends was George McBride, a Milwaukee boy, who played major league baseball starting in 1901 in Milwaukee* (with the Brewers, who moved to St. Louis and became the Browns in 1902). *He came to the games with us quite often. He was a very kind, gracious gentleman, never condescending at all, and I loved listening to George and my grandfather talk about baseball. He played most of his career (1908-20) with the Washington Senators and was their starting shortstop most of that time behind Walter Johnson, and in 1921 he managed the Senators. He married a local girl and stayed in Milwaukee his entire life (1880-1973). Anyway, he was a very nice man, soft-spoken, and loved baseball. He would tell stories about Cobb, Ruth, Wagner, Mathewson, Walter Johnson, all the greats. Said about Ruth: "Best ballplayer, by far, God ever created. Cobb or Wagner or*

Mays, they couldn't come close." He played with Wagner for part of the 1905 season (when both were with the Pirates), *and he said this about him: "Dominated the game and the National League, like Ruth later did with the American League and the Yankees. Wonderful person. Kind, generous. Second-best player in the history of baseball after Ruth." This was around 1965 ... he was in his early 80s, but he was a spry 80. Thin and lean. Moved well. Full head of white hair. Always wore a suit, with a hat. Both he and my grandfather - this is 1965 - said the game was far harder for the modern hitters than it was when George played. I asked them why. George said the ball fields were generally in very poor shape compared to (1965) fields. Lots of uneven bounces that gave the hitters hits that would not happen* (in 1965). *Both said the gloves players wore then were very small, not much bigger than your hand, so again, the hitters got more hits than they would today. There were no night games where it was much harder to pick up the ball. And there were no Negro players ... their word then. Shorter season with shorter travel distances gave players more time to rest.*

I was raised like many people of my generation ... I had a strong father who instilled core values. Don't lie, don't deceive, and I never wanted to be like those SOBs who did. I tried to live my life accordingly, and not just not lying ... you can play word games to hide your meaning or intent, and I don't do that either. I try to put my cards on the table and be somebody you can depend upon and trust even if they don't like what you're saying. I was born in 1953 at St. Mary's Hospital (now Columbia St. Mary's) *and grew up on the 2600 block of 46th Street right near Washington High and Sherman Park.* (County Stadium's address was 201 S. 46th Street.) *The zoo was at Washington Park then and I have very fond memories of that zoo, the uptown area and the Sherman Theatre. I really think that no kid could have had a better childhood than I did, and I felt blessed by that.*

I think the first real shock of my childhood was the assassination of JFK. I remember the announcement vividly ... the principal came on the speakers at our (Catholic grammar) *school and said, "all children, please get down on your knees and say a prayer; our President has been shot." We prayed for the President and then they let us go home, and that evening we learned that he had died. I was in shock. How could anyone be so evil as to shoot the President of the United States? That was probably my first step into a different life other than the innocent one that I had. The second step was the Braves ... finding out that adults could connive, could lie, that their words could mean nothing.*

I first remember hearing the rumors during the summer of 1963 and asking my grandfather, and he said not to believe the rumors, that they were just rumors and there was no way the Braves would ever leave Milwaukee. At that age, my grandfather's word was gospel, so I didn't think any more about it. Now fast-forward to 1964 ... a lot more rumors. William Bartholomay vehemently denied them. He said, "Where would we go? We bought the team to keep it here and it's going to stay here." He was not as eloquent as Old Lodge Skins in (the 1970 movie) *"Little Big Man," but it was kind of the same thing: "As long as the wind blows and the grass grows and the skies are blue, the land is ours forever." Certainly the point was being made that the Braves would be staying in Milwaukee. And at the end of the 1964 season* (general manager) *John McHale also said the team was staying, so it wasn't just Bartholomay ... McHale was singing the same tune. And then, just like that, the cat was out of the bag. The Brewers were going to leave Milwaukee. It really was an eye-opening experience for me as a child. I was an innocent. I was not cynical. I believed people were good and adults wouldn't lie. It was a huge betrayal. It opened my eyes. It showed me that adults could be sinister, even if I didn't really know the meaning of that word when I was 12. How could they do this? We were the first National League team to draw more than 2 million people, and we'd always supported the Braves and loved the Braves. And I still remember that asshole* (NL president Warren Giles, who was a vocal advocate of the move) *saying, "Milwaukee fans can now get their baseball in Chicago."*

It made me grow up quicker ... I'm not saying that's good, but it made me jaded before my time. When I turned 12, I got a paper route, and I didn't know any swear words before that but I learned them on that route. I knew what an SOB was, and that they (the Braves' decision-makers) *were SOBs. But my grandfather still had season tickets and we still loved baseball, so* (the Braves' imminent departure) *didn't stop us from going. I went to probably 15 games that year. I certainly was at the last one - September 22, 1965, with my grandfather. It was Dodgers vs. Braves. The Dodgers had Sandy Koufax going; they were chasing the Giants and needed the win while the Braves were just playing out the string. They started Wade Blasingame. In the bottom of the second Frank Bolling hit a grand slam off Koufax. In the top of the third, Mack Jones took Koufax deep. Then Aaron hit a sharp single, and Koufax was gone! Torre hit into a double play ... Joe did that often; he once hit into four double plays in one game, and three double plays and a triple play in another. Then Gene Oliver, one of the slowest guys in the history of the game, hit a ball in the gap that rolled to the wall. Willie Davis butchered the play and Oliver gets an inside-the-park home run. It was all downhill after that.* (The Dodgers rallied to tie the score at 6-6 and send the game into extra innings, and won 7-6 in the 11th.) *Just another straw on the camel's back. End of game. End of Milwaukee Braves.*

I guess what I remember most about 1965 was emptiness - how empty the ballpark was almost every night, how empty I felt after that last game when it finally really hit home for me that the Milwaukee Braves were gone forever. During the season it was mostly just apathy. Baseball was still here and there were some diehard fans. We were 12, and I don't think it dawned on us that that we might never have a team again. At the time, looking back, I wanted the Braves to stay (despite their deception) ... I was hoping Milwaukee would win the court fight and force the Braves to stay. But through 63-year-old eyes I see it differently, that it wouldn't have been a good thing either. It was the intent of those owners to leave, and how many more years would we have had left? My second choice was to get the White Sox up here, but we didn't get the White Sox. Baseball was mad at Milwaukee because we didn't go quietly into the night. They were going to make an example of us, and punish us. If you will, maybe it was divine intervention that the Pilots went bankrupt and they had to find a place to play with almost no time (during the spring of 1970). *The Pilots became the Brewers and it wound up being a great love story between the team and the city ... fortunately we had people like Bud Selig and others who worked hard and got us another major league team. We've only had one World Series appearance* (in 1982) *in 47 seasons, while we had two World Series and a world championship in 13 years with the Braves. Even so, I look at the bottom line: We have a team and it's our team, Milwaukee's team.*

During their years as perennial contenders, and even for a few years after that, most of the Braves' regular lineup was as familiar to their fans as their classmates or their co-workers or their wartime platoon comrades. Del Crandall caught, Joe Adcock played first, Johnny Logan played the league's most combative shortstop, and Eddie Mathews careened his way around third base. Hank Aaron was in right field and Billy Bruton was in center, and with those two in the outfield, it mattered relatively little who played left. Warren Spahn, Lew Burdette and Bob Buhl made up the top three in the four-man pitching rotation. (Buhl, whose career was interrupted by a stint as a paratrooper in the Korean War, beat the dreaded Dodgers eight times in 1956.) There were still gaps to fill in 1957, especially after Bruton and Adcock went down with season-ending injuries, but the Braves had the means by which to acquire their missing links, and did so. Red Schoendienst, ransomed from the cost-conscious and California-bound New York Giants, arguably was the best second baseman in baseball at the time, and he filled a void that had vexed the Braves ever since, as the Boston Braves, they had traded Eddie Stanky after the 1949 season. Bob "Hurricane" Hazle, a undistinguished outfielder (before and after 1957) who had been an after-thought acquisition in a deal with the Cubs the year before, was summoned from Triple-A Wichita and hit .403 with seven homers and 27 RBI in just 41 games down the stretch. And Don McMahon, who had signed with the Boston Braves in 1950 and had toiled for seven years in their organization without getting a major league promotion, was called up at the end of June and glued the bullpen. As a 27-year-old rookie, he went 2-3 with a 1.54 ERA and nine saves at a time when the save was not considered an official statistic and was doled out at the discretion of the official scorer at each game.

Most managers in 1957, including Milwaukee's Fred Haney, usually acted on the assumption that even a tiring starting pitcher was a better game-winning bet than any non-starter available. Being able to turn to a "closer" - a job description that didn't come into vogue in baseball for another 30 years - late in a game was an option Haney had not had before McMahon joined the team, and being able to entrust McMahon with a lead decreased

Haney's stress level while lightening the workload of his starters. In 1957, the eight NL teams hit 1,178 home runs and stole only 399 bases (compared to 1968, now known as the "Year of the Pitcher," when the 10 NL teams had 891 HRs and 704 SBs), so keeping the ball in the ballpark late in games against sluggers like Stan Musial, Gil Hodges, Duke Snider, Frank Robinson, Willie Mays, Ernie Banks, Roy Campanella, Del Ennis and Roberto Clemente was central to every team's pennant hopes. McMahon pitched 46 2/3 innings that season without allowing a single home run.

By the time the Braves were playing their 1965 epilogue season in Milwaukee, though, every one of those 1957 Braves paragons except Aaron and Mathews had retired or had been traded or released. It was still a talented team, and in 2016 remained one of only two National League teams (the 2003 Atlanta Braves were the other) to have six players with 20 or more home runs in a season, but 34 of the 37 players who wore Milwaukee Braves uniforms in 1965 offered scant nostalgia to their grieving fans.

There were three exceptions.

During the Milwaukee Braves' farewell game against the Dodgers on September 22, Aaron and Mathews unsurprisingly were bade farewell with standing ovations that increased in volume as the game progressed, and both reacted with acknowledgement that reflected the fact they knew and appreciated the fact they would never lose their deity status in Milwaukee. But Joe Torre, who had only been with the team since 1961, got a similar tribute and was moved to tears in the batter's box.

Fifty years later, Torre remembered that moment as one of the emotional pinnacles of his baseball career. By 2015, he was a newly enshrined member of the Baseball Hall of Fame after a distinguished playing career and his capture of four World Series titles in his first five years as manager of the New York Yankees. But that cold September night a half-century before, and the five seasons he spent in Milwaukee, still were vivid in his mind as he waxed nostalgic for a full hour.

It's been really fun coming back after all this time, seeing those plaques (on the Milwaukee Wall of Honor at Miller Park), seeing the same friendly people. Different generations, but the same friendly people. The memories it has brought back for me ... one was my first major league at bat, at County Stadium. I pinch-hit (on September 25, 1960, against Pittsburgh at County Stadium) *for Spahn on a Saturday afternoon against Harvey Haddix* (who, the year before in a game against the Braves at County Stadium, had retired the first 36 Braves he faced, only to lose 1-0 on an unearned run in the 13th inning). *We were losing by one run in the eighth, and I got a ground-ball single through the middle. I look over to the dugout and Lee Maye was coming in to pinch-run for me. Thank goodness for that, because my legs were shaking so bad.*

Milwaukee was really where I cut my teeth. I was fortunate enough to catch Spahn's 300th win (against the Cubs at County Stadium in 1961). *One thing he had a problem with was getting left-handers out, even though he was a left-hander. I remember this one night at old Busch Stadium* (in St. Louis) *and* (Stan) *Musial comes up. You all know Stan's classic stance* (a left-handed batter, Musial had a stance so closed that it looked as if he were peering over his right shoulder at the pitcher). *I signal for a fastball and Spahn shakes that off, and then he shakes off the slider. Finally he said yes to the curveball and he starts that big beautiful windup he had, and then he decides to drop down sidearm. Usually left-handed hitters will bail out against a pitch like that, but Musial proceeded to hit a line drive right back at Spahn at the area we don't want to think about. Those of you who remember Spahn's windup, with his high leg kick, and because of that kick, he couldn't wear a lot of protection there. Hit him right there. He's lying on the ground, but he gets up, throws to first for the out and lay back down again. At the time, the Cardinals' dugout was on the third-base side. As he crossed back to the Cardinals' dugout, Musial comes up to Spahn, who's still lying there, and says, "You OK, old folks?"* (Musial and Spahn were both 41 at the time.)

My brother (Frank, who was the Braves' regular first baseman in their World Series title year after Adcock was injured) *got to the big leagues in 1956, so as a 16-year-old I got to meet all those guys. When I was a rookie, guys like Spahn and Burdette and Buhl took me under their wings ... they'd take me to movies and stuff. Spahn was wonderful to work with ... he had one game where he never once shook me off the entire game. He was so good that if he didn't want to throw a pitch, he just wouldn't throw it for a strike. He made me look like a genius ... he spoiled the young guys that way.*

When I was over at (Miller Park) *today, I couldn't help but think of some of these stories. Eddie Mathews was my hero. I was a New York Giants fan growing up in Brooklyn, which was kind of a dangerous thing, but when my brother came up here in 1956, I kind of latched onto Eddie because he was everything I wanted to be. He played the game hard. He wasn't always pretty, but he just kept working at it, all the way through his career, especially on the defensive side. He made himself into a very good defensive player ... he was a very passionate player and I loved the way he carried himself. He was our captain ... I still remember the last time I saw him, at the 1998 World Series* (when Torre managed the Yankees to the second of their four World Series titles in five years), *when Bud brought him to New York as a guest. It was an emotional moment.*

Milwaukee has so many friends that will never go away. It all start- ed here for me. I'll always treasure Milwaukee and look back on it with a smile on my face. The friends I made here continued to enrich my life (even after the Braves left Milwaukee). *Bill Steinecke* (his man- ager in Eau Claire in the Class C Northern League in 1960) *had once caught for the House of David* (a touring semipro team noted for the fact all of its players wore long beards), *and that's why the Braves sent me to him that first year in pro ball. Steinecke helped me a great deal with the catching aspect, and Del Crandall and* (Braves backup catcher) *Del Rice both were totally unselfish in helping me once I came up to the Braves. Neither one of them ever considered the fact I was trying to take one of their jobs. They were just interested in helping me get better.*

Such a strange year, 1965. The fans knew the year before that we were going, and we had to stay there that one final year. It was sad. So many loyal fans in Milwaukee ... of course a lot of them didn't come out that year, which was certainly understandable, but that last game was certainly unforgettable. They gave Hank and Eddie standing ovations every time they came up that night, and I almost wanted to be up there applauding and yelling with them because I knew what they meant to Milwaukee. But my last time up, they gave me a standing ovation too. For a minute, I was looking around the ballpark to see who they were applauding before I realized it was me. After all, Hank and Eddie had been in Milwaukee since the team moved there (actually, Aaron didn't reach the majors until 1954, the Braves' second Milwaukee season. Mathews, who made his debut in 1952, was the only Braves player who was with them in Boston, Milwaukee and Atlanta) *and they were the heroes, the two guys the fans had come out that last night to see. They were telling me they appreciated what I'd done, and that meant everything to me, that they thought of me almost the same way they thought of Hank and Eddie. I've never forgotten that.*

You really didn't know what to expect that last night, especially with all that had happened during the year (as the franchise lingered in limbo), *but that night the fans showed their appreciation for all that the Milwaukee Braves had done for them up to that point. That level of loyalty is why the Milwaukee Brewers have become so successful. You know, they went through some very hard times* (from 1970 until their first winning season, 1978), *but they're back. It's just a very healthy franchise and it couldn't happen to a better city. They've taken this team to their hearts here, just like they did with the Braves* (in the 1950s). *One reason the Bartholomay group used to justify moving the team was that they didn't think they could draw a million people in Milwaukee again. So now they're drawing 3 million a year* (in 2008, 2009 and 2011), *and to see this happening in Milwaukee with the Brewers is something special to me.*

Allan H. "Bud" Selig in 2016 had retired only in the sense that he no longer held the position of Commissioner of Baseball for the first time since 1992. Approaching age 82 and retired from office for two years, he was teaching at the University of Wisconsin in Madison, maintained regular hours at the Milwaukee office from which he had ruled baseball during much of his commissionership, had his daily corned-beef lunch at Jake's (a delicatessen on West North Avenue that he has frequented since its opening in 1955), and was working on a book about his perspective and experiences during his tenure as the most powerful man in baseball. To some, he is and will remain the man who in 1994 failed to steer baseball away from the work stoppage that forced the first cancellation of a World Series since 1904, the man who looked the other way when lanky baseball players became record-breaking, home-run-hitting, strike-recovery cyborgs, and the man who essentially filibustered away the efforts of a friend and fellow member of his college fraternity to move the withering Oakland franchise to a proposed home 40 miles south to a far larger, far more affluent market in San Jose. But even Selig's detractors had to acknowledge that baseball prospered financially as never before during his time as commissioner, that it had maintained labor peace over his final two decades as commssioner, that it had taken belated steps to lasso the steroid stigma, and that baseball's mindset was transformed from relocation to reinvigoration when it come to maintaining individual franchises. With Selig as commissioner, only one city, Montreal in 2004, had to go through what Milwaukee - and Selig, as a lifelong Milwaukeean and as minority stockholder in the Braves - had endured in 1965 when Milwaukee lost the Braves. And in 2016, Selig was back where he started: He wasn't Commissioner Selig the power broker or even Owner Selig of the Milwaukee Brewers. He was Milwaukee Bud, just as he had been in 1957 when he began selling Fords alongside his father at Knippel-Selig Ford at the intersection of South 71st Street and National Avenue in West Allis.

I've thought often about my long career, and certainly one of the great moments happened on March 13, 1953, when (it was announced that) *Lou Perini decided to move the Boston Braves to Milwaukee. That first year, and we're honoring Billy Bruton tonight ... Billy hit the home run in the 10th inning of Gerry Staley to win the first (Milwaukee Braves) game ever played here. You think of those 13 years, and my memory of them is still pretty good. They were an amazing 13 years ... you think of the players who played here, all the Hall of Famers. Joe Torre and I were having a conversation the other day about Warren Spahn winning his 300th game, and this is a guy who didn't win a major league game until he was 25, and he wound up winning 363. I think of the legendary achievements of Henry Aaron. I see the Mathews (sons) are here ... what a great player, what a great competitor he was.*

We were lucky. We had 13 years of watching a team that was remarkable. It was a great thing for our city, especially the first six or seven years. It taught me a lot and served me well in the future in terms of what a baseball team could do for a community. Its sociological influence was just enormous ... the Braves transcended baseball, to be perfectly blunt. I can still remember Eddie Mathews' backhanding that ground ball by Moose Skowron (in Game 7 of the 1957 World Series) and realizing that hey, lil' ol' Milwaukee has beaten the mighty New York Yankees. We should have won in '58, too, up three games to one in the World Series, but their achievements were remarkable in every way. It galvanized the entire community. After that, yes, things began to move downward a little. That happens, but Braves management unfortunately didn't respond the way it probably should have. Their leaving was beyond heartbreaking, although it was a two-way street, of course. You can say it was unfair and wrong and a lot of other things, but we learned. Baseball learned.

There's that great photo of (Mathews) and Henry walking down that long runway at County Stadium for the last time, and that picture kind of told the story. Great sadness. We're playing the Dodgers in the last game for the Milwaukee Braves at County Stadium, maybe the last game there forever, for all we knew, at the time. I'm sitting with a couple of my partners - one was Ed Fitzgerald and the other was Ben Barkin.

(Barkin, who died in 2001, was a Milwaukee advertising executive and philanthropist who at one point was voted the nation's best publicist in a poll of 100 newspapers. Fitzgerald's father - the chairman of the Northwestern Mutual Life Insurance Company - probably is best known today for being the namesake of the cargo ship that sank in Lake Superior in 1975, taking with it 29 lives. Gordon Lightfoot in 1976 recorded a song telling the story of the sinking and memorializing the ship's crew. The younger Edmund Fitzgerald was CEO of Cutler Hammer, one of the biggest employers in Milwaukee. He died in 2013. Both were charter member of Teams Inc, the group that throughout the 1965 season tried to convince major league owners that Milwaukee deserved a replacement team. Fitzgerald later served as vice president of the Brewers.)

We drew 12,000 people, which was really pretty good for the last night because everyone was mad. There's also a sadness; this great story was coming to an end and it was stunning. A woman comes up to me and says, "Are you Bud Selig?" I'm thinking, uh-oh, what is she going to say? She was this handicapped woman, and tears were streaming down her face. She says, "Do you know how much this team meant to me? Do you have any idea?" I said, well, I think maybe I do, maybe as much as anybody. She pointed her finger at me - and I never forgot this during the 5 1/2 years we were fighting for a team - and said, "Don't you fail. You're all we've got." I never forgot that woman. She was a manifestation of how important the Milwaukee Braves were to so many people. The fewest games they ever won was 83, and that can win you a division title today. What she said helped get us through some difficult times, getting turned down (for an expansion or transferred team) *by both the National League and the American League.*

It wasn't just the caliber of players ... and even in the 1960s (after the team declined and contended only once, for the first five months of the 1965 season), *boy, you look at it and the talent was remarkable. It began a great baseball legacy. I was fortunate enough for my generation to pick that legacy up and I'm very, very grateful for that. I was thinking the other day about Andy Pafko.* (Pafko, a Wisconsin native and five-time All-Star during a career that began with the Cubs in 1943, was the most frequent starting left fielder for the Braves from 1953 until he retired in 1959. He died in 2013 at age 92.) *He was as nice a human being as you'd ever meet, and he loved Milwaukee. I remember the thrill of all of it, going all the way back to March of 1953 when Herb Kohl* (the future U.S. Senator, and a roommate of Selig's at the University of Wisconsin) *and I stood on Story Parkway. We look down into the valley and here's this beautiful red-brick stadium, and all I could think was, "Oh, my goodness gracious, we're getting a major league baseball team." And you're looking at somebody who'd been going to Wrigley Field and Comiskey Park for 10 or 11 years before that. So there's so many wonderful memories, and I can understand that the Braves are still celebrated and that people are keeping the spirit of that alive. You really had to live through it and see it.*

There's not much more I can tell you except that it was the start of a great baseball tradition in Milwaukee. Well, the (minor league) *Brewers started it, but it really started in April of 1953, and you always hear about what a great baseball town this is ... the way (the*

Brewers) draw is amazing considering the size of the market. (In 2016, Milwaukee was the 39th-largest media market in the country, and the smallest to have a major league baseball franchise.) *The Braves brought a lot of glory to this city and to this state, and so many memories. And I never stopped believing that, even after the Braves left and we thought sometimes that we'd never get another team.*

We thought we had the White Sox bought. Going back to May of 1968, we were in Chicago vying for a National League (expansion) *franchise (for the 1969 season) along with Montreal, Dallas, Buffalo and San Diego. It was reported at the time at one point in the owners' deliberation that Milwaukee had eight of the 10 owners' votes, but it had to be unanimous. The newspapers speculated at the time that it was Bill Bartholomay and* (Philadelphia Phillies owner Bob Carpenter) *who were voting against us. I remember that very well. We had worked for a year and a half to get an expansion team and I visited every own-er, over and over ... in fact we had some of the planning take place right here, at the Milwaukee Athletic Club. I've never said who voted against us - Bill Bartholomay and I are close friends today, but maybe that gives you a little hint. But as I've since learned, Yogi Berra was right when it comes to dealing with owners ... it's never over 'til it's over.*

We're ushered into a room; all the owners are there. Warren Giles (the NL president, who had championed the transfer of the Braves to Atlanta) *had gone to do a press conference, and I'm sitting there, my heart pounding. Walter O'Malley* (the Dodgers' owner and unquestionably the most powerful man in baseball at the time) *gets up, and it's like the Oscars. He says, "The winner is ..." and I see his lips mouthing an M, and for a split second I thought we had it. But he didn't say Milwaukee. He said Montreal. The American League had already expanded* (late in 1967 when it added Seattle and Kansas City, also for the 1969 season) *and at the time we knew the owners weren't happy with Milwaukee because all the litigation and a lot of other things had gone on.*

I walked the streets of Chicago that whole night. To their everlasting credit, Lou Chapman and Bob Wolf (the baseball writers for the Milwaukee *Sentinel* and *Journal* respectively) *followed me all night long. I don't know if they hoped I'd get mugged and they thought they'd have another story, and it was a tough night because i wondered if the dream of bringing baseball back was over. Fortunately by the next morning, I'd taken a shower and settled down a little, and I had to come back here the next day anyway because we had a White Sox-Orioles game at County Stadium that night. Day after that, we just started in again, and for the rest of that year, I thought we had the White Sox. John and Art Allyn owned them, and we had bought the team from Art. Problem was that John and Art got mad at each other, and John wound up buying Art out* (to keep the White Sox in Chicago), *and that ended that.*

That same day (during the summer of 1969) we heard that the Seattle team was in trouble, and I remember Ed (Fitzgerald) *telling me that we had to get out there.*

(Dewey Soriano, the Pilots' president, had been awarded the Seattle expansion franchise even though he was badly undercapitalized and Seattle had no existing major league-caliber ballpark. The Pilots already were deep in debt and had defaulted on their rental payments at Sick's Stadium, the home of the Pacific Coast League's Seattle Rainiers since 1937, and the domed-stadium proposal that had convinced AL owners to give Seattle a team didn't come to fruition until 1977.)

Of course that went on all winter. (Commissioner) *Bowie Kuhn wanted to keep the Pilots in Seattle, and I don't blame him; as commissioner, I had to make, frankly, some of the same kinds of decisions. But they couldn't find an owner in Seattle* (after Soriano turned the team over to the King County bankruptcy court) *and in early March I started getting calls, including one from the president of the AL* (Joe Cronin). *So I said to myself, well, maybe it's going to happen this time.* (Meanwhile, the team went to spring training in Tempe, Ariz., as the Pilots.) *The night of March 31, at 10:15 at night, I got a call from Lloyd Larson, the sports editor of the Sentinel. He even beat my lawyers to the phone. All he said was, "You got it," and hung up the phone because he was on deadline and had to get the story into the next day's paper.*

It was a long struggle, a long way from the Milwaukee Braves. I didn't think so at times in the early years ... the first few years were tough, because there was still a lot of anger at major league baseball in this community. Even I probably didn't understand just how angry they still were. But that disappeared, and hopefully over the years we merged the tradition of the Braves into the Brewers. The night we closed County Stadium (September 28, 2000) *was very dramatic and emotional. A lot of the old Packers* (who played some of their home games at County Stadium from 1953-94) *and the old Braves were there. My dad watched the ceremony from his hospital bed. Del Crandall and Hank and Frank Torre and a lot of other old Braves came. Bob Buhl was very sick, but he came.* (Buhl died on February 16, 2001, and two days later, Eddie Mathews passed away.) *The last two people we introduced were* (Brewers stars) *Paul Molitor and Robin Yount. I remember Del saying to me afterward, "You know, we had a great run here, but these guys have taken over, and that's as it should be."*

On whether Teams Inc had as its primary purpose convincing the Braves to stay or laying the groundwork for another team to come to Milwaukee: *All of the above. When we formed Teams Inc, the first thing we tried to do was buy the Braves, and that didn't do us any good. The front office told us that they weren't selling and they weren't going to stay here. That year we got some insight in terms of how to run a team. Frick just shrugged it off and didn't give us a lot of encouragement.* (Frick, in his last season as MLB commissioner, equivocated through the 1965 season, sometimes encouraging Milwaukee's efforts but more often emphasizing that MLB would expand on its own timetable and terms and that placing a team in Milwaukee wasn't a priority.)

CHAPTER 2

Braves Found

• • •

ON OCTOBER 5, 1957, THE newspapers and electronic media of
the world shrieked the news and implications of the launch of
Sputnik the day before. The beeps from the first man-made satellite as it orbited above and around the earth reverberated in
almost every American ear to a much greater degree than any
other Cold War development except the Cuban missile crisis five
years later.

Except in Milwaukee.

Milwaukee only five years earlier had been known primarily for the beers and gears that flowed off its assembly lines. On
October 5, 1957, though, "Today We Make History!" was the
banner headline in that morning's *Milwaukee Sentinel*, and the
history in question - the first World Series game ever played in
Milwaukee - was the final consummation of a marriage still unprecedented in American sports history in terms of scope and
passion. That *Sentinel* edition carried eight stories on its front
page. All eight were on the World Series - one was a story on
Yankee manager Casey Stengel's wife Edna - and if reportage
reflected readership, the *Sentinel's* editors probably were on the
mark that day.

The Milwaukee Braves, about to play Game 3 of the 1957 World Series after splitting the first two games in New York, were in their first World Series only five seasons after fleeing a Boston market in which the Braves' home attendance had plummeted from 1,455,439 in 1948 to 281,278 in 1952. Lou Perini had owned the franchise since 1943 and was a Boston native whose internationally-known Boston-based engineering firm was a primary contractor for the Toronto Transit Commission, Canada's first subway system, on which construction began in 1949 and concluded in 1954. Once his situation in Boston became untenable, Perini thought the postwar growth of the Canadian city and the opportunity to own a team with a full national constituency made Toronto the ideal location to which to introduce major league baseball and reap huge profits in the bargain. He already knew Toronto was a viable baseball town; the International League's Maple Leafs had drawn 446,040 in 1952 to lead minor league baseball in attendance.

Conversely, opinions within baseball circles were divided in the late 1940s and early 1950s on whether Milwaukee was suitable for a return of major league baseball. Its major league history, while encrusted in an era when baseball was little more than a patent-medicine industry, wasn't promising. Milwaukee had already had four major league teams - the Grays of the National League in 1878, the Brewers of the Union Association in 1884, the Brewers of the American Association in 1891, and the Brewers of the American League in 1901 - but none of the four lasted into a second season. The American League team moved to St. Louis in 1902 and became the Browns, who in turn became the current Baltimore Orioles in 1954.

The American Association's Brewers had led minor league baseball in attendance, with 286,979, in the wartime season of 1943 under the stewardship of Bill Veeck, who had purchased the Brewers in 1941 and made Milwaukee the testing ground for many of the promotional and team-building postulates that later were to transform the Cleveland Indians and Chicago White Sox and make Veeck the marketing paragon that he remained 30 years after his death in 1986. But the Brewers were playing at 11,000-seat Borchert Field - the oldest park in the American Association by the end of the 1940s, and a wooden anachronism four decades after concrete-and-steel ballparks had first come into vogue. The Brewers' best attendance count after Veeck sold them in 1946 was 266,061 in 1949 - the year minor league baseball drew 39,640,443, the highest total it would attract until 1999.

Borchert Field, which dated to 1888 and had been only cosmetically updated since its opening, was at the intersection of North 8th and Chambers streets, on Milwaukee's near north side about five miles from downtown Milwaukee. Like most ballparks of that period, it had to be constructed on a constricted plot of land within an existing neighborhood. The land parcel was rectangular, so Borchert Field was configured along the same lines as New York's Polo Grounds, with absurdly adjacent foul poles and almost unreachable distances to the left- and right-field power alleys. Borchert's plate-to-fence dimensions officially were listed at 267 feet to both corners, 450 to the power alleys, and 392 to dead center, but most players believed the power-alley distances were even greater and the foul-pole dimensions were even shorter. While the Polo Grounds was oval in shape, Borchert Field resembled a wafer, and fans seated on the edges of the main grandstand were unable to see all three outfielders at any one time - one of many inconveniences, the absence of nearby parking being another, with which Brewers fans had to deal in Borchert Park's final years. By the time Veeck bought the Brewers, it was at best substandard and at worst an assault on the senses. Warren Brown of the *Chicago Herald-American* wrote of Borchert Field in the early 1940s: "If anybody were to come out to see what was going on, it would be necessary to go through a fumigating plant after the visit."

Despite the ballpark, the Brewers generally drew reasonably well by Triple-A standards during much of their 50-year stay in the American Association, and had a rich baseball tradition that went far beyond the Brewers heritage. Chico Haines was a player, coach and manager in the Milwaukee-area baseball leagues from the 1930s into the 1970s, and after he stopped playing, he took up a far more grueling avocation - marathon-running. His son John became a renowned amateur golfer, and his daughter Anne spent the 1979 season as Bonnie Brewer, the sidekick of Bernie Brewer, the mascot who slid out of a chalet whenever the Brewers hit a home run at County Stadium.

Chico Haines remembers the period when amateur baseball in Milwaukee was at its zenith:

There was a pretty good group of people who followed the Brewers strongly at Borchert. Of course, it was easy to get to. It was at 8th and Chambers and the trolley ran right by it. We enjoyed going down there. We'd stand outside the fence and look through the knotholes and see the game for nothing. A guy I knew who lived across the street from the (adjacent) *pumping station was a park man at Borchert who helped take care of the baseball diamond, and he'd let me in for free once in a while, and he'd even let me sit in the bleachers sometimes.*

The Brewers had some pretty good hitters; one I remember was Carden Gillenwater, who was a really good outfielder. Another guy we had was Howie Moss; he could hit home runs, and the park was really made for him. Borchert Park made great hitters out of a lot of guys. It was only 258 or whatever it was down the lines so it wasn't a great feat to hit home runs. It was really something watching games there. We enjoyed going out there just to see those guys play. When you were young, you'd see guys play at Borchert, either for the Brewers or in the city and industrial leagues, and if they stayed around for a while you came to like them and follow them.

(Gillenwater and Moss were two of many players of the period who put up prodigious numbers in the high minors but never could adjust to major league pitching. Gillenwater, an outfielder, played for the Brewers in 1947 and hit .312 with 23 home runs and 92 RBI, and played 24 games for the Brewers before being promoted to the Washington Senators the following year. He played 18 professional seasons (1937-54), but was in the majors for only 335 games over five seasons with four teams, batting .260 with 11 homers and 114 RBI. Moss, a third baseman who had been moved to the outfield midway through his career, came to Milwaukee in 1949 at the age of 30. He was a five-time home-run champion in the minor leagues and finished his 13-season professional career with 279 homers, including 53 for the Baltimore Orioles (then in the International League) in 1947 and 33 in 1948 for the same team. He wasn't quite that prolific during his two-plus years with the Brewers, but still was one of the most feared sluggers in the American Association, putting up a .294-29-117 season in 1949 and following with a .285-62-87 season in 1950. His major league career, however, marked him as what would today be called a Quadruple-A player. He played in 22 major league games in 1942 and 1946 with the Giants, Indians and Reds, and got only seven hits in 72 at bats for a .097 average with zero home runs.)

Later, of course, Johnny Logan and Eddie Mathews came in. Billy Bruton turned into an excellent player while he was here ... he was a very good fielder and could run like the devil. Everybody liked Billy Bruton. We enjoyed the whole Brewer team; I think they were fairly popular, especially for a team that was switching. (County Stadium had been completed late in 1952, and during the Brewers' last season, all indications were that either the Browns, Cardinals or Braves would be in residence there when the 1953 season began. However, the Braves didn't announce they were moving to Milwaukee until mid-March of 1953, and the Triple-A Brewers franchise had to be moved on even shorter notice to Toledo. County Stadium was built with the idea that unless and until a major league team arrived, the Brewers would play there.) *We were happy, of course, when we got the Braves. But there were so many guys that we had down at old Borchert Field, both the Brewers and the* (amateur) *players we had down there, especially when they'd have the Hearst tryouts down there. I didn't really have the time to do as much as I would have liked, because I had a fulltime job by then, but we really enjoyed those tryouts.*

(The Hearst Games, played during the 1940s and 1950s, was a series matching a team of amateur players from New York City against representatives from all the other cities that had papers belonging to the Hearst newspaper chain. The *Milwaukee Sentinel* was a Hearst paper from 1924-62.)

We and our families could walk to Borchert. Even when we didn't watch through the fence, tickets weren't that expensive to begin with ... I believe it cost 75 cents to get in. Some of the players that were coming along (in the Boston Braves system) looked like they would be very good players, and in '57 when the Braves won the pennant, it was like one of our guys had done it.

I went to quite a few Braves games. They were pretty good pretty quick, but it took a while for them to really establish themselves (as a potential World Series winner). *Of course, the Dodgers were just about unbeatable them. Now we see some teams that take forever before they really establish themselves. The guys who were around for all that time did very well.*

(On the baseball climate in Milwaukee before the Braves arrived) *For myself, I don't know anyone who was more into it. We lived right by that filling station, on the corner of Humboldt and Chambers. There were muni leagues, industrial leagues* (at Borchert and at other ballparks throughout the city and county) *and you never missed a game. If you could get there in time and help the park man do the field, you got in for free. We loved it. I can remember even during polio trouble, it didn't stop baseball.*

(Polio outbreaks were not uncommon in Milwaukee in the years before Jonas Salk perfected his vaccine in 1954; in 1952, four children, ages 3 to 17, in one suburban Milwaukee family died of bulbar polio within five days. In early September 1955, after Salk's vaccine had been approved for general use, an outbreak that was described by news outlets as an epidemic hit the city. More than 600,000 doses of Falk's vaccine were rushed to Milwaukee and another 100,000 were sent to suburban areas.

The emergency actions helped bring the outbreak under control before it could fully take hold, and the Salk vaccine subsequently all but eliminated polio in the U.S.)

We followed baseball, every type of baseball, as close as you could follow it, and we loved it. There was a big rivalry between city and county ball teams, and it became kind of a feat to be around when you beat your rival. Even as a kid, you saw these guys play that would be in their early 40s; you went home and you tried to copy everything these guys said and did. We copied the announcers, too. Mickey Heath (the Brewers' play-by-play announcer) brought a lot of popularity to the team; he was top-flight. He had a unique way of saying something ... "It's a long drive to right field, and therrrrrrrrre she goes, out of the park for a home run." We got a kick out of it, and copied it (in casual conversation). *When Earl Gillespie came, he picked up on it. He was a great announcer too.* (Gillespie took over as the Brewers' play-by-play man on radio station WEMP in 1951, moved on to cover the Braves when they arrived in 1953, and stayed until the end of the 1964 season.)

Probably the biggest (amateur) *games were at Simmons Field, at 27th and Oklahoma. Simmons* (named after Hall of Famer Al Simmons, a Milwaukee native who often was called The King of Mitchell Street) *was one of the first parks to have lights, and it had the same home-run distances all the way around, and really good lights. Washington Park came in after that, and Lincoln Park had three fields that we played on. All the good games in the city and industrial leagues were either at Simmons or Washington Park or Lincoln Park, and that's where I played a lot.* (Simmons Park had almost no permanent seating, but had terraces beyond both foul lines that could accommodate several thousand people, and those terraces were packed for important city- and industrial-league games.)

For a city in a climate that didn't allow for year-round base-ball, Milwaukee and environs had a well-established baseball cul-ture and already had produced a number of major league stars in addition to Simmons. Outfielder Oscar "Happy" Felsch is best known today for being a participant in the Black Sox scandal in 1919, but he was an established major leaguer with the White Sox. George McBride played most of his 16-year career with the Washington Senators and was the shortstop behind Walter Johnson during most of that Hall of Famer's pitching career. Ken Keltner, considered by many the best third baseman who isn't in the Hall of Fame, was a Milwaukee native. So was Chet Laabs, an outfielder who had six double-digit home-run seasons during his 11 years in the majors, but is best known for hitting the two most important home runs in the less-than-hallowed history of the St. Louis Browns. Laabs, who had hit only three home runs in the 1944 season before the Browns' season finale, launched two two-run homers out of Sportsman's Park in a 5-2 win over the Yankees that clinched the only American League pennant the Browns would ever win.

One of Chico's contemporaries was Paul Schramka, a Milwaukee native who has the distinction of being the next-to-last Chicago Cub to wear No. 14. Schramka, who played both baseball and basketball at the University of San Francisco and was on USF's National Invitation Tournament championship team in 1949, played in two games for the Cubs in April 1953 before being sent down to the minors. Later that season, Ernie Banks was brought up by the Cubs and was given No. 14 - which, of course, has long since been retired by the Cubs in Banks' hon-or. Another Milwaukee native who achieved major league star-dom was Tony Kubek, the shortstop on the Yankees teams that went to nine World Series in 10 years in the late 1950s and early 1960s. Chico played and coached against both Kubek and his father. The younger Tony Kubek, a Bay View High graduate who signed with the Yankees out of high school in 1954, was the American League Rookie of the Year in 1957. His father, also named Tony Kubek, played in the minors, mostly with the Brewers, from 1931-36.

Harvey Kuenn, a West Allis native who was raised in Milwaukee and played for the University of Wisconsin before signing with the Detroit Tigers, had 2,092 hits during his 18-year career. While with the Detroit Tigers, Kuenn led the AL in hits four times in the 1950s and won the batting championship in 1959 with a .353 mark - earning him only the distinction of being a principal in one of the strangest trades in baseball history. He went to the Indians for Rocky Colavito, who'd won the AL RBI title that same year. Kuenn's career receded after that, but in 1982, he took over as manager of the Brewers midway through the season and led them to their only American League pennant.

Both Chicago teams had large fan followings in Milwaukee, the Cubs perhaps more so because the Brewers had a working agreement wth the Cubs in the 1930s and 1940s. Chico was an exception:

I was a White Sox fan because one of my first heroes was Chico Carrasquel (a four-time All-Star with the White Sox, and one of the first Venezuelan players to make an impact on the American major leagues). He came to the White Sox in 1950, and we'd go down to Chicago just to watch him play. I just loved the way he played and I tried to imitate him; that's why everybody started calling me Chico.

That was a good time to be following major league baseball. There were a lot of excellent players, excellent teams, like the Indians when they had Keltner, whom we liked a lot because we knew he was from Milwaukee. People associated more with the Cubs, but I liked the White Sox and I liked Bob Elson's announcing. We really liked Mickey Heath too. On Sunday nights, if we were playing games on Sundays and we missed the Brewers game, they'd have a scaled-down (re-creation) *broadcast that night. Heath told you what was happening but it wasn't* (in real time).

The Brewers weren't drawing too well until Bill Veeck got here. He did things. I remember he brought in Jackie Price and Max Patkin and everyone got a bang out of those two. (Price was a middling Brewers player who became known as a baseball stunt man. Among many other things, Price could play catch while standing on his head and hit while hanging from a trapeze. Patkin was a human ectoplasm who could contort his body in ways that left baseball audiences helpless with laughter, especially when he got on the base-coaching lines and mocked opposing players. Both went with Veeck to Cleveland when he bought the Indians in 1946, and both toured minor league parks for decades.) *Veeck was a really nice kind of guy. He'd be sitting in the stands or the bleachers and you could go up to him and he'd recognize you and say, "Hi, How you doing?" and talk to you. We always got a bang out of that. He had good teams in Milwaukee, and then of course he had the Cleveland Indians with Keltner, Lou Boudreau, Joe Gordon. Boy, that was an excellent ballclub.* (The 1948 Indians in 2016 remained the franchise's most recent World Series championship team, beating the Boston Braves in six games.)

We even got to play at County Stadium, and that was a thrill ... that's where they always held the state semipro tournament, and the winner always went to Wichita. (The National Baseball Congress tournament, held in Wichita, Kan., starting in 1935, determined the nation's best semipro team, and featured many future and former major leaguers. It is still held, but strictly as an amateur tournament.) *We loved it ... it was such a big deal that (the players' employers, which often were team sponsors) let us out of work and paid our wages while it was going on. You got to play against some great players. There were a lot of them who were ex-major leaguers. We played against* (Enos) *Country Slaughter* (the longtime St. Louis Cardinals and New York Yankees outfielder) ... *he was at the end of his rope by then, but he still hustled and he still gave 100 percent just like he did in the majors. We also played against Tom Seaver; I believe he was on an Army team at the time.* (After graduating from high school in Fresno, Calif., Seaver enlisted in the Marine Crops Reserve and served six months of military duty before enrolling at Fresno City College. He later played at the University of Southern California.) *He played for a team from Alaska* (the Fairbanks-based Alaska Goldpanners) *too, and we played against them a couple of times too. We were lucky to have a good enough team to get to the final four several times. It was nice getting to play against that kind of opponent, and the teams around here were very good. I remember Kubek, both the father and the son. Tony Kubek actually wasn't an established player when the Brewers were here. It took him a couple of years yet. He played in the Bay View area. His dad, of course, was outstanding. You'd find good players all around here; some played in the industrial league and others in the city leagues. It was a great place to grow up and live if you were a baseball player.*

Despite the fact baseball had been played and followed passionately in Milwaukee since before the turn of the century, the Brewers had struggled to stay afloat through Prohibition and then the Depression, both of which hit Milwaukee particularly hard. (The Miller brewing company, subsisting on the sale of non- and quasi-alcoholic products from 1920-33 while Prohibition was in effect, saw its revenue dip from $12,183,065 in 1915 to only $896,386 in 1932.) The Brewers drew only 98,000 during the 1941 season, despite the fact Veeck bought the team at mid-season and began promoting it in earnest almost immediately. When owner Harry Bendinger sold the team to Veeck, the franchise was broke and more than $100,000 in debt, and American Association president George Trautman had taken over operation of the franchise. One of the conditions of Veeck's purchase was that he agreed to assume the team's debts and provide the money to keep the park from being shut down for violations of the city's building, fire and health codes. The ballpark hadn't even been painted since 1924, and in 1944 it endured - barely - a tornado that blew in and through the park during a game, splintering much of the seating area and injuring more than 30 spectators. Attendance had tripled during the Veeck years, but declined again after Veeck sold the Brewers to Oscar Salinger in 1946 (and bought the Indians later that year). At the time Perini began actively shopping his moribund Boston Braves franchise, the Brewers' single-season attendance record of 365,473 in 1927 had remained unchallenged, even by Veeck's teams.

Many traditionalists throughout baseball remained reluctant in 1953 to alter a major league template that had remained un-changed for half a century. Almost every team in professional baseball, including the Boston Braves, had broken franchise at-tendance records in the late 1940s, and at the time, that level of prosperity seemed to reinforce the view that baseball would be best served by leaving the sport's map just the way it was. But by 1953, with attendance falling virtually everywhere and at every level, it was obvious that the stay-put advocates were fighting a losing battle with those who felt major league baseball had to expand and evolve beyond that template.

Even with its new ballpark, though, Milwaukee wasn't the universally-anointed choice as the first city to get a new or transplanted team. Many believed that baseball's most golden opportunities were in the Golden State.

Serious discussion about expansion to California circulated within the baseball establishment as early as the spring of 1932, when John McGraw, about to begin his 31st and last year as manager of the New York Giants, took his team to California for spring training. During one game at San Francisco's Seals Stadium, which had opened the previous year, McGraw - who by that time sometimes watched exhibition games from the stands rather than from the bench - was sitting with Seals owner Charlie Graham in the latter's box seats. A local reporter coaxed McGraw into a brief interview, during which McGraw declared Seals Stadium major-league ready and predicted that someday it would house a major league team. Little could McGraw, who resigned as Giants manager on June 3, 1932, and died less than two years later, have imagined not only that his prediction would come true, but that the team to occupy Seals Stadium would be the same Giants franchise of which he was still a part-owner at the time of his death. The Giants, after moving from New York to San Francisco, played at Seals Stadium in 1958 and 1959 before moving to newly-constructed Candlestick Park for the 1960 season.

The major leagues took a much more tangible step toward planting a flag on the West Coast in 1941, when the St. Louis

Browns stood ready and eager to move to Los Angeles for the 1942 season. The Browns' existence in St. Louis had been an abject one, with the franchise nadir coming in 1935 when the team drew only 80,999 spectators for the entire season. Even in 1940 with new ownership and an infusion of cash, the team's attendance total had increased only to 239,951. The Cardinals' 1940 attendance (324,078 in 1940) wasn't appreciably better, and it had become obvious to everyone in St. Louis that one team or the other would have to leave town at some point. The Cardinals, whose Gas House Gang teams of the early 1930s had won three NL pennants and two World Series, in 1941 still commanded the public imagination in St. Louis, and they had the added advantage of having their games broadcast on 50,000-watt KMOX and an extensive radio network that extended throughout the Midwest and deep into the South, making the Cardinals baseball's first truly regional franchise.

The Browns' owners, Don Barnes and William O. DeWitt, and the other seven American League owners had secretly been laying the groundwork for the move to Los Angeles since the summer of 1941. Sam Breadon, the Cardinals owner, had agreed to pay the Browns $350,000 in L.A. seed money to get them out of town, and Barnes and DeWitt had reached an accord with Cubs owner Phil Wrigley (who also owned the Los Angeles Angels of the PCL) to buy the Angels and Wrigley Field, the Angels' home park, for $1 million. The Southern California version of Wrigley Field was smaller (about 21,500 permanent seats) than its Chicago counterpart, but the parks had been designed by the same architect, Zachary Taylor Davis, and were virtually identical in almost every other respect except cost. Cubs Park, as Chicago's Wrigley Field was known until 1927, was built for only

$250,000 in 1915, while L.A.'s Wrigley Field cost $1.5 million to build in 1925 and was sometimes called "Wrigley's Million Dollar Palace." *The Sporting News* went even further in 1925, suggesting that major league owners would have "to acknowledge that (Cubs owner William) Wrigley has erected the finest baseball edifice in the United States."

L.A.'s Wrigley Field was built with the idea that it could be enlarged if major league baseball ever came to the West Coast, and when Dodgers owner Walter O'Malley moved his franchise to Los Angeles in 1958, he considered Wrigley Field as a temporary home. Instead, though, he made a makeshift baseball venue out of the mammoth Los Angeles Memorial Coliseum until Dodger Stadium opened in 1962. Wrigley Field would house major league baseball, but only for the 1961 season when the Angels played there as an American League expansion team. The Angels played at Dodger Stadium from 1962 until Anaheim Stadium was opened in 1966, the same year Wrigley Field was torn down. It is best known today as the site for the TV series "Home Run Derby," and for the fact that no less than 14 major movies were filmed there, the last being "Damn Yankees" in 1958.

AL officials, by December 1941, had worked out a 1942 schedule that included Los Angeles, with the other seven AL teams making two trips per season to Los Angeles (taking the Super Chief streamliner train out of Chicago) instead of three or four trips, as was the custom in the days when the major leagues included only 16 teams and each team played 22 games against each of the other teams in its league. All of the preparations for the move to Los Angeles were complete and the affirmative vote had already been orchestrated and was to be rubber-stamped at the AL owners meeting, scheduled to be held in Chicago on December 8, 1941. However, in the aftermath of the events of the previous day at Pearl Harbor, the proposal was postponed and subsequently shelved, and the Browns would continue to subsist in St. Louis for more than a decade.

Discussion of major league baseball on the West Coast resumed in 1946 after the San Francisco Seals drew 670,578 spectators - more than the Browns or Philadelphia A's attracted that year - to set a minor league attendance record that lasted until Louisville reached 868,418 in 1982. In 1947, the Los Angeles Angels drew 622,485. By 1952, the Seals, Angels and other PCL franchises were already considering proposals to reconstitute the PCL as a third major league, and some teams already had established player-development agreements with franchises in the lower-classification leagues. (PCL teams had been operating their own spring-training camps for decades, and sometimes played exhibition games against major league teams that were training in Southern California, as several, like the 1932 Giants, did at various times.) The quality of play in the PCL was thought to be on a par with that of the majors, largely because it was not uncommon for players who had opportunities to join major league teams to opt instead for the PCL, which often played 200 or more games per season compared to the major leagues' 154-game schedule. Therefore, PCL teams could pay their best players more than they could make as fringe players in the majors. By this time, too, the West Coast had blossomed as an important talent incubator, and it long had been common for top amateur players - Ted Williams in San Diego, Joe DiMaggio in San Francisco, Fred Hutchinson in Seattle and Jackie Jensen in Oakland, among many others - to sign with hometown PCL teams rather than with major league organizations. Once those players became PCL stars, of course, they were then sold to major league teams.

In 1952, the PCL was moved up in status from Triple-A, the level below the majors, to "Open Classification" - the only league ever to gain this distinction, which it kept until the Giants and Dodgers moved west in 1958. This meant, among other things, that PCL teams could not have conventional Player Development Contracts with major league teams, although several had unwritten understandings with big-league organizations that would loan or option players to PCL partners. It also meant that players taken off major league rosters had to pass through PCL waivers as well as those of the major leagues before they could be released or traded. Despite those moves, some PCL owners still wanted to unilaterally declare their organization a full-fledged major league, and although no official proposal is listed on any meeting agendas of the period, it's known that owners held private-session straw votes on an almost-annual basis on whether to forge ahead with that plan regardless of whether approval of MLB and its owners was forthcoming. One proposal reportedly called for the two weakest PCL franchises, the Sacramento Solons and the Oakland Oaks, to be relocated to Dallas and Houston, giving the PCL a broad enough geographic footprint to give it national credibility as a true major league. Nothing came of that proposal, or any of the others, but it was a foregone conclusion by 1952 that baseball's 50-year-old, 16-team cocoon would soon be reshaped.

Milwaukee, though the 13th-biggest city in the country by 1950, wasn't at the forefront of many plans to expand MLB's membership and reach, even after construction began on County Stadium. Most of the talk prior to 1953 had centered on the PCL-as-a-third-league concept, and on individual franchises - through transfer, expansion or a combination thereof - for Toronto, San Francisco, Los Angeles, Minneapolis-St. Paul and Baltimore. Minnesota's Twin Cities were planning publicly-funded Metropolitan Stadium, which opened in 1956 as the home of the American Association's Minneapolis Millers and then became home for the transplanted Washington Senators starting in 1961. Giants owner Horace Stoneham had a Player Development Contract with the Millers, in effect giving Stoneham first call on that territory if he decided to move the Giants out of the Polo Grounds. This was an option that he began to take seriously between 1954, when the Giants won the World Series and had home attendance of 1,115,067, and 1956, when their crowd count dipped to 629,179. (Stoneham also had lost the rental money from the football Giants, who moved to Yankee Stadium in 1956.) Baltimore in 1949 had already finalized plans to convert Baltimore Municipal Stadium - a horseshoe-shaped football stadium that already was serving, clumsily, as the home of the minor league Orioles - into a facility that was suitable for major league baseball. Houston, Seattle, Buffalo, Louisville and even Havana also presented themselves at various times as candidates for expansion or transplanted teams.

Yet Milwaukee had forged to the front of the line by the time Perini was ready to make a move. While other cities also were planning new ballparks and could offer some assets that Milwaukee couldn't match - particularly in terms of long-term population growth projections and proven major league-level support for minor league baseball - Milwaukee uniquely was in a political, practical and financial position to negotiate for a big-league team in earnest.

One element that was unique to postwar Milwaukee was its political climate, which throughout most of the city's history has been a eclectic brew of progressivism, lower-case socialism, municipal pioneering ambition, and the city's long-standing focus on trying to emerge from the glowering shadow of Chicago. Milwaukee elected the nation's first openly-Socialist mayor, Emil Seidel, in 1910, and after Republican Gerhard Balding's stewardship from 1912-16 (as of 2016, he remained Milwaukee's last Republican mayor), Socialist Daniel Hoan occupied the mayor's office from 1916-40. While much of the Midwest was embracing the resurgent Ku Klux Klan in the 1920s, Hoan made it clear after a KKK "klonvocation" near Racine drew an estimated 30,000 in 1924 that the Klan was not welcome in Milwaukee. Hoan said that if the KKK ever tried to organize on a broad scale in Milwaukee, it would find itself in "the hottest place in hell" and that it should "keep its hoods and nighties out of sight." Hoan continued to galvanize public anti-Klan sentiment in Milwaukee, and by 1928 it had virtually disappeared from the city.

Hoan and Frank Zeidler (1948-60), another Socialist, were champions of public works projects that would be based more on the widespread public benefits and wishes of the electorate than on municipal or business profits. Under Hoan, Milwaukee embraced unionism to a greater degree than was the norm in most industrial cities at the time, and during the Depression, Milwaukee put into place public-works, low-interest-loan and financial-stabilization programs that provided local relief while President Herbert Hoover was still trying to convince Americans that nothing was wrong with the economy that a second Hoover term couldn't solve. Hoan in May 1936 was featured on the cover of *Time* magazine, which described him as "one of the nation's ablest public servants, and, under him, Milwaukee has become perhaps the best governed city in the U.S." His approach dovetailed with the state's Progressive Party heritage that dated back to Robert (Fighting Bob) La Follette, the populist who had been governor of Wisconsin and a U.S. Senator and Representative, and won 17 percent of the popular vote in 1924 when he ran for President as a Progressive.

Spending on such public-works projects infuriated some of Milwaukee's big-business and anti-union interests, which equated Milwaukee's socialism with Communism and collectivism and had the ultra-conservative *Milwaukee Sentinel* as their editorial mouthpiece. But the local breweries, whose influence couldn't be ignored, were on board with progressivism as it applied to building public facilities, particularly those involving sports, that seemed to guarantee added profits for those businesses as well as providing much-needed recreational facilities for their workers.

As early as the 1890s, Milwaukee also had embraced the concept that parks and greenbelts should be staples in cities dominated out of economic necessity by the dismal haze and hues of heavy industry. Fredrick Olmstead, the urban landscaper whose early projects had included New York's Central Park and Brooklyn's Prospect Park, was a virtual vagabond late in his life as his vision of urban "emerald necklaces" wavered in and out of vogue on the national and state levels. Milwaukee, on the other hand, built three Olmstead parks - Riverside, Washington and Lake - in the 1890s, along with parkways to connect the urban oases and create a linear-park feel. Charles Whitnall, another Socialist and an urban planner on both the Milwaukee city and county levels, in 1923 drew up Milwaukee's first cohesive long-term urban compendium. It was based on the principle that housing and greenbelt not only could co-exist, but could complement each other. That same year, Milwaukee moved forward with a new neighborhood, Garden Homes, that became a national model for publicly-subsidized housing. In 1938, with First Lady Eleanor Roosevelt at the grand opening, Milwaukee County's sparsely populated southwest corner became Greendale, a federally-financed and planned community that was (and is) called a "village" and not a city. It was built strictly along federal guidelines and was conceived as an antidote for urban blight. Greendale, in particular, was seen as a reflection of the fact that "public housing" and "urban renewal" need not have the sinister connotation that many associate with those terms.

Another element that stamped Milwaukee as a major league city was the fact it had already proved it could and would turn out spectators in record numbers for events of broad-based interest.

In 1937, Marquette's football team scheduled a game against Santa Clara, which had won the Sugar Bowl over LSU that January and would repeat that feat on New Year's Day 1938. The game was played at Chicago's Soldier Field, and an estimated crowd of 60,000 fans - the vast majority of whom were from the Milwaukee area - attended the game, which Santa Clara won 38-0. While high school football wasn't as popular in Milwaukee as it was in some other similar-sized cities at the time, a crowd of 19,500 turned out at Marquette Stadium in 1949 as Bay View and Pulaski played for the city championship. (Pulaski won 30-0.)

On August 16, 1941, the Pabst Brewing Company and the Fraternal Order of Eagles co-sponsored a boxing match between Tony Zale and Billy Pryor. A ring was set up in Juneau Park, and an estimated crowd of 135,000 - still the largest ever to witness a boxing event anywhere - clambered onto the adjacent bluffs to watch the fight, for which no admission was charged. (Zale, the reigning world middleweight champion and a future Boxing Hall of Fame member, toyed with Pryor and knocked him out in the ninth round.)

Other events, such as the Milwaukee Midsummer Festival (1933-41) and the Circus Parade (1963-67), routinely drew six-figure crowds. In 1968, the various summer celebrations throughout the area were combined into Summerfest, which by 2016 was a music festival of international renown. Milwaukee also had pioneered in the area of entertainment-venue design. The Milwaukee Auditorium held more than 13,000 when it was completed in 1909 - it is now the Milwaukee Theatre, which seats about 8,000 - and the much-smaller Pabst Theater, also still in use, dates to 1895.

With events and turnouts like these in mind, Milwaukee and its leaders early embraced the idea of spending taxpayer money to construct multi-use buildings that could attract major league sports and become revenue producers. The city of Milwaukee in 1949 had begun construction of the downtown Milwaukee Arena, which opened the following year. Built to accommodate every type of sporting and entertainment event, and without any view-obstructing pillars, the Arena (renamed the UWM Panther Arena in 2014) was the first building of its kind in the country. The Los Angeles Memorial Sports Arena, opened in

1959, was largely based on the Milwaukee Arena, although the Sports Arena, which was demolished in September 2016, had a more futuristic saucer-like outer shape than the Arena's rectangular, brick-and-mortar exterior. An NBA franchise, the Hawks, moved into the new Milwaukee facility in 1951, and even though the Milwaukee Hawks were among the worst teams in the league (and drew accordingly), the building was considered the best in a league that was then in the midst of a painful formative process.

With the Milwaukee Arena under construction, Milwaukee County aldermen, by a 12-6 vote on January 11, 1949, approved plans for Milwaukee County Stadium, to be situated within an abandoned rock quarry on the west-central part of town. Actual construction began on the site on October 19, 1950. The city and county had visualized a modern sports stadium in the Story Valley since 1929, but the Depression consigned the project to the drawing boards until after World War II. Another obstacle had been aldermanic splits on where such a facility should be built. Even after the 1949 go-ahead vote committed funds for the ballpark, disputes - mostly pitting the predominantly-German northern enclaves against the heavily-Polish south side - continued through 1949 and well into 1950 before the compromise site was finalized.

Osborn Engineering Company, which had built Yankee Stadium and many of the other stadiums in use by MLB and NFL teams at the time, had been awarded the contract to build the stadium, and indicated that its preferred site was the intersection of North 60th Street and West Keefe Avenue, in the north-central part of the city. Other suggestions during the debate included Washington Park on the northwest side (provided the county zoo, located there at the time, could be moved, as it eventually was) and Haymarket Square at North Fourth Street and West McKinley Avenue. Residents and alderman who lived on the south side, though, argued for a parcel at the intersection of South 35th Street and West Lincoln Avenue. Even downtown Milwaukee was considered, as it would be in the late 1990s when it became apparent that County Stadium would have to be replaced if the Brewers were to stay in Milwaukee.

The Story Quarry site represented a grudging compromise, but in terms of Milwaukee's emerging new demographics that were transforming rural hamlets into suburban population centers, it made sense at the time, and for some years afterward. County Stadium could accommodate 11,000 cars at a time when owning an automobile was becoming less of a luxury and more of a necessity for most Americans, including Wisconsinites. It was the location most centrally located and most adjacent to the major arteries that connected the city with the expanding suburbs, especially those to the west. Milwaukee was one of the first major cities to embrace the concept of a transportation system built around auto travel, and planned its new ballpark around that vision.

County Stadium was completed late in 1952, with 28,111 seats and the capability of expansion to more than 40,000 if a major league team were to be obtained. But even at the time the park was finished, there was no certainty that a major league team would move in for the 1953 season. The Brewers had already made plans to abandon Borchert Field for good and move into County Stadium for the 1953 American Association season, and although the Braves had made little secret during the winter of their interest in leaving Boston to the Red Sox, they went to spring training in Florida as the Boston Braves. No major league franchise had been transferred from one city to another since 1903 when the American League's Baltimore Orioles moved to New York City and became the Highlanders (and, in 1920, the Yankees). The idea of altering a half-century-old footprint remained abstract, even though the Boston Braves weren't the only franchise in financial distress during the early 1950s as attendance in almost all cities that housed professional baseball teams declined from their postwar peaks.

Starting in the early 1950s, the advent and affordability of television and home air conditioning kept many former fans at home, and many others who had lived in the metropolitan core areas before World War II migrated to the suburbs that mushroomed in the postwar period. Attendance and interest in minor league cities were further eroded by the fact major league teams began televising games into minor league markets without compensating the minor league teams, and the fact aged ballparks like Borchert Field seldom could be replaced adequately because of the postwar building-material shortage.

Even so, baseball officials in the years immediately after the war saw little need to change the sport's geography or blueprint, mainly because Americans had plenty of money to spend but little on which to spend it while plants and companies converted from wartime to peacetime production. (Even Connie Mack, the much-beloved owner and manager of the Philadelphia Athletics, had to wait two years for delivery of a new car that he had first ordered in 1947.) The result was that baseball at all levels reached unprecedented attendance levels. In 1949, 466 teams (213 of which were affiliated with major league clubs) operated in 59 leagues, from the American Association, PCL and International League in Triple-A to the Wisconsin State League - home that year to the Appleton Paperjacks, Fond du Lac Panthers, Green Bay Bluejays, Janesville Cubs, Oshkosh Giants, Sheboygan Indians, Wausau Lumberjacks and Wisconsin Rapids White Sox - in Class D. (Wisconsin also had two teams in the Class C Northern League - the Eau Claire Bears, for whom 18-year-old Hank Aaron in 1952 played his first professional season, and the Superior Dukes.) The Brooklyn Dodgers in 1949 had 24 minor league farm clubs, the Yankees 21 and the Cardinals 20, and no team had fewer affiliates than the Boston Red Sox and Washington Senators with nine each.

But starting in the early 1950s once TV and home air conditioning became universal and consumer goods again became readily available, baseball markets on all levels that had flourished immediately after the war began to shrivel and, eventually, die. By 1965, the Minnesota Twins, with 10 affiliates, had the *largest* minor league system, and four teams - the Milwaukee Braves among them - were down to five farm clubs. Only 145 minor league clubs operated that year, in 18 leagues, and 20 of those teams were in "complex leagues" that operated out of major league teams' spring training facilities in Florida and played their games in virtual privacy. Only an agreement with Major League Baseball by which the major leagues would guarantee and underwrite a minor league structure with at least 100 teams saved the minor leagues from complete collapse during this period.

The Atlanta Crackers of the Class AA Southern Association typified the decay of the minor leagues during the 1950s. In

1947, they had drawn a league-record 404,584. In 1961, the final year of the Southern Association, the Crackers' attendance was 59,000. (Nonetheless, the franchise moved up to the Class AAA International League in 1962, and stayed in the IL until the Braves' arrival in 1966.)

Meanwhile, the fledgling freeway and interstate systems further broadened travel and commute horizons, and the GI Bill made home ownership a first-time possibility for millions of Americans. The suburbs burgeoned while property values in urban core areas deteriorated, and the ballparks themselves were becoming deterrents rather than attractions. Besides Cleveland Stadium (a taxpayer-funded facility that was opened in 1931 but didn't become the full-time home of the Indians until 1946) and Yankee Stadium (opened in 1923), every ballpark in use in the majors in 1952 dated at least to the 1909-1915 period when steel and reinforced concrete replaced wood as the ballpark construction material of choice.

Despite these trends and shifts, the idea of public funding for a private and profit-driven entity - even one that would be of widespread use and popularity - was still abstract in most municipalities in 1953, even though it was consistent with long-standing public policy in Milwaukee. Brooklyn Dodgers owner Walter O'Malley discovered this when he tried without success to convince New York City planning czar Robert Moses to use the then-newly-created power of eminent domain to obtain the land on which O'Malley wanted to build a new Brooklyn ballpark to replace crumbling Ebbets Field. (Ironically, the Barclay Center, now occupied by the NBA's Brooklyn Nets and the NHL's New York Islanders, was built on that very same site a half-century after the Dodgers left Brooklyn.) Other than Cleveland Stadium, no publicly-funded major league ballpark had been built in more than 50 years. And at the time ground was broken on County Stadium in 1950, no existing minor league ballpark was suited to serve as anything more than a temporary home for a major league franchise. San Francisco's Seals Stadium, McGraw's 1932 opinion notwithstanding, had only 18,000 seats and could be expanded only peripherally, and the same was true of Los Angeles' Wrigley Field and Seattle's Sick's Stadium, both of which held only about 21,000. Neither city had taken any quantitative steps toward replacing their Triple-A ballparks, as Milwaukee had. Toronto's Maple Leaf Stadium held 23,000, but it dated to 1926, couldn't be expanded, and wasn't much better suited than Borchert Field for major league baseball. The Maple Leafs left in 1967 and Maple Leaf Stadium was torn down the following year, leaving Toronto without professional baseball until the American League's Blue Jays moved into Exhibition Stadium, a loosely-reconfigured football venue, in 1977.

Other communities, particularly Minneapolis-St. Paul and Houston, also had major league baseball aspirations (and the will-ingness to spend public money to build new ballparks) in 1953, and in 1956, the Twin Cities followed Milwaukee's lead and built a new stadium without any guarantees that it would eventually house a major league franchise. But even after the introduction of eminent-domain laws in the late 1940s, the idea of building a ballpark for a private entity such as a baseball team remained anathema in the minds of many voters and public officials as well as the majority of baseball owners. And in terms of widening the scope of major league baseball beyond its half-century-old, self-imposed boundaries, travel in the pre-commercial jet-era remained an issue.

Most baseball people and municipal planners knew by 1953 that the sport's 1903 operational mode would have to change, and sooner rather than later. In Lou Perini's case, he knew by early 1953 that it had to change not sooner or later, but now. It was clear to Perini that his Braves had no future in Boston and that only one city - Milwaukee - was prepared to adequately accommodate him with virtually no advance notice. He also knew he couldn't wait any longer. Bill Veeck was waiting to move his St. Louis Browns to Milwaukee, the site of his first promotional triumphs.

Veeck had bought the Browns in 1951, the year he famously sent 3-foot-6 pinch-hitter Eddie Gaedel into a game against the Detroit Tigers. He later wrote that based on the relative success of his operation during the 1952 season, he was sure he could wedge the rival Cardinals out of St. Louis - especially since the Browns owned Sportsman's Park, where both teams played, and the Cardinals were the Browns' tenants. Veeck was further emboldened late in 1952, when Cardinals owner Fred Saigh, who had purchased that franchise from Sam Breadon, was forced to sell the club after being indicted for income-tax evasion. (He later pled no contest to the charge, and served five months in prison.) A number of bidders, including a Milwaukee consortium headed by brewing-company mogul Fred Miller, came forward. Miller's group, with County Stadium near completion, submitted a higher bid (more than $4 million) than that put forth by Gussie Busch and his Anheuser-Busch brewing company, and if Saigh had accepted that bid, the St. Louis Cardinals would have become the MIlwaukee Cardinals in 1953. But Saigh, wanting the team to stay in St. Louis, instead sold to Busch for a significantly lower price, estimated at $3.75 million.

Veeck had bought the Browns in 1951 with the intention of keeping them in St. Louis, but he knew by the end of 1952 that he couldn't compete with the Anheuser-Busch fortune and the Cardinals' regional, radio-driven reach, which he knew would soon extend to television. Veeck was friends with Miller going back to Veeck's Brewers days, and the two, at that time, had negotiated a contract that brought the Miller company its first ballpark-concession deal, at Borchert Field. Veeck was eager to move into Milwaukee after the Browns were doomed by the Busch purchase of the Cardinals. But Veeck couldn't move into Milwaukee either, because, after Veeck sold the Brewers to Chicago attorney Oscar Salinger in 1945, Perini had bought the team from Salinger, and the Brewers in 1947 became the Braves' Triple-A affiliate. The Braves thus owned the MLB territorial rights to Milwaukee, and thus the right to move there if they wished, as the 1953 season loomed.

Veeck already had been rebuffed in an effort to buy the Brewers from Perini, thereby gaining the territorial rights to Milwaukee, but Perini was not yet ready to commit to moving to Milwaukee, while Veeck was poised to move the Browns to Milwaukee at a moment's notice. It was reported at the time that Perini was negotiating with his preferred relocation target, Toronto, but couldn't get a commitment from that city to replace Maple Leaf Stadium. Baltimore, which had modified its municipal football stadium to accommodate major league baseball, also had perfunctory discussions with Perini.

Meanwhile, the team went to spring training in Florida still doing business as the Boston Braves. Veeck used the Milwaukee media - with which he was friendly, going back to his Brewer days - to maintain a sell-or-move mantra that he directed at Perini throughout the winter of 1952-53. Finally, Perini exercised his right to move to Milwaukee, making it official on March 13, 1953 - less than a month before the start of the regular season. (Veeck, knowing by then he would have to endure a lame-duck, financially-disastrous season in St. Louis with most of his financial backers having backed out after Saigh sold the Cardinals to the Busch brewery, sold the Browns to Baltimore interests after that 1953 season, and that team became the Baltimore Orioles in 1954.)

Perini made the move to Milwaukee belatedly and, by some accounts, reluctantly. But his arrival coincided with a confluence of time, energy, passion, middle-class affluence, political climate, and on-field talent that made the Braves the first sports-attendance phonomenon of the 1950s. The franchise flew in the face of the general decline that, along with the mushrooming popularity of football, already was beginning to threaten baseball's status as the nation's most popular sport. The Braves drew 1,826,397 to set a National League record in 1953, the year after the Brooklyn Dodgers (1,088,704) were the only National League team to chin the 1 million bar. The Braves led MLB in attendance their first six years in Milwaukee, and the Wisconsin euphoria culminated in 1957 when the Braves drew 2,215,404 fans, won the World Series and sent southeastern Wisconsin into a frenzy on a level only seen previously on V-J Day in 1945 and during the appearance of ousted Gen. Douglas MacArthur (who considered himself a native son of Milwaukee) in 1951. The flourishing of the Braves became known as the "Miracle of Milwaukee," and it begat a wave of transfers and expansion that lasted through 1971, when the second version of the Washington Senators abandoned that city for the Dallas-Fort Worth Metroplex.

Milwaukee, even before the arrival of the Braves, was flourishing. In 1950, it was the 13th largest city in the country with a population of 637,392 - a total that grew to 741,324 by 1960 and to 768,260 by 1965 - and already had flexed its municipal and industrial muscles. Just about any working man (and many working women) who wanted a job could easily find one in the factories and trainyards and breweries and docks. Along with its beer-brewing reputation, Milwaukee was known as "America's Gearbox." While it didn't build as many finished products as other cities like Detroit and Chicago, it produced parts for virtually everything - and a lot of jobs that came to Milwaukee during this period involved specialized skills for which employers were obliged to pay handsomely. The American Motors Corporation, formed in 1954, had a Milwaukee body-assembly plant that in 1965 employed 16,000, although it was slowed by a three-week strike that August. On the northwest side, A.O. Smith, the largest manufacturer of car and truck frames in the country, employed another 15,000. During the war, the giant Allis-Chalmers plant in suburban West Allis had 25,000 on its payroll and was responsible for more Manhattan Project components than any other U.S. corporate entity, and Milwaukeeans in every industrial field could justifiably say that they had done as much to win the war on the home front as any city in the country. This prosperity and industrial versatility had extended into the 1950s would continue to define life in Milwaukee into the 1970s.

This was particularly true in West Allis, Milwaukee's first western suburb and a factory city that was built around Allis-Chalmers. When Allis-Chalmers established its primary plant there in 1902, the community had 6,645 inhabitants; by 1930, it had 34,671, and it (and Allis-Chalmers) continued to grow through the Baby Boomer era, reaching a peak of 71,723 in 1970. But the city's economy was ravaged by the downsizing and closure of Allis-Chalmers in the late 1970s and early 1980s. Though West Allis still is home to a number of industrial concerns, along with the Wisconsin State Fair and the Milwaukee Mile auto-racing track, its population aged and dwindled and its per-capita income began a decline that never stopped. In 2015, West Allis' population, which had declined every year since 1970, was 60,620, including many Allis-Chalmers retirees. Most of the surviving Allis-Chalmers buildings have been repurposed in an effort to provide West Allis with the economic diversity that it lacked at the time Allis-Chalmers departed.

Jerry Weitzer, a concert pianist and professional jazz musician in the Milwaukee area for more than 40 years, in 2016 recalled growing up in West Allis as a Braves fan during their later years in Milwaukee.

We were like totally free as kids. You knew where every crack in every fence was, and everything ran around Allis-Chalmers. Everywhere you went, you passed a factory or a machine shop, and the smallest ones would be a block long. They'd all be feeding Allis-Chalmers, and you could tell what they were machining by the dust coating the sidewalk ... blue if it was steel, red if it was copper. There was so much smoke that it changed the sunrises ... you'd have these beautiful sunrises, every color, from Allis-Chalmers all the way to Allen-Bradley. You'd walk down the street and there would be the sidewalk and then the factory ... no clearance between them. They were all working three shifts and it was 24-hour everything ... the first shift would go from 8 to maybe 3:30, the second shift would go until 11:30 at night, and then the third shift. The clubs stayed open until 3:30 in the morning. It was just a massive movement of people. Parking lots were on every block. I think we had two movie houses, though I only remember going to one. There was a Sears, shoe stores, three or four grocery stores, music people, insurance people.

The best thing about growing up there was the park system. There were always balls and bats there, and coaches who'd direct us, but it wasn't that formal. If a team collapsed, you just formed another one. Bud Selig (whose father's Ford dealership was in West Allis) *used to run the punt-pass-and-kick contest. He'd go around the park handing out cards and you filled out the card and Bud would put it into the box. Everyone participated. They even had what I guess you'd call a midget football league in the park system.*

I started (playing events and celebrations of) *the Catholic Church in grammar school, from 1961* (at age 6) *to 1969. I started with the Roman Mass, epiphanies, Holy Names dinners. Later, I started doing the higher ed in the grade schools. (The schools had) music appreciation classes. I remember playing Beethoven's 7th Symphony* (in 1973) *because it was the death song of the Edward G. Robinson character in the movie Soylent Green.* (This was Robinson's last move; he died later that year.) *You were either getting ready for a concert or a parade or a service of some kind. It was fun. Everyone wanted you to play at their event, especially during Christmas season. We were allowed to perform, and* (that's how we) *learned how to play. The genius of the nuns was they took this great music and gave it to a bunch of second graders, letting us do whatever we wanted with it. We were composers, lyricists, vocalists, musicians, painters and poets. All before we knew who Beethoven was. God bless them*

I think my first game at County Stadium must have been when I was in third grade, around 1963. I remember we were way back in the upper deck ... you couldn't even see the seats below from where we were sitting. I was 10 when they moved, and what I remember was that none of my friends even wanted the Braves' baseball cards. It was like a death in the family. It was sort of like the factory noise (in the 1970s and 1980s when Allis-Chalmers cut back its production and workforce, then closed altogether). You'd hear the wet vacs and the grinding machines all the time, and then you didn't hear them anymore. The Braves leaving was kind of that way. They didn't tear down one lot one day and one lot another day. It was just poof, one day the sound was gone. Internally, they'd been moving everybody; we just weren't prepared for it. My brother bought a house around that time, and he said it was the worst deal he ever made because the taxes were all screwy (without the industrial tax base that Allis-Chalmers had provided). *If you were a business, you didn't get taxed, but the homeowners got taxed more. It was really a wacky tax system. It was No. 1 in the state* (in terms of homeowner tax liability per capita) *for I don't know how long.*

(The Allis-Chalmers decline and fall) *broke up families and broke up groups. It's like relying on religion and finding out that* (faith wasn't always rewarded). *All of a sudden, you're blind. I got home one night from working a gig, in 1972, and I didn't go in the house at all. Instead I went to George Webb's* (a local restaurant chain), *bought a pack of Kools and stayed out all night. I decided that this* (music) *was what I wanted to do* (instead of working in the factories).

In 1957, though, few could have envisioned any change in Milwaukee's industrial way of life, and the Braves' success in Milwaukee had been such that the Browns and Philadelphia Athletics had followed the Braves' lead and abandoned two-team cities in search of similar riches and unquestioning fan devotion. After the 1957 season, two of the most storied franchises in baseball, the Brooklyn Dodgers and the New York Giants, locked their rusting ballpark gates and began operation as the Los Angeles Dodgers and San Francisco Giants. Clearly, the Milwaukee Braves had been the vanguard of baseball's future - or so everyone at the time thought.

(Ironically, the Dodgers' move to Los Angeles, while considered a virtual certainty throughout their last-rite 1957 season, wasn't made official until the same day the Milwaukee Braves made their Sputnik-defying history by taking the County Stadium field for Game 3 of the 1957 World Series. The Giants, after casting coveteous eyes at Minneapolis-St. Paul for several years, in July 1957 had announced their plans to relocate to San Francisco for the 1958 season. Asked if he had considered the impact of the move on the kids who worshipped the Giants, Giants owner Horace Stoneham said he had. "But I haven't seen many of their fathers at the Polo Grounds lately," he added.)

The Braves, meanwhile, had established a presence in the Milwaukee community that radiated far beyond their actual games. Bill Streicher, a Milwaukee native who in 2016 was president of the MItchell Gallery of Flight Aviation Museum at General Mitchell International Airport, recalled those days: "Local businesses seemed to promote the Braves in simple but effective ways. For example, a local dry cleaner (I think their name was Spic n Span) offered promotional photos of the players to their customers (collect the whole set!). I think they also sponsored a kids baseball clinic at County Stadium at least once, taught by a few players. They issued 'how to' fold outs for pointers about playing each position. The local Johnston Cookie Company issued special Braves baseball cards (I think from 1953 to 1956). The cookie company was located on National Avenue southeast of County Stadium and the building and its big lighted sign could be clearly seen by fans seated in the stadium (the building is still there). Johnny Logan lived near my home on Milwaukee's southwest side and we occasionally saw him outside cutting his grass. My dad worked at Briggs & Stratton and one of his co-workers had a part-time job as a stadium usher for night games. I recall they wore some pretty loud uniforms including old taxi driver-style hats (typical 1950s fashions). The VA (Veterans Administration) Home was on a bluff overlooking right field of County Stadium. The VA built a small seating area on the bluff so the vets could watch the games (while listening to Earl Gillespie and Blaine Walsh do play-by-play on the radio). After the right field grandstand extension was built, their view must have been a bit obstructed."

It was a franchise built and seemingly destined to enhance multiple generations, in 1957 and for decades to come. And yet, just eight years after their World Series triumph, the "Miracle of Milwaukee" had dissipated, and the Braves and baseball were on their way south to Atlanta, awash in litigation and animosity and indifference. On November 16, 1962, a Chicago-based consortium led by Bill Bartholomay purchased the Braves from Perini, who had lost millions of dollars as the result of a failed real-estate venture in West Palm Beach, Fla., and had been primarily an absentee owner even as the Milwaukee Braves led the major leagues in attendance in each of their first six years of existence. Even in 1957, he had spent little time in Milwaukee and had delegated much of the day-to-day operation to a non-baseball functionary, Joe Cairnes, who assumed the title of president and had authority over all the baseball men in the organization, including general manager John Quinn, who was forced out after the 1958 season.

In July 1963, the *St. Louis Post-Dispatch's* Bob Broeg broke the story that the "Carpetbaggers" had no intention of keeping the Braves in Milwaukee and had bought the franchise with the express purpose of moving it to Atlanta and cornering the virgin market that the Deep South represented at the time. Later, the *Atlanta Constitution's* Furman Bisher wrote that Braves general manager John McHale approached him a year before, during the 1962 All-Star break, while Perini still owned the club. According to Bisher, McHale told him that Perini had already made up his mind to sell or move the club, and that he, Perini, saw Atlanta as an ideal location if a suitable ballpark could be built. If Bisher's story was accurate - and he was one of the most reputable and respected sportswriters of his era - the origin of the Braves' departure was not with Bartholomay, as generally has been assumed, but with Perini.

Bill Bartholomay and his fellow investors all had roots in Chicago, with the notable exception of Milwaukee native Del Coleman, who had made a Milwaukee-based fortune operating the Seeburg Jukebox Co. The rumors, despite management denials, festered through the 1963 and 1964 seasons, but Bartholomay didn't come clean publicly about his group's real intentions until

October 14, 1964, when it was announced that the franchise would be shifted to Atlanta as soon as Atlanta-Fulton County Stadium, then on the verge of completion, was ready for big-league play. Bartholomay and his group had one year left on the three-year lease at County Stadium that they had signed before the 1963 season, but they planned to either buy their way out of the lease or ignore it altogether.

They were able to do neither - Milwaukee County officials obtained a court injunction that forced the Braves to honor the last year of their lease - but MLB's commissioner, Ford Frick, and the other 19 owners made it clear after the injunction was issued that the Braves would receive official permission to move as soon as the lease expired and they were legally free to do so. Only one major Braves stockholder - a 29-year-old car-dealership partner named Bud Selig - voted against the move when it came up for a final vote, and the Braves thus began their final season in Milwaukee on a legal respirator. It was the first time - and the only time - in the 20th century that a major league baseball team was forced by a court order to play a complete final season in a city from which it had publicly and permanently estranged itself. That made - and still makes - the Milwaukee Braves' final season one unparalleled in major league history.

Even before the Braves assembled in West Palm Beach, Fla., for spring training prior to the 1965 season, almost everyone involved in the tug-of-war over the team knew this would be a six-month goodbye that would be interspersed and often over-riden by shouting and tumult and a sense of betrayal that remains, in some minds, as malignant 50 years later as it was in 1965. Meanwhile, a leaderless industry that already had been superseded in the public mind by the National Football League wallowed in chaos, confusion and cacophony that would last well beyond the advent of the Atlanta Braves in April 1966. Ford Frick, a former sportswriter who had been best known for being one of Babe Ruth's ghostwriters during the latter's career, became commissioner of baseball in 1951 and saw and defined his role as one of benign oversight. Even though he had the same virtually-unlimited power to act in the best interests of baseball that had been given to (and often used by) the original commissioner, Kenesaw Mountain Landis, the owners wanted no part of another autocratic, maverick czar. They liked Frick's management style - which rarely consisted of anything beyond the declaration "it's a league matter" - so much that when Frick he retired after the 1965 season, the owners elected retired Air Force Gen. William Eckert to the post. Eckert had no background in baseball and was even less willing to wield power (except in the interest of his friends) than Frick. When the election of Eckert was announced during major league meetings after the 1965 season, Philadelphia sportswriter Larry Merchant exclaimed, "My God. They've hired the Unknown Soldier." It was a nickname that would stick with Eckert throughout his short tenure as commissioner.

Amid the off-field tumult, the Braves' last season in Milwaukee was not without drama and accomplishment. They became the first National League team to have six players hit 20 or more home runs in a season: Hank Aaron, Eddie Mathews, Gene Oliver, Felipe Alou, Mack Jones and Joe Torre. Their pitching staff, while inconsistent and lacking the star power of the Spahn-Burdette-Buhl days, got 24 wins from Tony Cloninger - a total no Braves pitcher, as of the end of the 2016 season, had matched since - and 16 from Wade Blasingame. Ken Johnson, acquired early in the season from Houston, gave the Braves a reliable third starter, and Billy O'Dell, a starter throughout a distinguished career with the Orioles and Giants, registered a 2.18 ERA and 19 saves operating out of the bullpen. The Braves were a slow-footed team - they were ninth in the 10-team NL in triples, and had only 64 stolen bases compared to the champion Dodgers' 172 - and they never found a reliable fourth or fifth starting pitcher. Manager Bobby Bragan constantly bemoaned his team's inability to bunt and to produce during situational at-bats, and while Mathews was still a threat at the plate, his defensive mobility was now limited and the injuries he had ac-cumulated with his demolition-derby approach to the game were affecting his batting average and his ability to take the field every day.

Even so, the Braves nosed into first place on August 18, one of the strangest days of a strange season. That day in St. Louis, Hank Aaron hit a home run that didn't count because a base umpire, unseen by everyone, had called timeout just before the home-run pitch was released, but pinch-hitter Don Dillard hit the 14th and last home run of his five-year major league career, and his only HR as a Brave - a pinch-hit, three-run homer to beat the Cardinals 5-3. After a loss in the final game of that series the next day, the Braves won 4-3 in Pittsburgh on August 20 to move back into first place for the last time as the Milwaukee Braves. As it turned out, that was a final mirage. Starting with the two losses in Pittsburgh, the Braves unraveled, losing 26 of their final 42 games and dropping out of the race as the Giants and then the championship-winning Dodgers rampaged through September. Finally, it was September 22, 1965, and the Braves and Los

Angeles Dodgers - the same Dodgers whose move from Brooklyn had been greased by the Boston-Milwaukee transfer - played the Milwaukee Braves' last-ever home game.

In many ways and in many eyes - and since 1965, in most written and verbal accounts - the 13th and final Milwaukee Braves season is remembered as epilogue and asterisk. Of the paragons of the late 1950s, only Eddie Mathews and Hank Aaron - who were and still are joined at the hip in the memories of those who reflect upon the Milwaukee Braves - remained in 1965, and Mathews, hounded by injuries throughout the early 1960s, was on the downhill side of his career. Warren Spahn, whose 363 wins remains the record for MLB left-handed pitchers, had been sold to the New York Mets the previous winter after a public spat with manager Bobby Bragan, a native of Alabama who had made the mistake of stating for publication that he was looking forward to the Atlanta move and thought Milwaukee had run its course as a major league baseball town. Partly because of his ill-timed utterances and partly as the result of his dispute with Spahn, Bragan was booed by the scattered denizens throughout that final 1965 season. (Mention of his name at Milwaukee Braves Historical Society gatherings elicits boos to this day.)

Lew Burdette, who'd earned three of the Braves' four wins in the 1957 World Series, and Bob Buhl, who had beaten the transcendent Brooklyn Dodgers eight times in 1956, were both long gone - Buhl to the Cubs and Burdette to the Cardinals. Burdette had won 179 games for the Braves over 13 seasons in Boston and Milwaukee; Buhl had won 109 over 10 seasons. Del Crandall, the catcher who served as the pitching staff's navigator (and, some players have said, the nerve center of the team itself) had been traded to the Giants after the 1963 season; his career with the Braves had started in Boston in 1949. Also gone were Johnny Logan, the combative shortstop; Billy Bruton, the center fielder who congealed the outfield and was arguably baseball's best leadoff hitter during the glory years; and everyone else except Mathews and Aaron who had played a significant role in bringing the 1950s Braves to the brink of dynasty status. Mathews was the only one of the 168 men who had been a Milwaukee Brave when the franchise arrived and was still a Milwaukee Brave when it departed. The rest of what many considered a potential neo-Yankee Colossus - or at the very least, the equal of the Dodgers in their *Boys of Summer* period that was fading out as the Braves were barging in - was scattered to the winds with minimal return.

The irony of the Braves' decline into mediocrity after 1959 was that before the major league draft was introduced in 1965, the Braves' financial resources were such - especially in the 1950s, when TV and national-advertising money were minimal and most teams' budgets hinged on their gate receipts - that they could and did outbid even the no-ceiling-budget teams like the Yankees and Dodgers for amateur talent. But a lot of that money had been wasted on "bonus baby" busts. The Braves weren't the only team to lavish huge sums on untested (and ultimately unfit) players during the bonus-baby era when those players had to languish on major league rosters instead of learning their craft in the minor leagues, but they had the most money and therefore the most visible failures.

General manager John Quinn, who had built the Boston Braves' second and final NL pennant winner in 1948 and then transformed a seventh-place team into an instant contender in

Milwaukee, had been stripped of his decision-making authority by Lou Perini and then forced out entirely after the 1958
season. Charlie Grimm, who had taken over as Boston Braves
manager in 1952 after guiding the Cubs to three of their final
four NL pennants as of 2016, had been a player and manager
with the minor league Brewers and was immensely popular
both in Milwaukee and among his players. (He played left-
handed banjo in an impromptu clubhouse ensemble that also
included veteran outfielder and Wisconsin native Andy Pafko
playing the concertina and backup catcher Bob Roselli on
clarinet. Roselli, a native of San Francisco, settled on the San
Francisco Peninsula after he retired. As head of the American
Legion program in San Mateo, Calif., in 1982, he managed
Barry Bonds, and the following year, he took a San Mateo team
led by Gregg Jefferies to the Legion World Series title game.)

Grimm resigned during the 1956 season, saying he had loos-
ened the reins on his party-hearty players to the extent that he
had lost control of the team, and was succeeded by taciturn Fred
Haney. Few of his players liked Haney, and Johnny Logan more
than once said Haney's usual response to a crisis was to ask his
catcher, Del Crandall, what to do. But Haney got results. The
Braves went 68-40 in 1956 after Haney took over, and led the
NL for the better part of three months before the Dodgers over-
hauled them in the final weekend and finished one game ahead
of Milwaukee. Then came the 1957 World Series champions, the
1958 NL pennant winners who were ahead of the Yankees by
three games to one in the World Series before losing the final
three games, and the 1959 team that tied the Dodgers for the
NL title before losing the first two games of a best-of-three playoff. The second game, in Milwaukee, drew only 18,297, and the

Braves' attendance in 1959 was down a half-million patrons from the peak year of 1957. The team and the fan base eroded from there, and although it won at least 83 games during each of its 13 years in Milwaukee, by 1965 it was an aging, cobbled-together team that might have descended below the .500 bar after 1961 if it hadn't been for the advent of the Houston Colt .45s and New York Mets as league foils in 1962.

As the team faded, the relationship that had fused the team and the community in the 1950s had deteriorated. Players could no longer get loaner cars for the season from the Wally Rank dealership, and weren't able to stay in Milwaukee year-round, as they had done in the early years, because the off-season jobs that were theirs for the asking no longer were available to them. And although each of the Milwaukee Braves' final three managers - Chuck Dressen, Birdie Tebbetts and Bragan - tried to impose on-field structure and off-field decorum on their players, they were largely ignored and their authority was questioned. Players gained reputations for being more animated at Jackson's, a bar near County Stadium where many of the players lingered (and sometimes over-lingered), than on the field. The euphoria of 1953, when Braves fans would cheer even long foul balls by their beloved Braves, had morphed into expectation by 1956, demand by 1959, and outright cynicism by 1965. By the time the franchise's future in Milwaukee had begun to be questioned, emotions were as empty as the ballpark.

The world into which the Milwaukee Braves entered in 1953 had changed by 1965, too. In 1953 when the Milwaukee Braves played their first game, the No. 1 song in the country was "How Much Is That Doggie in the Window?" by Doris Day. In

September 1965, the song at the top of the charts was "Help!" by the Beatles, and the song that defined the national discomfiture was Barry McGuire's apocalyptic "Eve of Destruction." Milwaukee, though still a city where the architecture and the neighborhoods and the traditions extended back through multiple generations, had changed since 1953. The Korean War was still raging in 1953, but its acceptance as a vehicle of containing Communism was general, while in 1965 the anti-Vietnam War protest movement - with the University of Wisconsin as one of its epicenters - was engulfing Milwaukee and the nation. In 1953, the Ford Customline was the most popular vehicle in a country where foreign-built cars were only for the uber-wealthy. By 1965, the Chevrolet Impala was the highest-selling car, and the Customline, a model that in many ways resembled the Chevys that revolutionized the car world starting in 1955, was produced only until 1956, and was common only in junkyards by 1965. (In 1953, Ford sold 771,662 Customlines; in 1956, only 368,653 units were sold.) The McDonald's fast-food chain in 1953 had only three outlets that collectively grossed $1.35 million; in 1965 it had 710 restaurants and grossed $171 million. TV ownership had gone from 44.7 percent of U.S. homes in 1953 to 92.6 percent in 1965. The fastest available commercial airliner in 1953 was the propeller-driven L-749 Lockheed Constellation, which could reach 345 mph and had a fully-loaded range of only 2,600 miles, making it unsuitable for non-stop transcontinental service. In 1965, the Douglas DC-8 jet could cruise at 588 mph, and easily could accommodate not only transcontinental flights but cross-oceanic flights as well. In 1953, before the introduction of Jonas Falk's polio vaccine, more than 58,000 cases were reported, and the disease was regarded as a national scourge. By 1965, that total was down to 121.

Further, though Milwaukee's Menomonee River Valley heavy industry was still whirring and provided the bulk of the jobs for the dads who were taking their kids to games in 1965, ominous signs - both economic and ecological - that a day of reckoning was coming for Milwaukee and its economy. Between 1980 and 2014, the city, county, state and federal governments would spend a reported $5 billion to clean up pollution that lingered in the Menomonee watershed in the aftermath of more than a century of industrial use.

Meanwhile, the long-held concept and belief in Milwaukee as a city of distinct ethnic enclaves was giving way to a more sinister interpretation: That those neighborhoods were vehicles of segregation, *de facto* and otherwise. In 1965, North Division High School had 1,600 students, only six of whom were white, while eight of the other 12 high schools in the Milwaukee Public Schools district had student bodies that were at least 90 percent white. Father James Groppi was seen as a civil rights crusader and a purveyor of peaceful change in 1965, but he would attain national notoriety as a conduit of confrontation, marching with his supporters directly into the most resolutely conservative neighborhood in south Milwaukee and almost touching off a riot. In 1967, after a white police officer shot and wounded a young black man, Milwaukee narrowly averted the fates of cities like Detroit and Newark and Los Angeles only because martial law was declared before an outbreak of racial violence could spread beyond one neighborhood. A curfew was imposed by local officials, virtually shutting down the city, and aerial photos taken at the time show the city's freeways as devoid of traffic as if a science-fiction doomsday movie were being filmed in Milwaukee.

The Braves' third-to-last home game in Milwaukee, a 4-1 loss to the Phillies, drew their worst-ever crowd - 812 souls. A week and a half later, the Milwaukee Braves were no more, and while Bud Selig's group - now known as Milwaukee Brewers Baseball Club, Inc. - plotted and prodded and pleaded for a replacement team, those who had witnessed and participated in the "Miracle of Milwaukee" in the 1950s were left to ponder what had happened.

"I think there were mixed feelings," Bill Streicher said. "Bartholomay was a name not highly regarded. Some people were saying, 'good riddance.' There were others who were rather nostalgic. They remembered the days when the Braves first arrived. One thing that sticks in my mind is walking around my neighborhood during the summer. People would sit on lawn chairs in their yards to beat the heat, pre-air conditioning, and all the neighbors had the Braves game on the radio. You could hear Earl Gillespie's play by play from one end of the block to the other.

"A friend of mine, through junior high and high school, and I used to go to the games. He was a true baseball fanatic, and he and I would buy the yearbooks from all of the major league teams ... we'd mail away to the clubs and they'd send them to us. I quit doing that (during the Braves' final years in Milwaukee) but he kept doing it. And many years later (in 2000), once the final game at County Stadium was on the horizon, we decided to go. What I remember most is sitting in the grandstand and seeing Miller Park (then under construction, towering over County Stadium) and one of my first thoughts was that they're building a stadium that's going to block the view of the Johnston Cookie sign.

"It was a roller coaster, and everybody got on board and the city really supported them. Everything kind of hit a plateau in 1957 and 1958, and after that, rumors began to surface, the Braves started to make noises about moving, and the whole thing came crashing down. It affected the city's self-esteem because when the Braves finally came here, there was a lot of feeling that Milwaukee had finally made it. We now have a major league team, and that took Milwaukee to another level ... we're on an equal plane with some of the larger cities. I think there was still disbelief among other cities and teams that Milwaukee really was a major league city, as you saw with some of the comments during the 1957 World Series (when New York Yankees manager Casey Stengel referred tauntingly to Milwaukee as Bushville). Everyone was on a high then. Then everything eroded, and once they left here, there was a lot of despair. You have a taste of the major leagues and now it's no longer there. I don't think anyone really believed we'd get another major league team.

"The 1950s were a different era, more carefree. People were connected, and not through 'social media.' There was a lot more pride and trust. When the 1960s came along, things began to degrade, not only in Milwaukee but in many other cities. In 1967 when they had the riots (that were quelled when martial law was declared and a curfew was strictly enforced), I had a summer job and I couldn't go to work. Everything was shut down. Everywhere you turned, there was some kind of turmoil."

CHAPTER 3

Braves Founder

• • •

THE QUESTION HAS PERSISTED THROUGHOUT the half-century since the Milwaukee Braves ceased to exist: How did a franchise that led the major leagues in attendance in each of its first six seasons lose three-quarters of its constituency in just seven seasons - and winning seasons at that?

At least some of the answers don't come as readily as many thought at the time, and as some still think.

For decades after the Braves left Milwaukee and took up residence in Atlanta, their departure was explained through one overriding answer: The greed of Bill Bartholomay and the group of investors he organized to buy the Braves in 1962 with the express intention of moving them to Atlanta. Bartholomay, general manager John McHale and everyone else connected with the new ownership group repeatedly and emphatically denied that intent until October 14, 1964, when the new ballpark being built for the Braves in Atlanta was on the verge of completion. Their actions and Bartholomay's subsequent reflections on the Braves' final years in Milwaukee suggest that whatever thoughts he and his group had of restoring the attendance and passion of the 1950s lasted no more than a few months after he assumed control of the franchise. It's hard to assert that the "Carpetbaggers" were any less cynical in 1963 and 1964 than Walter O'Malley had been in 1956 and 1957 when he milked every last cent out of the Brooklyn Dodger fan base that he knew he would be abandoning for Los Angeles after the 1957 season.

But was ownership's dispassionate greed the *only* reason the Milwaukee Braves ceased to exist at the end of that final game in Los Angeles in 1965? There can be no question that it was *a* factor, and ultimately the deciding one. To put it a less incendiary way, it was a business decision, one that was based on basic business principles - moving out of a constricted, economically-limited market into a region that had never had major league baseball, had built a multi-purpose sports stadium, and was eager to prove that it had moved beyond the Jim Crow era. Ultimately, the courts were to rule that the Braves did not violate any laws by moving from Milwaukee to Atlanta after their lease at County Stadium ran out at the end of the 1965 season, although baseball's antitrust exemption - a premise, then and 50 years later, of the industry - came within one judicial vote of being overturned as a result of the transfer.

At the same time, the demise of the Milwaukee Braves can also be blamed on other elements, some of which came into play before Lou Perini sold the club to Bartholomay. Some negatively impacted the franchise even during the 1956-59 seasons when a string of four straight World Series championships was within the Braves' grasp. In fact, if one indulges in what-if speculation, it can be argued that the single biggest event that eventually transformed the Milwaukee Braves into the Atlanta Braves transpired in 1954, the year after the

Braves moved to Milwaukee and when the community was in full rapture over the Braves. This event wasn't treachery, but tragedy.

In 2014, at the age of 85, Bartholomay - who still lived in the Chicago area - granted an interview to David Sweet of *North Shore Weekend*, a Chicago-area publication, during which he explained, in more detail than in the past, his reasoning after the time he became the Braves' controlling partner. The story largely reads as an ode to Bartholomay, even though his ownership of the Atlanta Braves is as much of a blotch on his baseball legacy as his litany of deception in Milwaukee. He had sold the Braves to media mogul Ted Turner after the 1976 season, during which the Atlanta Braves' attendance had descended to 534,762 - fewer patrons than the Braves had attracted during their final year of court-imposed exile in Milwaukee. He remained, and in 2014 still remained, chairman emeritus of the Braves, who in 2017 plan to move into their *third* Atlanta-area residence - 30 miles away from their original base at Atlanta-Fulton County Stadium, and even farther from Turner Field, which became the Braves' home in 1997 after serving as the central venue of the Olympic Games in Atlanta the previous year.

The Atlanta Braves, of course, had attained artistic success unprecedented in professional sports while winning 14 straight division championships from 1991-2005. (They were second in the National League East in 1994, the season that ended without a postseason because of a work stoppage.) They had won the 1995 World Series, and participated in four other Fall Classics. But they won only the one World Series - the same total, in 50 years, that the Milwaukee Braves attained in 13. Bartholomay was long gone as an active participant in the operation of the franchise by then, of course, and during his ownership, the Braves went to the postseason only once, in 1969 when they won the NL Western Division title in the first year after major league baseball added four teams and grouped itself into four six-team divisions. The '69 Braves were eliminated in three straight games in the National League Championship Series by the eventual World Series champion, New York's "Miracle Mets." During their first 16 seasons in Atlanta, the Braves exceeded the Milwaukee Braves' 1965 win total of 86 only one other time, in 1974 when they went 88-74. Bartholomay sold the team in the midst of a five-year stretch during which it lost 474 games.

According to the *North Shore Weekend* story, Bartholomay's yearning to own a team began in the late 1950s, when he was on the governing board of the Chicago White Sox before Bill Veeck bought the team in 1959. Knowing that as a minority owner he would have no say-so in the direction of the White Sox under Veeck, who had bought 54 percent of the team, Bartholomay began casting his eyes on other major league franchises.

The story reads:

(In 1962) Bartholomay made inquiries into the availability of the Milwaukee Braves. Owned by Lou Perini, who had moved the team from Boston in 1953, Bartholomay had heard rumors the Perinis were getting no financial benefit from the team.

Tapped by his investor group, Bartholomay headed to Framingham, Mass., to visit Perini at the construction company he ran. I hung around his office for a couple of days. The only person I stalked in my life was Mr. Perini. Finally, his secretary took pity on me.

After speaking with Perini and then meeting with him a week later in Toronto, the Braves' owner said if Bartholomay brought a cashier's check to New York worth $6.2 million in three days, they had a deal.

"I was about $500,000 short," Bartholomay recalls. "I went to the Northern Trust. They gave me $600,000 — they said the extra $100,000 was in case I made a mistake."

In New York, Bartholomay carried two checks — one worth $6.2 million and one worth $5.6 million. Perini opened the envelope to the second one.

"I thought he would blow up," Bartholomay says. "I said, 'I want to pick your brain. I want you to stay.

"He started crying and said, 'No one's ever asked me to stay in anything.'"

Named the team's chairman, Bartholomay was quickly approached about moving to Atlanta. At the 1963 All-Star Game in Cleveland, Dr. Martin Luther King, the president of Coca-Cola and others told him they were building a $20 million stadium and wanted to recruit a pro baseball and pro football team. They wanted Atlanta to be the capital of the New South — a city not associated with people like Alabama Gov. George Wallace and Jim Crow laws.

With the Braves lease up in County Stadium in 1965, Bartholomay and his partners agreed to depart Milwaukee.

"You have to put the Atlanta move in perspective," says Bartholomay. "The second year in Milwaukee, we weren't drawing well. All the great players — Hank Aaron, Willie Mays, Jackie Robinson — had come from the South. But there were no pro teams playing down there."

Because of litigation, the Braves didn't move until 1966. Bartholomay still vividly remembers Opening Day on April 12 that year.

"I was disappointed because we lost the game in extra innings," he says. "But it was great. The whole city was electrified."

Despite some middling Braves' teams in the interim, the city and the baseball world were electrified eight years later when Hank Aaron smacked his 715th home run, topping Babe Ruth's record that was considered unbreakable.

"I was sitting in the front row with Hank's mother and father," Bartholomay recalls. "There's a place where you go beyond adrenaline — I carried his mother above the barrier and onto the field after he hit it."

It will be noted that Bartholomay - in the 2014 story, or in any others - made no mention of any efforts on his part to do anything to enhance either the attendance or the product in Milwaukee. After buying the club before the 1963 season, Bartholomay insisted on limiting the length of his new County Stadium lease to three years, giving himself a one-year cushion in case the new Atlanta park wasn't ready for the 1965 season (it was), and in case the Jim Crow discrimination laws that permeated the South at the time proved to be too substantial a deterrent to the move (they weren't).

The deal between the Bartholomay group and Perini, an absentee owner who felt no obligation or loyalty to Milwaukee despite the record-breaking attendance figures of the 1950s, included no limitations on when or where the team could move. From the time the purchase was finalized, the team was ticketed for Atlanta; the only question was when the move would happen. Once word of the Braves' intentions got out, Bartholomay, knowing that the environment in Wisconsin was certain to get hostile, even considered moving the Braves to Atlanta for the 1964 season. Besides breaking the County Stadium lease two years early, this would have forced the Braves to play their first season at 20,000-seat Ponce de Leon Park, the long-time home of the minor-league Atlanta Crackers. Ponce de Leon was almost as inadequate as a major league venue as Milwaukee's Borchert Field had been in 1952. It had no center-field wall; instead, it had a magnolia tree in dead center that was in play, and that still stands on the site, 50 years after the ballpark was torn down. While NL owners quickly told Bartholomay that they would not agree to the move in time for the 1964 season - American League owners had already rebuffed Charles O. Finley after the 1962 season when he went public with plans to move his Kansas City Athletics to Atlanta - Bartholomay also was told that he would have support among his fellow owners if he moved to Atlanta once the terms of the County Stadium lease were satisfied.

But even given the virtual certainty that Bartholomay and his group bought the Braves with the sole purpose of moving them out of Milwaukee, the franchise already was in trouble on several fronts when Bartholomay bought it. It drew 1.1 million in 1961, only five seasons after its record 2.2 million count of

1957, and while the Braves weren't the only MLB franchise to suffer from a drop in attendance during that period, one sees in retrospect an aging team, a tired and leaderless franchise, a farm system that failed to develop players on whom management had lavished hundreds of thousands of dollars in bonus money, and a disenchanted fan base that immediately assumed - often with justification - that every move made by management would turn out to be wrong, perhaps even intentionally so. This was the case before Bartholomay bought the team, and one can make the argument that moving the Braves was nothing more than what appeared to be a sound business decision, given the circumstances Bartholomay inherited.

Why, ultimately, did the Milwaukee Braves cease to exist after only 13 seasons in a market where they shattered baseball attendance records, won two pennants and a World Series, never came close to a losing season, and played a direct role in reshaping baseball's economic and geographic landscape?

Taking Bartholomay's unquestioned deception and pursuit of Dixieland profits out of the equation, one can outline four focal-point reasons and six secondary reasons Milwaukee lost the Braves.

1. Fred Miller's death.

More than 60 years after his death in 1954, Frederick C. Miller can still be described as Wisconsin's patron benefactor, both within and beyond the sports realm, and he still ranks with Al McGuire and Bud Selig among the most forceful advocates as Milwaukee as a big-tme sports city.

Miller had been a three-year starter at tackle for Knute Rockne's Notre Dame football teams from 1926-28, serving as captain and making several All-America teams during his senior season, and graduated with the highest academic honors the university could bestow. While establishing himself in the family business, Miller maintained close ties with Notre Dame, especially after his close friend - and former tackle understudy - Frank Leahy - became head coach in 1941. After Leahy returned from two years of Navy service in 1946, Miller became virtually an assistant coach - and lead recruiter - without portfolio. He also served as Leahy's personal public-relations man and social secretary, and he would walk the sidelines with Leahy during Notre Dame games. That relationship with Notre Dame and Leahy continued for the rest of Miller's life. Leahy would later say of Miller: "He had a tremendous capacity for loyalty; he idolized the very soil that Notre Dame rests on. That amazing loyalty just oozed out of him and into the players. I could feel it myself. He always seemed to give me a little added strength, a little extra feeling of confidence."

Miller had been friends with Bill Veeck since 1942, when the two were handball partners at the Milwaukee Athletic Club. After Milwaukee's three biggest breweries at the time - Blatz, Schlitz and Pabst - had rebuffed Veeck's efforts to enlist them as sponsors of the minor-league Milwaukee Brewers franchise he had purchased the previous year, Veeck had convinced Miller - then the general manager of the brewery, and known simply as "Fritz" to Veeck - to sponsor the team's radio telecasts and to buy the exclusive rights to sell beer at Borchert Field. This was the brewery's first-ever major sports investment, and the success of the venture confirmed Fred Miller's long-held idea that sports sponsorship and advocacy could be a springboard both for the company and for Milwaukee.

In 1947, Miller assumed the presidency of a brewing company that was struggling to survive against the "Big Three" in Milwaukee beerdom and had made only a faint footprint in the national market. In 1947, Schlitz was the No. 1 beer producer in the country, turning out 3.9 million barrels, while Miller was 20th, with 806,000 barrels. By 1952, after five years under Frederick Miller, his company was up to fifth after a $25 million plant upgrade. (In 1953, it dropped to eighth, partly because of a strike that shut down all of Milwaukee's breweries for 76 days, and in the late 1950s, after Miller's death, it fell to 10th before rebounding in the 1970s, largely because of its introduction of the first low-calorie beer, Miller Lite, in 1975. By 1980, it was second in national sales only to Anheuser-Busch.)

Meanwhile, Miller immersed himself in Wisconsin in general and in Milwaukee in particular, and in 1952 Pope Pius XII himself presented Miller with the Order of the Knights of St. Gregory title - one of the highest lay honors in Catholicism - for raising more than $1 million to benefit the St. Aemilian Child Care Center & Lakeside Children's Center, which until 1943 had been known as the Milwaukee Orphan's Asylum. His belief in sports and their benefits, both to the community and to his company, escalated as his power and influence increased.

According to Phil Eck, Miller's grandson and the author of a 2016 book about Frederick Miller's life and achievements, Miller made three attempts to purchase a major league baseball team for Milwaukee. The first was early in 1949, when the St. Louis Browns were put up for sale by Richard Muckerman, who had bought the team in 1945 when it was relatively flush financially after winning its only American League pennant in 1944 and outdrawing the Cardinals for one of only a few times during the 50 years that the teams shared the St. Louis market. Muckerman, though, spent the cash windfall to buy and improve Sportsman's Park, locking the Browns into St. Louis and leaving little money for player acquisition and development. Brothers Bill and Charley DeWitt bought the team, with the stated intention of keeping it in St. Louis, but soon were peddling it themselves. Miller made an offer. However, according to Eck, AL owners told Miller that Borchert Field would not be acceptable even on a temporary basis, and that his application would not be given consideration unless and until ground was broken on a new ballpark in Milwaukee. After Miller returned to Milwaukee, he told city and county officials of this mandate, and this brought about the start of construction on County Stadium, the financing for which already had been approved earlier in 1949.

Miller, with County Stadium construction underway in May 1951, tried to buy the Browns a second time, but this time lost out to Bill Veeck. "Veeck and (his grandfather) were buddies (going back to Veeck's ownership of the minor-league Brewers from 1941-45)," Eck said. "Veeck went behind his back with some (Browns) stockholders. He told them he intended to keep the team in St. Louis. He got enough shares to buy the club. After that, they (his grandfather and Veeck) weren't friends anymore."

Given Miller's reputation for transparency in his business and personal dealings, and the duration of the friendship between Miller and Veeck, it's easy to see in retrospect why Miller (and Eck) felt Veeck at least owed Miller the courtesy of informing him of his, Veeck's, interest in buying the Browns. At the same time, there is no concrete evidence that Veeck's intent was to undercut Miller or that any right of first refusal, implied or otherwise, was involved. Nor is there any evidence to suggest that Veeck, at the time he bought the team and for more than a year afterward, had any intention of moving it out of St. Louis. Instead, his stated objective, then and later, was to oblige the *Cardinals* to move. Paul Dickson, in his 2012 book *Bill Veeck: Baseball's Greatest Maverick*, wrote that Veeck became aware of the Browns' 1951 availability not through Miller but through close friend Roy Drachman, a real estate developer in Tucson, Ariz., where the Indians had moved their spring-training headquarters after Veeck bought that team, and where Veeck owned a ranch.

Veeck still had to acquire additional stock from individual investors in a previous stock sale before assuming control of the Browns on July 3, 1951, but contrary to Miller's apparent belief, no evidence exists that any of Miller's prospective investors switched their money from Miller's bid to Veeck's. All of Veeck's major investors also had been involved in his 1946 purchase of the Indians - and were repaid handsomely after Veeck sold the club in 1950, two years after it won the World Series - and some also had backed him in 1941 when he bought the minor league Brewers. Most of the investors, according to Dickson, were Chicago-based and had known Veeck since his days as a Cubs employee in the 1930s: meat packers Lester Armour and Phil Swift, Phil Clarke of City National Bank of Chicago, attorney Syd Schiff, and investment brokers Art Allyn and Newt Frye. Secondary stockholders included entertainer George Jessel, and

Abe Saperstein, the owner of the Harlem Globetrotters. Both also were long-time friends of Veeck. No mention was made in Eck's book, or in any other account of the transaction and its prelude, of any of those investors being involved with Miller - and even if Veeck did convince any of Miller's prospective stockholders to switch their commitment, their willingness to do so would not have been difficult to justify. Veeck had been immersed in baseball virtually his entire life - his father William had been president of the Cubs from 1919 until his death in 1933 - and Veeck already had two spectacularly successful stints as an owner, first in Milwaukee and then in Cleveland. Miller, on the other hand, had never been directly involved in baseball ownership or operations, and his overriding sports passion was Notre Dame football, not baseball.

Dickson wrote about Veeck's purchase of the Browns: "Before the sale to Veeck, rumors indicated that the American League would move the team to Baltimore, which had been crying for a major league team since the original Orioles left the city after the 1902 season to become the New York Highlanders (and then the Yankees). Some suggested the Browns should head for the West Coast, and another proposed shifting the team to Milwaukee." There is no other mention of Miller making an offer that the DeWitt brothers strongly considered; in fact, there is no mention of Miller in the book at all.

Veeck in 1961 wrote in his book *Veeck As In Wreck*, and maintained until he died in 1986, that he had bought the Browns in 1951 with the sole intent of winning a two-team survival battle in a one-team city at a time when the Cardinals seemed vulnerable. The Browns' attendance more than doubled from 247,131 in 1950 to 518,796 - more than they had drawn in 1944 during their only AL pennant year - in 1952, and Veeck later described his 1952 work as the most rewarding of his career. "I did not buy the Browns with the intention of moving them out of St. Louis," Veeck wrote in 1961. "If I did, I put on an awful good act of working 24 hours a day for a year and a half trying to (market) them. "

Veeck and Miller both thought they saw another window of opportunity after the 1952 season, when Cardinals owner Fred Saigh was indicted on income-tax evasion charges and had no choice but to sell the club. According to Eck, Miller, on behalf of the brewery, made an offer of $4.1 million to buy the Cardinals with the understanding that they would relocate to Milwaukee for the 1953 season. Saigh, wanting the Cardinals to remain in St. Louis, sold instead to Gussie Busch and the Anheuser-Busch brewery for $3.75 million. (Saigh also turned down another offer that was larger than the one that he accepted from Busch, and perhaps larger than Miller's offer. This one was from a Texas group that wanted to move the team to Houston, where the Cardinals had a Texas League affiliate, the Buffs, and thus had the territorial rights. Houston's support of its Double-A team had fluctuated over the years, but the Buffs had drawn a franchise-record 401,383 in 1948, and some took this as a reflection of Houston's readiness for major league baseball.)

Even though he was apparently outmanuevered by Veeck in his second effort to bring the St. Louis Browns to Milwaukee, and then thwarted in his attempt to buy the Cardinals from Saigh, Miller had not given up on the idea of bringing major league baseball to Milwaukee. He continued to believe

passionately that Milwaukee deserved and would enthusi-
astically support major league baseball, and he had become
Milwaukee's driving force for big-league status on many
fronts. Besides being the primary force behind the decision to
begin construction on $5.8 million County Stadium, Miller
in 1951 helped underwrite an NBA franchise, the Hawks, who
were to play in the brand-new Milwaukee Arena, which Miller
had helped convince the city to build. Even though he was
a Notre Dame graduate and one of its most ardent and influential backers, he helped bankroll the Marquette football
program, and without his backing, the "Golden Avalanche"
almost certainly would not have been able to stay in major college football as long as it did. (Marquette finally dropped football after the 1960 season after winning only 10 games in its
final seven seasons.) He also was central to the effort to save
the Packers, whose primary home until 1957 was a Green Bay
high school stadium and who probably could not have survived
in Wisconsin had they not been permitted by the Braves and
Milwaukee County to play half their home games at County
Stadium upon its completion in 1953. Before that, they had
played some games at Marquette's 24,000-seat stadium, which
was at the intersection of North 36th and West Clybourn
streets before it was torn down in 1976. The Packers also occasionally rented Borchert Field, and played a few games in a
makeshift stadium on the State Fair grounds in West Allis.

Veeck, knowing by the end of 1952 that he could not win
the battle for St. Louis against the Anheuser-Busch fortune, was
ready to move the Browns to Milwaukee in time for the 1953
season, but couldn't do so because Lou Perini, who had purchased the Triple-A Brewers, owned the major league rights to

the Milwaukee territory. This brought Miller and Perini, already friends, into collaboration.

They began working together during this interregnum, and Miller ultimately played a major role in convincing Perini that he would be best served by moving the Braves to Milwaukee. Miller, while not a stockholder or direct investor, orchestrated the final agreement, which was announced on March 13, 1953. Miller soon was named by Perini to the team's board of directors. He also bought WTMJ radio sponsorship on behalf of the brewery, paid $75,000 for the purchase and installation of County Stadium's scoreboard, and then bought $50,000 worth of advertising on that scoreboard. He also served as an invaluable go-between in other sponsorship arrangements that were worked out as part of the deal to bring the Braves to Milwaukee.

"The first thing they asked Lou Perini," Phil Eck said, "was 'is Fred Miller one of your stockholders?' Perini said no, that they were only good friends. I think this relieved the owners ... they weren't sure that they wanted a second brewery to own a team (after Anheuser-Busch had bought the Cardinals)."

Miller's confidence in Milwaukee was justified when the 1953 Braves set a National League attendance record with 1,826,397 paying spectators despite the fact the Dodgers were runaways in the NL race almost from its start, and in spite of spring weather that was savage even by Milwaukee standards. In 1954, the Braves broke their own NL record, drawing 2,131,888, and the franchise's success was heralded as a lifeboat for a sport that was suffering from dwindling attendance in almost every other market, major league or minor. Beyond Miller's justifiable pride in Milwaukee's having proved that it was profoundly a major league city, his belief that sports and beer could sell each other had been emphatically proved correct. In correspondence with the Miller brewery's board of directors late in 1953, Miller recommended the following commitments for 1954 - a time when most other breweries in Milwaukee and around the country were involved superficially, if at all, in sports advertising and promotion, and when beer sales throughout the nation were static:

⁘ Sponsorship of the Braves radio broadcasts for $250,000.

⁘ Underwriting the Packers, who did not yet have a commitment for a new Green Bay stadium and were one of the NFL's worst teams, for $110,000.

⁘ Sponsorship amounting to $250,000 for the NFL championship game. The brewery had sponsored the game the previous year, and Miller, who foresaw the emergence of the NFL as a powerful national sales medium long before it outgrew its regional and local bases, was enthusiastic about using that investment as a national vehicle to widen the brewery's reach and appeal.

⁘ An outlay of $30,000 to cover the radio and TV broadcasts of the NBA's Milwaukee Hawks. The NBA had only eight teams by the end of the 1954-55 season, including small-market franchises in Syracuse, Rochester and Fort Wayne. Its sustaining superstar, the Minneapolis Lakers' George Mikan, retired after the 1953-54 season, and its three big-market franchises - Boston, New York and Philadelphia - got lowest priority for dates in their cities' primary arenas. The Hawks drew poorly and never made the playoffs during their time in Milwaukee. But unlike almost all of his contemporaries in the sports-investment realm at that time, Miller believed the NBA had a future, and the 1954-55 Hawks had a rookie forward, Bob Pettit, who was to lead the St. Louis Hawks to an NBA title in 1958. Pettit went on to become one of the premier players in NBA history, and Miller thought, during the last months of his life, that a team built around Pettit could be successful in Milwaukee.

* Miller invested $7,500 in Marquette, one of Notre Dame's primary basketball rivals, to finance MU basketball broadcasts. This was in addition to his previous help for the struggling football program. He also helped bring a minor league hockey team, the Chiefs, to the Arena. Between Marquette, the Hawks and the Chiefs, the new Arena had three fulltime tenants, and that was crucial in the building's financial success.

"His ambition was to make Milwaukee a sports center and keep it that way," Eck said. "I'm not sure any of the other beer companies had anyone who was anything like Fred Miller. He was a doer. If he said he was going to do something, he did it, and I'd imagine he got a lot of that from (Knute) Rockne. People said they always felt better after talking to him."

The 1953 success was only the beginning for the Braves. But Fred Miller wasn't around to see the 1957 culmination.

During the afternoon of December 17, 1954, Miller hosted a Wisconsin State Brewers Association luncheon in the fermentation caves that had been opened below the main brewery the year before. Later that afternoon, Miller drove to Mitchell

Field, Milwaukee's main airport. One of his company's private planes, a two-engine, piston-driven Lockheed Ventura that originally had been built for the Army as a B-34 short-range bomber and had been purchased by the brewery from the Royal Canadian Air Force in 1951, was waiting in the company hangar along with the plane's two company-employed pilots, brothers Paul and Joseph Laird. Miller's 20-year-old son, Frederick Jr., a junior at Notre Dame who was on winter break, also was along for the trip from Milwaukee to Winnipeg, Manitoba, Canada. The purpose of the trip was twofold: The elder Miller wanted to survey a parcel of land that was owned by a husband and wife he knew; the plot was in foreclosure and Miller planned to pay off the mortgage so that the couple could own the land free and clear. He also wanted to enjoy a hunting trip with his son.

At 5:07 p.m., with light snow falling, the Ventura took off from Mitchell, but less than a minute later, one of the engines caught fire. The pilots radioed the Mitchell control tower and attempted to return to the airport, only to have the other engine fail. They were able to steer around homes surrounding the airport, but crashed well short of the runway, in an open field north of South Whitnall Avenue. The plane was loaded to its limit with aviation fuel, which immediately caught fire and engulfed Fred Miller Jr. and the two pilots; all three of them died within minutes in an inferno that couldn't be extinguished for several hours. Fred Sr. somehow escaped or was thrown clear of the plane. When rescuers reached him, he was still conscious but was burned over more than half his body and had suffered numerous other major injuries. His first concern was the safety of his son and the pilots, and he asked the emergency crews to try to extract them from the plane before tending to him.

Miller was rushed to Johnston Emergency Hospital on West Grant Street, and clung to life for five hours before his death at 10:10 p.m. He was 48. Both major Milwaukee newspapers put out special editions updating his condition and the circumstances of the crash on an hour-by-hour basis throughout the night. More than 3,000 attended his funeral, including Leahy, famed *Chicago Tribune* sports editor Arch Ward (a close friend of Miller's who conceived and promoted the major league baseball All-Star Game and the All-America Football Conference, among other high-profile sports entities), Hall of Fame manager Joe McCarthy, and Los Angeles Rams wide receiver Elroy (Crazy Legs) Hirsch. Numerous journalists both throughout and beyond Milwaukee mourned him as a man whose life and loss both would linger in Milwaukee for generations. *Sentinel* sports editor Lloyd Larson wrote: "Milwaukee suffered a loss so great as to be almost beyond comprehension. Fred Miller was a big leaguer through and through. No man ever did more or gave more of his time and himself to make Milwaukee a big league city in everything - sports, business, education and other worthwhile phases of community life almost too numerous to mention."

Although neither Miller nor Lou Perini ever offered confirmation, it was and still is believed by many that the two had a handshake agreement that gave Miller and the Miller Brewing Company the right of first refusal to buy the Braves and keep them in Milwaukee if Perini ever decided to relinquish his majority ownership of the club. Moreover, it was and is believed that even in the absence of an understanding between the two in 1953 or 1954, that Miller, if he had been alive in 1962 when Perini put the club up for sale, would have outbid Bartholomew's group or any other prospective buyers to buy the club and save it for Milwaukee. But for more than a decade after Miller's death, nobody emerged to fill the vacuum he left, and this absence of leadership among Milwaukee's movers and shakers was a significant factor in the sale to William Bartholomay's group and the franchise's subsequent move to Atlanta.

Would the Braves still be in Milwaukee if Fred Miller had not died in that plane crash? J. Gordon Hylton, a former Marquette law professor who has written and blogged extensively on the legal and financial elements of the Braves' Milwaukee stay and departure, isn't sure. In 2013, he wrote to the author:

That is a really interesting theory, and I certainly agree that the Braves' history could have been much different had Fred Miller survived. My only negative thought is Miller was first and foremost a profit-oriented businessman. He could have purchased the Cardinals in January 1953, but he declined to do so because he thought the asking price was too high. It was only after that episode that Fred Saigh decided that he would do his best to sell the Cardinals to a local buyer.

It is hard to know what the value of the Braves actually was in 1962 (when Perini sold the club to the Bartholomay group). The Braves lost money that season (after turning six-figure profits during the 1950s); Major League Baseball itself had entered into an era of declining per-game attendance, and the County Stadium lease had expired. The sale price was widely reported at the time as $5.5 *million, though later sources cite the figure of $6.1 million. Earlier that year, the Cincinnati Reds, reigning NL champions who were having an even better season in 1962 than they had in 1961, sold for only $4.5 million and that may have included* (Crosley Field, the Reds' antiquated ballpark). *Would Miller have believed that the Braves were really worth that much more than the Reds?*

Ironically, a good part of the Braves' value lay in the ability to move the team to Atlanta, which appears to have been what motivated Bartholomay to buy the team, although no one was aware of this in 1962 and most commentators described the new Chicago-area-based ownership group as "local."

Would Miller have been willing to overpay the team's market value to keep the team in Milwaukee when he (didn't do that) *to bring the Cardinals to Milwaukee in January 1953? I don't know the answer to that - but it may be yes, since he apparently thought that he could bring in partners and continue negotiating in 1953. On the other hand, Bartholomay was not publicly committed to moving the team in 1962, and he did keep it in Milwaukee for two years before announcing the move. I don't think we can assume that Miller would have definitely stepped in and tried to outbid the Bartholomay group. After all, Perini later reported that he had received numerous offers over the years for the Braves. Perhaps Miller was one of those unknown bidders, but he obviously never bid enough to tempt Perini to sell.*

What-ifs notwithstanding, there was no question in 1953 that Miller was a major player in the advent of the Milwaukee Braves. Miller was with Perini in the lead car of the motorcade that greeted the Braves when they arrived in Milwaukee before the start of the 1953 season. Though it is not certain, the circumstantial evidence, and many quotes from individuals who knew Miller well, strongly indicate that some kind of unwritten agreement between Perini and Miller did exist at the time Miller died - and that even if it didn't, Miller's sense of civic loyalty was such that if he had been alive in 1962, he would have used the brewery's financial might to outbid Bartholomay and anyone else after Perini put the club up for sale. Perini also kept a 10 percent interest in the team after he sold to Bartholomay, and though his interest in the Milwaukee market was little more that fidiciary at the time he was the primary owner, Perini might have backed any offer Miller would have made.

"I'm not sure of any agreement they had," Phil Eck said, "but I feel pretty certain that even if he couldn't buy the team himself, he would have found the people in Milwaukee to do it. He loved Milwaukee."

Bud Selig, who was 20 years old (and a rabid Milwaukee Braves fan) when Miller was killed, wasn't in a position to have first-hand knowledge of any agreement between Miller and Perini, and said so in 2016 when he was asked that question. But he added: "I (later) heard some talk about it. Fred Miller was a guy who loved baseball and got the park built; remember, County Stadium was built before anybody knew whether Milwaukee would even have a (major league) team. Fred Miller had an amazing ability to exercise vision. I'm sure he would have (at least tried to buy the team when Perini was ready to sell)."

But would the Braves have been a sound long-term investment to any ownership group in 1962, even if their permanence in Milwaukee had been ensured by a Miller brewery purchase that would have put an undeniably great and good man in control of the franchise? Perhaps not, even for somebody with Miller's business acumen and ability to bring out the best in people. Nobody will ever know how Miller would have proceeded if Perini had put the team up for sale and Miller had bought it, but the reality in 1962 was that on-field performance and attendance were sagging badly. This brings up Factor No. 2 in the demise of the Milwaukee Braves:

2. Management undermined the franchise throughout much of its time in Milwaukee by spending a disproportionate amount of money on massive bonuses given to amateur players who made little or no impact on the team.

As an industrialist who'd made his fortune outside baseball, Perini, who'd bought the Boston Braves in 1943, was in the vanguard of the new-breed ownership in major league baseball, which had been controlled by "sportsmen" like Connie Mack, Charles and Horace Stoneham, and Charles Comiskey throughout most of its history before World War II. Those men, and most other owners before World War II, depended on their baseball teams for their livelihoods, and basic business principles - other than hoarding every cent when it came to player salaries - were foreign to some of them.

Perini, conversely, got into baseball long after his construction company, which dates to 1894, became internationally prominent and enormously profitable (as it remained in 2016, reporting $4.2 billion in revenue in 2013 as the Tutor Perini Corporation). Perini believed in the business adage that making money meant first spending money, and even during the time his franchise was dissipating in Boston, Perini gave his scouts and other player-development personnel free rein in terms of signing top amateur talent at a time baseball had no first-year-player draft. Every winter, starting in the late 1940s, Perini would assemble Boston sportswriters, load them onto a plane that he called the "Rookie Rocket," and take them around the country to ceremonies where amateur players would sign with the Braves amid local (and Boston) fanfare. Eddie Mathews and Del Crandall, both Southern Californians, had signed with the Braves during Rookie Rocket junkets in 1949 and 1948 respectively. More conspicuously at the time, Johnny Antonelli, an 18-year-old pitcher, had signed for a $65,000 bonus in 1948.

For the first 50 or so years after major league baseball began with the founding of the National League in 1876, minor league teams usually operated independently of the majors, and made their money at the end of each season by selling their best players to higher classifications - or, in the cases of the most promising players, to major league teams. Sometimes the player would get part of the purchase price; more often, he got only a small salary increase and the opportunity to move one step closer to the majors. Lavish spending on promising players had occurred throughout baseball's history; the first player for whom a major league team paid $100,000 was Willie Kamm by the Chicago White Sox in 1923. But that money went to the PCL's San Francisco Seals, for whom Kamm, a San Francisco native, was playing at the time. Kamm had a distinguished 13-season career as a third baseman with the White Sox and Cleveland Indians, but he never cashed in himself on his notoriety as the "first $100,000 player." His highest salary was $12,500 with the Indians in 1929.

But the independent minor-league operation was essentially doomed after Branch Rickey introduced the "farm system" as president of the then-cash-poor Cardinals in the early 1920s, and popularized the notion that a major league team ought to have total control of all its prospects, from Class D through Triple-A. Through Player Development Contracts, or outright purchases, Rickey established a network of minor league affiliates, and the flow of talent from the vast Cardinal chain had much to do with the fact the team reached nine World Series from 1926-46, winning five of them. It also saved Rickey, always profit-conscious, the money major league teams had to pay their minor league counterparts to acquire new talent; he didn't have to pay any of the Cardinals' prospects more than a pittance unless and until they proved their major league capability. Other teams soon assembled their own sprawling farm systems, and by 1949, 59 minor leagues - far more than the talent pool of the time justified - were operating, most of them with major league ownership or affiliations.

It also meant that instead of negotiating with minor league operators for the top talent available, teams had to negotiate with the players themselves, and pay them what the market would bear, even though many of them were still in high school. The major league draft wasn't instituted until 1965, so before that, the teams that wanted the most promising talent had to outbid other teams for that talent - with all of the money going to the player, not a minor-league club as had been the case in Willie Kamm's time.

So began the "bonus baby" era, which started in earnest during the postwar prosperity in the late 1940s, and lasted until 1964 when the Los Angeles Angels signed University of Wisconsin player Rick Reichardt to a $400,000 bonus contract. The next year, baseball introduced the amateur draft, ostensibly to spread the talent more evenly, but in reality to protect the owners from their own profligate spending. Rick Monday, the first player taken in the first draft, in 1965, received a reported $104,000 from the Kansas City Athletics.

During most of the bonus-baby era, the major leagues had a rule requiring teams that had signed players for more than a designated amount to keep those players on their major league rosters for two years instead of sending them to the minors for the customary incubation period. Mathews signed for $5,999, one dollar less than the bonus threshold in 1949, so the Braves could send him to the minors rather than having him languish on the major league roster. He played three minor league seasons, the last (1951) with the minor-league Milwaukee Brewers. The previous year, Mathews, whose draft number made him vulnerable to callup when the Korean War began in 1950, enlisted in the Navy, but he was soon given a deferment and subsequently discharged because he was an only child and his father was suffering from tuberculosis, which took his life in 1953 during Mathews' second major league season and his first in Milwaukee.

The bonus rule was supposed to be a spending deterrent for major league teams, but it seldom was. The Braves, even in Boston, had invested considerably in young talent, and as a result, the team that migrated to Milwaukee in 1953 was far more talented and capable than its seventh-place finish in 1952 would have suggested. Once the Braves started accumulating unprecedented gate-receipt riches in Milwaukee, Perini authorized an even more aggressive approach.

The first of the Milwaukee Braves' big-money "bonus babies" were pitcher Joey Jay and infielder Mel Roach, both of whom received packages worth $40,000 during the 1953 season. (By way of comparison, the New York Giants in 1950 had signed Willie Mays for $4,000.) Jay, who became the first player from the nascent Little League program to make the majors, was only 17 and had just graduated from high school at the time he signed; Roach, 20, had played one season at the University of Virginia.

Both had to be kept on the major league roster through the 1953 and 1954 seasons. Roach played in only eight major league games during those two seasons, and didn't return to the Braves until 1957, after two years of military service. His eight-season major league career, which ended with the Phillies in 1962, included only 227 games, during which he batted .238 with seven home runs. Jay pitched in only 31 games during his first four seasons (1953-55 and 1957) with Milwaukee. He was a part-time member of the Braves' rotation from 1958-60, going 22-23, but his career didn't blossom until 1961 when he went to the Cincinnati Reds along with young pitching prospect Juan Pizarro for short-stop Roy McMillan in one of the most one-sided deals during the Braves' time in Milwaukee. Jay went 21-10 with a 3.53 ERA for the Reds as they won the 1961 NL pennant, and followed with a 21-14, 3.76 season in 1962.

The 1957 Braves won the NL pennant (and then the World Series) despite the fact they were, in effect, playing two major leaguers short throughout the regular season because two bonus babies were on the roster. The Braves that season had signed catcher-outfielder Hawk Taylor, 18, for $125,000, and spent another $100,000 to obtain West Bend native and Port Washington

High graduate John DeMerit, an outfielder who'd starred in basketball as well as baseball at the University of Wisconsin.

Taylor played in seven games in 1957 and four in 1958 before the Braves could send him to the minors to learn his trade, and even after he returned to the Braves in 1961, he played in only 56 games over the next three years before the Braves sold him to the New York Mets after the 1963 season. He was able to log 11 major league seasons with four different teams, mainly because of his defensive versatility, but he finished his 394-game career with a .218 average, 16 homers and 82 RBI. DeMerit was an even more profound washout, playing in 79 games with the Braves from 1957-61 and batting .172 with two homers and six RBI. The Mets took him in the 1962 expansion draft, and he played 14 games for that 40-120 team before being released, ending his major league career.

That same year, 1957, Mays - by then acknowledged as the best player in baseball and one of the best of all time - was paid $75,000 by the New York Giants. Stan Musial wasn't paid $100,000 until the 1958 season, and Ted Williams, in 1959, was paid $125,000 - the largest MLB salary ever at that point, and the same amount the Braves had laid out to sign Hawk Taylor.

In 1958, the Braves bestowed a $40,000 bonus on a 17-year-old high school player from Paducah, Ky., named Louie Haas. He was a middle infielder who was listed as 5-foot-10 and 165 pounds, but author Pat Jordan, a teammate of Haas in 1961 on the Palatka team in the Class D Florida State League, wrote that Haas was actually 5-foot-4 and 137 pounds. Other than one at-bat for Vancouver in the Class AAA Pacific Coast League in 1961,

Haas spent his entire four-year pro career in Class D, the lowest Organized Baseball classification at the time. In 328 games, he batted .250, and the only propensity he showed was for drawing walks (229 bases on balls, with 155 strikeouts).

In 1959, the Braves had an affiliate in the Class D Nebraska State League, which was in its final year of operation. The McCook Braves' starting rotation included, at various times, Pat Jordan, Bill Marnie, Bruce Brubaker and Dennis Overby - all of whom had been given bonuses of at least $30,000 each. Of those four, only Brubaker made the majors - for one game with the Los Angeles Dodgers during which he gave up three earned runs and three hits in 1 1/3 innings for a career ERA of 20.25. Jordan, who had signed for $37,000, finished that 1959 season with a 3-3 record and a 3.54 ERA. It was by far the best of his three seasons in the Braves' system. After he left baseball, he became a prolific and popular writer, working for *Sports Illustrated* for an extended period and publishing a dozen books - one of which, *A False Spring*, was a best-seller when it was released in 1973. *A False Spring* was perhaps, at the time it was published, the most thorough and insightful book about minor-league baseball life, and while much of it consisted of Jordan's reflections on the immaturity and absence of social skills that had much to do with the early dead-ending of his baseball career, it was also an indictment of the Braves' organization and its failures in terms of player evaluation, treatment and development. (One of the other McCook Braves pitchers that year was Phil Niekro, who had signed for a $500 "bonus" and went on to become a Hall of Famer.)

Meanwhile, in 1959, the Milwaukee Braves were paying Hank Aaron, the National League MVP two seasons before, only $35,000, although Aaron added an extra $13,500 to his income that winter when he was the top money winner on the "Home Run Derby" television show. Lou Burdette, who'd beaten the Yankees three times in the 1957 World Series and had been a fixture in the Braves' starting rotation since the team moved to Milwaukee, made $36,000. Warren Spahn and Eddie Mathews were the team's highest-paid players, at $65,000 and $50,000 respectively, and Red Schoendienst - who missed virtually the entire 1959 season after contracting tuberculosis - made $40,000. Schoendienst, a future Hall of Famer, had been in the majors since 1945 and was a 10-time All-Star at second base during his 19-year career. His acquisition from the Giants midway through the 1957 season was the final move that the Braves needed to win their only World Series title in Milwaukee.

To be sure, the Braves weren't the only team that wildly overspent on unproven talent during the bonus-baby era, and some of the amateur players who commanded big money did establish themselves as worthwhile. In 1965, the Braves' final season in Milwaukee, their two most consistent starting pitchers were Tony Cloninger (24-11, 3.29 ERA) and Wade Blasingame (16-10, 3.77), who had originally signed with the Braves for bonuses of $100,000 and $125,000 respectively. But neither pitcher again approached his 1965 level of excellence, and the Braves may have paid the price, in ways other than the huge cash outlays, for their empty investments on other players.

The bonus-baby system encouraged mistreatment, if not outright hazing, by veteran players who feared that their younger counterparts might get their jobs, or hurt their teams' chances of reaching the World Series at a time when a winning Series check could double the annual income of a middle-of-the-road major leaguer. Intimidation of younger players by their veteran counterparts had been an accepted part of major league baseball throughout its history - many attribute Ty Cobb's vicious play and demeanor to the way he was treated by his Detroit Tigers teammates as a 18-year-old rookie in 1905 - and David Lamb, in his 1991 book *Stolen Season,* interviewed 59-year-old Eddie Mathews, then a roving batting instructor with the Atlanta Braves. Mathews talked about his introduction to the Boston Braves after he signed with them in 1949 at age 17.

After Mathews signed and before he was assigned to a minor league team, the "Rookie Rocket" brought Mathews and other newly-minted prospects to Chicago to meet the Braves, who were playing the Cubs at Wrigley Field. Mathews in 1991 told of being threatened and intimidated, in the coarsest language he had ever heard, by veterans - like Bob Elliot, Red Barrett and Eddie Stanky - who had led the Braves to the 1948 NL pennant, and were players Mathews had idolized from afar in Santa Barbara, Calif. Later that night, though not of drinking age, Mathews went into a bar for a beer, and was given a free brew by the bartender. "This one's on the two gentlemen over there," the bartender said, pointing to Braves veterans Vern Bickford (who stayed with the Braves into their Milwaukee era) and Walker Cooper, who were sitting at a table in the tavern. "He nodded in thanks, feeling a touch of redemption," Lamb wrote, "The bartender leaned over to Mathews and added, 'They said to drink up and get the fuck out of here.'"

In the 1950s, before first-person books by Jim Brosnan and later Jim Bouton gave readers a behind-closed-clubhouse-doors insight to which the public hadn't previously been privy, most of what went on in major league clubhouses stayed there. Reporters didn't want to burn sources on the team by reporting untoward behavior or incidents, and many of them felt as much loyalty to the teams they covered as to the newspapers for which they worked. Most contemporary and retrospective accounts describe the championship-era Braves the same way most teams of that period are described: A collection of disparate players and personalities that didn't always mesh and tended to form cliques, many of them along geographic, age, racial (after 1947) and personality lines. Some Braves players, like Mathews, were relatively circumspect and uncomfortable with media scrutiny; others, like Warren Spahn, were extroverts who at least gave the appearance of enjoying their unique status.

The clubhouse environment can't necessarily be specified as a primary reason for the Braves' post-1959 decline and eventual departure from Milwaukee, Joey Jay's 1961 comment about the players' level of caring notwithstanding. But the presence on the team of so many bonus babies who had pocketed huge sums of money and done little or nothing to earn that money couldn't have added to team cohesion - especially in the 1940s and 1950s, when many older players had lost career time while in wartime service, and didn't take well to the idea of losing their jobs to young bonus babies who had not made such sacrifices.

More significant, the fact the bonus rule had the effect of taking away roster spots that might otherwise have gone to more capable veterans can be considered a reason the Braves, with more bonus babies and more money to spend than most teams, didn't earn the 12 additional victories that would have made them back-to-back-to-back-to-back World Series champions, likely cementing their status in Milwaukee permanently. And the fact the Braves' developmental system turned out so few adequate replacements once the 1950s paragons aged and departed can be considered a key factor in the deterioration of the team and its attendance, and eventually its departure from Milwaukee.

3. County Stadium.

The construction of County Stadium was considered visionary at the time, and in retrospect. The trouble was that the vision in question extended for less than a decade after the ballpark opened in 1953.

The cover photo of the very first issue of *Sports Illustrated*, dated August 16, 1954, shows Eddie Mathews at bat with packed stands and a Hollywood-premier level of light in the backdrop. To those who saw it in the 1950s when the Braves were breaking National League attendance records, County Stadium must have seemed like a beacon not only for Milwaukee's baseball future, but also for baseball itself. The park had been built for $5.8 million and had quickly paid for itself, and while it was no longer state-of-the-art by 1965, it was still clean, comfortable and structurally sound, if not particularly eye-catching. While it did have some view-obstructing columns, most of its seats offered a clear and proximate panorama of the action on the diamond. The ballpark had 11,000 parking spaces (compared to less than 1,000 at Brooklyn's Ebbets Field, abandoned by the Dodgers after the 1957 season and demolished in 1960) and was readily accessible from almost everywhere in southeastern Wisconsin, especially after the segment of Interstate 94 that was adjacent to County Stadium opened in 1958.

During the debate over whether Milwaukee deserved to be considered a major league city, County Stadium rarely if ever was mentioned as a reason it shouldn't. After all, the construction of the ballpark - only the second publicly-funded MLB venue of the 20th century, the first being Cleveland Stadium in 1931 - was the bait that hooked the Boston Braves and reeled them into Milwaukee. Players loved the fact that the field lighting was by far the best in the major leagues in terms of height, brightness and quantity. Before 1953, all the major league ballparks in use had been built without lights, and after 1935 when the first major league night game was played in Cincinnati, engineers had to improvise to mount lights on stadium rims not designed to support them. County Stadium's infield lights adjoined the upper-deck roof, but it also had four high towers with dozens of light banks in the outfield. This meant County Stadium's lights had superior range, and made it far less likely that a high fly could disappear into darkness during night games. Additionally, incandescent-light technology improved exponentially during the World War II years, and the quality of lighting available to County Stadium in 1953 was much superior to that of other ballparks, most of which had installed lights before or immediately after the war. Another County Stadium feature welcomed by players was the fact the new park's clubhouses were actually clubhouses and not simple dressing rooms. Players no longer were shoehorned together in claustrophobic, splinter-ridden clubhouses of the sort they'd had to endure in the older ballparks. For journalists and visiting dignitaries, County Stadium even had a built-in hospitality suite, called the Teepee Room, underneath the main grandstand.

County Stadium would serve Milwaukee and its baseball community well, and wound up having a life span of 46 baseball seasons from 1953-2000, counting the 1968 and 1969 seasons when the Chicago White Sox played a total of 20 games there, and not counting 1966 and 1967, the two years that followed the Braves' departure. Metropolitan Stadium, in Bloomington, Minn., was erected in 1956 under the same circumstances as County Stadium - with no assurance that a major league team would come there - and did not become a major league baseball venue until the Washington Senators moved to Minnesota in 1961. The Met, which cost $8.5 million and lasted only 22 major league seasons before being replaced by the Metrodome, was expanded several times, both for the Twins and for the NFL Vikings, and by the time it was abandoned, it looked more like a giant erector set than a major league sports facility. The other major league park built during this period was San Francisco's Candlestick Park, which opened in 1960 at a cost of $15 million, and a $16 million renovation and expansion to accommodate football was undertaken in 1971. Candlestick, from which the Giants finally moved after the 1999 season, had a 40-year baseball life during which talk of its replacement was virtually constant.

County Stadium was a better-than-adequate facility by major league standards throughout the time the Braves were there, and for some time afterward. At $5.8 million when it was finished in 1952 ($52.6 million in 2016 dollars), the ballpark was a bargain for the taxpayers who funded it. The luxury liner *SS United States* also was completed in 1952, and for the $79.4 million it cost to construct the ship, County Stadium could have been built 13 times over, with more than $4 million to spare. But for all the memories that were forged there by the Braves, Brewers, Packers and musical acts like the Rolling Stones (who played County Stadium in 1975), the ballpark did not remain an attraction unto itself - in 21st-century parlance, a "revenue stream" - for long. Milwaukee's baseball showplace was, in some ways, the first of the "modern" ballparks, but in more ways, it also was the last of the old ones.

The four ballparks that followed County Stadium, the Met and Candlestick Park were Dodger Stadium in Los Angeles and D. C. (now RFK) Stadium in 1962, New York's Shea Stadium in 1964, and the Houston Astrodome in 1965. Those parks ended forever the long-held premise that major league parks need not be anything more than basic baseball plants. While Dodger Stadium and Candlestick Park (before its 1971 remodel) were built exclusively for baseball, the multi-purpose "cookie cutter" sports monolith that would be an attraction unto itself - at least for a while - came into vogue starting with the Met, D.C. Stadium and Shea. Atlanta subsequently lured the Braves with the same type of state-of-the-art stadium, designed to attract and house not only major league baseball, but also football, concerts, convocations, conventions and the like. (County Stadium, of course, did house the Packers on a part-time basis from 1953 to 1994, but football was an afterthought when the stadium was built. One of the end zones was short of the required 10 yards in depth, and the playing surface was so narrow for football that both teams had their benches on one side of the field.)

And Atlanta's new park was a revenue stream, at least compared to County Stadium. Then, and a half-century later, luxury boxes were vital to professional sports operations not only because of the big-spending clientele they attracted, but because the income they generated didn't (and doesn't) have to be shared with visiting teams. Atlanta-Fulton County Stadium had 60 luxury suites when the Atlanta Braves began play in 1966. County Stadium in 1965 had two - one controlled by the county, the other by ownership. Atlanta's new digs also had 57 concession stands while County Stadium had only 37.

As it turned out, Atlanta-Fulton County Stadium (razed in 1997) was outlasted by County Stadium, which wasn't torn down until after the 2000 Brewers season. But beyond the fact it was more functional than futuristic, County Stadium didn't solve a problem that plagued the Braves (and later the pre-Miller Park Brewers) even when they were at their best: Milwaukee's capricious weather.

The Braves, whose first game in Milwaukee was on April 13, 1953, were able to play only one other home game before May 8, with four home games (and one in St. Louis) postponed because of weather during that span. They wound up having to play 32 games in 26 days, without a day off, later that season, shredding their pitching staff. Because they played 15 home doubleheaders, the Braves achieved their NL record-breaking attendance of 1,826,397 in only 62 home dates for an average of 29,458 per home opening in a ballpark that seated only about 36,000 even with temporary seating and standing-room areas. (Seven other Braves home games were shortened by weather that year.) The interference from the elements probably didn't matter that year; the 1953 Dodgers outdistanced the Braves to the finish by 13 games and often are prominently mentioned in discussions of the best teams ever, even though those Dodgers lost the World Series in six games to the Yankees.

But bad weather almost certainly played a role in the Braves being nosed out by the Dodgers in the 1956 race. The Braves had five games postponed in eight days during April, and had rainouts on May 18 and May 23 as well. Although the Braves went on an 11-game winning streak to take over first place after Fred Haney replaced Charlie Grimm as manager, and held that lead for most of the rest of the season, the doubleheader-heavy schedule eventually took its toll. The Dodgers won the pennant by one game over the Braves, whom they had trailed going into the final weekend of the season, and two over Cincinnati.

Decades later, of course, the Brewers' future in Milwaukee was directly tied to the construction of Miller Park and its re-tractable roof. It was argued - successfully, as it turned out - that the fact the Brewers were in the smallest market in baseball by the late 1990s made it essential that the franchise have a constituency throughout the state and beyond. This couldn't happen, the ar-gument went, without a weather-proof stadium because fans, es-pecially those from outlying areas, would not come to the games without knowing for certain that they would even be played. If this was true in the late 1990s, it stands to reason that it was true in the 1950s as well. Could or should Milwaukee, in hindsight, have built a weather-proof facility in the early 1950s instead of a fully functional but government-issue outdoor ballpark?

Doing so probably would have meant spending far more than the $5.8 million it cost to build County Stadium, and so far as is known, the idea of a retractable-roof or domed sports stadium in Milwaukee was never seriously considered during the run-up to the start of construction on County Stadium. But it would not have been impossible from the engineering or design standpoints. The concept itself was almost 2,000 years old, going back to the Roman Colosseum, which was completed in 80 A.D. It was built with an awning that could be stretched across the rim of the stadium during inclement weather.

If Milwaukee officials and politicians had looked for a model on which to base a domed-stadium plan, they wouldn't have had to travel far to find one that had been around for more than five decades when the Braves moved to Milwaukee in 1953 (and still was in place as of 2016). The West Baden Springs Hotel, built in 1902 in French Lick, Ind. (much better known, of course, for the fact basketball nonpareil Larry Bird grew up there) has as its distinguishing feature a dome that is 200 feet in diameter and 100 feet high and creates a huge atrium overlooked by six tiers of guest rooms. Even though the property went through several ownership changes and overhauls (and was closed and neglected for lengthy periods), the dome was never compromised until it suffered a partial collapse in 1991, 89 years after it was built. Both the dome and the hotel have been completely renovated and modernized since then.

The West Baden Springs Hotel dome was the largest free-span dome in the world until the Astrodome opened in 1965, and like the Houston facility, it was promoted as the "eighth wonder of the world" for decades after its construction. The Astrodome is more than three times larger than the West Baden Springs Hotel dome; its roof is 710 feet in diameter and the building stands 18 stories tall. But the Indiana dome proved that an indoor facility large enough to accommodate thousands of spectators was feasible from the engineering and architectural standpoints, even in 1902.

The first to put forth a serious domed-sports-stadium proposal is believed to be Charles C. "C.C." Pyle, the pioneer sports
promoter and agent who in 1925 had made both himself and
former University of Illinois football star Red Grange wealthy
by forming a team around Grange and barnstorming around
a country that to that point had considered pro football nothing more than a fleeting novelty. Grange was one of the biggest
names during the "Golden Age" of sports, spanning most of the
1920s, and that tour probably saved the 5-year-old NFL and certainly was the first step toward its emergence as the corporate
mammoth it later became.

Pyle, of whom it was said that the C.C. stood for "Cash and
Carry," believed in the future of pro football. He also felt major
league baseball, with new ballparks that weren't like boathouses with
diamonds and seats, could become an even more profitable industry
than it already was. In 1926 he paid an engineering firm $5,000 to
produce a set of blueprints for a 70,000-seat stadium with a retractable roof, escalators instead of steps in the aisles, magnifying glass
in the upper sections to improve the view, and even a landing pad
for helicopters, which were in their earliest stages of development in
1926. "Anyone who gets three or four of these stadiums will control
sports in America," Pyle told a news conference that he had called
to present the plans. Pyle for the rest of his life (he died in 1939)
insisted that such facilities could be built with existing technology
and engineering. However, he never took the idea any further. "It's
impossible," he said. "It's impossible because it would cost $3 mil-
lion." This was almost four times the $800,000 that had been spent
in 1923 to build the Los Angeles Memorial Coliseum, and well
over twice as much as the $1,245,000 it would cost the University of
Michigan to build 84,500-seat Michigan Stadium in 1927.

The idea of a domed sports stadium began to be more widely considered in the 1950s. Roy Hofheinz, the Houston politician and promoter who became the driving force behind the Astrodome, later said the basic concept for the building had first been presented to him in 1952, 13 years before the Astrodome opened, and that he never considered an outdoor stadium for Houston after seeing those blueprints. In 1955, owner Dewey Soriano of the PCL's Seattle Rainiers tried unsuccessfully to sell politicians on a domed-stadium project in an effort to attract a major league team. The blueprints that Soriano's architects had drawn up were incorporated into the design of the Kingdome two decades later, but two referendums intended to start the process were rejected by King County voters in the early 1960s.

In one of many spiteful gestures toward Milwaukee for forcing MLB into courtrooms before and after the Braves moved to Atlanta, Soriano in 1967 was given an American League expansion franchise, the Pilots, even though he was badly undercapitalized and even though Seattle was no closer to building a domed stadium in 1967 than it had been in 1955. Seattle got the franchise with the proviso that the domed stadium be approved by county voters and officials, and under construction, by the time the team began play in 1969. Those prerequisites were not met during the Pilots' one-year life span. The Pilots played at Sick's Stadium, the Rainiers' Pacific Coast League park, in 1969, and went bankrupt after the season. Bud Selig bought them from a bankruptcy court a week before the 1970 season and moved them to Milwaukee, where they began play as the Brewers in 1970.

In Brooklyn, Dodgers owner Walter O'Malley was keenly interested in the idea of a domed stadium to replace crumbling

Ebbets Field. O'Malley had first broached the idea in 1949, when, at his request, famed architect Norman Bel Geddes prepared preliminary blueprints for a stadium with a retractable roof. Bel Geddes' involvement apparently ended at that point, but in November 1955 - the month after the Brooklyn Dodgers won their first and only World Series title - O'Malley convened a press conference during which he and architect-futurist R. Buckminster Fuller displayed a model of a geodesic-dome, 50,000-seat edifice that O'Malley wanted to build on the same site that decades later became the location of the Barclay Center, where the NBA's Brooklyn Nets and the NHL's New York Islanders now play. Estimates of the cost ranged from $20 million to $30 million, much of which O'Malley was willing to absorb if New York City obtained the land and then deeded it to him under the then-new municipal right of eminent domain. Earlier in 1955, O'Malley had announced that the Dodgers would play seven home games - one against each of the other seven NL teams - in Jersey City, N.J., in 1956 and 1957. This was a warning shot across the bow of New York land czar Robert Moses, who nevertheless vetoed the use of eminent domain to acquire the land O'Malley wanted. It was at this point that O'Malley, who likely did want to stay in Brooklyn even after the Braves' success in Milwaukee upped the financial ante throughout baseball, finalized his decision to move the Dodgers to Los Angeles for the 1958 season.

New York Giants owner Horace Stoneham in 1956 was approached with a grandiose plan that would enable him to make good his escape from the Polo Grounds, which was in even worse shape than Ebbets Field and adjoined one of Manhattan's most dangerous neighborhoods. This stadium - which also was to house the football Giants, who had left the Polo Grounds for

Yankee Stadium after the 1955 NFL season - was to seat 110,000, and even its advocates in New York City government conceded that acquiring the necessary land, let alone building the stadium itself, would be a prolonged, difficult task at best. Stoneham, who was convinced even before O'Malley that he would have to leave the New York metropolitan area, never seriously considered the proposal. His plan was to move to the newly-completed ballpark in Minneapolis-St. Paul, where the Giants owned the major league rights by dint of their Player Development Contract with the Triple-A Minneapolis Millers. But O'Malley, after running out of New York City options he considered viable, convinced Stoneham that the Giants-Dodgers rivalry would be even more profitable in California than it had been in New York. Stoneham agreed, and the San Francisco Giants began play along with the Los Angeles Dodgers in 1958.

Finally, in 1961, the world's first retractable-dome sports facility - Pittsburgh Civic Arena - was opened. The $22 million arena, demolished in 2011, was best known as the home of the National Hockey League's Pittsburgh Penguins, and was far too small to accommodate baseball or football. The eight-panel roof was never opened for a sports event, other than some World Team Tennis matches in the 1970s. Its main function was to allow the Pittsburgh Civic Light Orchestra to perform in an open-air setting, and numerous concerts - including the Beatles' appearance there in 1964 - were held with the roof open. Plans for the arena were first unveiled in 1948. Various delays - including a five-year legal battle over eminent-domain land seizures - delayed its construction and opening 13 years, but once those obstacles were overcome, builders adhered to the original 1948 design.

What if, in Milwaukee in 1949 when the governmental go-ahead was given to build County Stadium, a dome or a retractable-roof stadium had been built instead of a modern but conventional outdoor baseball plant?

Obstacles to such a plan, of course, would have been numerous. Not the least of those would have been cost. A Milwaukee dome almost certainly could have been built for less than the $35 million cost of the Astrodome a decade and a half later - the Astrodome's scoreboard alone cost $2.1 million, almost one-third of the total cost of County Stadium - and probably for less than the $23 million cost of Dodger Stadium in 1962. But Milwaukee already had spent $5 million to build the Milwaukee Arena, now the UWM Panther Arena, which opened in 1950 after two years of construction. For a weather-proof County Stadium to be built, the Arena project probably would have had to be postponed or abandoned, and the City of Milwaukee, the State of Wisconsin and/or investors from the private sector would have had to become directly involved. This was an unlikely scenario considering the fact that Milwaukee was not guaranteed a major league baseball team even after County Stadium construction was completed in 1952.

It's also likely that a dome or retractable-roof stadium in the early 1950s would have taken much longer than the construction of County Stadium. As it was, building County Stadium took longer than expected because of a steel shortage that began because of the national postwar housing shortage and was exacerbated by the Korean War, which began in 1950. This would have forced any prospective occupant of a Milwaukee domed stadium to find a temporary home, and that wouldn't have been easy, especially since Borchert Field was not a consideration even on a temporary basis, as Fred Miller had been told by MLB owners in 1949. The new Milwaukee team might have been forced to play in one or both of the Chicago ballparks while its new home was under construction. Another option might have been to build a temporary ballpark, like Colt Stadium in Houston, where the Colt .45s played that franchise's first three seasons while the Astrodome was under construction. But this would have added even more expense to a project that would have been cost-prohibitive under any circumstances without a massive infusion of private capital.

Even so, the undisputed fact by the early 1990s was that the Brewers could not survive long-term in Wisconsin without a covered ballpark, and the result was Miller Park. Had the same not been true of the Milwaukee Braves as well, especially after the team's decline began in 1960? And record- and precedent-smashing as the Braves' attendance had been in the 1950s, would it not have been even greater - and easier to sustain - if the Braves had had an all-weather facility within which local fans would not have had to brave Milwaukee's brutal spring weather, and to which fans from outside the Milwaukee area would drive knowing they would see the game or games scheduled?

If an attraction-unto-itself stadium had been built, the Braves' attendance might not have nosedived after 1959 - which, of course, would have greatly increased their viability as the Milwaukee Braves, regardless of the ownership situation. Miller Park ensured the Brewers a statewide constituency, because fans could travel hundreds of miles knowing that the games for which they had bought tickets would be played. This promise never existed during the Braves' 13 years in Milwaukee, even when the Braves were setting attendance records.

4. Managerial choices

The Milwaukee Braves had five managers during their 13-year sojourn in Wisconsin. Each one was less popular than his predecessor, and the last Milwaukee Braves manager, Bobby Bragan, was - and still is - every bit as reviled as Bill Bartholomay and the "carpetbaggers" who were plotting to move the Braves out of Milwaukee.

When the team moved from Boston in 1953, it brought along as manager Charles "Jolly Cholly" Grimm, who in 1952 had taken over the Boston Braves from Tommy Holmes 35 games into a 64-89 season. Grimm, like Harvey Kuenn in 1982 when the West Allis native took over the Brewers in midseason and led them to their only American League title, was a friendly, familiar and convivial face when the Braves arrived in Milwaukee. He had managed the minor-league Brewers to the American Association regular-season title in 1943 while working for - and serving as an off-field sidekick to - owner Bill Veeck, whom he'd known when Veeck worked for the Cubs before buying the Brewers. Grimm loved Milwaukee's municipal joviality, and he loved its cuisine even more; Veeck once said of Grimm that he planned his daily tour of Milwaukee's eateries the same way a general would plot a winter offensive.

Grimm had managed the Cubs through most of the 1930s, and had a part in the Cubs' National League championships in 1932, 1935, 1938 and 1945. Like Kuenn, his was a Type B managerial personality that both rewarded and cost him. He had taken over for the hard-bitten Rogers Hornsby in 1932, but in 1938 was replaced by another Type A manager, Gabby Hartnett, midway through the season after owner Phil Wrigley determined that the Cubs had become too sanguine. After the Cubs began the 1944 season 1-9 under Jimmie Wilson, they brought Grimm back from Milwaukee, and the next season they won the pennant again. The Cubs faded after World War II and Grimm was let go in 1949, resurfacing with the tatterdemalion Braves three years later during their final season in Boston.

The same pattern that had characterized Grimm's time in Chicago manifested itself in Milwaukee as well. The town embraced him, and he embraced it back. His players appreciated the fact he wasn't a stern taskmaster and cared about performance more than he cared about their off-field haunts or personalities, and the Braves leaped from seventh place in 1952 to second in 1953. But as in Chicago, his permissiveness and patience began to be seen as negatives, and in 1956, with his team treading at 24-22, Grimm resigned, saying he felt he'd back-slapped and communicated his way out of his position of authority.

Most of the Braves disliked Fred Haney, a Braves coach who replaced Grimm, at least as much as they liked Grimm. After the Braves lost to the Dodgers in the 1959 NL tiebreaker series, Joey Jay said of Haney: "Fred Haney didn't manage the club. He sat in one corner of the dugout, gulping down pills and saying to Crandall, 'What should we do, Del?'" Johnny Logan, another vocal Haney critic, said of that 1959 season, "We should have won by 10 games without question."

Haney was 60 when he took the Braves job. He'd had two unsuccessful major-league managerial stints with two teams that were virtually without resources - the St. Louis Browns from 1939-41 and the Pittsburgh Pirates from 1953-55 - and had taken the coaching job with the Braves with little or no interest in becoming the manager, even temporarily. One reason was the fact that he was a Southern Californian who wanted to remain a Southern Californian, and while he was a relative unknown in major league circles, he was widely acknowledged and admired throughout the Pacific Coast League. Though born in what was then New Mexico Territory, Haney had grown up in Los Angeles, played and managed in the PCL, and established an insurance firm in L.A. that by 1929 had 29 branches, all in California. He also had done electrical work for Paramount Studios in Hollywood, and made important friends and contacts in the movie industry during that time. Much later, Bing Crosby said his friendship with Haney was the reason the Crosby character wore a St. Louis Browns jacket in the 1944 classic *Going My Way*. (That was the year the Browns won their first and only American League pennant.) Haney also became well-known as a broadcaster, doing play-by-play for both the Hollywood Stars and the Los Angeles Angels and hosting a radio talk show in L.A.

But Haney and Grimm were longtime friends, and Grimm talked him into taking the Braves coaching job, at least in part because Grimm realized Haney was strong in the respect - establishing structure and discipline - where he was weak. Haney was a lifelong friend of Ty Cobb, who was the Detroit Tigers' player-manager in 1922 when Haney made his major league playing debut with the Tigers, and Haney believed in the same orderly - some would say dictatorial - approach that characterized and sometimes demonized Cobb.

Haney's hiring was met with skepticism in Milwaukee and elsewhere, given his failures in St. Louis and Pittsburgh. The skepticism faded quickly when the Braves won their first 11 games under Haney and took over first place, where they stayed until the Dodgers overtook them during the final weekend of the season. During the team's final meeting before it dispersed for the winter, Haney told the players: "You had a good time, boys. Have a good time this winter. Because when we meet again next spring, you're going to have the toughest so-and-so you've ever run into. You may hate me in the spring, but you'll love me in the fall when you pick up your World Series checks." (Haney during the spring of 1957 also imposed a $500 fine on players caught out after curfew, and this had an impact at a time when only 21 players on the eight NL teams made more than $30,000 and none made more than $75,000.)

Of course, he turned out to be right on almost all counts. Haney was named NL Manager of the Year after the Braves won the 1957 World Series, and after they repeated as NL champions in 1958, he was given a contract for 1959 at $40,000 a year. (His highest salary during his six-year playing career had been $7,000.) But even in 1958, Haney sensed that his approach with what was now a veteran club was wearing thin, and he wanted to return to the West Coast, especially after John Quinn was forced out as general manager and John McHale was hired to replace him in January 1959. So Haney resigned after the 1959 season, resurfacing a year later - at the behest of Gene Autry, another old Hollywood friend - as the first general manager of the American League's Los Angeles expansion team, the Angels, with whom he stayed for six years before retiring. Haney also brought Roland Hemond, who had been with the Braves' organization since 1951, with him to L.A. in 1960. Hemond, who in 2011 received the National Baseball Hall of Fame Lifetime

Achievement Award for his 60 years of service to the sport, had been assistant farm director and scouting director of the Braves under John Mullen. Hemond was put in charge of both departments with the Angels, and he immediately hired three of the Braves' most respected scouts: Gil English in the Carolinas, Leo Labossiere in New England, and Nick Kamzic in the Midwest. All three had been shunted aside by McHale as he sought to remake the organization in his own image.

Haney, though a proponent of the type of aggressive baseball he had learned under Cobb, thought the Braves were best when they bided their time and waited for the home run and the big inning. That approach sometimes didn't sit well with the fans and some of the players, who thought the Braves should be more adept at producing runs via the hit-and-run, assertive base running, and bunting. Haney was booed at County Stadium even during the 1957 championship season, particularly in mid-June when the Braves fell out of first place by losing six of seven games, all but one of them at home. Haney also heard boos during September, when the eight-game lead they held on August 17 had withered to 2 1/2 games on September 15, and even as they won 10 of their final 12 games and finished eight games ahead of the field, doubts about Haney's ability to unify the team lingered. In a *Sport* magazine article in September, one unidentified Braves beat writer told reporter Irv Goodman: "The Braves don't have born leaders. They try to manufacture them. It won't work. And I have a suspicion the Braves know it." Elsewhere in the story, Russ Lynch, the sports editor of the *Milwaukee Journal*, was quoted by Goodman as saying that he believed the team had divided into cliques, one headed by Del Crandall and the other by Johnny Logan. The result, Lynch said, might be a repeat of the 1949 rebellion that had shattered the Boston Braves the year after they won the franchise's first NL pennant since 1914. Alvin Dark and Eddie Stanky, both fierce competitors and teetotalers, in 1949 led an open revolt against manager Billy Southworth, a recovering alcoholic who apparently had begun drinking again. The result was a one-sided trade that sent Dark and Stanky to the Giants, and started the Braves on the downward spiral that in 1953 landed them in Milwaukee.

But even if the Milwaukee players and fans never completely warmed to Haney, they won with him. The players apparently did as he asked, on and off the field. He kept his criticism private and his praise public, and whatever ego he had was well tethered, both with the media and with his players.

Charlie Dressen, who replaced Haney in 1960, changed all that - and not for the better. Even though he was fired late in his second season in Milwaukee, some accounts, both contemporary and retrospective, describe him as the man who bore more responsibility for the demise of the Milwaukee Braves than anyone except Bill Bartholomay and John McHale. While the aging of the team and the deterioration of a once-productive farm system undoubtedly undermined Dressen, the Milwaukee franchise, under his direction, sank into a morass from which it never really emerged.

Dressen, 62 when he took the Braves job, first became a major league manager in 1934 (the year after he retired as a player) when he was appointed to lead the Cincinnati Reds. He was fired midway through his fifth season, never having finished higher than fifth in an eight-team league, but hooked on with the Dodgers as a coach. He had impressed Reds president Larry

MacPhail with his baseball acumen, and before the 1939 season, when MacPhail left Cincinnati to assume the presidency of the virtually-insolvent Brooklyn Dodgers, he hired Dressen as a coach to work under first-year manager Leo Durocher, who was still a player-manager at the time.

Today, Durocher and Dressen sometimes are jointly identified as two of the last martinet managers, and both had multi-generational managerial careers. (Durocher managed in five separate decades, starting with the '39 Dodgers and ending with the 1973 Houston Astros. Dressen died in 1966 soon after relinquishing his position as manager of the Detroit Tigers, the fifth team he led, for health reasons.) Because Durocher is in the Hall of Fame and Dressen isn't, and because Dressen worked for Durocher while Durocher never worked for Dressen, some also think Durocher was Dressen's mentor. In reality, Dressen was eight years older than Durocher, and Durocher relied heavily on Dressen during his early years as Dodger manager. In his book *Nice Guys Finish Last*, Durocher wrote about how he and Dressen worked out an undetectable series of signs, and about how he, Durocher, almost resigned as Dodgers manager in 1942 after Branch Rickey took over from MacPhail as Dodgers president and fired Dressen (hiring him back a few months later) because of Dressen's fondness of horse racing. "Invaluable this man is to me," Durocher quoted himself as saying about Dressen. The two also are linked because they were managerial adversaries from 1951-53 when Durocher's Giants and Dressen's Dodgers took that rivalry to its zenith.

But Dressen was no Durocher. While Durocher was flamboyant and confrontational, and would stretch both the letter and the intent of baseball law to win, his real genius was his ability to find 25 ways to maximize return from 25 different play-ers. Dressen as a manager felt one approach - his - should fit all. Durocher acknowledged that he had managerial mentors early in his career, most notably Miller Huggins, his manager when he played briefly for the Yankees in the late 1920s, and Frank Frisch when Frisch was the player-manager of the "Gas House Gang" Cardinals during Durocher's time there in the mid-1930s. Dressen, on the other hand, never had mentors, other than per-haps MacPhail. Nor, he thought, did he have peers.

He thought - and told anyone who would listen - that he was baseball's foremost mind, and he tolerated no deviations from his course of thinking. When his team won, he accepted credit; when he lost, he assigned blame. His favorite dugout expression during a close game was, "Hold 'em til the eighth, boys, and I'll think of something." And that egotism was a major reason Dressen's time with the Braves was doomed to failure.

In Jim Brosnan's 1961 book *Pennant Race*, he wrote about Dressen: "If his own players didn't like him, Dressen could rest assured that most of the other players in the league had a simi-lar distaste for him. There are managers for whom players like to play; others whom players like to defeat." He further quoted his Cincinnati teammate, Joey Jay, who had played for Dressen in Milwaukee in 1960: "Let me tell you about Dressen. When he joined the club he said, in the very first meeting, 'I know you guys hate my guts. But I don't care! I don't care!' And he pounded his fists together to emphasize his point."

Even given that state of affairs, the Braves still had the core of their 1957 championship team in place, and finished second under

Dressen in 1960, seven games behind the Pirates. But the Braves of 1961 were no longer young, and had wearied of Dressen. He was even more strict than Haney in terms of policing his players away from the field, and the players resisted accordingly. After sweeping a doubleheader from the Cubs at Wrigley Field on July 26 to move to 52-36, the Braves lost 11 of their next 16 games to fall to fourth place, seven games out. They never got closer than five games behind after that.

In 1961, the Braves tried to improve their infield defense by acquiring second baseman Frank Bolling from Detroit and shortstop Roy McMillan from Cincinnati. Hank Aaron was moved to center field with newly-acquired Frank Thomas taking over in left and Lee Maye in right, and Joe Torre supplanted Del Crandall as the regular catcher. Dressen, unlike Haney, also tried to remake the Braves' batting approach in the image he preferred, with more stealing (the Braves stole 70 bases that year, their most since 1951) and an emphasis on the hit-and-run and the bunt. But the personnel didn't fit the tactics, and the Braves didn't permanently chin the .500 bar until July 21, when they beat the Pirates at Forbes Field to go to 44-43. A 10-game winning streak in mid-August pulled them to their high-water mark of 64-51, but they still were in fourth place and trailed the first-place Reds by eight games. They finished fourth, 10 games out of first, and Dressen didn't finish at all.

The two-game tipping point began during a home game against San Francisco on August 29. The Braves won 7-6 on a walk-off homer by Eddie Mathews in the 13th inning, but not before Dressen made a move that seems to have convinced his superiors that his expertise was waning, if not gone altogether.

The *San Francisco Examiner* reported it thusly: "In the 11th, after Joe Amalfitano had chopped his third single of the game and (Ernie) Bowman sacrificed him to second, (left-handed-hitting Willie) McCovey was intentionally passed (by right-handed reliever Don Nottebart) with two out. The crowd of 21,407 sent up a roar of disbelief - an intentional walk with Willie Mays the next hitter? (Earlier in the season, Mays had hit four home runs against the Braves in a game at County Stadium.) When did anyone last try that? But Mays ... was an eyelash out at first on a grounder to McMillan, and there went the final Giant threat."

The next day against the Giants, with the Braves trailing 2-1 going to the bottom of the ninth, Aaron led off with a single, bringing Joe Adcock to the plate. Giants manager Alvin Dark brought in relief specialist Stu Miller, a slow-slower-slowest craftsman of the sort that always bothered Adcock, a free swinger who had trouble with off-speed pitches. In 1961, even sluggers were expected to be able to bunt in game-deciding situations, and Adcock, with 52 sacrifice bunts in his career and 11 during both the 1954 and 1956 seasons, was more than capable of doing so. With the Braves at home and the tying run at first with no outs, and two of Milwaukee's most capable hitters, Frank Thomas and Joe Torre, coming up behind Adcock, the expectation throughout the ballpark was that Adcock would be asked to bunt, given the fact one of baseball's oldest adages is that late in a one-run game, the home team should play for the tie and the road team should play for the win. Another possibility would have been to have Aaron, who had 21 stolen bases that season, try to pilfer second against Miller, whose lack of velocity and painstaking motion made him a mark for steal-minded baserunners.

Dressen didn't agree. He had Adcock hit away. Adcock bounced a comebacker to Miller, who started a 1-6-3 double play. Thomas and Torre then singled, but Dressen - who still had a well-stocked bench, including, on that particular day, regular right fielder Lee Maye - sent up 29-year-old outfielder Neil Chrisley, who had been acquired from Detroit in the Bolling deal and had spent most of the season in the minors, to bat for McMillan. Chrisley, who had only 10 at-bats with the Braves that season (the last of his five years in the majors), grounded out to second base to end the game and, for all intents and purposes, the Braves' pennant hopes.

Three days later, with 25 games remaining, Dressen was fired, and Braves fans and players wondered anew why he had been hired in the first place. After Haney resigned, the Braves had more than a few options, including no fewer than *five* men who won World Series titles with other clubs and were all eminently and imminently available during the winter of 1959-60.

- One was Ralph Houk, who'd managed Denver of the American Association to a pennant in 1955 and to second-place finishes the next two seasons. He then was promoted to a coaching seat alongside Casey Stengel in the Yankees dugout. Houk succeeded Stengel as Yankees manager in 1961 and won three pennants and two World Series in three years before moving up to the general manager post.
- Alvin Dark, though still an active player, had made clear his managerial aspirations, and had spent part of 1960, his last season as a player, with the Braves. (Of course, he also had been the shortstop on the 1948 Boston Braves team that won the NL pennant that year.) In 1961, Dark

was named manager of the San Francisco Giants, with whom he won an NL pennant in 1962 and had his team in contention for four straight years before being fired at the end of the '64 season, largely because of remarks he made during the season to the effect that black and Latino players did not respond to pressure as well as white players. He then managed in Kansas City and Cleveland before Charles O. Finley, who'd once fired him when the A's were still in Kansas City, hired him back to direct the Oakland A's in 1974 after Dick Williams resigned. That season ended with the A's as World Series champions for the third straight year.

* The Braves also could have selected Hank Bauer, who during World War II had been wounded twice in the Pacific theater - once during the Allied invasion of Okinawa - and survived several near-fatal attacks of malaria. Bauer was one of the most respected players in baseball in terms of leadership. He had played in nine World Series and won seven rings with the Yankees from 1949-58. At the end of the 1959 season, the Yankees traded him to the A's. Bauer, 37 at the time, played two seasons for Kansas City, the first as a player-manager. After Charley Finley fired him in 1962, he accepted the job as Baltimore's non-playing manager, and in 1966 the Orioles swept the Dodgers in the World Series.

* At a time that Leo Durocher proteges like Dark, Eddie Stanky, Gene Mauch, Bill Rigney, Herman Franks and Sam Mele were seeping into the managerial ranks, Durocher himself wanted back into baseball. Giants owner Horace Stoneham had fired him after the 1955 season - one year after Durocher managed the Giants to the last World Series title the franchise was to win for 56

years. Durocher spent the next five seasons working for NBC as a color commentator on its Game of the Week, playing golf, and discussing employment with "several" teams. In his autobiography, he wrote that Cleveland general manager Frank Lane offered him a contract that would be worth $53,000 a year after taxes, "considerably more than I was able to keep on a $100,000 salary." Durocher makes no mention of whether he talked to the Braves after the 1959 season, but he did write that Stoneham tried to hire him back in 1960 after he fired Rigney during the previous season, and that Kansas City, Baltimore and even Fred Haney's expansion Los Angeles Angels also made offers that he turned down, for various reasons. Finally, he signed on as a coach with the Los Angeles Dodgers before the 1961 season and stayed there through 1964 - even though, some claimed, he tried to undermine Dodgers manager Walter Alston during much of that time. In 1966, he was appointed manager of the Chicago Cubs, and in 1969 Durocher led a team that hadn't finished as high as third since 1946 to the cusp of an NL East title before it was chased down and passed by the "Miracle Mets."

Those '69 Mets were managed by Gil Hodges, who in 1959 played the 14th year of his illustrious career. Hodges, though, was a part-time player after that, and when he retired in 1963, he was immediately named manager of the Washington Senators. In 1967, the Senators traded him to the Mets for pitcher Bill Denehy - one of only five times in major league history that a player was traded for a manager - and the Mets' reward was the '69 World Series title.

Even with all those high-profile names and resumes potentially in the mix, if the managerial choice had come down to player preference - although, in those days, even elite players rarely had significant influence on front-office decisions - it seems likely the Braves would have chosen Ben Geraghty to replace Haney.

Geraghty, 47 at the time of the vacancy, had been a minor league manager, mostly in the Braves' system, since his playing career - which included 70 games with the Braves and Dodgers - had ended at age 30. In 16 seasons as a minor league manager, Geraghty won six pennants during one nine-year stretch, and never finished below second place in his final 10 seasons. In 1957, after taking the Braves' Triple-A affiliate in Wichita to the American Association championship, *The Sporting News* named him Minor League Manager of the Year.

Perhaps even more important, he was loved and idolized by virtually every player he had ever managed. Hank Aaron, who played for him in Jacksonville, Fla., of the South Atlantic League in 1953 - the year before Aaron was called up to the Braves - described Geraghty as the greatest manager who ever lived, and without question the best for whom he ever played. Jacksonville, of course, was in the segregated South, and Aaron - the first black man ever to play in the Sally League - later described how Geraghty would search through every Sally League city until he found restaurants and hotels that would serve both whites and blacks, and how Geraghty would eat dinner with him every night, whether the restaurant at which they dined was "white" or "colored." Author Pat Jordan, who played in the Braves' organization from 1959-61, described Geraghty this way:

When I arrived in Bradenton in the fall of 1960, Ben Geraghty was already a legendary figure in professional baseball. His former players spoke of him in mystical as well as mythical terms, or so it seemed to one who had never met him. They said he was the game's most brilliant strategist. He had the highest winning percentage of any manager in baseball history. He was a master at inducing aging veterans like Ed Charles to surpass their own self-defined limitations, while at the same time and on the same team, he coddled and prodded young prospects into fulfilling their potential ... His players spoke of him with an awe and reverence one associates not with a minor league manager who had enriched their careers, but with a man who had enriched their lives in a way that had nothing to do with baseball. They spoke of him the way football players speak of Vince Lombardi.

The only asset Ben Geraghty didn't have going for him at the end of 1959, when the Braves job opened, was health, and that may have been the primary reason that the Braves didn't hire him. In 1946, his first year as a minor league manager, he guided the Spokane Indians of the Class B Western International League. On June 24 in the Cascade Mountains during a road trip, the team bus veered off the highway in a heavy rainstorm, crashed, and burst into flames. Nine of the 15 passengers died. Geraghty survived, but suffered life-threatening lacerations and head trauma, and, as Jordan put it, "he was never again a healthy man." While managing Jacksonville in 1963, Geraghty suffered a heart attack and died at age 50.

Whether Geraghty or any of the other potential candidates to take over the Braves for the 1960 season would have fared better than Dressen is, of course, a matter of speculation. But it seems certain that none of them could have done any worse.

Dressen was replaced, ostensibly on an interim basis, by Birdie Tebbetts, a Braves executive vice president who'd been a standout catcher from 1936-52 and then managed Cincinnati, with indifferent success, from 1954-58. After the Redlegs fired him, Tebbetts said, "I will definitely never manage again." And there are Braves fans who will tell you he was true to his word, at least during the season and change in 1961 and 1962 when he was the Braves' skipper.

The '62 Braves needed a late rush to finish a dreary season at 86-76. They never were in the pennant race, finishing fifth, 15 1/2 games behind the Dodgers and Giants, as they continued with a rebuilding process that to Braves fans looked more like scaffolding than structure. Attendance fell to 766,921, eighth in the 10-team league. The Braves won if they hit home runs (181, second in the National League) and lost when they didn't. Their team batting average of .252 was the lowest in the league aside from the two expansion teams, the Houston Colt .45s and the New York Mets, that entered the league that year. Tebbetts, who neither angered nor inspired anyone during his time in charge, apparently decided he liked managing after all, but that he didn't like doing it in Milwaukee. He resigned after the 1962 season to accept the Cleveland Indians' managership. In 1964, after the Indians traded relief pitcher Pedro Ramos to the Yankees, Ramos, who was Cuban-born, said: "I never want to play for Birdie Tebbetts again. He's a maniac. I don't like the way he treats human beings. He's worse than Fidel Castro in a town that's free."

His replacement was Bobby Bragan, who had been the Phillies' regular shortstop from 1940-42 before being traded to the Dodgers. Because of wartime manpower exigencies, Bragan found himself catching as well as playing shortstop in 1943 and 1944. He missed the 1945 and 1946 seasons because of military service, but returned to the Dodgers in 1947 and played the final 34 games of his career for Brooklyn in 1947 and 1948. Branch Rickey, president of the Dodgers from 1943-50, liked Bragan's baseball knowledge and his ability to communicate it, and hired him as a minor league manager in the Dodgers system. When Rickey became president of the Pittsburgh Pirates in 1951, Bragan went with him, and managed in the PIrates organization until he was hired as the Pittsburgh manager in 1956. He lasted only 1 1/2 seasons there before being fired. He began the 1958 season as manager of the Cleveland Indians, but was let go after only 67 games.

Bragan's hiring raised eyebrows among Braves fans and others in the baseball community, and not because of the racial controversy in which he had become involved in 1947. A native of Alabama, Bragan and Dixie Walker during the spring of 1947 had helped orchestrate a petition drive intended to prevent Rickey from bringing Jackie Robinson to the Dodgers. Manager Leo Durocher, just before being suspended by Commissioner Happy Chandler for the 1947 season for "conduct detrimental to baseball," emphatically quashed the petition, and Bragan later said Rickey convinced him that his opposition to black players was misguided. Bragan subsequently renounced that position, and in fact became known for working productively with young black players, including Hank Aaron and Maury Wills.

More to the point, for Braves fans, was the incident that occurred on July 31, 1957, at County Stadium when Bragan was still managing the Pirates. In the next day's *Milwaukee Journal*, Cleon Walfoort wrote:

Bobby Bragan ... enjoyed the most expensive drink of orange juice in the history of organized baseball right out in the center of the dia-mond at County Stadium in the fifth inning (of the game against) *the Braves. He insisted that he had enjoyed the orange juice and that it was worth every cent it is going to cost him - $100 - but he didn't finish it. He offered to throw the rest in an umpire's face after he had been ordered from the field.*

Bragan has been carrying on a season-long feud with the crew of umpires, of whom Frank Dascoli is senior member. His main target has been Stan Landes, Milwaukee's contribution to the National League staff. (Landes, a former Marine who served in both World War II and Korea before umpiring in the NL from 1955-72, was one of the biggest umpires in baseball at the time. He was 6-foot-2 and was listed at 215 pounds, although most believed he weighed considerably more than that. He also was Jewish, making him a target of anti-Semitic barbs from players and fans, especially in the early seasons of his career.) *Dascoli was operating behind home plate and Landes at second base as Bragan went into his act. Bob Buhl, Braves pitcher, had progressed from first base to third on a double by Red Schoendienst. Bragan, from his place of business in the dugout, thought Buhl had failed to touch second base. He called to his pitcher, Bob Purkey, to throw the ball there and demand a ruling of Landes. The umpire spread his hands, palms down - "Safe!"*

Bragan did not immediately leave the bench but held his nose with his fingers in an elaborate gesture of disdain. Landes promptly pointed him out of the game and went all the way to third to make sure that

Bragan no longer was on the premises. "Just a minute, Stan," Bragan told the umpire. "I want to talk this over, but first I have to get comfortable." One of Bragan's players - "Whammy" Douglas, the one-eyed pitcher, it was - got a carton of orange from a vendor in the stands and gave it to his boss. Bragan wanted a hot dog, too, but decided not to wait for it. Instead he sauntered out on the diamond, sipping his drink through a straw. He politely offered to share his drink with the four umpires who met with him behind the pitchers mound. "What are you guys trying to do, keep your record intact?" Bragan inquired of them. He had been ejected by these same umpires three times this summer.

*"You get out of here or I'll forfeit the game," Dascoli ordered. "You don't have that much guts," Bragan told him. Frank Secory, who had been officiating at first base, warned Bragan to "cut out the bush league stuff." "I'll throw this drink in your face," Bragan threatened. Secory spread his arms to move Dascoli and Landes out of the way and stuck out his jaw. "Let's see you do that," he challenged. Bragan finally decided on a more discreet course - the one leading through the dugout and into the visiting clubhouse. He was still seething after the game. "Yeah, I know, you can't fight City Hall," he said. "But I was just fed up with this crew. I told (*NL president Warren*) Giles he should break them up. I wanted to show them up. It was worth whatever it costs. If it's not more than $100, that is. Fifty bucks is my previous high but the fines have added up to $750 or $1,000. It's the only way I have of getting back at them. I've never had any trouble with the other 12 umpires in the league - ask them. Just this crew. I never defied an umpire before and I never put on a clown act in the majors. You might say this was my debut.* (It was not. Bragan had a reputation for loutish behavior as a manager in the minors. As manager of the Hollywood Stars of the PCL, he once laid down on home plate and refused to move after an umpire's call went against him.)

"But that Landes has rabbit ears. Let somebody call him "Jumbo" or "Lummox" and he's out of the game. You can't even say "Hi-Ho, Silver" to Dascoli because he couldn't get a job in the Western League once."

Bragan disclaimed any participation in a recent incident in Cincinnati in which Pittsburgh players splashed water from a bucket from their dugout to indicate that Raul Sanchez, Redlegs pitcher, was throwing spitballs.

While Landes was making his report to league headquarters in Cincinnati from the wall telephone in the umpires room at the Stadium, Dascoli volunteered his opinion of Bragan. "He's a busher and a clown who thinks he's a comedian," the veteran umpire spouted. "He's got a ballclub that has all kinds of potential, and look where he's got 'em. He'll push you around if you let him."

Bragan got the expected $100 fine and a stern rebuke from Giles, even though Giles was well-known for tolerating disrespect and verbal abuse of umpires. Bragan got an even stronger rebuke three days later when Pirates management fired him and replaced him with Danny Murtaugh, who led the Pirates to World Series championships in 1960 and 1971. Bragan's managerial career appeared to be over after the Indians fired him midway through the following year, but he hooked on with the Los Angeles Dodgers and later the Houston Colt .45s as a coach before taking the Milwaukee job before the 1963 season after Tebbetts' resignation.

While Bragan as Braves manager never behaved as badly as he had at County Stadium in 1957, he wasn't any more of a catalyst of improvement than Dressen or Tebbetts had been. Attendance continued to dwindle, especially as more paragons of the 1950s either retired or were traded, and the decline accelerated after Bob Broeg's *St. Louis Post-Dispatch* story in July 1963 confirmed the already-widespread rumors that the Braves were on their way to Atlanta. The Braves finished sixth, 15 games behind the Dodgers, in 1963, with one of the few diversions coming on July 2 at Candlestick Park, where Spahn and the Giants' Juan Marichal collaborated to craft perhaps the best-pitched game in major league history. Both future Hall of Famers worked 15 scoreless innings, with Marichal giving up only seven hits and Spahn eight. In the top of the 16th, Marichal gave up a two-out single to Denis Menke, but retired Norm Larker on a comebacker to end the inning. After Harvey Kuenn flied out to lead off the bottom of the 16th, Mays hit a solo homer to give the Giants a 1-0 victory. Marichal threw 217 pitches that night and Spahn 201. Marichal said later that he could hardly stand up on the mound by the end of the game, and when the game went to the top of the 14th, Giants manager Alvin Dark, after watching Marichal warm up for the inning, came out to remove him. Marichal told him: "See that old guy out there? He's 42! I am *NOT* coming out of this game until he does or we win!" Dark shrugged and went back to the Giants' dugout.

Spahn went 23-7 with a 2.60 ERA and an NL-high 22 complete games that season, but the duel with Marichal represented one of the last instances of the mastery that won him 363 games, more than any lefthander in baseball history. The next year, he went 6-13 with a 5.29 ERA and was removed from the rotation by Bragan. The two feuded for the rest of the 1964 season, lobbing verbal, on-the-record broadsides at each other. It was one of many examples of Bragan's proclivity for fighting battles he could not win. Another came late in the 1964 season, when Bragan was asked - for one of the countless times during his tenure - about whether Milwaukee deserved to retain major league baseball. He replied: "I remember a story about a crooked creek down in Alabama. That creek is so crooked that no matter how hard or often people tried to jump over it, they always came down on the wrong side. Eventually the people learned to walk around it."

It didn't matter whether or not the quote was intended as a repudiation of Milwaukee, because most fans took it as a declaration of war against Milwaukee by the Braves' own manager. Bragan had been booed since his arrival on a number of counts, among them his penchant for shuffling his lineup, using players at positions that they had never played and subsequently proved they could not play, and using the media to express his dissatisfaction with players. But the spat with Spahn and the crooked-creek remark made him a target every time he stuck his head out of the dugout during the remainder of his stay in Milwaukee, and most of his remarks about the Atlanta move did more to anger Braves fans than to soothe them, especially when he was addressing the by-now-hostile Milwaukee media. His wife Gwenn also was outspoken to a fault. In an *Associated Press* story late in the 1965 season, she said, when asked about managing a household while her husband was managing a team: "(Because husbands don't want distractions from kids when they're home), I whale the daylights out of them right then and there." She also claimed that "I know one or two players were shipped out just because of their wives." And there was more: "I had a pretty good scare in Brooklyn (when the Dodgers still were playing there and Bragan was managing the Pirates) when a man tried to get into the room, and right after that I got a little .22. There are times I'll sleep with it under my pillow when Bobby is on the road. The gun is loaded, by the way."

On the field in 1964, the Braves continued to plod along during the first half of the season; on July 4, they were 37-40 and in eighth place, 10 1/2 games behind the surprising Phillies, and as late as August 14 after a loss to the Giants, they were 58-56 and in sixth place, 12 games back. At that point, they surged, probably saving Bragan's job for 1965. With Aaron and Mathews still productive and young players like Joe Torre catching, Rico Carty at first base, Denis Menke at shortstop and Felipe Alou at first base and in the outfield giving fans hope that a renaissance might be at hand, the Braves went 30-18 the rest of the year and won 13 of their last 15, including a four-game sweep in Philadelphia as the Phillies lost 10 straight to blow a 6 1/2-game lead and the pennant in the final two weeks of the season. (The Cardinals, who came from behind to win the pennant and then the World Series, were only one-half game ahead of the Braves on July 4.). The Braves were not serious contenders that season, mainly because they had only two reliable starting pitchers (Tony Cloninger and Denny Lemaster) and a vulnerable bullpen, and although the Braves finished only five games behind the Cardinals, that margin was the closest they had come to first place since June 14. Yet Braves fans, many of whom likely were motivated by the hope that improved attendance might yet save the franchise for Milwaukee, turned out in surprising numbers. After drawing only 773,018, ninth in the 10-team league, in 1963, County Stadium in 1964 had 910,911 paying patrons (sixth in the league) in 1964. Season-ticket purchases increased from 3,685 in 1963 to 4,470 in 1964. This was taken by some people (none of them National League owners) as a strong indication that Milwaukee still cared about keeping the Braves, or, at the very least, about getting a replacement team if they did move.

Two weeks after the end of the season, this optimism was quashed when the Braves finally announced that they intended to move to Atlanta for the 1965 season, given the fact Atlanta-Fulton County Stadium construction was ahead of schedule. Milwaukee County obtained an injunction holding the Braves to the final year of their County Stadium lease, and NL owners ruled that the Braves would have to play in Milwaukee in 1965.

$$\bullet \ \bullet \ \bullet$$

What other factors entered into the transfer of the franchise? Some of the following probably were relatively inconsequential in relation to the bigger picture that emerged primarily because of the four pre-eminent factors outlined in this chapter. But in a perfect-storm situation for Milwaukee fans, secondary winds and currents worked against them as well:

5. The Packers. The arrival of Vince Lombardi as Packers coach in 1959 coincided with the start of the Braves' decline from their 1957-59 apex. There is no documentation to prove conclusively that some Wisconsinites who had been spending discretionary money to watch the Braves diverted that money to Packers tickets instead. But it is a viable conclusion, especially considering the fact that in 1956 while the Braves were still eclipsing MLB attendance records, the Packers were on the verge of going the route of the Portsmouth Spartans, Pottsville Maroons, Frankford Yellow Jackets and other relics from the NFL's Hupmobile days.

(The league had been founded in 1920 during a meeting in a Hupmobile showroom in Canton, Ohio.)

The Packers had been playing most of their games in a high school stadium in Green Bay before City Stadium (now Lambeau Field) opened in 1957, the year after Green Bay voters overwhelmingly approved a bond issue to build the stadium. Before City Stadium opened, the Packers had played some games at various Milwaukee venues - including, starting in 1953, County Stadium, where the Packers continued playing part of their schedule until 1994 - and could not have survived long enough to benefit from Lombardi's work had it not been for the fact they had a presence in a large metro area.

At the time Lombardi arrived, the Packers hadn't won an NFL title since 1944 or had a winning season since 1947, and were barely subsisting financially even with their Milwaukee income. But that changed almost immediately. In 1959, Lombardi's first season, the Packers went 7-5, and the following year, he took them to the NFL title game, losing to Philadelphia. In 1961, the Packers won the first of the five NFL titles they were to capture during Lombardi's nine seasons. They became, and remain, Wisconsin's focal-point sports entity, pushing the Braves to secondary status in many minds and, at least during the fall and winter, most sports pages. It also didn't help the Braves, from the fan-dollar-competition standpoint, that the University of Wisconsin football team was reasonably successful during the years of the Braves' decline. The Badgers won Big Ten titles in 1959 and 1962, playing in the Rose Bowl after both of those seasons, and finished the latter regular season as the No. 2-ranked team in the country.

Lombardi conceivably could have lent moral support to the effort to keep the Braves in Milwaukee, but there is no record of Lombardi having done so. In fact, Lombardi is on record, in David Maraniss' biographical tour de force *When Pride Still Mattered*, as making it clear he disliked Milwaukee and avoided going there whenever possible. Lombardi tried during his Packers tenure to end the Packers' relationship with Milwaukee entirely, although the Packers, who had separate season-ticket bases in both cities, didn't become a full-time Green Bay entity until 1995. Shortly after the Anerican Football League began operation in 1960, Lombardi had a no-compete clause written into the Packers' rental agreement with County Stadium, rendering it unavailable for any pro football games except those of the Packers. In 1965, Lombardi used this contractual veto power to torpedo an effort, led by former Notre Dame coach Terry Brennan and Milwaukee realtor Marvin Fishman, to land an American Football League franchise for Milwaukee.

In 1963, after Bartholomay and his group bought the team, the Braves did try one ploy that had worked three times for the Packers in their lean years: A public stock sale. The Packers, in 2016 the only publicly-owned major league sports franchise in the U.S., first sold stock in 1923 to establish themselves as a corporation, and followed with issuances in 1935 and 1950. In all three cases, the influx of stockholder cash helped save the tottering Packers franchise. The Braves' stock sale worked far less well. The new owners put 115,000 shares (representing 36.4 percent of the team's total stock) on the market at $10 per share. But only 15 percent of the stock was purchased, even after the value of the stock dropped to $3.50 per share. Bartholomay and other

NL owners later used this failed stock sale as leverage in the effort to secure permission for the move to Atlanta, and some believe he gave the go-ahead for the stock sale knowing full well it would fail, thus giving him enough justification to move the franchise.

6. Eugene Grobschmidt. Grobschmidt (1906-73) represented a south Milwaukee district - where a public park is named for him - on the Milwaukee County Board of Supervisors from 1954-72, and was that body's president from 1960-72. He had little, if anything, to do with the Braves' original decision to abandon Milwaukee; that call, by all accounts, had already been made by the Bartholomay group by the time it purchased the Braves from Lou Perini in 1962. But Goldschmidt's actions and rhetoric after the Braves' intention to move became public knowledge had three effects: It ended any possibility of constructive compromise, especially between the Braves and Bud Selig's Teams Inc group during the 1965 season as Teams Inc tried to obtain a replacement franchise. It led directly to the expensive, seemingly-interminable and ultimately-unsuccessful antitrust lawsuit against Major League Baseball that had as its main effect the treatment of Milwaukee as a baseball leper colony for four years after the Braves left. And it demonstrated that Grobschmidt knew next to nothing about baseball as a sport or as a business. Clearly, both at the time and in retrospect, he was intent on one goal and one goal only: Punishing and angering the Braves by any and every means at his disposal, regardless of the consequences. Early in 1965, he was quoted as saying: "Speaking as a supervisor, I must tell you (his constituents) to support the Braves (during their final season in Milwaukee). But speaking as an individual, to hell with the Braves."

Grobschmidt was admired by many as the voice of those who were angry over the Braves' departure, but his anger wasn't limited to the Braves. He constantly feuded with County Executive John Doyne, and not only on matters involving the Braves. Grobschmidt technically had no power to speak for the county as a governmental entity, while Doyne did, but that didn't stop Grobschmidt from projecting his churlishness as that of the collective voice of Milwaukee County government. He was fond of making grand, unilateral pronouncements that achieved nothing other than souring the already-testy relationship with the team - and, more important, with Major League Baseball and the other 19 owners. Nor did it stop Grobschmidt from trying to undermine Doyne - who, like Teams Inc, favored a more measured approach in the county's dealings with the Braves - at every turn. At least twice during meetings involving the Braves, Teams Inc and political leaders, Doyne and Grobschmidt had to be physically separated outside the meeting room. In 1965, Doyne put forth a proposal by which any major league team that occupied County Stadium in the future would be offered a lease far more lucrative than the one under which the Braves had operated. Grobschmidt promptly said that he would use his power with the county board to prevent such an arrangement, even if doing so meant Milwaukee would never again host major league baseball.

7. **Lou Perini's television policy.** From the time Perini moved the team to Milwaukee in 1953 until 1962, when he permitted 15 road games to be shown on TV in Milwaukee, Perini would not allow *any* Braves games - even road and national network games - to be aired in the Milwaukee area. The Braves were the only franchise in major league baseball at that time to enforce such a complete TV ban. His reasoning, shared by many owners

in the early days of electronic media, was that "giving the product away" would discourage fans from paying their way into County Stadium. The only way one could see the Braves on TV from 1953-62 was to have a set and a TV antenna that could pick up WGN in Chicago when the Braves played the Cubs.

That "giving away" major league baseball kept fans away from the park may have been partly true in the short term, but it has long since been demonstrated by every major league team in every major sport that day-to-day TV exposure has the long-term effect of introducing and endearing a much larger body of fans to the team and the sport. In the 1920s and 1930s when home radio ownership became virtually universal, many owners took the same attitude toward "giving away" their product on radio as Perini later embraced with TV. When Larry MacPhail took over as Brooklyn Dodgers president in 1938, the Yankees, Dodgers and Giants had a radio-ban agreement that had kept all their games off the airwaves in New York City for several years. MacPhail, who had already seen the benefits of radio as president of the Cincinnati Reds, immediately let it be known that the Dodgers would no longer be party to the ban. He signed a radio contract with WOR, the most powerful station in the New York area, and brought Red Barber from Cincinnati to announce the Dodgers' games. Barber soon became as closely identified with the franchise as any of its players, and the Dodgers, who were on the brink of bankruptcy when MacPhail arrived, in 1939 broke the 1 million attendance barrier for the first time in franchise history. The Giants and Yankees were soon forced to follow the Dodgers' lead, ending the radio ban, and the success of MacPhail's maximum-exposure approach continued into the TV era (and still continues today).

Would television exposure, when the Braves had the attention not only of Wisconsin but of the entire baseball world, have made any difference later when the team and franchise weakened? It's possible, maybe even likely, that allowing at least some telecasts might have helped the Braves build a new fan generation that might have sustained them indefinitely even after they lapsed into mediocrity and saw their attendance drop by nearly one-half from 1957-61, and then by another one-half from 1961-65. In any case, the Bartholomay group in 1964 allowed telecasts of all Saturday home games and some road games, and the Braves' attendance did increase that year, though that was more likely attributable to the team's strong finish and the sense among Braves fans that their turning out in large numbers might yet save the Braves for Milwaukee.

Under Perini, the Braves missed not only that potential exposure, but also the revenue that the team's TV rights likely would have generated, especially during the peak years. In 1956, the Brooklyn Dodgers, already with one foot out the door on their way to Los Angeles, received $880,270 for their TV and radio rights. (The Dodgers in those days televised all their home games and about 20 road games per season.) The Dodgers, despite an aging team and a decaying ballpark in a dangerous neighborhood, reported a $487,462 net profit in 1956 with the help of the proceeds from a seven-game World Series against the Yankees.

The Braves accrued only $135,000 for the WTMJ radio rights, and had no television revenue at all. This largely negated the gate-receipt advantage of the Braves, who in 1956 drew 2,046,331 compared to the Dodgers' 1,213,562. (The latter total included the seven "home" games the Brooklyn team played in New Jersey in 1956.) Perini could, and did, argue that fans in the stands at County Stadium spent money for parking and concessions that Dodger fans watching on TV In New York City weren't putting into owner Walter O'Malley's coffers. But even in 1956 when TV's impact on sports finance wasn't yet fully anticipated or understood, revenue from TV rights and advertising quite likely would have more than offset any parking and concession losses that Perini would have incurred if he had allowed the Braves to be shown on TV.

In any case, by 1959, the Los Angeles Dodgers - in their second of four years playing in the L.A. Coliseum - were outdrawing the Braves while still collecting far greater TV and radio rights, simply because of the comparative market sizes. In 1960, the Dodgers' attendance of 2,253,887 broke the National League record set by the Braves in 1957, even though Los Angeles finished in fourth place, 13 games behind the champion Pirates. By 1965, the Braves' final year in Milwaukee and the Dodgers' fourth season in Dodger Stadium, Los Angeles outdrew the Braves almost five-fold - 2,553,577 to 555,584.

At the time the Giants and Dodgers moved West, both Giants owner Horace Stoneham and O'Malley planned to implement pay-per-view operations, so both kept their TV visibility to a minimum in the years after the move, usually only televising the nine road games each played against the other. The Giants weren't able to implement pay-per-view TV until the early 1980s, and Stoneham maintained the team's policy of showing only the Giants' nine road games against the Dodgers until 1969. The Dodgers in 1964 became the first team to offer telecasts on a subscription basis, airing a pay-per-view home game against the Cubs on July 17 of that year. Otherwise, they too offered minimal over-the-air TV exposure. But neither the Giants nor the Dodgers needed to air many of their games for free to make a profit via the emerging medium. The Dodgers and Giants received $1 million each for their TV and radio rights. The Braves in 1965 took in only $150,000, all of it from the rights to games that were televised or carried on radio in Atlanta. They went to spring training in 1965 without any radio or TV contract at all in Wisconsin, and though a makeshift airwave coalition was put together before the start of the season, all parties acknowledged that it would lose money and represented more of a public service than a for-profit endeavor.

8. **The carry-in beer ban**. In 1961, fans who had become accustomed to bringing their own food and beverages (including beer) into County Stadium were prohibited from doing so by the Milwaukee County Board of Supervisors. This was the season that the Braves' attendance drop went into full plunge mode, and even though it was the county and not the team that imposed the ban, some blamed the Braves, who did want it because it helped concession sales at the stadium and used it as a secondary complaint when they made their case to be allowed to move to Atlanta.

In retrospect, the premise that the ban drove fans away in significant numbers appears mostly false, mainly because it didn't turn out to be permanent. The ban was lifted in 1963 and reinstated in 1965, and when it was in effect, it had no appreciable impact on the Braves' home attendance. While some fans complained about the ban when it was in effect, the county board wasn't flying in the face of MLB convention. One team that was still allowing carry-ins when the 1961 season started was the Philadelphia Phillies. And the Phillies abandoned that policy on June 28 of that year after a near-riot during a game against San Francisco. Phillies catcher Jim Coker was ejected from a game after an argument with home-plate umpire Tony Venzon, prompting a cascade of beer bottles and cans from the stands and almost resulting in a Phillies forfeiture.

9. The Braves' promotional vacuum. Like most teams of the postwar period - the most notable exceptions being the Indians, Browns and White Sox when those teams were owned by Bill Veeck - the Milwaukee Braves had few giveaways or discount-seat programs during their 13 seasons. Ball Day and Bat Day were annual staples in Milwaukee, as they were in all major league parks, and the Braves also had Knothole Days (allowing children in for free on certain dates when accompanied by an adult) and Ladies Days on weekday afternoons. Another promotion the Braves employed was Camera Day, during which fans were allowed on the diamond for a short period before games to have photos taken with their favorite players. Sometimes visiting players participated as well; Michael Curley, whose remembrances of the Milwaukee Braves are included in the opening chapter, recalls having his photo taken with the Cardinals' Stan Musial. To the Braves' credit, they maintained those promotions even during the 1965 season as the contempt with which Milwaukee and the Braves regarded each other intensified. Otherwise, though the franchise's "marketing" plan throughout its time in Milwaukee consisted mainly of contending every year, and once the team fell from championship-caliber status in 1960, it made no effort to augment the conventional promotions to which most teams limited themselves.

10. The Milwaukee metro area's public-transit short-sightedness. By the time the Braves arrived in 1953, the suburbs surrounding Milwaukee, like many such communities throughout the country, already were teeming with young families making their way out of the central city. The seven southeastern Wisconsin counties' population had increased by 35 percent from 1950-63, even though the population of Milwaukee itself was experiencing its first downturn since the city's earliest years, falling from a high of 741,324 in 1960 to 717,099 in 1970 (and to 636,212 in 1980). The suburban counties had experienced a 143 percent increase in amount of land converted from rural to urban use. Retail outlets mirrored the population shift; Southgate Shopping Center opened on South 27th Street in 1951, and the Bay Shore Shopping Center in suburban Glendale began operation in 1954. Part of the reason for choosing Story Valley as the County Stadium site was the fact state officials and political leaders were committed to the Interstate Highway system and other high-volume expressways as the main transportation modes between Milwaukee and its suburbs. This made sense at the time given the existing and projected demographics of southeastern Wisconsin. But Borchert Field had been easily accessible from almost anywhere in the city; a electric-trolley system and multiple bus lines ran down North Eighth Street, Burleigh Street and other thoroughfares in the vicinity of the old ballpark.

County Stadium from the time it opened was served by county bus Route 90, a baseball-game-specific line that still runs from downtown to Miller Park along Wisconsin Avenue. But Milwaukee had eliminated its electric-trolley system in 1958 and its trackless-trolley system in 1965, and as more and more families left central Milwaukee for the suburbs, the only way for them to get to the ballpark was by car - and Milwaukee had commuter-traffic problems even in the Braves' early years. Two proposed freeways originally designed with ballpark access in mind - including one that was to be called the Stadium Freeway, running along the eastern edge of the County Stadium property and extending to the intersection of 60th and Burleigh - were deferred, postponed and eventually abandoned. The first snippet of Milwaukee's projected freeway grid was completed in 1953. Twelve years later, Interstate 94 from Milwaukee to Madison was only 70 percent complete, with a 19-mile stretch just west of Milwaukee scheduled for opening later in 1965.

Meanwhile, light-rail, subway, and commuter-bus systems that might have augmented the new freeway grid and made County Stadium accessible from the suburbs as well as the city proper were never seriously considered. Milwaukee and the rapidly-suburbanizing counties surrounding it were almost never on the same wavelength on any subject. This was particularly true of affordable housing. Henry Maier, mayor of Milwaukee from 1960-88, complained loudly and often during his tenure about the surrounding counties' refusal to assume any responsibility for affordable housing, and a half-century later, Tom Barrett was voicing the same frustrations.

Whether the lack of access to County Stadium via means other than the automobile played a more-than-incidental role in the Braves' attendance problems in the 1960s is difficult to ascertain. But as with some of the other secondary factors, it can't be discounted as a reason the Braves' attendance slipped to the point where their Milwaukee future was compromised.

It seemed clear in 1965, and a half-century later, that the overriding reason Milwaukee lost the Braves was that the Bartholomay group from Day One of its stewardship was hell-bent on moving them to Atlanta as soon as legally possible. But the attendance drop after 1959 that endangered the franchise in the first place was largely the result of factors, outlined in this chapter, that began to manifest themselves before the Bartholomay group bought the team from Lou Perini.

At any rate, from mid-October 1964 on, the Milwaukee Braves were doomed. And so began 1965, the year of Milwaukee's sad riddance.

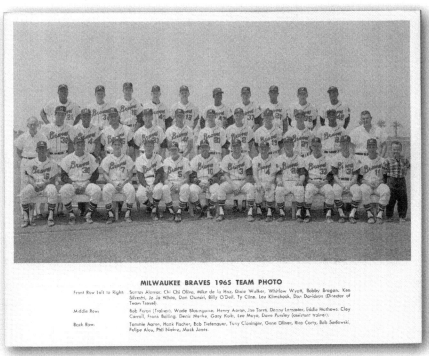

MILWAUKEE BRAVES 1965 TEAM PHOTO

Front Row left to Right: Santos Alomar, Chi Chi Olivo, Mike de la Hoz, Dixie Walker, Whitlow Wyatt, Bobby Bragan, Ken Silvestri, Jo Jo White, Dan Osinski, Billy O'Dell, Ty Cline, Lou Klimchock, Don Davidson (Director of Team Travel).

Middle Row: Bob Foron (Trainer), Wade Blasingame, Henry Aaron, Joe Torre, Denny Lemaster, Eddie Mathews, Clay Carroll, Frank Bolling, Denis Menke, Gary Kolb, Lee Maye, Dave Pursley (assistant trainer).

Back Row: Tommie Aaron, Hank Fischer, Bob Tiefenauer, Tony Cloninger, Gene Oliver, Rico Carty, Bob Sadowski, Felipe Alou, Phil Niekro, Mack Jones.

The 1965 Milwaukee Braves.

An aerial view of Milwaukee County Stadium as it neared completion
in late 1952. The minor-league Milwaukee Brewers were set to
play their 1953 season at County Stadium before the Boston
Braves announced their move to Milwaukee in March 1953.

Warren Spahn in a New York Mets uniform during spring training in 1965. It was the first time since his major league debut in 1942 that Spahn had worn a uniform other than that of the Boston/Milwaukee Braves.

Joe Torre, the future Hall of Famer who joined the Braves in 1960 and emerged as a star during the latter stages of the franchise's Milwaukee era.

A ticket stub and a page from the game program of August 11, 1961, when
Warren Spahn earned the 300th of his 363 major league pitching victories.
Owner Lou Perini would sell the Braves late in 1962 to a group, led by Bill
Bartholomay, that would move the Braves to Atlanta after the 1965 season.

This card was given to fans who showed a ticket stub from
the game in which Spahn earned his 300th victory.

From left, Bobby Bragan, the Milwaukee Braves' last manager; Dan Osinski, a productive relief pitcher for the Braves in 1965; Eddie Mathews, a Hall of Famer and the only man to have played for the Boston, Milwaukee and Atlanta Braves; and Denis Menke, the shortstop whose injury problems in 1965 forced Bragan to improvise throughout the season.

Opening Day 1965 at County Stadium. The crowd of 33,874 was by far the largest of the Braves' farewell season in Milwaukee.

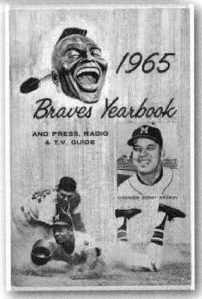

On previous page, a pennant, a yearbook and program from the Braves' stay in Milwaukee. Above, Bragan working with Hank Aaron before a game. Though Bragan was reviled by Braves fans, especially during the Braves' farewell season, Aaron was one of many players who later said Bragan's individual instruction played a key role in their successes.

The day the 1965 National League pennant race - in which the Milwaukee Braves were on top as late as August 20 - turned violent. San Francisco pitcher Juan Marichal (27) has just hit Los Angeles catcher John Roseboro over the head with a bat during a Giants-Dodgers game at Candlestick Park on August 22. Giants infielder Tito Fuentes (26) also is wielding a bat. (Photo by Neil Leifer)

Joe Torre, Gene Oliver, Bob Sadowski, Felipe Alou, and Eddie
Mathews leave the field after a home victory in 1965.

The sadness of 1965. The photo at top is of a typically-empty County Stadium seating section; the other two photos are from September 22, 1965 during the Milwaukee Braves' last-ever home game.

Part Two: The 1965 Season

· · ·

Bracing

• • •

THE FIRST MONTH OF THE last year of the Milwaukee Braves can be described as the end of happy days, at least from a Milwaukee baseball fan's perspective, and the start of As The World Turns.

Or churns.

Happy Days, of course, was the period-piece television show that ran on ABC from 1974-84, and was set in Milwaukee in the late 1950s on the premise that it was the place and time that best reflected the pinnacle of postwar prosperity and the emergence of the middle class. Unemployment and racial unrest and foreign wars and Baby Boomer discontent and the disintegrating environment existed, but they weren't readily visible in the *Happy Days* Milwaukee, and the utopian elements of the series were still celebrated in southeastern Wisconsin long after they became past-tense. A statue of Arthur Fonzarelli, whose leather-jacket mix of contempt and cool became the lasting personification of the TV show, stands on a promenade alongside the Milwaukee River in downtown Milwaukee.

Much of the *Happy Days* mythology was based on a factual place and a factual way of life, at least as they are remembered through the prism of time and distance. Milwaukee's unemployment rate at the start of 1965 was 2.2 percent, and 489,600 were employed by manufacturing firms in the metro area, breaking the previous high of 488,000 in 1953. Personal income was up 27 percent over 1957 levels, and from May 1964 to May 1965, the Milwaukee economy had added 17,000 jobs. The only overriding omission of the *Happy Days* TV run was that the singular Milwaukee phenomenon of the 1950s - Milwaukee Braves baseball - was virtually ignored throughout the show's run. Although the team was a real-life municipal obsession when it led the major leagues in attendance during each of its first six years in Milwaukee, the Braves and the passion with which they were followed were mentioned only in distant passing, if at all, during most *Happy Days* episodes. (Hank Aaron did make a cameo appearance on the show in 1983, during its ninth season and seven years after Aaron retired as a Milwaukee Brewer.)

That oversight notwithstanding, the Milwaukee that the TV show projected still existed in January 1965, at least for young people who at the time had little inkling of what the rest of the year and the rest of the 1960s would hold for them - especially after they reached draft age and the spectre of America's longest war loomed. And even though anybody with any sports consciousness knew that the Milwaukee Braves would play out one more season and then flee to Atlanta, life as it had been continued, for the most part, as 1965 dawned. The October 1964 announcement of the move had angered many but surprised few, given the fact it had been rumored almost from the time Lou Perini sold the team to Bill Bartholomay and his group, two years earlier. To some, it was almost a relief. To many, it meant only a shrug of the shoulders, reflective of an environment where a franchise had lost two-thirds of its constituency during the six seasons from 1959-64.

If you were a kid in Milwaukee at the start of 1965, you probably were listening to the world through one ear - the ear that didn't have a transistor-radio earpiece in it. You were listening, most likely, to one of the two warring Top 40 radio stations on the AM dial - WOKY (920) and WRIT (1340). Both played what their young listeners wanted to hear, especially the Beatles music that some of them had heard in person the previous year when the Fab Four played the Milwaukee Arena. If you listened to WOKY, which pulled in the best ratings of any station in southeastern Wisconsin except for the flagship-for-grownups WTMJ, you would adjust your schedule so that you didn't miss your favorite DJ, whether he was Jack Lee or Bob Barry or Paul Christie or Ron "Ugly" Thompson, and if there was a malt shop or a drugstore near you that had a jukebox, a quarter would get you five singles.

You might have eagerly awaited the emergence at the top of the playlists of your own favorite group: Herman's Hermits, or the Dave Clark Five, or the Byrds, or maybe even Bob Dylan if you liked both folk and rock 'n roll and sensed a convergence of the two in Dylan's early music. Maybe you even followed or attended dances featuring local groups, like Tony's Tigers (who charted with a song called "Little By Little") or the Skunks. You anxiously awaited any or all three of the music-based network dance shows: *Hullabaloo*, *Shindig*, or *Where the Action Is*. The song that brought about the most youthful disquiet in 1965, Barry McGuire's "Eve of Destruction," wasn't recorded until July and didn't reach the top of the Billboard charts until September (and did so despite the fact many stations refused to play it because they feared backlash from their conservative advertisers), but one new group's first single was climbing the charts in January and reached No. 9 in February. Its title and its angry overtones, if not necessarily its lyrics, must have darkened the mood of the Milwaukee Braves fans within the young listenership: *"(This Will Be) The Last Time* by the Rolling Stones.

Pop psychologists, educators, and some Baby Boom parents were beginning to bemoan the "generation gap," and at least musically, it was more than a gap. The parents of the kids of January 1965 had grown up listening to music - particularly polka - that was radically different from the soundtracks of their kids' childhoods.

In 1948, many of those whose kids were listening to rock 'n roll in 1965 had been among the 8,000 polka enthusiasts who had jammed the Milwaukee Auditorium (now the Milwaukee Theatre). Few stayed home to watch TV that night; only a handful of households in Milwaukee owned TVs, and they had only one station to view - WTMJ, which was carrying the Brewers' American Association baseball game against the Indianapolis Indians that evening. (This was also the same night that the Lutheran Federation Dartball League title was decided, with the Ascension beating the Heptatha Cubs 13-3, 1-5, 18-12. Though Milwaukee was the 13th-biggest city in America in 1948, the fact an item like that was considered newsworthy speaks to the sense of small town and neighborhood that continued to exist in Milwaukee in the postwar years.)

Polka, of course, had been a staple in Wisconsin for genera-tions, especially within the city's German enclave on the north side and the Polish community on the south side, and in 1948 it was bridging the gap between the diminishing Big Band era and whatever was to come next. (Rock 'n roll didn't emerge as a mass musical genre until the mid-1950s.) This night - June 9, 1948, the same day that Chuck Yeager broke the sound barrier on an XS-1 test flight in California - all ages, lineages and musical inclinations descended on the Auditorium for a "Battle of the Bands" that had four home teams and only one visiting team - Frankie Yankovic and the Cleveland Kids. The rest of the field included the Six Fat Dutchman ("led by tuba-booping Harold Loeffelmacher," according to the *Sentinel* story the next day), and Lawrence Duchow and His Red Ravens from Fond du Lac, "who made some barnyard noises during the Clarinet Polka (prompting) the fans to break out into shouts and squeals like cowboys at roundup time." All five polkafest bands already had major recording contracts, and Frank W. Van Lare of Oconomowoc, who had been in the business of booking bands and scouting talent for more than 40 years, told the *Sentinel* that polka bands were outselling Big Band icon Tommy Dorsey and that the Red Ravens' version of *Swiss Boy* had already sold 500,000 copies. Yet Yankovic's work pre-empted that of all others; according to the *Sentinel*, "Teenagers are jumping from jitterbugging to polk dancing ... more than 8,000 students of the 'jump and toss' school of the dance gathered to crown the king ... 73-year-old twins, a preteen boy with his mom, and two young girls with lacquered upsweeps twirled until their full skirts flared out like open umbrellas ... Frankie Yankovic and the Cleveland Kids were popularly acclaimed the best of the five polka bands ... and Mayor (Frank) Zeidler made it official by personally presenting Frankie with the Oscar of rural rhythm."

Yankovic, who died in 1998 at age 83, became known as the King of Polka after his *tour de force* in Milwaukee. He recorded several gold albums, in 1986 became the first polka artist ever to win a Grammy, and was one of Milwaukee's few constants before, during and after the time of the Milwaukee Braves, even though he lived in Cleveland throughout his career.

Polka was passe among kids (if not their parents) in Milwaukee in 1965, but the generation gap notwithstanding, youngsters and adults alike were inundated and imbued by the written word if they grew up in Wisconsin after World War II. Madison, home of the University of Wisconsin, was considered the Berkeley of the Midwest, and UW's string of satellite campuses was already well established. And because of the nature and the ferocity of the newspaper rivalry in Milwaukee, it was difficult to live there in 1965 and not have an opinion on the issues of the day. To a large extent, at a time when the evening *Milwaukee Journal* claimed 383,215 subscribers (compared to the *Milwaukee Journal Sentinel's* circulation of 258,000 in 2014, 10 years after the *Journal* and *Sentinel* combined their editorial staffs and products) your world outlook depended on which newspaper you and your parents read.

The morning *Sentinel*, which had about 175,000 subscribers in 1995 when it was folded into the *Journal*, had peaked at approximately 200,000 readers in 1957. Like many morning newspapers of the era, the *Sentinel* routinely was out-circulated by the *Journal* in the postwar years because most adults read the paper after their workday and not before. The *Sentinel* leaned toward bombast in its headlines and content. Its two above-the-fold stories on Jaunary 1, 1965 were about four children who had died in two separate house fires in Milwaukee the night before, and about the record-high 1,057 people who had died in accidents on Wisconsin roads in 1964.

The *Sentinel* had much such gore to chronicle because such tragedies were all too common in Wisconsin in 1965. Many of the city's homes, especially on the near north side in neighborhoods that had been fragmented by the construction of Interstate 43 in the early 1960s - straight through the lot that had once housed Borchert Field - were tinderboxes that had been built before the turn of the century and had fallen into disrepair. And driving, especially in wintertime, was dangerous in Wisconsin in 1965. Even though Wisconsin in 1961 had become the first state to require drivers-side seat belts, the law was loosely enforced and the seat belts worn loosely, if at all. It wasn't until 1968 that the federal government mandated installation of seat belts in all new cars, although later in 1965, it did mandate 17 safety-related features such as padded dashboards, dual brakes and standardized gear shifters for the 1966 model year. Sen. Abraham Ribicoff (D-Conn.), a longtime critic of the American automobile industry, had formed a subcommittee to study how cars could be made safer. He claimed that for an additional $100 per new car, the death toll on U.S. highways could be cut in half.

Unsurprisingly considering Wisconsin's brewing and drinking heritages, drunken driving was even more of a problem in Wisconsin than in other U.S. states. This was true even in 2016, as Wisconsin remained the only U.S. state where a first-offense OWI (operating while impaired) was still considered an infraction rather than a misdemeanor. Local-option laws exacerbated the problem; while the minimum drinking age in Milwaukee was 21 in 1965, it was 18 in several surrounding counties. Bars also stayed open later outside Milwaukee than within it, putting too many drivers who shouldn't have been on the roads behind too many steering wheels.

There was also the application of "planned obsolescence" - an idea, brought to the American automobile industry by famed Milwaukee industrial designer Brooks Stevens in the late 1950s - that cars ought to be made with the idea that they would be up to date (both in terms of style and safety) only until the next model year. Competition from foreign manufacturers that were making smaller, safer, more economic cars pre-empted and eventually ended this business model in the 1970s. Design and construction of new roads also improved after 1965, and seat-belt use was virtually universal by the turn of the 21st century. In 2015, the death toll on Wisconsin roads dropped to 556, its lowest total since 1942 - a year during which non-essential driving was limited because of tire and gas rationing that was imposed throughout World War II.

Still, tragedy-based stories were all too common in 1965, and the *Sentinel*, much more than the *Journal*, based much of its content on ambulance (and Communist) chasing. The *Sentinel* was a former Hearst paper that had ceased operation in 1962 after a lengthy strike eroded most of what was left of its readership. (Soon after, the *Journal* purchased the *Sentinel* subscription list and machinery, and hired some of its former employees.) Like most Hearst papers and the *Chicago Tribune*, which then circulated widely in Milwaukee, the *Sentinel* never had made any secret of its ultra-right-wing editorial stance. In 1932, it even openly campaigned for Herbert Hoover, who had become a political pariah as the Great Depression deepened and Hoover increasingly distanced himself from both problems and solutions. Voters in a liberal-leaning state where Progressives and Socialists were integral parts of the political tapestry cast their ballots for Franklin Delano Roosevelt, who won Wisconsin by nearly a 2 to 1 margin. In 1965, when civil-rights and anti-Vietnam War demonstrations began in earnest at the University of Wisconsin in Madison, the *Journal* reported them as legitimate protest and sometimes tacitly sympathized with them, while the *Sentinel* scolded those who fomented the unrest and questioned, not so tacitly, their patriotism - a right-is-right stance that remained in place in the *Sentinel* newsroom and editorial offices through the rest of the 1960s and well beyond. The *Sentinel* had closely covered the 1964 presidential campaign of segregationist Alabama Gov. George Wallace in 1964, though it stopped short of endorsing him. The Journal Company in 1965 was 80 percent owned by its workforce of 1,076, so neither of the papers had corporate or political interests for which they were obliged to be a mouthpiece. Even so, their political stances remained the same as they had been when the *Sentinel* was a Hearst paper.

But even though it had the Milwaukee market largely cornered (at least financially) by 1965, the *Journal's* ownership thought having two such disparate editorial voices in the city stimulated healthy debate. So it maintained the *Sentinel* and treated it as an editorial rival even though the two papers' circulation, advertising and production were combined. After Congress passed the Newspaper Preservation Act of 1970, this business-operation combination of two papers with different editorial products became common as the newspaper industry declined after the advent of cable television and later the Internet eroded its reader-ship and its advertising base. Milwaukee thus became a working model for papers that entered into Joint Operating Agreements (known in the industry as JOAs) after 1970.

Journal Sentinel editor George Stanley, who grew up in Green Bay and De Pere and graduated from the University of Wisconsin, in 2013 wrote in an e-mail of the relationship be-tween the two Milwaukee papers: "The *Journal* bought the *Sentinel* before the JOA was written, so there was never a JOA concerning our papers. The *Journal* kept the *Sentinel's* separate editorial voice going because it thought it was good for the com-munity, not because it had to. It actually could have closed the paper at any time if it had wanted to. From a business perspec-tive, I think they thought it was good to have both an AM and PM paper during those decades (from 1962-95) and that could sell ads into both to maximize an adertiser's reach ... Because of the continuing national shift toward AM papers and the move by advertisers to follow that trend, I think (management decided) in 1994 that the market would not be able to support a PM daily much longer, so (the move was made) to merge the two papers into one."

Part of the JOA law, which was written into Federal Commu-nications Commission rules, specified that newspapers that had entered into a JOA could not operate television or radio stations in the same market, but that didn't apply to the *Journal-Sentinel* agreement in 1962 or to the 1995 editorial merger, Stanley wrote.

"If the *Sentinel* had been the PM rather than the AM, (man-agement) might've just closed it," Stanley wrote. "The company had the legal ability to do whatever it wanted without hurting its FCC licenses (it also had been the longtime owner of the WTMJ TV and radio stations, and TMJ stands for *The Milwaukee Journal*) because its ownership of the *Sentinel* and the local broadcast properties all predated later laws and broadcast restrictions and so were grandfathered in."

As the Milwaukee newspapers evolved after the *Journal* absorbed the *Sentinel*, much of what they reported presaged 1966 and beyond. Some of the headlines, like the *Sentinel* fire-fatality banner on the first day of 1965 and a story about "rioting" in South Vietnam three days later, were not feel-good in nature. And the *Sentinel* showed its off-the-edge-of-the-right-wing editorial sentiments on January 6 when it headlined a story on a health-care milestone: MEDICARE HURDLE FALLS and adjoined the story with a related column that was topped by a one-word head: PATERNALISM.

There were ominous signs of the social, ecological and economic upheaval that would befall Milwaukee in the coming generation. On January 28, with the low temperature at minus-20, an inversion layer, car exhaust, and industrial emissions from the Menomonee Valley created what the *Journal* described as a "Londonesque fog." Visibility was down to virtually zero, causing several automobile accidents that shut down the 16th Street Aqueduct, and several plants on the Menomonee River were ordered closed for the day. Grant Park Beach, in South Milwaukee, had been closed for six years due to pollution from adjacent factories that had been spewing raw sewage directly into Lake Michigan. (The beach reopened during the summer of 1965, but few went near it because of the residual stench.) In 1965, as in most years during the 1960s, millions of dead alewives (a type of herring) washed onto Milwaukee beaches from Lake Michigan.

In 1980, Congress created the so-called Superfund to tax serial industrial polluters to help the federal government pay for the most massive cleanup jobs. Two Milwaukee County sites were among the top-priority Superfund locations. One was Moss-American (Kerr-McGee Oil Co.) off North Granville Road, where the T.J. Moss Tie Company in 1921 established a wood-preserving facility west of the Little Menomonee River in Milwaukee. The plant treated wooden railroad ties, poles, and fence posts with creosote, a preservative that consists of a mixture of numerous chemical compounds derived from coal tar and fuel oil. The practice continued until 1976, when the plant was shut down. Also named on the Superfund priority list was the Fadrowski Drum Disposal site in Franklin. At that location, Wisconsin Department of Natural Resources investigators found thousands of buried drums containing dangerous quantities of mercury, benzine, chromium, barium, lead and cyanide. Cleanup of the Fadrowski site was completed in 1995; the Moss-American location, first listed by the national Environmental Protection Agency as a Superfund site in 1984, was still on that list in 2016. Those two sites were cited by the EPA as the Milwaukee area's most egregious polluters, but they were far from the only red-flag locations long before and during the 1960s. Though most of the heavy industries, especially those lining the Menomonee River, were long gone by 2016 and the valley had largely been restored to its original pristine state, city officials in 2016 recommended that residents install filters on their drinking-water taps because of the possible existence of residual lead in the city's water supply.

Labor unrest was in the news, including strikes at Milwaukee's American Motors Corporation plant and at the George Meyer Company (where Happy Felsch, a Milwaukee native and the center fielder on the Chicago White Sox team that threw the 1919 World Series, worked as a crane operator in the 1940s and 1950s). So was the Fraternal Order of Eagles and its Milwaukee headquarters on West Wisconsin Avenue, because its charter specifically barred blacks from joining. The FOE in 1965 was one of Milwaukee's most influential and prestigious fraternal orders. Its lodge had been built in 1927 (it still existed, as the Rave nightclub, in 2016) and was an entertainment and social magnet throughout the next four decades. FOE members included many dignitaries from the sports and entertainment worlds, including Bob Hope, Gordie Howe, Max Baer, Arnold Palmer, Danny Thomas and Art Rooney. Warren Spahn was a member during his years in Milwaukee, and so was Red Schoendienst. (None of those individuals was known to have been involved with the drafting or enforcement of the whites-only rule; most probably did not even know about it until 1965 when the Eagles' exclusionary policy became front-page news in Milwaukee and elsewhere.)

Milwaukee's emerging demographics, in 1965 as in 2016, were reflective of schisms that cut largely along racial lines and underscored what came to be called "*de facto* segregation" in the city. While 56 of the employed white men in Milwaukee held white-collar jobs, only 21 percent of the city's black men did so. The "inner core" - i.e., the near north side - had 16 percent of the population and 7 percent of the acreage in the city, but was 90 percent black and was the site of 59 percent of Milwaukee's crime. Fewer than one of four of adults in that area who had jobs made more than $3,000 per year, and 25 percent of the families in the inner core were single-parent households, compared to 4 percent elsewhere in the city. In a city where 21.6 percent of the students were non-white, North Division and Lincoln were virtually all-black, Rufus King had gone from 32 percent black to 42.8 percent since 1960, and three high schools - Bay View, Pulaski and South Division - had a total of six black students between them. In Pulaski's case, this would change dramatically after 1965. The school, built in 1933 at the intersection of South 27th Street and Oklahoma Avenue, in 2016 was as reflective as any Milwaukee high school of the city's evolving demographics. In 1965, Pulaski served a south-side neighborhood that had been predominantly Polish for decades. By 1988, however, it was 57 percent white and 36 percent black. In the 1990s and thereafter, the area surrounding Pulaski became an Hispanic enclave, and in 2010, Pulaski was 48.6 percent black, 34.6 percent Hispanic and 9.4 percent white.

The Milwaukee Police Department in January 1965 got the OK to permanently beef up patrols at North Division and King, where 15 to 20 students were being arrested weekly at the two schools. At North Division, a teacher's jaw was broken by a vocational student. Racial tension, while not yet at a boiling point, clearly was festering in what sociologists were already calling the most segregated city outside the South. On May 18, 1964, a one-day walkout of Milwaukee public schools was organized by integrationists, resulting in a 60 percent absentee rate that day, and more were planned for 1965. (A three-day boycott took place in October, during which many parents sent their children to "freedom schools" hastily set up in Milwaukee's predominantly black neighborhoods.) To try to alleviate that tension, the Milwaukee business community in 1963 had formed the We Committee to establish communication between white and black community and business leaders. In 1965, it had 127 members employing 120,000 persons, and its stated goal was taking strides to ensure that "true integration, and including the poor in solution seeking, should trump the 'problem approach' to the Negro." Ben Barkin, the advertising executive who was serving on the board of the Bud Selig-led Teams Inc group that was trying to keep big league baseball in Milwaukee, in January 1965 called the We Committee's work "a kind of local, exemplary United Nations. I firmly believe explosions that rocked other communities will never happen here. We are here to talk to each other, to try to understand each other. We are out of the crawling stage, and as a result, I firmly believe we can set an example for other communities."

But for the residents of Milwaukee who weren't being ground down by poverty and urban decay, the *Happy Days* correlation still held mostly true in January 1965. Even in the dead of winter, you could take your date to the Starland drive-in to see Kim Novak and Lawrence Harvey in "Of Human Bondage." If your car defroster didn't work, the Varsity at 14th and Wisconsin was showing "A Shot in the Dark" starring Peter Sellers and Elke Summer, and the Warner at 214 W. Wisconsin Ave. had Tony Curtis and Natalie Wood in "Sex and the Single Girl." Even more titillating was the movie showing at the Strand: "The Pleasure Seekers," starring Tony Franciosa. The subhead on the movie's TV ad read" "Where do good little girls go when they want to be bad?" In March, Myrna Loy, one of the most prolific and critically acclaimed movie actresses of the 1930s and 1940s, appeared for a week at the Pabst Theater at the head of a touring company that performed "Barefoot in the Park." Or, for those with non-mainstream entertainment tastes, there were always the Adult Trike Races as Bruno's Hall in Muskego. Parents with young children likely preferred Holiday on Ice, which in January 1965 was in the midst of a weeklong run at the Milwaukee Arena.

Wisconsin, particularly southeastern Wisconsin, was urbanizing at an unprecedented pace in 1965; according to the U.S. Census Bureau and the Wisconsin Farm Bureau Federation, 63.8 percent of Wisconsinites lived in urban or suburban areas, and for the first time since it became a state in 1848, Wisconsin had more people (3,952,485) than cows (3,773,000). Young families looking for homes could spend anywhere from $35,900 for a four-bedroom white-brick Colonial in Shorewood to a two-bedroom duplex in West Allis for $14,900. Milwaukee now had six TV stations, including two on the then-newfangled UHF dial, and on Monday night, viewers had to make a choice between the *Andy Williams Show*, *The Lucy Show* and Bing Crosby's variety show. On the night of January 13, the handful of Milwaukeeans who cared about the NBA could watch the All-Star game on independent Channel 18. Some households also had to decide whether an investment in color TV was worthwhile. One could buy a 23-inch Philco 23 at MilTV Inc. on West North Avenue. Musical variety was plentiful on the radio as well, with 30 radio stations in Milwaukee - including 15 FM stations, five of which were broadcasting in stereo.

On the economic front, all appeared to be as it had been throughout the postwar economic boom, which had benefitted Milwaukee as much as any American city. The county unemployment rate, though higher than that of Milwaukee itself, held steady at 3.9 percent compared to the national average of 4.9

percent, with 529,000 employed overall and 196,000 working in factories. Allis-Chalmers, one of the county's biggest employers, announced it had landed a contract to build a superheater for a nuclear power plant in Sioux Falls, S.D. Two months later, Allis-Chalmers announced it had signed an even bigger contract, valued at $105 million, to build 55 guidance systems for NASA, with some of those systems earmarked for what became the Apollo program that eventually landed men on the moon.

The presence of the St. Lawrence Seaway, opened in 1959, continued to be a boon to Milwaukee's shipping and cargo-processing industries, with 644,294 net tons handled - a 140 percent increase since the opening of the seaway. (In 2012, the Milwaukee harbor's total tonnage was 2,016,161.) Despite the inner-core poverty, crime was relatively negligible in comparison to cities of similar size, though it was increasing: Twenty murders were reported in Milwaukee in 1964, down one from the previous year (and compared to 121 in 2005 and 90 in 2014), but 44 forcible rapes (up from 32 in '63), 170 robberies (up from 153) and 2,975 burglaries (up from 2,470) were also reported. Caterpillar, which had built tanks for the military during the war, had come to Wisconsin in 1952 and by 1965 had a local workforce of 600. By 2016 it was the world's largest producer of construction and mining equipment and diesel and natural-gas engines.

Educationally, Wisconsin fared well compared to its 49 counterparts: 92.4 percent of residents ages 14-17 were enrolled in high school compared to the national average of 87.4; a teacher's average salary was $5,985 compared to the national average of $5,963, and Milwaukee Public Schools teachers made an average of $7,237. Per-pupil spending was $498 in Wisconsin compared to $455 nationally. While 24.5 percent of Americans who took the military's mental-health test failed it in 1964, Wisconsin's failure rate was only 8.1 percent. In a survey reported by *Christian Herald* magazine, 89 percent of Protestant respondents said they wouldn't object to having a person of another race as a next-door neighbor. Despite Milwaukee's *de facto* segregation problem, the magazine ranked Wisconsin 11th nationally in overall racial tolerance; only Minnesota among Midwest states ranked higher. Then as later, Milwaukee was a focal point for the hospital industry; in 1965, 25 general hospitals were operating in the metro area, employing 1,900 physicians.

The Miller Brewing Company was coming off a 1964 record output of 3,284,164 barrels of beer, up 50 percent from 1954, the year of Fred Miller's death. (Schlitz, however, still had a big lead in Milwaukee beer-brewing with 8,250,000 barrels, second nationally only to Anheuser-Busch, and Pabst, with 7,440,000, was third.) And the city, while already more than 100 years old, was still building. The Milwaukee Harbor Bridge, later to be named in honor of longtime mayor Daniel Hoan (who ironically had opposed its construction), was in the beginning phases of the approval process. The climate-controlled Mitchell Domes opened in 1965 as well; in 2016, they were closed temporarily while the first major repairs since their opening were undertaken.

The high school basketball season was well underway at Cedarburg, Port Washington, Granville, Mequon Homestead, Brookfield Central, Hamilton, Glendale Nicolet, Menomonee Falls and Brookfield East - all members of the Braveland Conference, which soon would require a new name. (In 2016, it was called the North Shore Conference.) Eddie Mathews Jr., at age 10, wasn't yet in high school, but he was a basketball fan even though his father had been the Braves' third baseman since before Eddie Jr. had been born. The father had already told the son and the rest of the family that they would continue to live in their ranch-style home in the then-rural north-central area of Brookfield, at 18145 Brookdale Drive, regardless of where the Braves played in 1965 and beyond. Brookfield then was so rustic that the Mathews home bordered a chicken farm. In 1957, the family's German shepherd got loose from the Mathews yard and into the neighbor's chicken coop, killing 76 chickens and six rabbits before it could be subdued. The chicken-farm owner sued Mathews for $500, and the matter was settled out of court.

Staying in Brookfield was fine with Eddie Jr. because he had his own unique gig - as a Marquette basketball ball boy under the auspices of a first-year coach who was struggling through an 8-18 season. But Al McGuire already was making strides toward assuaging those in Marquette circles who were angry over the firing the previous season of highly-regarded coach Eddie Hickey, who'd taken the Warriors to three postseason berths in his six seasons before being fired at the end of the 1963-64 season.

"My parents were not the kind of people who involved their children in adult matters (such as the ramifications of the Braves' impending move to Atlanta)," recalled Eddie Mathews Jr., who went on to medical school at the University of Wisconsin and in 2016 was in the midst of his career as an anesthesiologist at a Waukesha hospital. "We had the old 'children should be seen and not heard' thing going on, though I knew what was happening. But I remember being a ballboy that year very well. There were three or four of us, and Al would take us out to pizza sometimes after games. He even let us ride behind him on his motorcycle."

Bowling, another element of the Milwaukee image widely held then and later by outsiders, was in full swing in 1965. Milwaukee that year had 68 bowling alleys - 21 on the north side, 20 on the west side and 27 on the south side. The city was considered second only to St. Louis as an American bowling mecca at a time when the sport was at its zenith from a participatory standpoint. Land for alleys was still readily available in most cities, including Milwaukee. The advent of the automatic pinsetter and ball return, first introduced in 1946 and virtually universal in public bowling alleys by 1965, lessened both the time and the cost of participating in a regular bowling league. Some of these bowling centers were owned and operated by fraternal organizations, private clubs, YMCAs, and even bars. Milwaukee in 1955 had 2,200 taverns, and in 1965 it still had 1,908 despite a law that limited liquor licensing to one establishment per 500 residents.

Although industrial, municipal and youth baseball (including the Stars of Yesterday program) had long been popular in Milwaukee, Little League was a late arrival on the scene, partly because of Wisconsin's harsh spring weather. (Little Leagues in warmer climates usually start their regular season in early March and end it by mid-June to accommodate the international All-Star tournament, which culminates with the Little League World Series in Williamsport, Pa. in late August.) This finally changed in 1965 with the organization of the Milwaukee area's first chartered Little League - the eight-team Beckum-Stapleton Little League, which celebrated its 50th anniversary in 2015. (Though 242 Wisconsin natives had reached the major leagues as of 2016, the state had never sent a team to the Little League World Series, and the only national championship ever won by a Wisconsin youth baseball team came in 1987 when Stevens Point captured the American Legion tournament.) Felix Mantilla, a member of the Braves' 1957 World Series title team, became a permanent resident of Milwaukee and was still there in 2016. Throughout and after his baseball career, he was heavily involved in area youth baseball and other endeavors benefitting Milwaukee kids, and a Little League on the south side of the city is named for him.

While Ben Barkin was serving on the We Committee, he, Bud Selig and the other members of Teams Inc - formed in November 1964, a month after the Braves announced they were leaving for Atlanta - faced a daunting task. The Braves already had moved their offices to a temporary location in Chicago that just happened to be in the same building as Bartholomay's insurance agency, and Bartholomay, after finally having confirmed all that he had been denying for more than two years, also indicated that the Braves would try to buy their way out of the final year of their County Stadium lease in time to begin the 1965 season in Atlanta. A week after the announcement, the Braves board of directors had voted to seek National League permission to make the move in '65. During a meeting in Phoenix on November 6, NL owners - faced with legal action by Milwaukee County if the Braves broke the lease - ordered the Braves to operate in Milwaukee in 1965 but approved their move to Atlanta for the 1966 season. After that, the Braves signed a 20-year lease to operate out of Atlanta-Fulton County Stadium starting in 1966. But rumors that they would proceed with Bartholomay's original plan - to try to pay off the last year of the County Stadium lease and move to Atlanta immediately - still persisted. The Braves, in fact, tried three times in 1965 to get Milwaukee County to nullify the lease and allow the Braves to move to Milwaukee as soon as they could pack their equipment and files.

The dilemma facing Selig and his organization was simple: Should Teams Inc, county and city government, and the Wisconsin baseball community try to stop the move by litigation or by trying to buy the team from Bill Bartholomay's group? Or should they encourage what was left of the Braves' fan base to frequent County Stadium in 1965, even with the knowledge that the Braves would be gone at the end of the season, in the hope that Major League Baseball would see that Milwaukee was still fertile baseball ground and give the city the next available franchise? Some supported the latter approach. A letter to the editor that was published in the *Sentinel* on January 1 read, in part: "Since we can see the Braves another year, let's give the manager and the players a hearty Milwaukee welcome in 1965. And when the time comes to say farewell, let's shed a few tears and wish them all good luck."

By January 1965, Selig and Teams Inc had decided to proceed on the assumption that the Braves couldn't be bought. Teams Inc had made a preliminary inquiry of Bartholomay regarding the possibility of his selling the franchise late in 1964, and had been brusquely rebuffed. It also seemed unlikely that Milwaukee could immediately garner enough support among major league owners to obtain another team by 1966. White Sox owner Arthur Allyn, though, voiced his support for Milwaukee, saying that commissioner Ford Frick should have vetoed the move out of hand (as he had the power to do) and that he, Allyn, would push to get his fellow American League owners to insist on such a veto during their meetings in New York in February. "I fought ... to get Frick to squash the move, but he wasn't about to do anything," Allyn said. "Milwaukee is a major league city. It's too bad the people running the baseball operation there had to goof it up." (After the Braves moved, Allyn's White Sox played a total of 20 games in Milwaukee in 1968 and 1969, and he made it clear that he wanted to move the White Sox there. But he was blocked, and then bought out, by his brother John, who insisted that the franchise stay in Comiskey Park.)

Even Lou Perini, who still owned 10 percent of the Braves' stock after selling the team to the Bartholomay group late in 1962, thought Milwaukee should get something more than the back of Major League Baseball's hand. "It (the move) was a lousy job and we have only ourselves to blame," he was quoted as saying on January 15. "What worries me is the Braves' image in Milwaukee, especially if it's a bad season. The image will suffer, and so will Milwaukee ... within a few years, the conditions might be right for another team. But if the image suffers this summer, that future might be completely wiped out."

But even though it made intellectual sense to acknowledge the inevitable, let the Braves go and concentrate on the effort to obtain another team, the Braves' continuum of dishonesty couldn't be ignored, and wasn't. As recently as April 11, 1964, Bartholomay had said: "We are definitely not moving. We're playing in Milwaukee, whether you're talking about 1964, 1965 or 1975. I hope this is the last time anybody tries to link us with Atlanta or any other city."

On January 5, 1965, United Press International reported that general manager John McHale had offered Milwaukee County

$1 million to vacate the final year of the stadium lease and allow the Braves to play out of Atlanta as soon as the All-Star break. The story was denied by McHale, by Milwaukee County Board of Supervisors president Eugene Grobschmidt and by Milwaukee County Executive John Doyne, with whom Grobschmidt and other supervisors were in constant discord over the Braves and many other governmental matters. Doyne said he was waiting for a report from Selig's group before deciding how to proceed, and hadn't heard anything from the Braves about their intentions since September. Grobschmidt was far more blunt. "We will never release the Braves unless we have assurance that 40 to 50 major league baseball games will be played here each season until Milwaukee gets its own team under expansion." A week later, Grobschmidt had this to say: "If each of the 20 teams played only five games here next season, Milwaukee fans could see a total of 100 games."

A subsequent letter corrected Grobschmidt's math and his logic; the most games that could have been played in Milwaukee under his formula was 50, since two teams are needed for every game, and it was apparent by now that MLB was unsympathetic to Milwaukee's situation and cared only about steering the franchise south by the most expedient means possible. This was confirmed on January 25, when Teams Inc submitted its report to John Doyne. The headline in the next day's *Journal* told the whole story: "Braves Lost, Teams Inc Reports."

In its report, according to the *Journal*, Teams Inc recommended that the county keep in effect the injunction it had obtained to force the Braves to stay in town through the 1965 season. "At the same time," the *Journal* reported, "the group of civic leaders painted anything but a rosy picture of Milwaukee's baseball future ... (and said) that most people in Organized Baseball and much of the general public outside Wisconsin feel that Milwaukee has lost interest in baseball and in recent years has failed to properly support the Braves." The report also referenced "a substantial belief on the part of these same people that within the past four years, definite anti-baseball attitude has developed there."

According to the *Journal*, the committee met with nine of the 10 NL owners, along with Frick and National League president Warren Giles. It came away with the conclusion that "there is no question but that erroneous information has been fed to baseball officials for the last year or more ... Knowing what we know today, it is apparent that our recent visits to NL officials should have been initiated a year or more ago and then maintained on a regular basis so that the Milwaukee situation could be kept before these men ... (Owners and officials) have very real questions as to whether Milwaukee is a good baseball town. They have indicated that they feel Atlanta is a better one."

The Teams Inc report further recommended that Wisconsin fans should support the Braves in 1965, and said that turning out in numbers characteristic of those drawn by the Braves in the 1950s might fast-track the efforts to get a replacement or expansion team. This likely was prompted by remarks by Bill Veeck, who had suggested to Lou Chapman of the *Sentinel* that the best course of action might be for Teams Inc to begin accepting 1966 season-ticket applications and soliciting advertising support for a team - even one that existed only on paper - other than the Braves. Selig and Teams Inc eventually did this after the 1965 season, when Teams Inc was dissolved and a new corporation, Milwaukee Brewers Baseball Inc., was established to do what Veeck had suggested.

The "definite anti-baseball attitude" to which the report referred probably was a reaction by owners to the threat of litigation by the county, and particularly the bellicose stance taken by Grobschmidt. If they thought that the sentiments they expressed to Selig and his group would silence Grobschmidt, they were wrong. On January 21 during a speaking engagement in Sheboygan, Grobschmidt said he believed the Braves had an "escape clause" in their contract with Atlanta that would indemnify Atlanta if a federal antitrust lawsuit succeeded in preventing the move. He also said, based on his discussions with members of Wisconsin's Congressional delegation, that the federal government could void the move if the antitrust litigation succeeded. Further, he said he had knowledge to the effect that the Braves' move had been planned since 1962, "and I believe Mr. Perini was in on the deal." (As it turned out, in this case, Grobschmidt had correct information.) The corollary implication was that in a federal antitrust lawsuit, the Braves, Perini and Bartholomay and his group could also be guilty of conspiracy to defraud Milwaukee County if the antitrust suit succeeded. Indictments along those lines potentially could have been even more damaging to MLB and its owners than the antitrust suit.

Then came an outlandish declaration, even by Grobschmidt's standards: He said that the move to Atlanta could be prevented altogether if 10 Wisconsin businessmen kicked in $30,000 each to create a salary fund for the Braves' top players. "Next, they (the top players) would tell Atlanta they're quitting baseball," he said. "If they (the Braves) have to lose a half-dozen to a dozen of their top men, they just wouldn't have a baseball team worth the name." That, according to Grobschmidt's master plan, would mean Bartholomay would have to sell the team to Teams Inc, which would keep the franchise in Milwaukee.

No response to Grobschmidt's remarks is recorded, either from the owners or from Selig and Teams Inc - presumably because it was too ludicrous to even be contemplated by players, management, ownership or anyone else who followed baseball with anything more than cursory interest. But it made abundantly clear the ferocity with which Grobschmidt and his allies in county government were prepared to attack the Braves in the coming year and beyond.

Meanwhile, amid the turmoil and tumult, reporters dutifully submitted stories on baseball outside the courts and boardrooms, and what might be expected from the 1965 Milwaukee Braves. Most of those stories were not widely read, partly because many in Milwaukee had resigned themselves to the reality of the franchise's situation, and partly because the main story about the Braves' personnel during that forlorn winter had been about a player no longer on their roster - Warren Spahn.

Spahn, who was to turn 44 on April 21, was both a wonder of the ages and a wonder of age. He had first signed out of South Park High in Buffalo in 1940, when the Boston National League team was known (for the fifth and final season) as the Bees. He came up to the majors with the Braves in 1942 - wearing No. 16 instead of the soon-to-be-familiar No. 21 - but was sent back to the minor leagues after four outings with no decisions because he refused an order from manager Casey Stengel to throw a bean-ball at an opposing hitter. Soon after, he went into the Army and was assigned to an engineering unit, and by 1945 had risen to the rank of staff sergeant. On March 17, 1945, just seven weeks before the end of World War II in Europe, Spahn and his unit were performing maintenance on the Remagen Bridge, one of the last intact bridges across the Rhine River into Germany. "We were trying to complete repairs on the Remagen Bridge so that our trucks could carry supplies to the front," Spahn recalled years later. "I checked all the main points and then started to walk toward the bridge. Suddenly, there was a terrible, deafening roar as the bridge collapsed, throwing many of the men and much of the equipment into the deep gorge and water below. We did manage to rescue some of the men, but many had been crushed by the falling debris, and others drowned." In all, 28 American troops - including 11 from Spahn's battalion - were killed in the Remagen Bridge collapse, and 93 were wounded. "In only a matter of minutes," Spahn recalled, "I would have been on that thing." Spahn already had suffered shrapnel wounds to the neck and leg for which he was later given a Purple Heart, and became an officer after the incident at Remagen with his promotion to second lieutenant.

Returning to the Braves - who had fired Stengel in 1943 - at war's end, Spahn went 8-5 in 1946, then began his journey to baseball's pantheon in 1947, when he was 21-10 with a 2.33 ERA and made the National League All-Star team for the first of 14 times. With Johnny Sain also winning 21 games that year, newspapers began to refer to the Braves' rotation as "Spahn, Sain and two days of rain," although the 1948 NL pennant winners got considerable help from Vern Bickford and Bill Voiselle with 13 and 11 wins respectively. Spahn would have only one more season with fewer than 17 wins until 1964, and he finished his career with 11 seasons of 20 wins or more, even though he won only one Cy Young Award, in 1957.

In 1963, he had earned his 327th pitching win to top the career games-won-by-lefthanders list that previously had been headed by Eddie Plank. More than a half-century after his major league career finally ended in 1965, he was sixth in total wins by any pitcher with 363, and still well ahead of Steve Carlton (329) among lefties. His 1963 season, at age 42, had been one of his best: 23-7 with a 2.60 ERA for a sixth-place team. He led the NL in complete games for the seventh straight year, with 22, and was second only to Sandy Koufax with seven shutouts. But in 1964, the 5,000-plus innings that he had logged as a major league pitcher finally won out over his will. He finished with by far the worst year of his career: 6-13, 5.29 ERA, only four complete games, and his 63rd and last career shutout. That came on May 5 at County Stadium, when Spahn two-hit the Mets, who went 53-109 that season. He was 6-11 with a 5.13 ERA at the end of July when manager Bobby Bragan pulled him from the starting rotation, and he started only three games the rest of the year. He did rack up four saves in the final two months, but logged only 10 innings pitched during that time.

Spahn wasn't happy about his demotion or about some of Bragan's comments to media members to the effect that he, Spahn, had little left to contribute as a major league pitcher. He was even unhappier about the way the news was conveyed to him, saying he found out not directly from Bragan, but from sportswriter Lou Chapman. On November 23, 1964, he was sold to the Mets - managed by Stengel, who had detoured Spahn's career in Boston 22 years before. Both said at the time of the sale that the 1942 incident was long forgotten and forgiven, and that Spahn would serve the Mets as a part-time pitcher and full-time pitching coach. But by January, Spahn, in an article by Al Hirshberg for *Sport* magazine entitled "I Can Still Pitch," made it clear he still expected to be an effective, full-time pitcher with the Mets. "I'm a *pitcher*," Spahn told Hirshberg. "Age isn't a factor, as Satchel Paige has proved. When he helped pitch the 1948 Indians to a pennant (and a World Series title), he was almost certainly older than I am now. (Paige was at least 42, and may have been as old as 48, in 1948, and he pitched his last major league game for the Kansas City Athletics in 1965, when he may have been as old as 65.) And Satch had two things going for him that I've got going for me: He was in good physical condition and there wasn't anything wrong with his arm."

Spahn told Hirshberg he had found a mechanical flaw in his delivery that he had corrected after being taken out of the Braves' rotation. "All I needed was my regular turn and the confidence of my boss," he said "I didn't get either." Later in the month, he told another reporter that he'd be "busting my butt to beat the Braves above and beyond the call of duty. If I were leaving the Braves in the late 1950s or early 1960s, that would be a different matter. But the club is leaving Milwaukee. There's been such a drastic change in personnel (that) actually I'm better off."

Though he rarely if ever talked about it to newspapermen, Spahn no doubt had one last historical milestone in mind: Surpassing Christy Mathewson and Grover Cleveland Alexander and becoming the No. 1 winner in National League history.

Both had won 373 games, and Spahn at the start of 1965 stood at 356, well within reach of Mathewson and Alexander if he could regain his 1963 form. That this goal was important to him was borne out after his 1965 season, which turned out to be his last in the majors. With 363 NL wins, and needing 11 more to pass Mathewson and Alexander, he continued pitching for two more years in hopes of returning to the big leagues. He worked in three games for the Mexico City Tigers in the Mexican League in 1966, then signed on with the Cardinals and pitched three games for their Class AAA affiliate in Tulsa - his first minor league appearances since 1942 - before finally retiring for good at age 46.

Bragan, already unpopular among Milwaukee fans, tried at first to avoid getting into a battle of incendiary quotes with Spahn, and the two didn't speak in person until January 25, during the 12th annual Milwaukee baseball writers dinner at the Schroeder Hotel (which by 2016 had become the Hilton Milwaukee Civic Center). This dinner had long been the highlight of the Braves' off-seasons. For this affair - which most people thought would be the last such dinner because of the Braves' imminent move - two of the honored guests this night were Charlie Grimm and Red Schoendienst. Joe Torre and Rico Carty, the Braves' MVP and Rookie of the Year respectively for 1964, were presented with those awards. Spahn, Bragan, Del Crandall, Johnny Logan, Jack Dittmer (the starting second baseman for the Braves in 1953 during their first season in Milwaukee), Eddie Mathews, Andy Pafko and John Quinn (the general manager of the Braves from their Boston days through the 1958 season) were there, along with various Milwaukee dignitaries, officials and baseball luminaries. Mathews, noting the overhaul of the team's roster in recent years, said, "It looks like I'm the last of the Mohicans, with the right haircut too."

Instead of the festive occasion it had been since its inception, the 1965 writers dinner turned out to be a three-hour collective vent that disavowed any notion that the Braves' 1965 season would be baseball as usual.

Toastmaster Lloyd Larson, the sports editor of the *Sentinel*, began the "festivities" by saying: "Three years ago, Warren Giles was late to our dinner because he was fogged in at the Cincinnati airport. The fog hasn't lifted yet." Milwaukee Mayor Henry Maier recalled the time, immediately after Bartholomay and his group had purchased the team, that he had given Bartholomay a trophy key to the city. "It turned out to be a skeleton key," Maier said, "and apparently it worked in Atlanta too." Jim Major of television station WTTI said, presumably in jest, that he owned a John McHale doll. "You wind it up," Major said, "and it says, 'Today, tomorrow, and as long as we are welcome.' They'll also have an Oliver Kuechele doll. You wind it up, and it believes the John McHale doll." (Kuechele, the longtime *Journal* sports editor, had angered much of his readership by writing that the Braves' contention that they weren't planning to leave was to be believed, and earlier in the month, he had written a column urging Milwaukee fans to support the Braves during their final Milwaukee season. He'd also been one of the many Milwaukee journalists who, in effect, had told Eugene Goldschmidt to keep his mouth shut, lest he further poison Milwaukee's relationship with the Braves and MLB. Some of the quotes attributed to Goldschmidt on the Braves situation in 1965 seem comical in retrospect, but they did reflect to a large degree the vigor and venom of many in Wisconsin who wanted the Braves punished in any way possible for their duplicity.)

Finally, the time came for Spahn to be honored with an engraved gold ashtray in the shape of a baseball glove, and a silver trophy. Bragan, trying to make light of the tension surrounding Spahn's departure from Milwaukee, said just before the presentation that he wanted to apologize to Spahn for previously having said that Spahn and Stengel "have in common not only age (Stengel, still the Mets manager, was 74) but wealth." At the dinner, Bragan, with his usual ham-handed sense of humor, composed a poem that read, in part, "Whatever I said in anger, whatever I said in spite, I'm sorry I said those words 'cause I thought of some worse ones last night." His quip was met by stony silence. Spahn didn't mention it in his subsequent acceptance speech; asked by a reporter whether he accepted the "apology," Spahn said tersely, "If I had any comment, I would have made it in my speech."

Spahn would return to Milwaukee in 1965, both as a Met and as a San Francisco Giant, but other than reunions and other commemorative events (such as the final game at County Stadium in 2000), this January 1965 trip to the dinner was essentially Spahn's face-to-face farewell to Milwaukee. Interestingly, he had never bought property in Milwaukee, even though it had been his baseball home from the day the franchise arrived there. Aaron had bought a home in Mequon, a rural suburb 15 miles north of Milwaukee, and Mathews had made Brookfield his home since 1953. Johnny Logan and Felix Mantilla were among the other players who had made Milwaukee their year-round home, especially in the early years when off-season jobs - a virtual necessity for all but the highest-paid players - were plentiful in Milwaukee.

After he retired, Logan even ran for Milwaukee County Sheriff twice, losing on each occasion. But Spahn had bought a ranch in Hartshorne, Okla., early in his career, and made Oklahoma his primary home for the rest of his life. (In 1965, his 16-year-old son Greg was a regular halfback on the Hartshorne High football team, and his father said in 1965 he was interested in playing football for the University of Wisconsin, though that never materialized. After his father died in 2003, Greg took over the operation of the family ranch.)

During the baseball season, the Spahn family lived in Wauwatosa, in a leased home on Martha Washington Drive that had been built in 1952 on a 5,401-square-foot lot. The two-story, 1,766-square-foot home, which still stood in 2016, has four bedrooms, two bathrooms and a basement, and in 2015 was valued at approximately $350,000. The first story was brick; the second had wood framing. It was, and still is, a comfortable residence in a comfortable neighborhood, but in the 21st century, it seemed like an unusually modest home for the pitcher who won more games than any lefthander who ever lived. But Spahn was a practical man, and while he enjoyed his notoriety in Milwaukee and the atmosphere of the clubhouse, he never was captive to his fame. People who were kids when Spahn was with the Braves tell of meeting the great man himself at the grocery store or on the streets surrounding County Stadium, or even when he'd pick them up as they were hitch-hiking to the ballpark. He'd talk baseball with them, gently admonish them about the dangers of hitch-hiking, and often give them autographed balls as he pulled up to Gate X, the players' entrance to County Stadium. When the kids would thank him, Spahn invariably said, "No, thank *you*."

With Spahn gone, only Hank Aaron and Eddie Mathews remained from the 1957 World Series championship team, and Aaron had made it clear he expected to be paid on a par with what Spahn had made during his final season in Milwaukee. (Spahn's 1964 salary was reported at the time to be $85,000, though it probably was closer to the $73,500 that the Mets agreed to pay him as a player-coach in 1965.) The Braves knew that 1965 would become a financial sinkhole because of the growing ennui and anger in Milwaukee (on January 26, they had sold only 36 season tickets compared to 4,470 the year before), the expenses they would incur while trying to establish a presence in Atlanta, and the imminent legal fight over the move. Even so, they knew they would have to pay Aaron more than the $61,000 he made in 1964.

His home-run production had slipped from 44 in 1963 to 24 in '64, and even superstars, in an era during which multiyear contracts were rare, could expect their teams to try to cut their salaries if their output diminished in any way. The reserve clause, binding players to their teams in perpetuity unless they were sold, traded or released, wouldn't be struck down for another decade, and players rarely had bargaining power based on knowledge of other players' salaries. Front offices almost never revealed terms of contracts when they were signed; they also admonished players not to tell reporters - or even each other - how much money they were making. Most players in 1965 still complied, fully mindful of the power the owners held over them.

Some players whose sense of responsibility to their team and their conscience even volunteered to take cuts if they didn't think they had done enough the previous year to justify their full salary. Mathews was one such player; in 1956, after hitting at least

40 homers and driving in at least 101 runs in each of his first three seasons in Milwaukee, he "slumped" to 37 homers and 95 RBI. Mathews in 1991 told *Stolen Season* author Rick Lamb that general manager John Quinn asked him: "What are we going to do with your contract after a year like that?" Replied Mathews: "I'll take a $5,000 cut (to $50,000)." Mathews was up to $67,500 by 1961, at age 31, but he never made that much money again. He took a $2,500 cut in 1965, from $57,500 to $55,000, after hitting only .233 with 23 homers and 74 RBI in 1964. Bragan occasionally platooned Mathews with the right-handed hitting Mike de la Hoz in 1964, and he played some first base as well. Plagued by shoulder and groin-muscle injuries, he missed 21 games in '64 and was not at full strength for numerous others, and had more strikeouts (100) than walks (85) for only the second time in his career.

In light of the Braves' financial situation - they had unloaded players making a total of $330,000 since the end of the 1963 season - rumors persisted throughout the winter that Mathews, who would turn 34 in October, would be traded, though none of those rumors turned out to be true while the Braves were still in Milwaukee. Bragan in January 1965 said the platooning system would end, that the Braves had no intention of trading Mathews, and that he would play against any and all pitching. "Eddie played the best third base of his career during the last two months of last season," Bragan said. "His shoulder is as good as new now. He's our third baseman. Period." Indeed, Mathews wasn't traded until 1967 (to the Astros), and thus has the distinction of being the only player ever to play for the Braves in three different cities.

Bragan's reassuring words notwithstanding, Aaron clearly had supplanted Mathews as the face of the franchise, especially with Spahn gone. Aaron was 2 1/2 years younger than Mathews and was at the apex of his game. Even with his 1964 power reduction, he had batted .328, third-best in the NL behind Roberto Clemente (.339) and teammate Rico Carty (.330). He also had played with calcium deposits in his ankle, and missed 17 games because of other injuries. The Braves by 1965 had abandoned their brief defense-pitching-speed focus. In 1964, they had hit 159 home runs, second in the NL to the Giants' 165, and their .272 team batting average was best in the league. To pose any kind of pennant threat in 1965, they needed power, particularly from Mathews and Aaron.

In an interview with the *Sentinel's* Lou Chapman in January during contract negotiations, Aaron vowed improvement, especially in the power categories.

"I'm going to be strictly an offensive hitter," he said. "Last season I was worried too much about striking out (his K total of 46 in 1964 was his lowest since his rookie season, 1954). As a result, I was strictly a defensive batter. This year, I have made up my mind to go up there swinging from the time I leave the bench instead of taking and waiting.

"I'd like to come back and win that home-run title (as he had done in 1957 and 1963). Normally, I hit at least 35-40 a year, and if I get lucky, I could take it all. In any event, I should do a lot better than last year."

After protracted negotiations, Aaron got a raise, from $61,000 to $67,500 - still not close to what he wanted, and not close to the $75,000 figure that the *Sentinel*, quoting an anonymous friend of

Aaron's, reported on January 28. He didn't reach the $100,000 mark in salary until 1970 - after it became apparent he had a realistic chance to break Babe Ruth's career record of 714 - when he signed a contract with the Atlanta Braves worth $125,000. His highest baseball salary came from the Brewers in 1975 and 1976, the final two years of his career, during which he made $240,000 each year while serving mostly as a designated hitter and gate attraction.

After signing his 1965 contract, he predicted that the Braves would contend during their last year in Milwaukee and urged the fans to come out to support them. "We've got the best hitting team in baseball," he said. "It all depends on our young starting pitchers and the kind of help we get in the bullpen. Tony Cloninger (a 19-game winner in 1964) should easily be a 20-game winner. I also look for Wade Blasingame (16-10 in 1964) to win 20, and for fellows like Bob Sadowski and Hank Fischer to win 15 each. They all talk about how great (Hall of Fame catchers) Roy Campanella and Yogi Berra were. Joe Torre should be even greater someday - and soon."

Aaron also predicted that if the Braves started well, the uptick in their attendance in 1964 would continue. "All we have to do is get off to a fast start and you'll see a lot of interest among the fans. A good attendance will go a long way toward getting the city another franchise." He also pointed to the fact six different teams (the Braves, Pirates, Giants, Cardinals, Dodgers and Reds) had won pennants in the previous seven years, and that the Phillies had led most of the way in 1964 before their epochal collapse. "St. Louis, Cincinnati, the Dodgers, San Francisco or the Phillies could be favorites," he said, "and there isn't much difference between them and the Braves."

Bragan, in a separate interview, went so far as to predict the Braves would draw a million fans in 1965. "When the people fail to come out and see stars like Aaron, Mathews, Joe Torre and Denis Menke, they're the ones who are being hurt," he said. "It will be the last chance for them to see their old favorites." Bragan, apparently misreading the degree to which he was disliked in Milwaukee, even said he would come to Milwaukee in February from his home in Texas to help the Braves' promotional efforts, such as they were.)

Aaron, and the Braves' other black players, had another decision to make as the 1965 season loomed: Whether to become fulltime Atlanta-area citizens once the Braves were ensconced in the South. Aaron in 1964 had said that he had no intention of living in Atlanta full-time after the franchise moved, noting that he had been treated well while living in Mequon and saw no reason to leave. But after a visit to Atlanta in January, while contract negotiations were in progress, his refrain - no doubt scripted by management - was considerably different.

In October 1964, Aaron had said: "I'm going to keep my family in Milwaukee. You know how the South is. I have lived in the South (during his season with Jacksonville in the Sally League) and I don't want to live there again. We know everyone here and have our friends here. Our children are in integrated schools here. Atlanta is in Georgia, and that's a concern," he said.

By January 1965, though, Aaron had changed his tone and tune. "Atlanta isn't as segregated as most of the rest of the South. It's more integrated than Milwaukee," he said. "The only thing that's bad about (Atlanta) is it's in Georgia, and that throws a lot of people off. The (Atlanta) schools will be fully integrated next year. We looked in some mixed neighborhoods, but actually don't mind as long as the neighborhood is halfway presentable. We're not staying in any ghetto ... the Negroes there have made tremendous progress there in all phases. The Negroes there are way ahead of the Negroes here (in the Milwaukee area). It's no contest. Sure, they've got segregation problems, but they've got them in Milwaukee too. Up here, they call it *de facto* segregation. There, they just call it segregation ... I haven't said we will move, and I'm keeping an open mind. We've been treated good here and you can't live in a town for 11 years and expect to pull up roots just like that. But I have to think of my family, and I certainly don't want to stay away from them nine months of the year." (In February, Aaron confirmed that he would purchase a home in the Atlanta area before the 1966 season. He still lived in Atlanta in 2016.)

Massed Fieldpieces

• • •

FIELDPIECES WERE MASSED BUT BARRELS were largely muzzled in February 1965 as the combatants on the Milwaukee baseball front surveyed the various battlefields looming before them.

Meanwhile, Braves management was putting together what virtually everyone knew, by the start of February, would be the last Milwaukee Braves team. And despite the fact it would be trying to operate under circumstances not seen before in 20th-century major league baseball - as a team that not only planned to play a lame-duck season in a city that couldn't have cared less about it, but actually was plotting to leave during the season - the team looked fearsome even by 1965 National League standards. And those standards arguably were higher in the National League in 1965 than at any time in major league history.

A total of 352 players appeared in at least one NL game during the 1965 season, and 97 of them - 27.6 percent - were All-Stars at least twice during their careers. This was at a time when making an All-Star team was considerably more difficult than it was a half-century later. In 1965, 53 players (28 in the NL, 25 in the AL) were selected for the All-Star Game at Minnesota, while 79 players (38 from the AL, 41 from the NL) were chosen for the 2016 All-Star Game in San Diego.

Twenty-nine of those 97 players were future Hall of Famers. In order of the teams' 1965 finish, they were:

* Los Angeles: Sandy Koufax, Don Drysdale
* San Francisco: Orlando Cepeda, Willie Mays, Juan Marichal, Gaylord Perry, Willie McCovey
* Pittsburgh: Roberto Clemente, Willie Stargell, Bill Mazeroski
* Cincinnati: Frank Robinson, Tony Perez (and Pete Rose, if his lifetime ban ever is lifted)
* Milwaukee: Eddie Mathews, Joe Torre, Hank Aaron, Phil Niekro
* Philadelphia: Jim Bunning, Ferguson Jenkins
* St. Louis: Lou Brock, Bob Gibson, Steve Carlton
* Chicago: Ernie Banks, Billy Williams, Ron Santo
* Houston: Robin Roberts, Nellie Fox, Joe Morgan
* New York: Warren Spahn, Yogi Berra (in 1965 a Mets coach who was activated briefly and finished his playing career with two hits in nine at-bats over four games)

In addition to the 29 future Hall of Fame players, 13 of the NL's other 1965 players made at least five All-Star teams: Rose (17), the Cubs' Harvey Kuenn (8), former Brave Del Crandall of the Pirates (8), the Phillies' Richie Allen (7), the Cardinals' Ken Boyer (7), the Astros' Rusty Staub (6), the Cubs' Don Kessinger (6), the Cardinals' Bill White (5), the Dodgers' Maury Wills (5), the Cubs' Ed Bailey (5), the Phillies' Cookie Rojas (5), the Cardinals' Dick Groat (5) and the Reds' Leo Cardenas (5).

John Roseboro of the Dodgers, Glenn Beckert and Larry Jackson of the Cubs, Turk Farrell of the Astros and Mike Cuellar of the Astros were on four All-Star teams each. St. Louis' Curt Flood and Bob Purkey were three-time All-Stars, as were the Braves' Felipe Alou; the Phillies' Johnny Callison, Gus Triandos, Ryne Duren and Frank Thomas; the Astros' Jim Wynn and Jim Gentile; the Cardinals' Curt Simmons; the Pirates' Bob Friend, Roy Face, Bob Veale and Wilbur Wood; the Giants' Tom Haller; the Reds' Johnny Edwards and Lee May; and the Dodgers' Claude Osteen and Johnny Podres. (Thomas played for Philadelphia and Houston before joining the Braves for the final month of the 1965 season.)

Two-time All-Stars who played in the NL in 1965 included Milwaukee's Frank Bolling, Clay Carroll, Denis Menke and Billy O'Dell; Philadelphia's Chris Short, Art Mahaffey, Ray Culp and Lew Burdette; San Francisco's Matty Alou; Cincinnati's Vada Pinson, Joe Nuxhall and Tommy Helms; New York's Ron Hunt, Roy McMillan, Frank Lary, Tug McGraw and Bud Harrelson; Los Angeles' Wally Moon, Bill Singer, Ron Fairly, Willie Davis and Jim Gilliam; St. Louis' Julian Javier, Bob Skinner and Tim McCarver; Chicago's George Altman and Ken Holtzman; Pittsburgh's Gene Alley and Hal Smith; and Houston's Larry Dierker. Another was the Dodgers' Tommy Davis, who had won NL batting championships in 1962 and 1963 and seemed destined for a position in the baseball Pantheon before breaking and dislocating his ankle on May 1, 1965 - an injury from which he never fully recovered, even though he continued playing until 1976.

The Cardinals, Cubs, Astros and Mets, the four bottom feeders in the NL in 1965, had more Hall of Famers (11) that year than the entire American League, which in '65 included only nine future Cooperstown enshrinees: Brooks Robinson, Luis Aparicio, Carl Yazstremski, Hoyt Wilhelm, Al Kaline, Satchel Paige, Harmon Killebrew, Mickey Mantle and Whitey Ford. (Paige pitched in one game for the Kansas City A's in 1965, and was at least 59 years old at the time.) This was a period during which the NL won 25 of 29 All-Star Games from 1960-85, and clearly was the superior top-to-bottom league by any yardstick, the Yankees' domination of the AL during and immediately after the Casey Stengel era notwithstanding.

That was largely attributable to the two leagues' comparative eagerness to mine the rich vein of emerging black and Latin American talent. The Yankees, who won 15 of 18 American League pennants from 1947-64, did not have any black players until Elston Howard joined them in 1955 - eight years after Jackie Robinson and Larry Doby became the first blacks to play major league baseball in the 20th century, six years after the Giants (Monte Irvin, Hank Thompson) integrated, and five years after the Boston Braves did likewise with Sam Jethroe. The Tigers didn't employ a black player until Ozzie Virgil (who was also the first native of the Dominican Republic to play in the majors) in 1956. Even as late as 1968, when the Tigers won the World Series and by which time Detroit had become a predominantly black city, only five of the 33 players on the team that year - Gates Brown, John Wyatt, Lenny Green, Willie Horton and Earl Wilson - were black, and Wyatt and Green played in only 22 and six games respectively. The Red Sox were the last team to integrate, adding Pumpsie Green in 1959.

The 1964 season had ended with the top five National League teams within five games of each other, and given the quality and quantity of the talent and the fact six teams had won pennants since 1958, another demolition derby seemed likely if not inevitable. The Dodgers, who had toppled out of the 1964 race after Koufax was sidelined in August by the onset of the pitching-arm circulatory problem that would end his career two years later, made the boldest off-season move. They sent their only legitimate power threat, Frank Howard, to the Washington Senators in a trade that landed them lefthander Claude Osteen.

The move constituted a final acknowledgement that these were no longer the Dodgers who'd transformed baseball into jai alai during their years at claustrophobic Ebbets Field, and then in the L.A. Coliseum with its 42-foot left-field screen looming only 251 feet from home plate where fair territory met foul. Playing now in the spacious confines and the marine-layer-heavy air of Dodger Stadium, they would pin their pennant hopes and their developmental template almost exclusively on pitching, speed and defense. One important element in their ability to do that was the fact they had the only all-switch-hitting infield in major league history - Wes Parker at first, Jim Lefebvre at second, Wills at short and Gilliam at third. This enabled the Dodgers to keep their best defensive infield on the field at virtually all times, even when opposing teams switched from a right-handed pitcher to a left-hander, or vice versa. Roseboro behind the plate and Willie Davis in center field were defensive pillars as well. The Dodgers had finished sixth in 1964, but even after trading Howard, they believed their pitching, defense and speed would enable them to contend in 1965. Nevada's Stateline sports book, which had operated since 1949 when Nevada became the first state to legalize sports gambling, agreed in February that the Dodgers' chances were as good as anyone else's. The oddsmakers there had the

Dodgers, Phillies, Cardinals and Giants as 4-1 pennant bets, followed by the Reds (5-1), Braves (10-1), Pirates (12-1), Cubs (50-1), Astros (100-1) and Mets (100-1).

In their objectives and process, the Dodgers were the antithesis of the Braves, whose total of 159 home runs in 1964 was second only to the Giants' 165. But Milwaukee in 1965 had pitching question marks that had rarely existed during the 1950s and early 1960s when Warren Spahn, Lew Burdette and Bob Buhl were fixtures in the starting rotation. Tony Cloninger had gone 19-14 with a 3.56 ERA in '64, but the remainder of the staff paled in comparison to that of the Dodgers. And the pitching was made to look worse than it was because the defense was porous. The most frequently used first baseman in 1964 had been Gene Oliver, a catcher by trade who'd been moved to first upon the emergence of Joe Torre behind the plate. Frank Bolling had been a Gold Glove second baseman for Detroit in 1958 and was an All-Star for the Braves in 1961 and 1962, but at age 33, his range was narrowing and he was coming off a .199 season in '64. Mathews, too, was limited defensively by 1965, so much so that Bragan had played him at first base occasionally in 1964 and in the outfield for 42 games in 1963. Rico Carty, who had made his debut with the Braves late in 1963, was such a prolific hitter (.330, 22 homers and 88 RBI in only 455 at-bats in '64) that his presence in the lineup seemed a necessity, but he hadn't shown more than minimal aptitude either at first base or in the infield. Lee Maye likewise looked like a budding star at bat, but in 1964 he had committed 11 errors, more than any other center fielder in the league. And room likely would have to be made, either in the outfield or at first base, for Felipe Alou, who had been acquired from the Giants before the 1964 season in a trade that sent pitcher Bob Shaw and catcher Del Crandall to San Francisco.

Alou had been a disappointment in 1964; limited by injury to 121 games, he had batted only .253 with nine home runs and 51 RBI, but he had been a .319-27-87 performer in his final season with the Giants in addition to being part of the only all-brother outfield in major league history, with Matty and Jesus.

The Braves on February 1 made a lightly-trumpeted but highly-beneficial move, sending catcher Ed Bailey back to the Giants, from whom they'd acquired him before the 1964 season, for lefty Billy O'Dell.

Bailey was a five-time All-Star, but at age 34 he clearly was on the downside, and the emergence of Torre and the acquisition of Oliver rendered him expendable. Nor did the Giants see much future use in O'Dell, 32, who had gone directly to the major leagues with the Orioles after they signed him out of Clemson University in 1954, and would end his career in 1967 without ever having participated in a minor league game. His 19 wins had been central to the Giants' National League pennant in 1962, but he was removed from the starting rotation in 1964 during an 8-7, 5.40 season. He had been a starter virtually his whole career, and Bragan and McHale hadn't ruled him out of the starting-rotation mix, but they also saw him as a potential bullpen talisman. Bob Tiefenauer, a knuckleballer, had led the Braves with 13 saves in 1964, and Bragan in 1965, like Fred Haney during the World Series title season of 1957, thought the Braves needed a "fireman" with conventional stuff in the back of the bullpen. In 1957, that turned out to be Don McMahon, and Bragan had similar hopes for O'Dell.

O'Dell, for his part, welcomed the move for many reasons. He wanted out of San Francisco partly because of his exile to

the bullpen, and partly because he felt some of his Giants teammates had quit on manager Alvin Dark in 1964, particularly after his ill-considered remarks regarding black and Latino players
and their ability to handle pressure. "There were guys who broke
their backs for Dark, but there were other guys who didn't hus-
tle," O'Dell said. "They gave him only 60 percent. It was pitiful.
The Giants may have a new manager (Herman Franks), but the
players are the same ... I would name names, but that would serve
no purpose. Besides, those guys know who they are." Rebuttal
from the Giants wasn't long in coming. Franks, who had been a
Giants coach in 1964, said: "I know of nobody who wasn't putting
out. But why dignify his remarks by answering them?" Willie
Mays' response: "If he meant me, I was playing at times when
I was hurting, and I played the best I could all the time. If he
meant (Orlando) Cepeda, he had an injured knee (later surgically
repaired). If he meant (Juan) Marichal, he had a bad back. If he
meant (pitcher Jack) Sanford, he had an arm that needed surgery."

O'Dell also liked the idea of getting the run support the
Braves surely would provide, and of pitching anywhere other
than Candlestick Park, which most pitchers regarded as the
maximum-security prison that its critics said it architecturally
resembled. A gust of wind had blown Giants reliever Stu Miller
off the mound during the 1961 All-Star Game there, and pitchers
complained that the gales that howled through Candlestick made
it difficult to get loose, especially during night games. Moreover,
O'Dell lived in South Carolina, and said he looked forward to
playing only a short drive away from home in Atlanta in 1966.

Though O'Dell did not try to hide the fact he was looking
forward to the Atlanta move, most of the 37 men who constituted

the final version of the Milwaukee Braves avoided speaking ill of Milwaukee and its soon-to-be-abandoned fans, or sidestepped the subject of the move altogether. Mathews, who had the most leverage as well as the most seniority on the team, went about as far as any of the players would go all season on that touchy subject when he said in February: "Milwaukee fans have a right to feel resentful. They are not upset at the players, but rather at the owners and management. Atlanta will have a lot of living up to do to match Milwaukee as a baseball city."

Pitcher Denny Lemaster, embroiled in a contract dispute after winning 17 games but posting a 4.15 ERA in 1964, worried about how difficult the fans could make matters on the players. "There's a lot of resentment in Milwaukee against the players themselves," he said from his California home. "You tell them it's not you who wants to move, but they can't believe this." And it would not be a stretch to suggest that more than a few other Braves would have embraced the idea of making the move before the 1965 season if it had been their decision to make. Seventeen of the 37 players on the 1965 Milwaukee Braves, along with Bragan and coaches Dixie Walker and Whitlow Wyatt, had been born in former Confederate states, though five of those players, including Mathews, had been raised outside the South. Two others who weren't from the South had wives who were. Privately, at least some of the Braves - maybe even most of them - also must have been looking forward to the opportunity to play closer to home, in a warmer climate and in a brand-new ballpark with a brand-new audience in 1966.

Another Braves player, speaking on the condition of anonymity, was quoted in the *Atlanta Constitution* as saying: "If (the

Milwaukee business community) had been so free with their money when the Braves were trying to establish themselves there, all this mess might not have happened. We were never offered a chance to establish ourselves in off-season jobs there. They never did anything to make us feel at home. (All we got was) a dairy product and a quart of milk a day, and one time we got free cookies and our laundry done." This was quickly and angrily refuted by the Milwaukee papers, in which it was pointed out that Braves players had received free loaner cars from the Wally Rank dealership with the option to buy them at cost, and that local restaurants (especially those in the George Webb chain) routinely picked up meal checks for Braves players, especially in the early years. Del Crandall had at one point been vice president of a cleaning firm. Mathews had helped start a construction business in MIlwaukee. Ernie Johnson had sold insurance. Frank Torre had a public-relations job. Aaron and Billy Bruton had been set up in the real estate business. Wes Covington had opened a bar. Milwaukee native and former Boys Tech (now Bradley Tech) student Bob Uecker had worked for a savings-and-loan company. (Uecker and Don Pavletich, a Reds catcher who was from West Allis, planned to attend the Milwaukee police academy after the 1965 season.) The Braves players also had numerous endorsement offers, even during the 1965 season. "Ah, yes," sarcastically wrote Oliver Kuechle. "T'was ever this: Ingratitude."

Four days after the Braves obtained O'Dell, Bragan arrived in Milwaukee after having driven from his home in Fort Worth, Texas. Bragan had promised he would make a trip north to try to promote ticket sales for the final Milwaukee season. It's unknown why he thought he would be more help than hindrance in that regard, especially given his "crooked creek" disparagement of Milwaukee as a major league city and the fact many fans still recalled the 1957 tantrum at County Stadium that had cost him his job as Pirates manager. But he claimed to have personally sold 400 to 600 season tickets on a similar offseason trip in 1964, and didn't let negativism creep into his initial remarks to the Milwaukee media. "I'll be on the phone every morning promptly at 9 o'clock each morning (until the start of spring training in early March)," he promised.

He also promised to be less of a grab-bag manager in 1965, at least in terms of the lineup he planned to put on the field. He said that barring injuries, the players who started on Opening Day in Cincinnati on April 12 would be in the lineup almost every day as long as their performances merited it.

"It'll be a club like the Yankees - solid in every position," he said. "There's no question as to our offense; it's the best in the league. But our defense needs shoring up."

According to Bragan, the Braves' projected defensive deployment in 1965 was Torre catching, Alou at first, Bolling at second, Mathews at third, Denis Menke at short, Carty in left, Lee Maye in center and Aaron in right. Carty and Alou, Bragan said, could wind up exchanging positions, and he also said he would give 20-year-old middle infielder Sandy Alomar a chance to move into a three-man weave with Bolling and Menke. The Braves had signed Alomar as a 16-year-old out of Puerto Rico in 1960, and though his offensive numbers at Triple-A Denver in 1964 had been pedestrian - .263 with little power and 110 strikeouts in 662 plate appearances - and even though he had made 42 errors in Denver and 61 while with Austin of the Texas League in 1963,

Bragan thought him a potential Gold Glover defensively. Alomar never won a Gold Glove, but he played 17 major league seasons with six teams. He also sired Roberto Alomar, who became a Hall of Famer, and Sandy Alomar Jr., who played 20 major league seasons (1988-2007) and was a six-time All-Star catcher.

It was a formidable-looking lineup, and many were picking the Braves to win their first pennant since 1958, despite the turmoil surrounding the franchise shift and the questions about Milwaukee's defense and pitching. Mets manager Casey Stengel said that if longtime Dodger starting pitcher Johnny Podres - who'd beaten Stengel and the Yankees in Game 7 of the 1955 World Series to give the Brooklyn Dodgers their only World Series title - could rebound after an off-year, "I gotta take the Dodgers to win the flag. (Podres didn't, but the Dodgers did.) But Milwaukee has the best hitting team in the league. If they get the pitching, they're the best team." Houston manager Lum Harris concurred. "I like the Braves because of their great power and the fact their pitching improved greatly last season. O'Dell can help them either starting or relieving." Harris also said he expected a seven-team race that didn't include his Astros, the Cubs or the Mets. So did Leo Durocher, out of baseball again in 1965 after four years as a coach with the Dodgers. "I'll have to say Eddie Mathews holds the key," Durocher said. "If he makes a comeback, look out. And he's certainly capable of having that good year."

Mathews' ability to coax at least one more Hall of Fame-type season out of himself certainly was central to the Braves' 1965 hopes, and his value was unquestioned even though he was 33 and was coming off his least productive year as a major leaguer.

it was reported that the Mets had offered the Braves $500,000 for him late in 1964, and McHale said the Braves had rejected at least two similar offers in the previous two years. In retrospect, especially considering they were spread thin financially by their impending move and court battles by 1965, perhaps selling Mathews in 1963 or 1964 might have been their most prudent course of action. But at the time, there were persuasive reasons why they couldn't.

Hank Aaron by 1965 had long since supplanted Mathews as the Braves' most numerically productive player. Aaron averaged .317 with 177 homers and 599 RBI during the five seasons from 1960-64, while Mathews batted .269-146-463. But the Braves' farm system had not produced a suitable replacement for Mathews. Moreover, for many of the Braves' remaining Milwaukee fans, seeing even a diminished Mathews still evoked memories of the heady days when the franchise first came to Milwaukee - particularly the first year, 1953, when Aaron was still in Double-A. Mathews had perhaps the best offensive season by a 21-year-old in the history of the game, before or since, banging away at a .302-47-135 clip to finish second to the Dodgers' Roy Campanella in the MVP balloting. (The home run and RBI totals remained the best of his career when he retired in 1968.) And even after injuries and age began taking their toll later in Mathews' career, he never lost the swing that Ty Cobb had once called one of the four most perfect he had ever seen.

Even in 1965 when the Milwaukee Braves were about to disappear from the baseball scene, people would still pay to see Eddie Mathews or to have their sons see Eddie Mathews before he and the Braves left for good - and the Braves still had to try to eke out some level of financial solvency before they made good their escape to Atlanta. Mathews was a partner, with Aaron, in what would become the most productive home-run-hitting combination in the history of baseball, and he had been a constant during the years after the 1950s championship teams faded into mediocrity. And much like motorcycle-riding Robin Yount with the Brewers a generation later, Mathews personified the work ethic of an industrial city. He didn't play with the grace and seeming effortlessness that characterized Aaron, and he didn't have the steel-cable wrists that Aaron did. But he played hurt and he played to the hilt. He still careened around third to get to balls that seemed out of his reach, he still caromed into second to break up double plays, and he still understood the strike zone as well as any slugger of his time. In 1963, he led the NL in walks drawn for the fourth and final time, and he ended his career with almost as many walks (1,444) as strikeouts (1,487). He also was determined to treat younger players in a helpful and civilized manner, unlike the "greeting" he'd received from the Boston Braves as a 17-year-old in 1949, and while his leadership wasn't of the back-slapping, rah-rah variety, the younger players deferred to him partly out of seniority but mostly out of admiration.

Defensively, Mathews even at the apex of his career had some liabilities. *Sport* magazine's "secret ratings of NL players" in late 1957 described him as the best third baseman in the NL, but with disclaimers: "One of the authentic sluggers of our day … in addition to his power, he has a good arm and is faster on the bases than he is generally given credit for being. This speed makes him tough to double up on ground balls. He is only fair defensively; his hands are not too sure and he is often uncertain going after a grounder. Despite his running speed, he doesn't cover much ground at third." But that didn't matter much to his Milwaukee idolators, many of whom were women. In 1957, *Sport* published a story purportedly written by Gussie Moran, who had been one of the best women's tennis players in the world and in 1957 was working as a TV sportscaster. Moran was asked to rank "baseball's 10 handsomest men," and Mathews was on the list. Wrote Moran: "The pretty boy of the whole group is apple-cheeked Eddie Mathews. For all of his 6-foot-1, 192-pound body, he has the look of a spoiled cherub. To me, Eddie Mathews is the Tyrone Power of baseball. Brown eyes, brown hair, big white teeth, petulant lips, small ears, nice nose and good neck - he'd look handsome in one of those magazine shirt collar ads. He's not all beauty, either - he's also brute. For before he was 25 (he's now 26), he hit more home runs than any other man in baseball did up to that age, including the one and only Babe Ruth. At one time, Mathews and not Mickey Mantle was thought to be the likely slugger to break the Babe's record mark of 60 homers for one season. He hasn't done it yet, but with those beautiful muscles, he can make a girl believe anything."

Author David Lamb had another perspective on Mathews, having first met him in the Braves clubhouse in 1954, when Lamb was only 15 years old. Lamb, who died in 2016, originally was from Boston and mourned the loss of his beloved Braves to Milwaukee, but he continued as a fan of the Milwaukee Braves. Lamb, who had writing aspirations from an early age, wrote to *Journal* sports editor Russ Lynch asking about the possibility of writing a outside-looking-in, kids-eye-view column on the Braves. In 1954, the Milwaukee papers covered the Braves beyond the point of saturation, and to Lamb's surprise, Lynch authorized the column. Later that season, a Milwaukee family offered to bring Lamb to Milwaukee for a week, at the family's expense, and through Lynch, Lamb got game credentials during a late-season homestand and interviewed and wrote about many of the players.

Lamb did indeed become a writer - an internationally-known war correspondent for the *Los Angeles Times*. In 1991, sickened by what he had seen "in places that had no heroes," he took a leave of absence from his job and set about writing a book, *Stolen Season*, that stood a quarter-century later as baseball's version of *Blue Highways*. Lamb retraced some of his old baseball steps and discovered new pathways while traveling around the country in a motor home. He went to Durham, N.C., to meet Mathews, who was a roving minor league batting instructor for the Braves at the time. Mathews had a difficult time after Milwaukee and after his playing career, and by 1991 had faded into relative obscurity - unlike Aaron, especially after Babe Ruth's career home-run record beckoned. But Lamb, in *Stolen Season*, wrote admiringly of Mathews nonetheless: "To me, (cowboy-Western movie actor) Randolph Scott would always ride off alone into the sunset, having brought justice to another frontier town. Eddie Mathews was also indestructible (as a player). He was young and tough and talented, my chosen symbol of the Braves' phoenix-like rise from unworthiness, and I rated his perfection as falling somewhere between that of God and of Randolph Scott." At the end of their talk, Mathews told Lamb: "I'll tell you the truth ... if I (died) tomorrow, I wouldn't have many regrets. I wished my father had lived to see what I did with the Braves. That's about it. I've had a hell of a lot of fun. People say, 'Slow down. Aren't you afraid of dying?' I tell them, 'I just want a week to apologize to everyone before I go.'"

Taking all of those value-to-the-franchise factors, both tangible and intrinsic, into consideration, few who followed the Braves in 1965 thought a trade of Mathews was either likely or imminent. (He wasn't moved until after the 1966 season, when the Atlanta Braves dealt him to Houston.) The Milwaukee Braves would largely be built around him in 1965, just as they had been from the day that they relocated from Boston.

At the same time, the *Journal's* Bob Wolf pointed out that the fulcrum of the season might be perhaps the franchise's most enigmatic player. Originally signed out of Atlanta's Henry McNeil Turner High in 1958, Mack Jones reached the majors with the Braves in 1961 at the age of 22. In his debut, on July 22, he got four hits off the Cardinals' Bob Gibson, and it looked as if the Braves had found a Billy Bruton with power. (In fact, Bruton, the Braves' regular center fielder since their arrival in Milwaukee, was traded after the 1960 season largely because of Jones' potential.) Jones had exceptional raw tools - speed, power, acceleration, lateral movement and a quick bat that enabled him to hit for both speed and power. But for the next 3 1/2 seasons, the debut against Gibson looked like a mirage. Jones started the 1962 and 1963 seasons with the Braves, but was unproductive and was sent back to the minors both times. In 1964, with Bragan's impatience with Jones reaching the tipping point, the Braves conditionally traded him to the Tigers, who could keep him if they wished after the 1964 season or send him back to the Braves.

At the Tigers' Triple-A affiliate in Syracuse, Jones regained his confidence and had a breakout year, batting .317 with 39 homers and 102 RBI. (In seven minor league seasons, starting with Salinas of the Class C California League in 1958, Jones was a .306 hitter with 102 homers and 368 RBI.) He played equally well in the Dominican Republic winter league as well, but Detroit had no room for Jones in its 1965 outfield, and sent him back to the Braves. Wolf wrote that Jones "(has been) perhaps the most consistent failure in major league baseball. Four times he has tried to win a job with the Braves, and four times he had drifted back to the minors. Now he is preparing for his fifth try." Bragan said in February 1965 that Jones "is very much in the running for the center field job (in competition with Lee Maye). He has always been a bridesmaid and this might be the year for him ... Mack has all the tools. He has cut down on his strikeouts and the word we have is that he is swinging the way we always felt he could. The big thing, of course, is whether he is over the mental bloc."

But other than the O'Dell trade, Bragan's tub-thumping, the re-acquisition of Jones and some peripheral contract-signing news, the Braves' on-field outlook for 1965 was virtually ignored by the Milwaukee media in February 1965. (The signing of pitcher Tony Cloninger, a 19-game winner in 1964, rated one paragraph in the *Journal* on February 23.) In earlier years, "hot stove" baseball discussion dominated the Milwaukee papers even during the winter - except, after 1959, when the Packers were playing. But by 1965, if the papers mentioned anything about "Reds" in a headline, they usually were referring to Communists, not the Cincinnati baseball team. And the multi-front legal fight over the Braves was providing ample kindling for the "hot stove," both in Milwaukee and around the nation.

As the drama deepened and the stances of the opposing sides hardened, the national media began to chime in on the confrontation. The Milwaukee situation, many reporters and columnists wrote and said, wasn't only about whether Milwaukee was a major league city or even whether the Braves' diminished attendance warranted moving a franchise that had led the major leagues in attendance during each of its first six years at County Stadium. Some saw it in a larger, more ominous context of dishonesty and mismanagement, if not outright collusion, by major league baseball's leadership, and thus saw merit in the antitrust lawsuit that Milwaukee County was about to pursue against the Braves. One who took that view was the *Washington Post's* Shirley Povich, whose column was one of the most widely-syndicated in the country at the time. Povich wrote:

"Just before deserting the city which they ransacked of its major league baseball franchise, the owners of the A-bound Braves have asked the good burghers of Milwaukee for a season-long kiss. This came about when Braves owners, faced with immense losses as a lame-duck team and hated by the citizenry for their announced defection, came up with a new ploy: Support us next season and we will cut your team in on some of the profits. (Milwaukee's leaders) rose to a lure that would stifle all the walleyed pike in all of Wisconsin's lakes ... tacit here was the threat that if the fans did not support the team, it would be taken as a lack of baseball interest in Milwaukee and a setback to any attempt to bring a new club in. The Braves owners thus were applying a Chinese knot to Milwaukee. The more the city's fans determined to punish the defecting owners by staying away, the tighter would become the tether to baseball in the future. It appears that Milwaukee has bought itself a strange package which calls for support of the owners who kicked the city in the pants while responding to the goo-goo eyes of the hussy Atlanta,

which has been flouncing her skirts at the Braves for two years. The Braves' operational losses, which threatened to become staggering, could now be modest, by the simple expedient of hauling their victims into their own leaky boat."

The "leaky boat" in question was the Braves' announcement on February 9 that they would "donate" up to $675,000 (by the Braves' calculations) to help bring a replacement team to Milwaukee as soon as 1966. The Braves' formula called for them to contribute to an escrow account at the rate of 5 cents per ticket sold in 1965 up to 766,921 - a figure representing the Braves' lowest-ebb Milwaukee attendance, in 1962. Once that plateau was reached, the ante would increase to 25 cents per ticket, and if the Braves crashed the 1 million barrier, they would contribute $1 for every additional ticket sold. "It is an offer we make freely and in the friendliest spirit for the good of Milwaukee and the Braves," general manager John McHale said. "We invite Milwaukee to become our partners in our final season here." Meanwhile, Bragan said the team - which had sold only 36 season tickets at the end of January - was up to 500 such commitments. "Everyone knows now that he'll have company (at the ballpark)," Bragan said. "Before, people looked at that 36 figure and sort of shied away. A lot of people are playing a waiting game, but even that's encouraging." (Exactly 10 years before, thousands of fans had camped overnight in sub-freezing temperatures at County Stadium while waiting in line for Braves tickets to go on sale.)

Another encouraging note, from Milwaukee's standpoint, was the formation by NL president Warren Giles of a committee to explore the possibilities of returning baseball to Milwaukee in 1966. Three NL general managers - John Holland of the Cubs,

Joe Brown of the Pirates and John Quinn (the former Braves GM) of the Phillies - were selected to serve on the committee, along with four members of Teams Inc, the group of local civic leaders and businessmen that had been formed in November 1964 to pursue the same course of action. Teams Inc was to be represented by Edmund Fitzgerald, Donald Slichter of Northwestern Mutual Life Insurance Co., Irwin Maier of the Journal Company, and County Stadium manager William Anderson. Fitzgerald said the Braves' "donation" plan was similar to one that Teams Inc members had discussed, "but this particular plan was their own. The specific figures, attendance levels and amount are all theirs." Nevertheless, Fitzgerald said, the Braves "can be useful in helping Milwaukee achieve its objectives in securing another team after 1965." Bartholomay, who had claimed for more than a year - with some justification - that he didn't know which individuals and groups truly represented Milwaukee interests in discussions with the Braves, said the members of the new committee were the "real leaders of the Milwaukee community rather than segments outside of it." He added that the club was not for sale at any price; Teams Inc's first move after its formation had been to offer to buy the Braves from Bartholomay.

Teams Inc and the Braves came to a quick agreement on the mutual-assistance pact, and on February 15, the *Journal* and *Sentinel* both ran full-page ads urging Milwaukee fans to support the Braves during their final year at County Stadium. "We all have a stake in keeping Milwaukee a major league city," read the ad. "It is vitally important that the opening (home) game April 15 against the Cubs be a rousing, enthusiastic sell-out ... Be a partner with your neighbors and friends in making the 1965 season something we will all remember with pride."

Three days later, Teams Inc released a promotional booklet, put together by advertising mogul and Teams Inc member Ben Barkin. But having made what seemed like a goodwill gesture, the Braves again incurred public wrath by cancelling, because of what Braves management called "obvious and unusual circumstances," the Wisconsin Silver Slugger program that the *Sentinel* had sponsored. The program had been similar to the "academy" that the Brewers were promoting half a century later. It featured Braves players and coaches providing hands-on instruction, followed by scrimmages broken down by age and skill groups.

The newspapers' house ads notwithstanding, the *Journal* and *Sentinel* editorial staffs were not given specific orders by management to let up on their criticism of the Braves. While some writers on both staffs advocated cooperation with the Braves, others contended that the Braves should be treated as the brigands many of their former fans now considered them to be. *Sentinel* sports editor Lloyd Larson made an interesting suggestion to the effect that if cities could use the power of eminent domain to obtain land for professional sports teams, could the principle not be reversed in terms of forcing teams to say in government-owned and operated facilities like County Stadium? Wrote Larson: "Why not place the quasi-public utility stamp on a baseball club that occupies facilities built with public funds? Then it would be subject to regulation that does not apply to a club owning its own plant ... It might be possible to go a step further and make it a part of the law that a franchise can't be moved from a city where public facilities are used. The club naturally would be privately owned, as now, but it could only be sold to new owners, not shifted to another city, when business judgment dictates ... Isn't it logical, then, that any club that must rely on public subsidy also must accept the 'here to stay' concept when it comes to franchises?"

The legal wheels also were turning. On February 14, attorney John MacIver of the law firm of Michael, Best & Friedrich released a legal opinion sought by both Teams Inc and the Braves regarding the likely outcome of an antitrust suit by Milwaukee County against the Braves and MLB. It read, in part, "We do not believe that the county would prevail in such an antitrust suit action," and that even if it did, no court would order the Braves back to Milwaukee "as part of a remedial order." (This was proved correct after the Braves left Milwaukee, but only by a 4-3 vote in the Wisconsin Supreme Court, after a lower court had ruled in the county's favor.) Ford Frick applauded the law-firm finding, saying: "I submit that the displeasure of a community at the prospect of losing a club is not a sound reason for subjecting every aspect of baseball to the antitrust laws."

McHale, who had returned to Milwaukee from Atlanta for the first time since September, said: "Baseball has never been scared of (losing) any antitrust exemption. Neither are we. Besides, any suit that may be started now is after the fact. It's a fact (that the Braves had received NL permission to move), isn't it?" Nevertheless, the U.S. Senate had begun holding subcommittee meetings on whether baseball should be allowed to keep its antitrust exemption, and Wisconsin Sen. William Proxmire, who had sponsored an amendment to eliminate the exemption, called the Braves' actions "irresponsible."

Rep. Clement Zablocki, who represented Milwaukee's 4th Congressional District from 1949 until his death in 1983, had introduced a similar bill in the House of Representatives. He said his bill had several elements beyond the Braves' situation: He thought CBS' purchase of the Yankees earlier in the year represented a violation of the Sherman Antitrust Act because CBS intended to use the public airwaves to exclusively promote a private company, and he believed that MLB already had violated antitrust law by blocking two third-major-league efforts, by the Pacific Coast League in the early 1950s and then the Continental League spearheaded by Branch Rickey after the Giants and Dodgers moved to California in 1958. (The threat of the Continental League had been a major factor in MLB's decision to expand from 16 to 20 teams in 1961-62.) "Baseball is sick and badly in need of some bitter medicine," Zablocki said. "It's not the new stadium or prospective attendance which have lured the Braves to Atlanta (and the Yankees and CBS to each other). It is the lure of extremely lucrative contracts for radio and television broadcasts (that prompted the Braves' decision to leave Milwaukee, and CBS' decision to buy the Yankees). Organized Baseball cannot have the best of both worlds. Either it is primarily a sporting activity or it is strictly a profit-making adjunct of the entertainment industry, and (in the latter case) therefore should be subject to antitrust laws."

Eugene Grobschmidt, president of the county Board of Supervisors, was working with both Proxmire and Zablocki to form a joint front to push the antitrust-exemption legislation, and the county board already had voted for a resolution to that effect. Arthur Montgomery, chairman of the Atlanta stadium authority, accused Grobschmidt of "employing a strategy to break the Braves financially." Retorted Grobschmidt: "Montgomery is putting his foot where his mouth ought to be. We're doing the same thing that Teams Inc is doing - trying to keep major league baseball in Milwaukee."

Montgomery may have been right about the existence of a movement to force the Braves into bankruptcy, and in any case, the Braves were feeling the heat. It turned out that McHale's visit to Milwaukee hadn't been intended to boost the joint ticket-selling effort with Teams Inc, nor had he come back to reminisce with the few friends he still had in Milwaukee. *United Press International* reported that McHale, with Bartholomay's approval, had offered Milwaukee County a buyout of $500,000 to allow the Braves out of the last year of their County Stadium lease and let them begin the 1965 season in Atlanta-Fulton County Stadium, on which ground had been broken on April 15, 1964 with a projected completion date of April 9, 1965.

The offer was tendered by Alan Bell of the Braves' New York public-relations firm to Ben Barkin and Edmund Fitzgerald of Teams Inc. According to McHale, the offer included not only the $200,000 rental that the Braves owed the county for the use of County Stadium during the last year of the lease, but also $300,000 for future rent even though, obviously, the Braves had no intention of continuing to play in Milwaukee. McHale thought this proposal eminently fair; Fitzgerald and Barkin did not. They told Bell that as citizens of Milwaukee, they found the offer unacceptable, and in any case couldn't speak for the Milwaukee County board. When the board did speak for itself, it rejected the offer out of hand - as it would do at least twice later in 1965.

On February 23, Anheuser-Busch and Coca-Cola signed a three-year contract to be co-sponsors of the Braves' radio and TV broadcasts in Atlanta, beginning with the start of the 1965 season. Under the agreement, reported to be worth $1 million per year over its duration, 55 of the Milwaukee Braves games would be available on radio in Atlanta and on the regional radio network the Braves had already set up. Another 18 games would be carried on Atlanta TV, and the Braves already had scheduled six in-season exhibition games (common in baseball at the time) in Atlanta-Fulton County Stadium. But at the same time, Schlitz had not renewed its $400,000 sponsorship of Milwaukee Braves broadcasts in Milwaukee, instead shifting that portion of its advertising budget to Houston, where the Astros' move to the Astrodome was certain to dramatically enhance the value of that market. This left the Braves, at least for the time being, with no radio or TV sponsorship for 1965 except the $150,000 it received for the rights to the games that were to be carried by radio or TV in Atlanta. This was by far the smallest total broadcast revenue of any team in MLB in 1965; the next-lowest totals were those of the Washington Senators and Kansas City Athletics, both of which collected $300,000.

The decisions by Anheuser-Busch and Coca-Cola to sponsor broadcasts and telecasts of the Braves in Atlanta caused a backlash in the Milwaukee area, at the time and for some years thereafter. Though no boycott of Anheuser-Busch and Coca-Cola products was ever formally organized in Wisconsin, many Braves fans stopped buying them, and some never resumed. Coca-Cola had held the soft-drink concession rights at County Stadium throughout the Milwaukee Braves' existence; in 1970, when the Seattle Pilots moved to Milwaukee, the Brewers sold the soft-drink rights in the stadium to Pepsi, which still retained them at Miller Park in 2016. Cardinals owner Gussie Busch also incurred the wrath of Milwaukee fans by voting in late 1964 in favor of the Braves' move, after saying repeatedly he opposed it. Anheuser-Busch's share of the Wisconsin beer market, never high because the Milwaukee-based breweries had virtually cornered their home market, plummeted in 1965 in response to Busch's about-face.

Despite such skirmishes, and despite the Braves' abandonment of the Silver Slugger program, Teams Inc and the Braves continued to work together to fill County Stadium for the season opener and, Milwaukeeans hoped, beyond. Bud Selig and Bragan appeared in a photo with a caption that described them as Milwaukee baseball's "advance task force." Bragan said more than 2,000 single-game tickets had been sold on the first day of the joint campaign, and that 1,848 season tickets had been sold since it began. Said Selig, who had been chosen by his fellow Teams Inc members to head the Braves ticket sale: "Only three months ago, people didn't think it was possible to sell 200 season tickets. Now the temper seems to have changed."

McHale also sounded a conciliatory tone. "We plan to do everything we can to have as many people in the ballpark as we possibly can," he said. "Of course, our staff is not as big as it used to be, with many of our men in Atlanta, and that restricts us somewhat ... we would like to work with Teams Inc ... (they) communicated with us that they wanted to be as much help as possible. If it helps in the long run to get another baseball team (in Milwaukee), we are certainly not averse to that. If there are any profits, we have no objection at all to (the profits) staying in Milwaukee."

Martin Beckman, 58, who said he had attended all but about 15 of the Braves' home games in 1963 and 1964, re-upped. "Teams Inc persuaded me that (working with the Braves) was the only way for Milwaukee to keep major league baseball," he said. But his opinion was far from universal. The Milwaukee Athletic Club, which had purchased 30 season tickets for the 1964 season, did not renew in 1965, even though former Braves shortstop Johnny Logan - who had retired earlier in the month after an 18-year career, including nine seasons with the Braves - was a long-standing MAC member and was participating in the Selig-directed effort to sell tickets for the Braves' final Milwaukee season.

In Chicago, the Cubs also were looking anxiously at the Braves' season-ticket sales. Even though owner Philip K. Wrigley had gone on record as opposing the Braves' move, he never said outright that he wouldn't vote for it, either. The Cubs, more than any of the other 19 major league clubs, stood to profit from the Milwaukee Braves' departure. The Cubs hadn't finished higher than fifth since 1946 or drawn a million paying spectators since 1952 - the year before the Braves moved to Milwaukee. At the time, it was faster and less stressful to drive from many of Chicago's northernmost suburbs to County Stadium than it was to get to Wrigley Field (or, for that matter, Comiskey Park, home of the White Sox). The Cubs had drawn 751,647, ninth-best in a 10-team league, compared to the Braves' 910,911 in 1964, but Cubs ticket manager Jack Maloney predicted that once the move was consummated - or even before - the Cubs would pick up a minimum of 100,000 disgruntled Braves fans per year. (He was wrong. The Cubs' attendance actually fell in 1965, to 641,361, and again in 1966, to 635,891, dead last in the NL. It wasn't until 1969, when Leo Durocher's Cubs led the National League East most of the season and drew 1,674,993, that they regained their pre-World War II status as the team of choice in Chicago, and began to draw in significant numbers from territory that once had been dominated by the Braves.)

Milwaukee, meanwhile, settled in for a final season of watching and listening to the Braves - and, at least in some cases, still rooting for them. Despite the legal and political posturing by the Braves and those who sought to punish them for their calumny, it still appeared at the end of February 1965 that the issue could be solved to both sides' relative satisfaction. Teams Inc, the theory went, would help the Braves sell enough tickets and generate enough interest to insure the team against financial ruin during its last year in Milwaukee; Organized Baseball, in turn, would prioritize Milwaukee as soon as another franchise became available, either through transfer or through expansion.

The outside world was seeping in on the baseball realm, diverting some attention from the Braves' situation. Few of the news stories during the month seemed to presage calamity, but they did foretell the changing of society as the oldest of the Baby Boomers approached adulthood.

The *Journal* ran a series on a subject that rarely made it onto American front pages in 1965: Would the Catholic Church change its long-standing position of absolute opposite to birth control? Meanwhile, the *Sentinel* maintained its usual reactionary bent, giving much coverage to a charge made by Bob Siegrist, a Madison right-wing radio commentator, that John M. Gruber, the editor of the University of Wisconsin's student newspaper, should be fired because he lived in the same Madison home as relatives of former Communists. Gov. Warren Knowles, who had taken office the previous month, quickly jumped into the fray on Gruber's behalf - calling the accusation a "witch hunt" even though Knowles was a Republican - and UW regents flatly refused to take action against Gruber. Despite the *Sentinel's* best efforts to sustain the story and by doing so reviving McCarthyism, the story gradually faded from public view. The *Sentinel* also ran a four-part series called "The Homosexual," describing homosexuality as if it were a plague that had to be contained. "The *problem* of homosexuality is being discussed in medical, legal and social-service circles," an editorial reported, "(and) the *Sentinel* offers this explanatory, scientific series of articles as a public service."

In the affluent northeast suburb of Fox Point, the Brown-Port Theatre insisted that it would show the movie "Sex and the Single Girl" despite protests by women's groups who said showing the movie would detract from the status of Fox Point (Bud Selig's hometown) as a family-oriented community. A $30,000 claim was filed against a Milwaukee police officer who was accused of "mistreating" two black boys on the near north side. Governor Knowles, in opposition to many within his own party, presented a budget for fiscal-year 1965-66 of $832 million, 27 percent larger than the budget of the previous fiscal year. Revenue-raising options suggested by Knowles and some Democrats included an increase in the $1-per-barrel beer tax that had remained unchanged since the end of Prohibition in 1933, and a state lottery, which Knowles estimated would raise $20 million per year.

Civil rights protests in Alabama led by Dr. Martin Luther King were covered by both papers, though rarely from the violence standpoint because most of the protests in Alabama and elsewhere in the South were relatively peaceful in January and February 1965. (This, of course, would soon change, in the South and throughout the country.) The *Journal* focused on localizing the national story, covering in depth a march by the NAACP and the Milwaukee Unified Schools Integration Committee (or MUSIC) on a Milwaukee Public Schools board meeting, and noting approvingly a teen meeting of the Wisconsin Catholic Action convention in Milwaukee during which the 3,000 delegates, almost all of whom were white, sang the civil-rights anthem "We Shall Overcome" when asked to do so by a convention speaker.

The Vietnam War had not yet reached critical mass as it would do later in the year; U.S. troop strength there was "only" 23,500 at the end of February, and a Harris Poll taken in February indicated that 83 percent of Americans supported President Lyndon Johnson's decision to bomb Communist supply bases in southern North Vietnam. But on February 10, one of the earliest antiwar protests was held on the UW campus in Madison. The *Sentinel* responded to the news story with an editorial headlined, simply, "Ignore Them." The editorial accused the protesters of having leftist ties. "Jealous of the attention the Berkeley rioters got (during a demonstration at the University of California's main campus a few days earlier), they may be hoping to provoke an even better show in Madison. It is an embarrassment to have a bit of

Peking crop up in Madison. The one thing they can't stand is to be ignored."

Milwaukee and its business commiunity still appeared to be booming, despite the increasingly ominous ecological situation in the Menomonee Valley and along the shores of Lake Michigan. The mayor's office announced that $38 million in federal money was earmarked for Milwaukee projects, and the Milwaukee County Zoo prepared to take delivery of 20 Adelie penguins shipped directly from Antarctica. Milwaukee's police force, which included 1,800 employees, got a 5.5 percent raise on top of a 3 percent increase that had been granted to all municipal employees - much, predictably, to the dismay of the *Sentinel*, which declared in an editorial that the raises were excessive and would unnecessarily increase homeowners' tax burden. A strike that eventually lasted for 6 1/2 years had shut down the Kohler plumbing-fixture company, which didn't reopen until the end of December, but the American Motors plant in Milwaukee averted a strike that would have affected all of its 8,891 employees. The United Steel Workers District 32 reached an all-time membership high, with 25,000 card-carrying workers. A.O. Smith, which manufactured a variety of products ranging from boilers to car frames in peacetime and bombs and airplane propellers during World War II, announced plans to expand its workforce to 8,000 - the most since the end of the war, and a significant increase from its 6,300 workforce only two years earlier. The Kohl corporation, owned by founder Max Kohl and later run by his son, future U.S. Senator and Milwaukee Bucks owner Herb Kohl, announced a $12 million expansion. Already the largest grocery-store chain in the state, Kohl's planned to expand into the department-store and eventually the shopping-center realms.

FMC Corp., which had a plant in Port Washington, announced sales and earnings of $830 million for 1964. Allis-Chalmers, in West Allis, was building a 120-foot screening tower that was expected to produce 500,000 kilowatt-hours of power for the Dairyland Power Co-op.

With the month coming to an end, the Milwaukee Braves were en route to Florida for spring training. But like just about everything else associated with the final season of the Milwaukee Braves, March in West Palm Beach, Fla., presented its own set of problems.

The Last Spring

• • •

On Monday, March 1, 1965, the Milwaukee Braves convened in West Palm Beach, Fla., for the first workout of their last season. Hank Aaron and Eddie Mathews, by now the only two players on the roster who lived in Milwaukee year-round, no doubt were eager to get out of weather that was typical of Wisconsin in spring: 40 degrees, winds up to 20 mph, rain likely, snow possible. But few of the other players who had been to spring training with the Braves before considered West Palm Beach any sort of tropical paradise - aside, of course, from the fact they would be back to doing what they did best after a five-month hiatus.

Like many of the issues that had confronted the Braves both on and off the field in their latter years in Milwaukee, the negatives literally and figuratively surrounding West Palm Beach Municipal Stadium had been the handiwork of Lou Perini. Perini and his construction company had branched into real estate in 1958, and he had entered into an agreement with the Atlantic Coast city of West Palm Beach to convert thousands of acres of vacant Florida wasteland into what amounted to a brand-new community - including a new spring training home for the Braves, who had trained in the Gulf Coast city of Bradenton since before World War II.

The facility, opened in 1963, had been an unmitigated disaster from the start, and Perini found himself in somewhat the same position as Hall of Fame manager John McGraw in the late 1920s when McGraw had been convinced to lend his name and invest some of his money in a Florida land-speculation scheme. Unlike Perini three decades later, McGraw was essentially a front man for the "developers" who had initiated and then bailed out of the project. McGraw had not been directly involved in its conception or its failure, but many disgruntled property buyers who had seen their investments disappear held McGraw responsible, and some sued him. He settled all of those claims, but doing so took him most of the rest of his life (he died in 1934) and nearly bankrupted him. In Perini's case, many believe the money he and his company lost during the first years of the West Palm Beach development was a deciding factor - if not *the* deciding factor - in his decision to sell the Braves to Bill Bartholomay and his group after the 1962 season.

In West Palm Beach, swampland had to be drained, palmetto groves had to be cleared, and land had to be leveled before any construction could begin. Flooding further slowed the progress, and even the homes that were built proved difficult to sell because of the barren location and the uncertainty regarding how much of the project would ever be completed. The Perini firm, at the start of 1965, had put a total of $21 million into the project, and had recouped only $4 million. It also had stopped making the $1 million annual payment to West Palm Beach that had been part of the original agreement, and Perini already had renegotiated the contract, giving his company until 1978 to finish the project. In 1965, the spring-training complex that was part of the deal was one of the few elements of the project that could be called even remotely finished, and even at that, it was hardly satisfactory in its first few years of operation. The main ballpark, which also was to became the home of the Braves' Class A affiliate in the Florida State League, was built with hardly any accouterments, even lacking a roof to protect the mostly-older spectators from the withering Florida heat. Symbolically, in 1963 when the Braves assembled for their first spring training in West Palm Beach, they found that the ballpark's home plate had been installed backward. (Eventually, the stadium was improved and an adjoining baseball complex was built, but in 1998 the park and the site were abandoned and the ballpark was torn down in 2002.)

Because most of the property surrounding the ballpark retained its natural habitat in the years immediately after the Braves came to West Palm Beach, it also retained its natural wildlife, including snakes and alligators - much to the consternation of outfielder Len Gabrielson, who had signed with the Braves out of the University of Southern California in 1959. (His father, also named Len, had played briefly for the Phillies in 1939, and his son Randy followed him to USC in the early 1980s.) Gabrielson, a 6-foot-4, 210-pound left-handed-hitting outfielder who also could play first base, was brought up for four games at the end of the 1960 season. He returned to Milwaukee in 1963 and played in 46 games, then took part in 24 games in 1964 before being traded to the Chicago Cubs. He hit only 37 home runs during his 10-year, five-team major league career, but one of them, early in the 1963 season, embedded him in the memories of the Braves fans who saw it. Gabrielson's blow struck the Longines clock at the top of the scoreboard that overlooked the bleachers in straightaway right field. (The third of Willie Mays' four home runs on April 30, 1961 is generally considered the longest homer at County Stadium while the Braves called it home. The ball, hit on a pitch by Seth Morehead, cleared the left-field bleachers and the picnic area behind them on the fly before landing on the asphalt of the parking lot. The Giants hit eight home runs in that game, which they won 14-4, and Hank Aaron hit two for the Braves.)

Gabrielson's imposing physical stature, and the intelligence and business acumen that made him a millionaire in the real estate business in Northern California after he retired from baseball, didn't help him in one respect while he was with the Braves: He was an ophidiophobe (one who is abnormally terrified of snakes). This made West Palm Beach a torture chamber for him, and at one point during spring training in 1963, Gabrielson made the mistake of reacting to the sight of a snake while Warren Spahn and Lew Burdette were watching.

The two, roommates from the time the team was still in Boston until Burdette was traded to the Cardinals in 1963, were notorious, not only among the Braves but throughout baseball, for the fiendishness of their clubhouse pranks. If they weren't wiling away their off-hours at the Cock and Bull - a bar in downtown West Palm Beach where Bob Uecker in 1968 had a beer bottle broken over his head in a fight, creating a wound that required 48 stitches to close - Burdette and Spahn were busy catching all the snakes they could find. For the rest of that spring of 1963, Gabrielson could count on being greeted by a snake at any time that he might not be expecting it.

Players disliked spring trainings in West Palm Beach during the Braves' early years there not only because of the abundance of creatures and the absence of creature comforts, but also because of the fact the ballpark was surrounded by lots that had been cleared and drained but hadn't yet been developed, leaving only huge mounds of dirt. With the natural windbreaks having been bulldozed, that dust was transformed into tiny projectiles that pockmarked players' faces throughout games and practices until the area surrounding the ballpark was finally built out, far behind schedule and long after the Braves had moved to Atlanta. One building that had been included in the original plans for the parcel was the 5,000-seat West Palm Beach Municipal Auditorium, which wasn't completed until 1967. When it finally was finished, it had a cone-shaped roof that neither held nor deflected water well, prompting locals to dub it the "Leaky Teepee." In the 1990s, it was sold to the Jehovah's Witnesses, who renovated it, then converted it into a place of worship that was renamed the West Palm Beach Christian Convention Center.

In 1965, a decade before free agency became a reality and salaries began to soar, many players had to work offseason jobs - readily available in Milwaukee during the Braves' glory years, less so afterward - to remain financially solvent. Consequently, those players rarely worked out or played year-round, as became the norm in later decades, so spring training was used for conditioning as much as for polishing baseball tactics and techniques. It also was rare in 1965 for pitchers and catchers to show up at spring training before the mandated time, and during an era when only stars rated multi-year contracts, players sometimes missed the early - and most taxing - segment of spring training while negotiating with management. Usually, only players who felt they had jobs and careers on the line showed up before the mandatory reporting date.

Frank Lary, who had been acquired the previous August from the New York Mets, still hadn't signed with the Braves as of March 1, though he did report to camp and pitched some batting practice. Lary, who would turn 34 in April, had been the longtime ace of the Detroit Tigers pitching staff; he had earned 21 wins in 1956 and 23 in 1961, and was best known for his work against the Yankees, against whom he was 28-13 for his career. But he won only 19 games after his 23-win season. The Braves had invited him to spring training in 1965, but he didn't impress Bragan, and was sold back to the Mets on March 28. He went 2-3 with a 3.32 ERA in 28 games with the Mets and White Sox in 1965, then retired. (Lary Sorensen, a pitcher who finished with 18 wins for the Brewers in 1978, was given his first name because his parents, both of whom were from the Detroit area, were fans of Lary and of the Tigers.)

Two of the players who did arrive before their teammates in 1965 were pitchers Bob Sadowski and Hank Fischer, both of whom were coming off disappointing 1964 seasons but remained candidates for positions in a starting rotation that would be without Spahn for the first time since 1946. Sadowski, 27, said he had been too heavy to maximize his stuff in 1964. After weighing 208 pounds in 1964, he was down to 195 by the time spring training officially opened, and intended to pitch at 185 during the upcoming season. He also had another reason for wanting to establish himself in the Braves' long-term plans. Although he was originally from Pittsburgh, he had played for the minor league Atlanta Crackers in 1962 and '63, and had made his permanent home in Atlanta. Fischer, 11-10 with a 4.01 ERA as a second-year player in 1964, had been in West Palm Beach for almost two weeks before the arrival of most of his teammates. He encamped early to work on his changeup, which he predicted would transform him from a good young pitcher into a fixture in the Braves' starting rotation, which needed a fourth member behind Tony Cloninger, Wade Blasingame and Denny Lemaster. "I know I'm going to win 15 games and I'm shooting for 20," Fischer told the *Journal*. "With our power, all a pitcher has to do is hold a club under five runs. I don't see any way I can fail to win 15. (It didn't work out that way. He went 8-9 with a 3.81 ERA in 1965, lasted only two more years in the majors, and finished his career 30-39 with a 4.23 ERA.)

On March 1, after the arrival and settling-in of most of the players, McHale addressed the club. He warned the players about involving themselves in the controversy surrounding the franchise shift. "This is going to be an unusual day (with the Milwaukee and national media arriving in West Palm Beach) for us," McHale said, "but I'm sure you realize that the only thing for everybody is to do his best. And don't get involved in that controversy." It was a controversy that continued to tear at prospective ticket buyers in Milwaukee. Despite Bragan's proclamation in February that the team had sold 1,848 season tickets for 1965, Selig said on March 1 that the actual total was 840, compared to 4,470 the year before.

For the first time in their Milwaukee history, the Braves' first full day of camp wasn't the lead story in the Milwaukee sports sections. That distinction belonged to Bob Pettit, who announced his retirement from the NBA, effective at the end of the 1964-65 season. Pettit had become one of the NBA's all-time greats during his 10 seasons with the St. Louis Hawks, but many in Milwaukee remembered 1954-55, Pettit's rookie season, when he was the lone redeeming quality of a Milwaukee Hawks team that in 1954-55 ended, unmourned, its four-season stay at the Milwaukee Arena. Pettit finished fourth in the NBA in both scoring and rebounding in his lone season as a MIlwaukee Hawk. He was named Rookie of the Year, played in the All-Star Game - as he did every year of his NBA career - and in 1957-58 led the Hawks to their only NBA title as of 2016, scoring 50 points in Game 6 against the Boston Celtics as the Hawks wrapped up the best-of-seven title series. "Bob Pettit fan clubs flourished (in Milwaukee)," read a story in the *Journal*, "especially among teenaged girls who, though they seldom saw the 6-foot-9 rookie play, hung around the Arena entrances like feminine stage-door Johnnies ... Pettit was easily the most popular man on the Milwaukee pro club. He received most of the mail (sent to the team) ... the other letters were mostly bills which owner Ben Kerner shuffled from one drawer to another in an attempt to forget where they were." (The Hawks played their final Milwaukee home game on March 4, 1955, losing 99-96 to the Syracuse Nationals before 3,438. Miller Brewing Company president Fred Miller had been one of the franchise's primary financial supporters, and his death in December 1954 ended whatever chance the Hawks had of staying in Milwaukee beyond the 1954-55 season.)

The *Journal* also carried a story by Bob Wolf on Tony Cloninger, a one-time bonus-baby variable who had become a constant in 1964 with his 19 wins at the age of 24. Cloninger had reached the majors in 1961, only two years after going 0-9 with a 9.59 ERA and walking 58 in 47 innings while spending part of the season with Cedar Rapids in the Class B Three-I League.

But after being sent to Class C Boise, Cloninger strung together 34 straight scoreless innings to get himself back in the organization's good graces.

Author Pat Jordan marveled at Cloninger's grit when both were in the Braves' minor-league organization. "When told to run 10 wind sprints," Jordan remembered, "he ran 20. He seemed always to be sweating, always working painfully hard at tasks that were either senseless or so much easier than he made them. At first I thought this was simply his desire to prove that despite his ($100,000) bonus he did not expect a free ride through the system, as many bonus players did. Eventually I realized that Tony was proud of his ability to do things the hard way, proud of his refusal to quit even when *he* knew his efforts were senseless." This would be a quality that Braves fans would come to fully appreciate in 1965.

In his March 1965 interview with Wolf, Cloninger - who was a longtime major league coach after his retirement as a player - gave Braves pitching instructor Whitlow Wyatt much of the credit for his emergence as a pitching-staff anchor. "I can't say enough about Whitlow Wyatt for all the help he has given me. He changed my motion slightly and it made a world of difference. I used to pitch high a lot so he had me bend my left knee slightly. That pulls my body down and I have to pitch lower." (Ironically, Wyatt, a mediocre major league pitcher from 1929-37, resurrected his career while spending the 1938 American Association season in Milwaukee with the Brewers. He went 23-7, was purchased by the Dodgers and went on to become a National League All-Star each of the next four seasons.) Cloninger also wanted to be stronger, particularly in the late innings, so he reported to camp at

219 pounds, five pounds heavier than he had been in 1964. He'd kept in shape during the offseason by raising and tending to four quarterhorses on his farm in Iron Mountain, N.C. His $100,000 bunus had been well-invested; it helped pay for the farm and for the horses.

While Bragan knew with some certainty that Cloninger, Blasingame and Lemaster would be at the top of the Braves rotation, a week of spring training had done little to clear up the uncertainties in the infield. Mathews, of course, would be entrenched at third. Denis Menke, the nominal shortstop who had batted .283 and hit 20 homers in 1964, said he preferred to remain at short, but Menke had played all four infield positions and said he was willing to move to another spot as long as he was in the lineup every day. Besides Sandy Alomar, the Braves also thought Woody Woodward had possibilities at shortstop, and either or both could replace Frank Bolling at second base if he didn't show signs of improving his .199 batting average of 1964. Bolling was still one of the best defensive second basemen in baseball - he had committed only seven errors in 1964 and his fielding percentage of .985 was the best among NL second basemen that year - but his range was beginning to be called into question.

At first base, no less than four viable candidates had to be evaluated - Gene Oliver and Joe Torre, both long-ball-capable catchers who had first-base experience; Felipe Alou, acquired from the Giants the year before, and Rico Carty, who had burst into the forefront as a rookie in '64 by batting .330 to finish second behind Roberto Clemente in the NL batting race, even though he wasn't installed as a regular (usually in left field) until June 1964. When asked if he feared the so-called "soph-omore jinx," he replied, "What's that?" Carty, a native of the Dominican Republic whose English was limited, also gave the Braves an ebullience that many of their other players lacked. His teammates enjoyed his perennial smile and *joie de vivre* whenever he was on the field, and he had some quirks that marked him as truly unspoiled in the ways of the U.S. In the on-deck circle, he would amuse himself by pointing his bat at the pitcher as if it were a rifle. In 1965, and for years afterward, he would always appear on the field with a large object bulging from the left back pocket of his uniform pants. It turned out that he didn't trust banks, or the clubhouse lockbox, and the object in question was his wallet. Carty also made it clear he preferred the outfield to first base. He wore his outfielders glove even when he was used at first, but he also had chronically sore feet that limited his mo-bility in the outfield. The pain was such that Carty would run around the infield dirt on his way to the outfield at the start of innings.

Both Carty and Alou, who was coming off knee surgery, were more comfortable in the outfield than at first, but play-ing either or both in the outfield would mean sitting Lee Maye and/or Mack Jones and thereby diminishing the Braves' team speed and outfield defense. It was a dilemma with which Bragan would wrestle until Maye was traded early in the regular sea-son. Carty's bat was so valuable that the Braves even considered using him at catcher, his original position, with Torre play-ing first and Oliver coming off the bench. But farm director John Mullen remembered a previous experiment with Carty behind the plate in the minors in 1960. "He couldn't even catch a pitched ball," Mullen recalled. "He spent most of his time running back to the screen to pick up the ball." Oliver wasn't a particularly adroit catcher or first baseman either, but in 1964 he had hit 13 home runs (11 of which had either tied a game or given the Braves the lead) and had driven in 49 runs in only 279 at-bats. (Oliver also had the unusual distinction of being a hallowed figure among fans of a team for which he had never played. While with the Cardinals in 1962, he had hit a game-winning home run against the Dodgers in the final game of the regular season, forcing the Dodgers into a playoff with the Giants that San Francisco won to reach the World Series. For the rest of his career, Oliver was cheered heartily by Giants fans whenever his team visited Candlestick Park.)

Clearly, the Braves would have a glut both at first and in the outfield, especially after Aaron returned, and *The Sporting News* reported that the Braves and Astros were discussing a trade that would send Oliver to Houston for pitcher Bob Bruce. Another rumor was that the Indians, who needed a second baseman, had made overtures to the Braves in an effort to acquire Frank Bolling. The *New York Daily News* reported that the Mets wanted to add power and had offered the Braves left-handed starting pitcher Al Jackson, who must have salivated at the thought of working in Milwaukee with the Braves' offense behind him. Jackson and Roger Craig had been the Mets' two best starting pitchers during their first three years as the National League's expansion laughingstock. Jackson had pitched at least 213 innings each season for the Mets from 1962-64, and had a 31-53 record to show for it. The Mets wound up keeping him for the 1965 season, during which he went 8-20, but finally, in 1966, sent him to St. Louis, where in 1967 he was a member of the Cardinals' World Series championship team.

In Milwaukee, Selig on March 6 reported that season ticket sales for 1965 were up to 934, and estimated the total would be up to 1,700 by Opening Day. Meanwhile, McHale announced that the Braves' net losses for 1964 were $45,270, slightly higher than the $43,378 he claimed they lost in 1963. Few believed him, given the fact the Braves, like most major league teams by 1965, could and did claim player salaries as business expenses and deduct them from their income-tax assessments.

Other sports news continued to push the Braves below the fold in the Milwaukee newspapers. On March 6, the *Journal* played two stories ahead of the Braves in its sports section: The University of Wisconsin winning the Big Ten track title, and the fact Marquette's basketball team drew a respectable 6,359 per game at the Arena despite going 8-18 in Al McGuire's first season, approaching Marquette's record average of 6,697 in 1959-60. (That same season, the UW Badgers, who hadn't made the NCAA tournament since 1947 and wouldn't do so again until 1994, averaged 6,382 for their games at Wisconsin Field House.) McGuire, even then a tireless promoter, promised at least a .500 season in 1965-66, and suggested that Warrior fans buy season tickets for 1965-66 because the program would be selling out the building consistently before long.

Two days later, the Braves-Teams Inc agreement began to unravel, with Edmund Fitzgerald claiming that the Braves had co-opted the nickel-per-ticket arrangement and tried to incorporate it into their own sales pitch. The idea, of course, had been for Teams Inc to use its credibility in Milwaukee to help sell tickets while keeping the Braves in the background, and Fitzgerald said the Braves' attempts to sell tickets on their own negated

Teams Inc's efforts. Teams Inc also lashed out at the Braves for emphasizing the increased payments to the escrow account if 1965 attendance reached the agreed-upon milestones. "Nobody here is going to sell out," Ben Barkin of Teams Inc declared. "Everything the Braves have done is calculated to get them out of Milwaukee *this season*."

Teams Inc, the Braves, radio stations WTMJ and WEMP, and the Majestic Advertising Agency also came to a grudging agreement by which Braves games would be carried in Milwaukee as well as in Atlanta. They agreed that the arrangement, which was described as a "co-op," would be a money-loser for all concerned and would not put a dent in the deficit that the Braves were rapidly accumulating as operators of a franchise that had no future in Milwaukee. But Edmund Fitzgerald called it a necessary sacrifice "to once again prove (Milwaukee's) major league status." This would become harder to do once the regular season opened. The Braves had already relocated most of their operational staff to Atlanta, and many of their Wisconsin-based employees were leaving as well. Earl Gillespie, who had been the radio play-by-play voice of the Braves since their arrival in 1953, already had resigned the year before to take a job with television station WITI (a job he kept until his retirement in 1985), though his radio sidekick Blaine Walsh stayed for the 1965 season, during which he worked with play-by-play man Merle Harmon. In March 1965, William S. Eberly, who had been ticket manager at County Stadium from 1953-61 and then business manager since 1961, quit to accept a non-baseball post in Toledo, Ohio, his hometown.

While few out-of-the-ordinary baseball stories emanated from West Palm Beach or Milwaukee in March 1965, the world beyond was becoming more incendiary by the day. President Lyndon Johnson had begun to lay out in detail his Great Society plan, the centerpiece of which was the Voting Rights Act of 1965, that he promised would provide equal opportunity for all Americans. The civil rights marches led by Dr. Martin Luther King, Jr., in Selma, Ala., were becoming national catalysts. In Berkeley, Calif., sit-ins and demonstrations that had begun the previous December had disintegrated into a riot during which 800 demonstrators were arrested, and on March 10, University of California president Clark Kerr and chancellor Martin Meyerson both resigned. This triggered demonstrations at many other colleges, including little Beloit College, where 175 students staged a march in support of the Selma demonstrations. Wisconsin Gov. Warren Knowles and Lieutenant Gov. Patrick Lucey both applauded the students. Lucey, a Democrat who was to serve as Wisconsin governor from 1971-77 and later as the U.S. ambassador to Mexico, in 1964 had said that Wisconsin had been besmirched by the fact 200,000 voters in the state had cast their votes for segregationist George Wallace in the 1964 presidential election. In March, Lucey said, after the Beloit demonstration, that "we might look on this march as penance to help remove that mark on the state's conscience." In Milwaukee, where NAACP president Whitney Young had spoken a few days earlier, 130 members of MUSIC (Milwaukee Unified School Integration Committee) staged a silent protest at an MPS board meeting. MUSIC's role in the civil-rights movement in Milwaukee would become increasingly active and influential in the coming months.

After a minister was beaten to death during an outbreak of violence in Selma on March 11, eight Wisconsin priests made the trip to Selma to lend their support to the integrationists. One was

Father James Groppi, an assistant priest at St. Boniface Church on West Clarke Street. Groppi was virtually unknown outside his parish at the time, but by the end of the month, he would be in the headlines after defying arrest at the Alabama state capitol in Montgomery and joining 34 other clergymen in reciting the Lord's Prayer on the capitol steps. "God is the father of us all," he said, "and we are all brothers in him. We have an obligation to help our brothers. If we go to church Sunday and preach the doctrine of Christ and then do nothing, we are hypocrites." In subsequent years, Groppi would go much further than that both within and beyond the Milwaukee civil-rights movement; in fact, he would become one of the more polarizing figures in Milwaukee's history.

The U.S. involvement in Vietnam also was beginning to undergo outside scrutiny from unexpected sources. *Washington Post* columnist John G. Norris, who had been an information officer in the Navy during World War II and later had written extensively about the Cold War, became one of the first mainstream reporters to describe in detail the escalation of the U.S. intervention in Vietnam. Norris warned of "more marked escalation of the war than generally has been realized" and told of bombings and Marine deployment that the Pentagon had not previously disclosed while bringing U.S. troop strength in Southeast Asia up to a reported 27,000. Up to this point, most U.S. newspapers had either applauded the U.S. involvement in Vietnam, or had downplayed it. In Milwaukee, the *Sentinel*, as it had done during the demonstrations in Madison in February, questioned the motives and particularly the patriotism of anyone who dared protest U.S. domestic or foreign policy. The *Journal*, as usual, took a broader-based editorial stance, expressing support for the containment policy the U.S. had adopted toward Communism since the beginning of the Cold War, but warning, with pre-science as it turned out, of the U.S. invention in Vietnam escalating into a full-scale war. It quoted Sen. George McGovern, an outspoken opponent of U.S. involvement in Southeast Asia, who had said that "the American Eagle comes with both the arrows of war and the olive branch of peace. We should be extending both. Instead, we extend just the arrows."

With the outside world and the franchise-shift machinations commanding the bulk of attention and the Braves still awaiting the start of their exhibition season in Florida, the *Journal* ran an innoculous piece on Braves utilityman Lou Klimchock, a 25-year-old utility infielder who had been commuting between Milwaukee and the minor leagues since the Braves had acquired him from Kansas City in 1962. Klimchock had played in only 42 games during the fragments of three seasons he spent in Milwaukee. He got into 34 more games in 1965, and did not accompany the team to Atlanta. Klimchock never spent a full year in the majors, and played in more than 90 major league games only once (with the Indians in 1970) in 12 seasons. But he accumulated 5,075 at-bats (and 1,481 hits) during 15 seasons in the minors, and he holds the distinction of being the last former Milwaukee Brave to maintain an on-field, in-uniform baseball position. After his retirement, he settled in Scottsdale, Ariz., and managed the travel team on which his grandson, Mitch Nay, played. Nay, a third baseman, in 2012 was drafted in the second round (58th overall) by the Toronto Blue Jays. He signed with the Blue Jays, foregoing a scholarship offer from Arizona State, and in 2016 was in his fourth season in the Toronto organization.

On March 12, the Braves played their first intrasquad game, with a team captained by Gene Oliver defeating an Eddie Mathews-directed team 7-4. Hank Fischer, still working on his new changeup, pitched for Mathews' team and gave up all seven runs, in the fifth inning. The Braves also added Bill Southworth to the roster. Southworth, 19, was a cousin of Billy Southworth, who had managed the Boston Braves to the National League pennant in 1948 after taking the Cardinals to three straight World Series and winning 316 games from 1942-44. (He also had a fine career as a player, and in 2008, 39 years after his death, was inducted into the Baseball Hall of Fame.) He was also the father of Billy Southworth Jr., an Army Air Corps pilot and promising baseball prospect whose looks were such that he reportedly received casting-call overtures from Hollywood. At age 27, after completing 25 bombing missions over Germany and attaining the rank of major, he was killed on February 15, 1945, when the B-29 he was piloting crashed into Flushing Bay near New York City. This led, indirectly, to the advent of the Milwaukee Braves.

Southworth, who had been a heavy drinker throughout his adult life but had renounced alcohol before the Cardinals hired him, resumed drinking after his son's death. The '48 Braves, a hard-partying ensemble themselves, apparently weren't side-tracked by this, but in 1949 when the Braves slumped, a group led by teetotalers Alvin Dark and Eddie Stanky took complaints about Southworth to management, and both players demanded to be traded. They were sent to the New York Giants for Sid Gordon, Red Webb, Willard Marshall and Buddy Kerr in a trade that helped the Giants win two pennants and a World Series, and undercut the Braves to such an extent that their fan base nearly disappeared, leading to the move to Milwaukee. Only Gordon was still with the Braves when they moved to Milwaukee (he hit .274 with 19 homers and 75 RBI in 1953), and he was traded that winter to the Pirates in the deal that brought second baseman Danny O'Connell. Southworth took a medical leave of absence in 1949, returned in 1950, and resigned during the 1951 season, the Braves' next-to-last season in Boston. But he was retained as a scout and was involved in the scouting and signing of Hank Aaron, who had been playing Negro League baseball for the Indianapolis Clowns. (Bill Southworth had totaled two hits in seven at-bats in three games for the Braves in 1964, but never returned to the majors after that, and played only three minor league seasons before retiring at age 21.)

Aaron didn't play in the intrasquad game, and reported after the game that the ankle injury that had hindered him in 1964 still lingered. He subsequently underwent minor surgery to address the calcification of the injury, and it was hoped he would be ready for Opening Day four weeks hence.

The Braves beat the Dodgers 6-1 in their first full-scale exhibition game, with Joe Torre hitting a three-run homer off Sandy Koufax. Bob Sadowski and Denny Lemaster each worked three scoreless innings, and Dan Osinski, a 31-year-old who had drifted into and out of the Angels and A's organization as a starter but hoped to resurrect his career as a reliever with a newly-learned forkball, came in with the bases loaded and got the final out. Frank Bolling singled twice and started two brisk double plays. At the Mets training camp in St. Petersburg, Warren Spahn made his first spring-training appearance wearing a uniform other than that of the Braves. Against the

Cardinals, he went three innings and gave up four hits, three walks and three runs.

One of the umpires in the Braves-Dodgers game was Wisconsinite Bruce Froemming, a 25-year-old who had begun officiating in the Milwaukee recreation leagues when he was still attending Custer High School., from which he graduated in 1957. He then went to former major league umpire Al Somers' instructional school with the goal of plying his trade in professional baseball, and was hired by the Class D Nebraska State League in 1958 at the age of 18, making him the youngest ump in the professional ranks at the time. Froemming advanced to the Class C Northern League and worked there two seasons before a two-year stint in the military. He umpired in the short-season Class A Northwest League in 1963 but had been out of baseball entirely in 1964. "I didn't want to go back to the Northwest League," he said, "and when no other good spot opened, I decided to wait."

A position for the 1965 season opened in the Class AA Texas League, and Froemming accepted it, self-imposing a 10-year deadline for making the major leagues. He got there in 1971 and worked 37 seasons as a big-league umpire before retiring in 2007, and in 2016 he was still working as an MLB umpire supervisor. Another Wisconsin resident, Paul Pryor, already was well-established as an NL umpire in 1965. Pryor, who originally was from Rhode Island, was an NL umpire from 1961-81. He settled in Racine early in his career, and taught school there during the off-season.

That same day (March 15), Teams Inc members met with state, county and city officials in Madison in the first real attempt to present a united front in the effort to guarantee Milwaukee major league baseball in 1966 and beyond. Setting the tone for the rest of the year and beyond, the meeting accomplished little, with no joint action agreed upon. Milwaukee County already was in the process of initiating antitrust litigation against the Braves and Major League Baseball, and neither Teams Inc nor the other governmental bodies wanted to compromise that outcome. "It was agreed by all present that any further comment would not be appropriate at this time," a post-meeting statement read. From now on, Teams Inc and the three governmental jurisdictions generally would work independently, with Eugene Grobschmidt and the county pressing the antitrust litigation, the city and the state (and eventually Wisconsin's Congressional delegation) piggy-backing onto the county's actions, and Teams Inc dealing on its own with the Braves.

Grobschmidt, meanwhile, continued to grapple politically with County Executive John Doyne. During one of his anti-Braves jags, Grobschmidt had suggested that the county buy the team or seize it through the power of eminent domain, and then put it under the auspices of the county parks department. Doyne, as tactfully as he could manage under the circumstances and given the mutual loathing between the two men, pointed out that such a scheme was impossible even if Bartholomay were to put the team up for sale - as he had been saying since November that he would not do.

Trying to be oblivious to the upheaval to the north, the Braves played two games that would both, in their own ways, turn out to be Milwaukee's *nom de guerre* during the 1965 season. Mack Jones, to whom the Milwaukee papers still referred as a "four-time minor league failure," and Eddie Mathews hit two-run homers, and the Braves beat the Orioles 4-2 in West Palm Beach. Mathews earlier had been named the Braves' captain, their first since Del Crandall in 1956, after which Fred Haney had discontinued the practice.

The next day, the same teams met in Miami, with the Braves losing 4-3 and Jones going 0 for 5, striking out three times and not hitting the ball out of the infield. Lee Maye dropped a fly ball in left field to cost the Braves two unearned runs, and Woody Woodward, playing second base, misplayed a popup into a single, muffed on a suicide-squeeze attempt, and failed to run out a line drive that he thought was foul but turned out to be fair. Billy O'Dell also failed to impress in his Braves debut, giving up only one run in two innings but surrendering five hits. Denis Menke was in a slump that eventually became a 3-for-35 famine, although he was still getting most of the playing time at shortstop. The second-base job remained up for grabs between Alomar, Woodward and Bolling, according to Bragan. First base also remained open, especially after Carty made three errors there (and could easily have been charged with a fourth) in a 9-8 loss to the White Sox in West Palm Beach on March 20. "He got his indoctrination," Bragan said. "But he's learning, and I'm going to keep him there (at least for the moment)." The bullpen situation looked unsettled as well, with Bob Tiefenauer surrendering three hits, two walks and two earned runs in two innings against the White Sox.

Bragan, trying to remain upbeat with the regular season still four weeks away, submitted to a perfunctory interview with *New York Times* columnist Arthur Daley, who had been with the *Times* since 1926 and its lead sports columnist since 1942. Daley was far removed from the "chipmunk" genre of sports journalists - led by Dick Young of the *New York Daily News* - who in 1965 were challenging the long-held belief that reporters should be mouthpieces for the teams they covered and write as fans rather than as impartial observers. Daley's column the next day read predictably: "The Braves know that they have aroused bitterness and resentment in Milwaukee and they realize that they may be boycotted by once-frantic fans whose hearts are currently as cold as the Wisconsin winter. But brash Bobby Bragan, the Machiavellian manager, is working on a diabolical plot to thaw them out. 'Last year we won 20 of our last 26 games. If we can start out the same way, we'll still have a good year at the gate. And if everything works out the way I hope it will, fans will be clamoring for tickets in Wisconsin.'" But the question of whether power alone would be enough to win in the NL in 1965 was answered differently in other quarters. Fresco Thompson, a Dodgers vice president whose team was confronting the opposite problem - overpowering pitching, underwhelming hitting - was asked about that conundrum when the Braves and Dodgers played earlier in March. "You can get beat 9-8 as well as 1-0," he replied - prophetically, as it turned out. "In 1929 when I was with the Phillies, we had six .300 hitters and I was the worst - at .329. Where did it get us? In the ashcan, as usual."

Daley was right about the "boycott" by Milwaukee fans, who had made it clear, despite Bragan's lofty pronouncements, that they would not buy tickets to 1965 Braves games in significant numbers if the Braves themselves would directly profit. On March 18, Teams Inc announced that it had purchased outright, for $35,000, *all* of the remaining tickets for the Braves' home opener on April 15. "Opening Day is now a Milwaukee promotion," Edmund Fitzgerald said. "It is no longer a Braves promotion." Teams Inc's estimate was that a crowd of 25,000 would enable the group to recoup its investment, including the 27 1/2 cents per ticket it would owe the visiting Cubs under major league rules at the time. Any proceeds beyond that would be put into the escrow fund to obtain a replacement team for Milwaukee; a capacity crowd, Fitzgerald estimated, would net between $20,000 and $25,000. "We're not looking to just break even," Fitzgerald said. "If we are to show others that Milwaukee is truly major league, we must fill the stadium to (its 43,000-seat) capacity and more."

Teams Inc called the buyout "Stand Up For Milwaukee Day." Ticket prices would not be raised from 1964 levels, which ranged from $4.10 for mezzanine boxes and $3.10 for lower-deck boxes to 75 cents for bleacher seats (50 cents for kids). Selig, in charge of ticket sales under the previous agreement with the Braves, said 1,150 season tickets had been sold. After Opening Day, the Braves would have to sell tickets on their own. But Selig remained optimistic. "The Phillies sold 1,500 season tickets in 1964," he said, "and they ended up drawing 1.5 milion (actually 1,425,891). The club you put on the field is your best salesman." As a more tangible salesman, Selig brought on Johnny Logan, who had announced his retirement as a player the previous month after spending 13 years in the majors (10 1/2 of them with the Braves) and had obtained a job selling paint in Milwaukee. Logan sold about 40 tickets on behalf of Teams Inc despite his misgivings about having anything to do, even indirectly, with the Braves. "I don't think the Braves ever had good public relations," he said. "The McHale regime has really hurt us, and Birdie (Tebbetts) engineered those bad trades (that cost the Braves Logan, Bob Buhl, Billy Bruton, Joe Adcock and Don McMahon, among others). I'm not here to spread moral support for those carpetbaggers. I'm trying to help the civic-minded people in Teams Inc to keep major league baseball alive here."

The Braves in 1961 had traded Logan to Pittsburgh, where he played until the end of the 1963 season when he went to Japan and played for the Nankai Hawks in 1964 at age 38. His team won the Japanese World Series despite his .189 average over 98 games. Logan at his peak was known for his lightness on his feet at shortstop, but he also was known as the Upper Midwest's answer to Yogi Berra when it came to the English language. Asked, at the time he retired, whether he had established a residence in Japan during his year there, Logan replied: "Nah, it cost too much to live there. So I communicated." Logan as a player was almost as well known for his malaprops as for his All-Star caliber work at shortstop. Once, upon receiving an award, he said, "I will perish this trophy forever." Another time, told that a newspaper's mistake was a typographical error, he replied, "The hell it was. It was a clean base hit."

Teams Inc also sent out pamphlets prepared by advertising exeuctive Ben Barkin to sports editors and political figures around the country, explaining its plight and its proposed remedy. Though Barkin had no illusions about national opinion changing the view of almost all MLB owners that major league baseball would be better off long-term in Atlanta than it would be in Milwaukee, the pamphlets and the overriding concern over the long-term effects of the Milwaukee abandonment did prompt a number of columns and editorials that called attention to the

Milwaukee situation. It also gave credence to those who thought, even before the Braves' move became official, that the ship of baseball was rudderless and headed toward reefs, one of which was on the western shore of Lake Michigan.

Perhaps the most widely-read sportswriter during this time was that of Jimmy Cannon, who in 1965 was composing a syndicated column for the *New York Journal-American* and winding down a sportswriting career that was the last of its kind in a profession that already was beginning the process of consolidation, condensation and homogenization. In his 1973 book *No Cheering in The Press Box*, Chicago sportswriter Jerome Holtzman chronicled the history of sportswriting up to that time by interviewing 18 sportswriters whose work collectively spanned almost three-quarters of a century. Holtzman described Cannon as the last of the sportswriters whose skills were such that they often were sent to cover non-sports stories - such as, in Cannon's case, the kidnapping and murder of Charles Lindbergh's infant son and the trial and execution of Bruno Richard Hauptmann in connection with that crime. Holtzman, in *No Cheering in The Press Box*, wrote of Cannon: "Jimmy Cannon was the most distinctive sportswriter of his time, as his big-brother friend Damon Runyon had been in the previous generation. But Cannon, unlike Runyon, never wrote fiction. He was an essayist, a master of the epigram and the memorable phrase. Though he generally viewed the sporting scene as entertainment, an extension of show business, he was also a vigorous curmudgeon, alert and eager to strike at hypocrisy and social injustice."

Cannon was a lifelong New Yorker who rarely wrote about goings-on in other cities, especially late in his career, but his outrage over the Milwaukee situation oozed through his column on March 24. It read, in part: "The Braves are being run like a floating crap game. But a guy dealing dice up an alley would get slugged with a piece of lead pipe if he rousted - repeat, rousted - the suckers with such brutal contempt. The guys who control the Braves don't even recognize contracts. A document held them in Milwaukee for another year, but they attempted to welsh on it. It didn't matter that the stadium was built for them with public funds ... it (the uprooting of the franchise) is one of the most disgraceful propositions in American sports. What they are doing damages all baseball. But the speeches go on and baseball is described as the noble endeavor of principled men. The hell it is ... Kids will learn many things from this, and none of it will make this nation a better place to be."

San Francisco Examiner sports editor Curley Grieve, like former *Milwaukee Journal* sports editor Russ Lynch in 1952 and 1953, had played a leading role in the successful effort to bring major league baseball to his city. On the Braves' situation, he wrote: "It is a melodrama framed in black ... Milwaukee's fate is unfortunate and undeserved ... the striking success of baseball there must have had some influence on the Giants and Dodgers moving west (because) Milwaukee had broken a 50-year pattern (with no major league franchise moves). To lose the Braves is surgery without anesthesia and County Stadium will be a painful and expensive monument to a better past."

The *Minneapolis Tribune's* Dick McCollum, whose constituency also could thank Milwaukee for the major league status that the Twin Cities had attained in 1961, wrote: "It must be kept in mind that the owners of the Braves did not leave Milwaukee because baseball failed there. They left because they saw more lush pastures elsewhere. Had the Braves ownership identified itself with the city as the Twins' owners have identified themselves with Minnesota, Atlanta would have to look elsewhere for a team." McCollum further predicted that Milwaukee, "with its new aggressive line, will have no trouble establishing itself as a logical site, maybe the most logical site, for an expansion franchise. If it results in an American League team, so much the better. A Minnesota-Wisconsin rivalry in baseball would be good for everyone (as it became and remained after the Brewers joined the AL in 1970)."

Lou Perini, though only a 10 percent owner of the Braves and completely distanced from their day-to-day operation by 1965, couldn't resist chiming in, even though by 1965 few in Milwaukee cared much about his take on the situation. He repeated the sentiment earlier expressed by Braves' officials - that the team, for the good of baseball, should be allowed to move to Atlanta as soon as it could get its vans packed, though he did suggest Milwaukee be provided with neutral-site games until a new team moved there. "We'll suffer through 1965," he said, "but the one that will be hurt will be Milwaukee. The (courtroom) game that Milwaukee is taking is a very serious one. If attendance falls off badly, and I'm afraid it will, Milwaukee will kill itself (as a future home of major league baseball)." Perini also blamed the Milwaukee press for the sentiment against the Braves, just as he had blamed the Boston press for the demise of the Boston Braves.

Local teenagers, almost all of whom had grown up with the Braves, took a somewhat more neutral - some might say, indifferent - view of the Braves' likely departure. The *Sentinel* interviewed about a dozen students at Wauwatosa West High, and some of their responses were more insightful than the rhetoric that was spewing forth from the combatants. From Gilbert Sutcliffe: "I don't think that pleading with the people to get them to the games is the answer ... if they don't have the interest, maybe Milwaukee doesn't deserve to have a major league team. I go to the Braves games quite a bit, and I think the Braves have done everything it's conceivable to do." Linda Schierow said: "I think whoever wants to go (should attend games) just the way they did before, not because of (the franchise shift). They should go to enjoy the game, not to prove that Milwaukee isn't a bush league town." Opined Timothy Wax: "No matter what you do, you're going to have trouble. There are people who, because of the ill will that has been aroused, will say, 'Why should I support them?' But I think we should support the Braves. If you don't, it's going to give Milwaukee a bad reputation as a baseball town." Deborah Landmann: "I really think it's hopeless to try to get the support of the people. Everything they've tried to do to keep them here has failed." Kristin Sauter: "The Braves are just moving away so they can be appreciated. I don't think they are appreciated any more the way they used to be. I think there are more important sports. With baseball, you have to sit there and wait and wait for action."

Everybody knew that a bad Braves team would play before acres of empty seats in 1965, but nobody knew how Milwaukee would react if the Braves were to become contenders, and the signs from Florida continued to be largely promising. Cloninger and Blasingame pitched well (seven shutout innings between them) against the A's, although the Braves lost 5-4. Gene Oliver hit a home run in the same game, and Ty Cline and Mike de la Hoz, both of whom were given little chance of making the club when spring training convened, were 6 for 13 and 6 for 14 respectively after that game. Aganst the Pirates in Fort Myers on March 24, the Braves won 12-10 as Torre hit two homers and drove in five runs, Felipe Alou got two hits to run his spring total to a team-high 13, and Mack Jones homered, tripled and drove in three runs as the Braves bombarded Bob Friend, a longtime nemesis. Friend finished his career 31-30 with a 3.61 ERA against the Braves. Those were extraordinary numbers when one considers that during most of Friend's career, which began in 1951, the Braves were among the best teams in the league while the Pirates almost always were among the worst - especially from 1951-57, when Pittsburgh finished last in the eight-team NL four times and seventh the other three seasons. Despite this, Friend had more wins against the Braves than against any other NL team.

The dispiriting news for the Braves was that Phil Niekro, Frank Lary and Dick Kelley all were shelled, and that the Braves almost blew an 11-2 lead before Dan Osinski shut the Pirates out in the ninth. Osinski had allowed only six hits and one earned run in eight innings to this point, and looked as if he would begin the season as the Braves' late-inning "stopper."

The Braves' next exhibition game was against the Mets the following day, and pitcher-coach Warren Spahn, to whom Mets manager Casey Stengel had completely entrusted the pitching staff, was scheduled to start against his former team. But Spahn changed the rotation so that he wouldn't face the Braves in this game or in any exhibition contest. "Why should I pitch against them now?" Spahn asked rhetorically. "I'll see them in May."

Spahn also said of Stengel, the same man who in 1942 as manager of the Boston Braves had cut him from the roster after he refused to intentionally hit a batter: "He's the most wonderful person I've ever been associated with. He has given me free rein with the pitchers, and whatever I've done, he's backed me up." His opinion of Bragan? "No comment." Bragan, on the other hand, had plenty to say about Spahn. "I hope he pitches every time they come to our park. We'll fill the park. Winning 12 games for the Mets is the equivalent to winning 16 for the Braves, and if I felt he could win 16 for the Braves, he'd still be with us ... I figure the loss of Warren Spahn is addition by subtraction."

The Braves lost the game 6-1, committing four errors and a passed ball and dropping their spring-training record to 6-6. Billy O'Dell started and worked four innings, giving up five hits and one earned run as Bragan continued to deliberate over whether to use O'Dell as a starter or as a reliever during the regular season.

On March 26, Sandy Alomar made a belated bid to earn a middle-infield position, collecting three hits and turning a game-ending double play with a slick pivot in a 9-5 win over Minnesota in Orlando. The Braves cuffed Twins starter Mudcat Grant, who would go on to win 21 games for the AL pennant-winning Twins that summer. Milwaukee amassed seven hits and six earned runs against Grant in three innings. Bragan, whose stated opinions on players were as variable as the steamy spring weather in Florida, said of Alomar: "He has been absolutely amazing. You'd think he never had played anywhere but second base. (Alomar had been primarily a shortstop through his career.) I almost think that if the season were to start today, I'd go with him at second base (instead of Frank Bolling)." Cloninger pitched five innings, giving up only one hit and retiring 14 straight batters, but he was upstaged in the Milwaukee newspaper reports by Warren Spahn. Pitching for the Mets against the Yankees in Fort Lauderdale, Spahn spaced six hits and a single run over six innings and drove in three runs with a home run, a single and a sacrifice fly. (Spahn batted .194 with 35 homers and 189 RBI over his 21-season career. Don Drysdale, generally remembered as the best-hitting pitcher of the 1950s and 1960s, batted .186 with 29 homers and 113 RBI over his 14-year career.)

The next day, onetime $500 acquisition Phil Niekro got his first extended work of the spring, and shut out the Pirates over 4 2/3 innings in a 3-2 Braves loss. Bragan had been trying to convince Niekro, who had pitched in 10 games (all in relief) in his 1964 major-league debut season, to diversify his pitching portfolio so that he could use his knuckleball as an off-speed pitch rather than as a tactical mainframe. The Braves' starting pitcher that day was Arnold Umbach, who had pitched in one game for the Braves in 1964 but didn't appear in the majors in 1965. The next year, after the Braves moved to Atlanta, he was in 22 games, then disappeared from the majors. During the spring of 1965, though, Niekro and Umbach were fighting for jobs, and Bragan thought Niekro might have the advantage if he could emerge as a starter and as more than a knuckleball specialist. Consequently, Niekro threw his knuckleball sparingly during most of the 1965 season. It wasn't until Bragan was fired during the 1966 season and Billy Hitchcock took over that the Braves committed to Niekro, then 27, as a starter and as a knuckleballer. The result, of course, was a 24-year career that included 318 wins and a plaque in the Hall of Fame.

The rest of the starting lineup against the Pirates consisted of Ty Cline in center field, Mathews at third base, Felipe Alou at first base, Lee Maye in left field, Joe Torre catching, Mack Jones in right field, Denis Menke at shortstop, and Alomar at second base. Even without Aaron, it was a formidable batting order. Jones at this point was playing well enough to seriously threaten Lee Maye's center-field job; he was second on the team in homers (3) and hits (15) and led in RBI (9) and triples (4). Bragan also indicated that Rico Carty, who had left the team briefly to attend to a family matter, would be used primarily in the outfield. Felipe Alou, Bragan said, was a more reliable first baseman and would play at that position much of the time. (Like many of Bragan's spring pronouncements, this was to change soon enough.) The pitching, meanwhile, continued to show promise. On March 29 against the Phillies in Clearwater, Wade Blasingame, saying he had "pitched out" of shoulder soreness that had hampered him throughout the spring, logged seven shutout innings in a 5-0 win. In his four previous outings, Blasingame had given up 10 runs in 11 innings. In the eighth, Niekro walked the bases loaded with one out, but Dan Osinski came on to strike out Dick Stuart and Alex Johnson - two of the more menacing, if not proficient, hitters in the NL - to retire the side. In the ninth, the Phils loaded the bases again as Osinski gave up two walks and a hit, but he struck out Johnny Briggs and got Johnny Callison on a game-ending grounder.

That same day, Eugene Grobschmidt was in Washington, D.C., conferring with Rep. Emanuel Cellar (D-N.Y.), who during his 50-year Congressional career had established himself as the baseball industry's most persistent political opponent. The Supreme Court in 1922 had upheld a challenge by the defunct Federal League to baseball's antitrust exemption, in effect ruling that baseball's internal affairs were its own business and nobody else's, but Cellar had long believed that MLB's exclusionary control of professional baseball's product, locations and operations constituted monopoly and restraint of trade as defined by the Sherman Antitrust Act. As chairman of the House Subcommitee on Study of Monopoly Power, Cellar in 1951 - at a time when no franchise had shifted since 1903 - began holding hearings, and continued to do so periodically into the 1960s. During Ford Frick's tenure as commissioner of baseball (1951-65), he was called to testify during Congressional antitrust hearings no less than 17 times. In the long run, the hearings changed nothing; in 1965, baseball's antitrust exemption read exactly as it had in 1951 - and in 1922.

One of the more famous hearings brought Casey Stengel to the stand. Stengel, the Yankees' manager at the time, responded to a question with a rambling, aimless discourse - "Stengelese" - of the sort into which Stengel, a shrewd and calculating man who knew how to cultivate reporters to his advantage, often launched when he wanted to avoid a direct answer to a question but didn't want "his" reporters to walk away with empty notebooks. At this subcommittee hearing, he achieved just that, talking for a half-hour and saying virtually nothing. Mickey Mantle followed him to the witness stand, and when he was asked how he felt about baseball's antitrust exemption, he replied, "My opinion on that is just about the same as Casey's." The room broke into hysterical laughter, and the hearing soon was adjourned.

In 1965, Cellar's most significant achievement in opposition to the antitrust exemption had been to force Walter O'Malley to turn over financial records that proved O'Malley's Dodgers, despite his claims to the contrary, had turned a significant profit in Brooklyn before moving to Los Angeles in 1958. But after he met with Grobschmidt and other county and state officials, Grobschmidt reported that Cellar had told him he believed the Braves' behavior represented a strong case against baseball and the antitrust exemption. Cellar offered to turn over to Grobschmidt the paperwork involved in previous litigation against baseball. Grobschmidt subsequently used this feedback to convince the county board, and John Doyne, that the antitrust action was worth pressing even as the expenses of doing so became prohibitive.

The month ended on what some must have thought was an optimistic note, though it almost certainly would not have turned out well if it had been true. Frank (Trader) Lane, who had sued Kansas City A's owner Charley Finley shortly after Finley had fired him as general manager in 1961, was quoted as saying that Finley intended to move his team to Milwaukee as soon as the Braves vacated County Stadium, even though Finley's lease at Kansas City Municipal Stadium ran through the 1967 season. Finley, who ran an insurance agency out of Chicago and had once bid unsuccessfully to buy the White Sox, twice previously had been blunted by AL owners when he asked to move, first to Atlanta and then to Dallas-Fort Worth. He quickly dismissed Lane's Milwaukee comments, and nothing further came of them.

The opening of the 1965 season was now less than two weeks away. The Braves by the end of March had sold 1,225 season tickets and Teams Inc had sold 12,000 tickets for the home opener April 15 against the Cubs. But the Braves were operating, by their own admission, with about one-third of the Milwaukee staff they had employed at the start of 1964. Tickets for 1965 games had not yet been printed, and would not be available until at least April 7. Even the County Stadium kitchen where food was prepared for staff and players had been ransacked. Its stove, refrigerator and other necessary equipment all were gone. Presumably, they were on their way to Atlanta.

Primacy, then Privacy

• • •

AFTER ALMOST THREE YEARS OF uncertainty that morphed into betrayal, the question of whether the Milwaukee Braves would become the Atlanta Braves in 1966 - if not sooner - no longer lingered as the 1965 swan-song season approached.

It was replaced by another question: Had the Braves' ownership deliberately created an artificial hardship case to foment indifference in Milwaukee and hasten the Braves' departure for Atlanta?

In many minds, then and 50 years later, the answer was yes, though in retrospect, the evidence has to be described as circumstantial.

The Braves since 1960 had unloaded players whose salaries added up to more than $300,000: Spahn, Burdette, Buhl, Logan, Crandall, Bruton, Schoendienst and other key members of the team that had come so close to winning four straight World Series from 1956-59. It wasn't a purge of the sort Charles O. Finley undertook in 1976, at the start of the free-agency era, when he reduced an Oakland Athletics team that had won five straight division titles and three consecutive World Series to a 54-108 team within four seasons. Nor did it approach what Connie Mack twice did with Philadelphia A's squads that were arguably among the best teams of all time. In 1915, Mack broke up a team that had won four pennants and two World Series in five years because of the incursion of the outlaw Federal League - the organization that lasted as a major league for only two years, but prompted the upgrading of the two existing leagues' salary structure and forced the question of baseball's antitrust exemption into the Supreme Court. Mack, who had invested heavily in the stock market during the 1920s and lost most of his personal wealth in the 1929 crash, performed a similar dispersal starting in 1932 with a team that had won three straight pennants and two World Series with future Hall of Famers Mickey Cochrane, Lefty Grove, Jimmie Foxx and Milwaukee native Al Simmons. Later, toward the end of his 50-year tenure as manager of the A's, Mack said candidly that the ideal scenario would be to have his team finish fourth - good enough to encourage the fans to come out in significant numbers, but bad enough that he wouldn't be forced to pay his players championship-team-level wages.

Ownership's howls of indignation throughout the 1965 season notwithstanding, the Braves were hugely profitable throughout most of their first 10 seasons in Milwaukee, and most of their losses in 1963 and 1964 - perhaps $100,000 in all during those two years - were due to the diminished product on the field. But even though they hadn't been serious National League pennant contenders since 1959, the Braves still had two of the game's luminaries, Hank Aaron and Eddie Mathews, and at least from the long-ball standpoint, their lineup still was as intimidating as any in baseball, save perhaps San Francisco's. Distant and aloof as Lou Perini and Bill Bartholomay were as owners of the Milwaukee

Braves, there's little concrete evidence to support the assertion that either deliberately undermined their own product, as Finley and Mack (and other owners throughout the 20th century) had done to their teams. The Milwaukee Braves, after all, never came close to having a losing season, and even in 1965, tempting cash offers for at least two players, Mathews and Torre, are known to have been turned down. And when it became apparent early in 1965 that the Braves desperately needed another starting pitcher, they got one, trading Lee Maye to the Astros for Ken Johnson.

Perhaps the integrity-of-the-product question, then, is best asked this way: Did the Braves, unwilling to risk the fallout from taking a pennant-winning team out of Milwaukee, deliberately do less than they could have done in 1965 to improve the existing product after the Bartholomay group bought the team? After all, the last thing Bartholomay and his partners wanted was to dispel the notion they themselves had created - that Milwaukee no longer was a financially viable baseball territory and that moving the franchise to Atlanta was the only realistic alternative?

Frank Thomas thought the franchise had been putting profit ahead of productivity throughout the 1960s, and used himself as an example in 2013 when he visited Milwaukee and gave a talk at a Milwaukee Braves Historical Association dinner. Thomas, an outfielder who also could play both corner-infield positions, hit 286 homers during a 16-year career that ended in 1966. The Braves had acquired him from the Cubs early in the 1961 season, and at age 32, he had responded with a .284 average, 25 homers and 67 RBI in 124 games for a team that led the league in homers with 188. "After the season," Thomas said in 2013, "I asked (general manager John) McHale about '62, and he said I would be his left fielder. I said, 'If that's the case, you bring out any contract you want, and I'll sign it. But if you intend to trade me, please don't let me sign the contract.' He said fine, and I signed. Then in November, I was sold to the Mets. And they didn't have anyone to replace me. McHale was a pup out of Branch Rickey."

Rickey, in the days before player agents were in vogue, was a master at circumlocution and was notorious for misleading or outright lying to players during salary talks, paying them at less than market value and then unloading them even when they were still productive, even if it damaged his team in the short term. Usually, his motive was making money not only for his owner, but also - maybe *especially* - for himself, because he always insisted on a clause in his contract that gave him a share of his team's profits at the end of each season (much as Billy Beane did many years later with the "Moneyball" Oakland Athletics, of whom he was also a part owner). The best example of Rickey's operating procedure came in 1953, when Rickey was president of the Pirates. His only player of any quality was future Hall of Famer Ralph Kiner; even though Kiner was at his peak and was the team's only legitimate drawing card, Rickey cut Kiner's salary from $90,000 to $75,000, then traded him to the Cubs in a 10-player deal that also involved the Cubs paying the Pirates $150,000.

Eight years before, when Rickey was with the Dodgers, he took full - and, under 21st-century scrutiny, probably illegal - financial advantage of the Jackie Robinson signing. Robinson was a member of the Kansas City Monarchs at the time Rickey signed him for the Dodgers organization in 1945, but Rickey simply ignored Robinson's contract with the Negro League team. The

Monarchs got nothing in the transaction because there *was* no transaction, and they weren't in position to protest because of all that Robinson's signing meant to black players hoping to reach the majors. And Rickey, who so often was and is projected as a paternal figure in Robinson's life and career, didn't extend any such affection to his financial dealings with Robinson. He paid Robinson $5,000 in 1947, and $21,000 in 1949, the year Robinson won his only MVP award.

Conversely, later in 1947 when Bill Veeck signed Larry Doby and made him the American League's first black player, Veeck purchased Doby's contract from Effa Manley, owner of Doby's Negro League team, the Newark Bears. In 1952, the Boston Braves bought Hank Aaron's contract from the Indianapolis Clowns for $10,000.

Braves fans who stood by them during their last year in Milwaukee grew increasingly suspicious during March, when the Braves, despite their need for at least one more starting pitcher, didn't pursue deals that could have landed them Al Jackson and Bob Bruce, among others. On the first day of April 1965, another disgruntled ex-Brave, Billy Hoeft, made an even more specific accusation. Hoeft was from Oshkosh and was one of only seven Wisconsin natives to play for the Braves while they were in Milwaukee. (Andy Pafko was the best-known of the others.) Hoeft was a well-traveled lefthander who had been a 21-game winner for the Tigers in 1956 and then had several good years as a reliever with Baltimore.

After joining the Braves in 1964, he had helped congeal a vulnerable Braves bullpen with 42 appearances, a 4-0 record, a

3.60 ERA and four saves. At only 32, Hoeft seemingly remained of use to the Braves in 1965, especially given the fact the Braves had no other experienced lefties in the bullpen. (The Braves, of course, had picked up Billy O'Dell from the Giants in February 1965, but on April 1, Bragan still hadn't decided whether O'Dell should start or relieve.) And Hoeft saw sinister overtones in his release by Milwaukee the previous October.

Hoeft told *Journal* reporter Bob Wolf that in his opinion, the Braves management's main concern in 1964 had been to win just enough to keep the fans interested, but not enough to make the World Series and perhaps, by doing so, save the franchise for Milwaukee. He said the fact Bragan used 110 different lineups during the 162-game NL season "was aimed at preventing the Braves from winning the pennant." He also verbally flayed Bragan and his handling of the pitching staff, pointing to the use of Clay Carroll and Dan Schneider as starting pitchers in a Labor Day doubleheader at Wrigley Field when better pitchers were rested and available. "We still had a chance (at the pennant)," Hoeft said. "Fortunately, we won both games, but the starters didn't last more than two or three innings apiece. The lineup changes were demoralizing to the guys. They didn't know where they were hitting. They didn't know where they were playing. The way he (Bragan) did things, you had to get teed off. And they would have been better off if they had come out and told the people they were moving. They told little white lies all year, and that made the people mad.

"I pick the Braves to win this (1965) year. They've got great power and their pitching staff is good enough if Bragan leaves them alone. They're only hurting in one place: They got rid of me. Before the season's over, they'll wish they had me back." (As it turned out, Hoeft was released by the Tigers before the start of the season, and although he pitched two more seasons, with the Cubs and Giants, he never regained his former effectiveness.)

"I see that Hoeft has been reading Warren Spahn's copy," Bragan said. "It would have been better to take a champion-ship team than a fifth-place team to Atlanta (if the transfer had been approved and consummated in time for the 1965 season). Actually, I don't think it's worthy of comment."

Neither was Hank Fischer's pitching in his bid to establish himself in the starting rotation and win "at least 15" games, as he had predicted the previous month. Fischer worked four innings in a 4-2 loss to the Tigers on the same day as Hoeft's tirade, giving up five hits and three runs, one of which was unearned because of an error by Fischer as he tried to throw out a runner at second after a sacrifice bunt. Jim Northrup hit a home run later in the game off Phil Niekro, another starting-rotation candidate, and Denny McLain limited the Braves to three hits over seven shutout innings. The loss left the Braves 10-9 in the Grapefruit League, although Eddie Mathews was batting .349 for the spring and Sandy Alomar (.314) continued to press Woodward and Bolling for middle-infield playing time. Bragan, in fact, said his intention at that point was to position Alomar at second and Denis Menke at shortstop. Frank Bolling would remain on the team, but as a reserve. Alomar could play either position, but he expressed a preference for second base. "You can bobble the ball once or twice (at second) and still throw the man out," he said. "if you play shortstop and you bobble it, you get an error. I like second base."

Another Sandy, though, cornered most baseball conversation on April 2, when the Dodgers sent Sandy Koufax back to Los Angeles from their spring base in Vero Beach, Fla., to be examined by famed orthopedic surgeon Robert Kerlan. The Dodgers, of course, had ridden Koufax's left arm to World Series championships in 1959 and 1963, and had disappeared from the 1964 NL race - of which, at 58-57, they were only peripheral participants anyway - after Koufax injured his left (pitching) arm on August 16 and was lost for the season, taking with him a 19-5 season and a 1.74 ERA.

Koufax's circulatory problem had aggravated a "traumatic arthritic condition" in Koufax's arm, and even though he had pitched 30 innings during spring training in 1965 and had completed two games, he awoke on the morning of April 2 with his arm virtually immobilized. The 1965 and 1966 seasons were probably the two best of his career, but after 1964 he never pitched without excruciating pain. Kerlan also told him the circulatory problem was non-operable, and that if he continued to pitch, he might lose the use of his left arm later in life. Two years later, that possibility was the primary reason he retired from baseball at age 31; it also played a role in his tag-team holdout with Don Drysdale during the spring of 1966. (In 1964, Giants pitcher Jack Sanford underwent what could be called the first version of "Tommy John surgery" in an effort to relieve a circulatory problem similar to Koufax's. During an 11-hour operation, a blood vessel was grafted from Sanford's ankle and implanted in his pitching arm. Sanford, a 24-game winner for the Giants in 1962, won four of his first five starts in 1965, but didn't win a game for San Francisco thereafter, and was sold to the Angels in August. He enjoyed a rebirth in Anaheim in 1966, going 13-7 with a 3.83

ERA, but was only 4-4 with a 5.12 ERA with the Angels and A's in 1967, and retired after that season at age 38.)

The Dodgers, of course, had fortified their starting rotation by acquiring Claude Osteen from the Senators in the Frank Howard deal, but neither they nor anyone else in baseball needed to be told that the Dodgers without Koufax (and virtually without long-ball power) would be hard-pressed to challenge teams like the Giants, Reds, Pirates and Braves. Even so, the latest Las Vegas odds had the Dodgers as the 2-to-1 favorites to win the pennant, followed by the Giants and Cardinals (3-to-1), the Phillies (4-to-1) and the Reds (5-to-1). The Vegas bookmakers, apparently mindful of the Braves' pitching quandary and their dependence on the long ball, had dropped them to 8-to-1.

If Braves management was concerned over the team's inconsistency in the spring, it was jubilant over one other announcement: The Braves already had sold 25,000 tickets for their three-game exhibition series at the brand-new Atlanta-Fulton County Stadium later in April. It would be the first athletic event at the park that would house the Atlanta Braves in 1966. Teams Inc, meanwhile, had decided that given the fact it had bought out County Stadium for the final Milwaukee Braves opener, the event should be treated as a showcase of Milwaukee as a baseball city. Toward that end, it considered a reunion of the 1953 Braves, though some of them wouldn't be available because they were still in baseball in 1965 and would be playing elsewhere that day, and two were dead. Vern Bickford had died of stomach cancer in 1960 at age 39; and Dave Jolly had succumbed to a brain tumor in 1963 at age 38.

Mets pitching coach-pitcher Warren Spahn said he would change the Mets' rotation so that he could pitch the day before the Braves' home opener, and sought and received permission from the Mets to travel to Milwaukee for the Braves' final Opening Day there. "If I can be of any service to the people of your city and state, I owe it to them," Spahn told *Sentinel* sports editor Lloyd Larson. "I mean the people of Milwaukee and Wisconsin - not the Braves' management."

Charlie Grimm, in 1965 a Cubs vice president, and Lew Burdette and Bob Buhl, who were on the Chicago roster, were obliged to be there. Of course, Eddie Mathews, the only original Milwaukee Brave who was still with the team in 1965, would be there, and so would Johnny Logan, now a fulltime Milwaukee resident. Andy Pafko, who was managing the Braves' Class A farm team in West Palm Beach, indicated he would come; so did Billy Bruton, who had hit the 10th-inning home run - the first homer of his career, and the only HR he was to hit that season - against the Cardinals to win the 1953 home opener. Bruton in 1965 had retired from baseball and was working in public relations for Chrysler in Detroit, and later became right-hand-man to chairman Lee Iococca after Iococca joined the automaker. Jack Dittmer had an auto dealership in Iowa, and Sid Gordon was in the clothing business in New York City; both indicated they would come. Max Surkont, the winning pitcher in the 1953 season opener, also accepted Teams Inc's invitation.

While Selig and Teams Inc were trying to maximize the Opening Day buyout, Bragan still had roster decisions to make, though in 1965 some roster moves could be deferred until more than a month after the start of the season. Major league rules then allowed teams to keep 28 men on their active rosters until May 15, at which point they had to be trimmed to 25. And at a time when pitching staffs usually consisted of nine or 10 pitchers (instead of the 12- and 13-man staffs that had became commonplace by the 2000s), managers had multiple options at the other eight positions. Tommie Aaron, Hank's younger brother, had worked his way into the conversation at first base with a strong spring, and the *Sentinel's* Red Thisted, who had covered Milwaukee professional baseball continuously since 1926, guessed that the younger Aaron would open the season at first, with Carty in left field and Felipe Alou in right. (Hank Aaron was still questionable for Opening Day because of his ankle ailment, and it was announced he would stay in Florida for treatment after the Braves broke camp on April 7.) Maye and Jones, Thisted thought, would alternate in center, and Ty Cline seemed likely to make the club as a defensive specialist and pinch-hitter after leading the NL with 14 pinch-hits (in only 40 at-bats) in 1964.

Among the pitchers, Clay Carroll was making a bid to start the season in the rotation. He lost 3-2 to the Phillies in Clearwater on April 2, but gave up only five hits and an unearned run in seven innings, and had surrendered only two earned runs in 20 innings during the spring. The next day, the Braves sent infielder Woody Woodward and pitcher Arnie Umbach down to Triple-A, reducing the active roster to 26 - two under the Opening Day limit. This seemed to indicate that Bragan and McHale, contrary to what their detractors had been saying and writing, actually were considering adding players before Opening Day instead of conducting a fire sale. Starting pitching was an obvious priority. After Tony Cloninger authored a nine-hit complete game in a 3-1 victory over the Astros on April 4, coach Ken

Silvestri said Cloninger was "the only starter who's ready (for Opening Day)." Cloninger had thrown 26 innings during spring training, allowing only 20 hits, five walks and six earned runs. Although Bragan had not confirmed it, the assumption was that Cloninger would be the Opening Day starter. "I've never started an Opening Day game before, even in the minors," he said. "I'd certainly consider it a big privilege." It also appeared that Bragan had backtracked - as he often did - on his earlier pronouncement that Sandy Alomar would open the season at second base. Frank Bolling was at second and Menke was at shortstop for the game against the Astros.

In Los Angeles, Dr. Robert Kerlan said it remained possible that Sandy Koufax would be able to pitch in 1965 despite his career-threatening arm injury. "We will try to get him to the point where he can play with the condition," said Kerlan, who said limiting Koufax to one outing per week was a possibility. "We're not trying to cure anything." As it turned out, the treatment during the last two years of Koufax's career usually involved administering painkillers, and despite Kerlan's assessment, numerous baseball men were quoted as saying they believed Koufax's career might be over. But he was back pitching within a week, and the one-game-work-week suggestion never was put into practice. In fact, Koufax, whose inning load in a season had surpassed 255 innings only once before 1965, pitched 335 innings in 1965 and 323 in 1966, leading the NL both years.

In Fort Lauderdale, Fla., Yankees third baseman Clete Boyer was released from jail on $500 bail after being accused of slugging a male model (the charge soon was dropped, and Boyer threatened a lawsuit), and Kansas City A's first baseman Jim

Gentile was fined $500 by owner Charles O. Finley for directing an obscene gesture at fans in Bradenton, Fla., during an exhibition game there. Gentile said he would not pay the fine, and demanded to be traded. Gentile, 31, had hit 152 home runs in the previous five years, including a 1961 season during which he hit .302 with 46 homers and 141 RBI for the Orioles while finishing third behind Roger Maris and Mickey Mantle (and ahead of Detroit's Norm Cash, who hit .361 that year with 41 homers and 142 RBI) in the AL Most Valuable Player balloting. But his skills diminished precipitously after 1964; in June 1965, Finley traded Gentile to Houston, and he was an undistinguished reserve for the Astros and Indians before retiring after the 1966 season. At the Minnesota Twins' spring-training site in Orlando, Fla., manager Sam Mele and his mercurial shortstop, Zoilo Versalles, argued heatedly, and Mele fined Versalles $300 for "failure to give me his best effort." Versalles apparently got the message, going on to win the American League Most Valuable Player award that season as the Twins cruised to the franchise's first AL pennant since 1933, when it was still located in Washington.

In Austin, Texas, McHale appeared at a banquet and, in response to a question by an *Austin American* reporter about the Braves' intention of keeping their Texas League affiliate in the Texas capital city, said: "We'd like to stay as long as we are welcome. It is our desire to stay here as long as we can, not just one or two years." It was almost a word-for-word playback of what Bartholomay and McHale had said in 1963 and 1964 about Milwaukee when the rumors of an imminent move first made print. As it turned out, the Braves had no more intention of keeping their Double-A affiliate in Austin than they had of keeping their parent club in Milwaukee. They moved their Double-A farm team from Austin to Shreveport, La., after the 1967 season, and the Austin area was without professional baseball until 2000 when the Express, operating out of suburban Round Rock and owned by Hall of Fame pitcher Nolan Ryan, joined the Pacific Coast League.

As the regular season crept closer, so did the national realization that the conflict in Southeast Asia was not going to be a quick-thrust "banana war" like the numerous American interventions in Latin America and the Caribbean during the first half of the 20th century. The military on April 3 deployed 2,000 more enlisted personnel to Vietnam, increasing the troop presence there to 30,000. The first Wisconsin fatality was reported the same day: Army Captain Gerald C. Capele, 30, of Fond du Lac. Oregon Sen. Wayne Morse, one of the few Congressmen who had opposed the Vietnam intervention from the beginning even though both he and President Lyndon Johnson were Democrats, said: "Our hands are dripping with blood in Asia, to our everlasting discredit ... (The U.S.) is guilty of aggression in Vietnam and history will condemn us for it." Morse made his comments during a debate in Portland with Wisconsin Sen. William Proxmire, also a Democrat, who had won a special election to fill the Senate seat vacated by Joseph McCarthy's death in 1957. While the Proxmire-Morse discussion ostensibly was a debate, Proxmire echoed Morse's sentiments and remained a strident critic of the U.S involvement in Vietnam for the next decade. Johnson that same day announced a $1.3 billion federal commitment, as part of his Great Society template, to public education. The *Sentinel*, hewing to form, editorialized against LBJ's plan, insisting that the program was being steamrolled through the Democratic-controlled Congress for political reasons. It complained along virtually the same lines two days later when the House of Representatives approved Medicare, which the *Sentinel* described in a headline as a "$6 billion welfare bill." It also suggested, in a piece on its op-ed page, that "surrendering" in Vietnam meant endangering Alaska.

With world and national news events roiling, the Braves kept toiling. In West Palm Beach on April 7, the Braves beat the Dodgers 1-0 in 12 innings, with Bob Sadowski shutting out Los Angeles for eight innings and Osinski doing likewise over the final four. Gene Oliver singled home the winning run. The next day, the Braves traveled to Fort Lauderdale and beat the Yankees 4-1, with Clay Carroll registering 5 1/3 more shutout innings. "I'd say our trouble spot (starting pitching) is shaping up real well," Bragan said. Eddie Mathews, apparently settled in at No. 2 in the batting order, had two hits to raise his spring-training average to .357, and Felipe Alou hit his third homer of the spring. The Braves finished the Grapefruit League season with a 13-12 record; Gene Oliver was the team's leading hitter with a .370 average, and Osinski's 0.82 was the best ERA among the pitchers. Bragan announced that Carroll had beaten Fischer out for the "swing" spot in the starting rotation, which also would include Cloninger, Sadowski, Blasingame and Lemaster. O'Dell and Osinski would be the late-inning relievers.

Almost every edition of both Milwaukee papers continued to carry letters to the editor regarding the Braves' situation. One, printed in the *Journal* on April 8, suggested that the Hall of Fame be sent a package including Lou Perini's bank statements, and "several animated reproductions of famous baseball mouths, mainly McHale's with a foot in it and Bill Bartholomay talking out of the side of his." Oliver Kuechele added the thought that the package should include the plaque that Perini had sent Milwaukee after the 1953 season, thanking "the finest fans in all baseball." (The plaque remained in place at County Stadium until the park was torn down in 2001.) Warren Spahn, preparing for his new role as the Mets' pitcher-pitching coach, assigned himself to the Opening Day pitching slot. Asked by New York writers how he felt about the turmoil surrounding his old team, he said, "I wound up with the statement that it's not a matter of Milwaukee needing baseball but rather of baseball needing Milwaukee."

On April 9, the "Eighth Wonder of the World," the $35 million Houston Astrodome, was unveiled as the Astros played the Yankees in an exhibition game. Mickey Mantle had the first hit (a single), scored the first run and hit the first home run amid the orange, yellow and cerise hues and the architectural bedazzlement in the Astrodome that day as a capacity crowd of 47,879 was transfixed by the structure that many felt represented baseball's future. From the advertising standpoint, it did. The Astrodome's $2.1 million scoreboard, the first capable of animation, would net $18,000 per game night in 1965 for the Astros and Harris County. (The stadium's official name was the Harris County Domed Stadium.) Immediately, though, problems became apparent, particularly the glare from the opaque roof panels that made fly balls almost impossible to track. Astros outfielder Ron Davis said he caught only two of the 12 fly balls hit to him during batting practice, "and one of them was an accident. I just found the ball in my glove." General manager Paul Richards said it was "impossible" to play under those conditions. All 4,596 panels that comprised the roof subsequently was painted over, but with no sunshine penetrating the roof, the grass began to die. The field had to be reseeded several times during the 1965 season - leading, within the next year, to the search for an artificial surface. Monsanto won the contract to design and install the carpet, which became known - and before long, reviled - as "AstroTurf."

The glare situation notwithstanding, most NL players looked forward to playing in the Astrodome, and the Colt .45s-turned-Astros became baseball's prime attraction in 1965. After the Colt .45s drew an NL-worst 725,773 in 1964, the Astros played before 2,151,470 - second only to the Dodgers - in the Astrodome in 1965. Imposing and eye-popping as it was, though, the element that visiting players liked most about the Astrodome was that it wasn't Colt Stadium, the ballpark it replaced.

Houston had been granted its NL franchise on the condition that the Astrodome be built - plans for it had first been unveiled in 1952 - but the Colt .45s were to begin play in 1962, so they needed a temporary home. Buffalo Stadium, where the Texas League Buffs had played since 1928, was too small (14,000 seats) and too rickety, and unlike San Francisco's Seals Stadium and Los Angeles' Wrigley Field, couldn't be expanded or upgraded, even temporarily. So the Astros, at a cost of only $2 million, flung together Colt Stadium in what was to become the Astrodome parking lot. It held 33,000, but had no roof to protect the fans from the Texas heat. "No matter what ballpark they talk about, Colt Stadium was the hottest ballpark in the major leagues, ever," Rusty Staub, one of the franchise's early paragons, said later. As much of an inferno as the ballpark was, it was made even more uncomfortable by winged invaders. Richie Ashburn, the future

Hall of Famer who was winding down his career with the Mets in 1962, said after his first game at Colt Stadium: "Women in Houston don't wear perfume. They wear insect repellent." After the Astrodome was finished and the Colt .45s became the Astros, Colt Stadium sat vacant for several years until Harris County placed a lien on it to recoup back property taxes from the team. It was then sold to a group that transported it, piece by piece, to Torreon, Mexico. Later, the remnants of the park was sold to another Mexican League team, in Tampico. It was that team's regular-season home until 2000. Parts of it still remained at the Tampico site in 2016, though most of its accouterments had long since been cannibalized and sold.

Almost incidentally from a national standpoint, the fact the Milwaukee Braves would not be the Milwaukee Braves much longer was emphatically brought home the same day as the Astrodome's debut. The Braves played the first game, an exhibition contest against Detroit, in what was to become their new home - $18 million Atlanta Stadium. Earlier in the day, a motorcade consisting of about 40 vehicles transported the Braves from the Atlanta airport to a downtown reception as thousands lined the streets to welcome the team. (When the Braves arrived in Milwaukee from Boston in 1953, 12,000 people mobbed the train, and 60,000 turned out for a downtown rally.) *Journal* reporter Evans Kirkby covered the day's welcome-to-Atlanta activities, and wrote: "Under sunny spring skies, the city of Atlanta laughed Friday. For this was the day that the Braves came to town ... two young ladies daringly risked sunburn in scanty 'bunny' costumes, and Miss See Georgia First's costume was such to guarantee that Georgia would be seen second." Kirkby did grudgingly acknowledge that the park "has several advantages over Milwaukee. It's prettier, it's bigger and it's even more conveniently located. Atlanta's stadium is circular, eliminating all obstructive support columns. For another $9 million, they could even add a roof."

Bobby Bragan not surprisingly was both irrelevant and irreverent in his remarks at the reception. "I was reading where it was exactly 100 years ago to the day that Lee surrendered at Appomattox," he said, "and I couldn't help but think that now a band of Wisconsinites really surrendered to the city of Atlanta." Atlanta Mayor Ivan Allen apparently was still fighting the Civil War in his mind as well. "This is the happiest moment for Atlanta since General Sherman decided to head south for Savannah," he said.

As an afterthought, the Braves beat the Tigers 6-3 that night before a well-under-capacity crowd of 37,232, with Tommie Aaron hitting a three-run homer and Joe Torre contributing a two-run homer and a double that hit the first-base bag and caromed into the outfield. O'Dell shut down Detroit over the final 2 1/3 innings in relief of Denny Lemaster. The stadium operation indicated that if the Braves had indeed moved to Atlanta in time for the 1965 season, neither Atlanta nor its ballpark - on which ground had been broken only 51 weeks before - would have been ready. The parking-lot gates were not opened until an hour before game time, and only one-third of the 4,300 parking spaces (compared to County Stadium's 11,000) were available because of construction delays, creating a massive traffic jam that prevented many of the fans from getting into the stadium until well after the game began. Many of the concession stands and restrooms were unfinished and therefore not open. Some of the seats had not yet been installed, and others had not yet been painted. Unlike the early years in Milwaukee, the Braves' arrival in Atlanta was virtually ignored by the city's high-society exemplars. The *Atlanta Journal's* society editor wrote that "we're just recovering from the Jack Benny appearance last week. That was *terribly* social." The Braves and Tigers played two more games in Atlanta that weekend, drawing a total of 106,133 for the three-game series despite competition from a NASCAR race and the Masters golf tournament.

Milwaukee, meanwhile, was working toward securing what government officials thought was its transportation future. The county earmarked $135 million, most of it federal money, for a 14.3-mile link between the Stadium Freeway and what later became Interstate 794. Like much of the Interstate project in Milwaukee, this link was never built (nor was all but a two-mile stretch of the Stadium Freeway), but 800 buildings had already been acquired, most through the use of eminent domain, so that they could be leveled to make room for the new freeway. The Milwaukee County Parks Commission recommended that the county spend $2,259,000 on improvements to County Stadium, regardless of whether the Braves played there beyond 1965 or not. Racial tensions continued to escalate; a 36-year-old widow with four sons reported a cross-burning on the front lawn of their home on North 116th Street in Wauwatosa. The family had lived at that location since 1955, and had experienced no previous racial problems, and the woman expressed thanks to the white neighbors who came to her aid and comfort after the cross-burning.

By April 12, three days before the Braves' final Milwaukee home opener, Teams Inc reported that 17,000 tickets had been sold. Twelve thousand people showed up for a hastily-arranged "open house" at which Johnny Logan and other former Braves and Brewers signed autographs. The scoreboard, though, had only one advertisement, purchased by Marshall & Ilsley Bank; otherwise, it was blank. In 1953, the Miller Brewing Company had paid $75,000 for the scoreboard and purchased advertising on it for an additional $50,000.

After the end of the Tigers series, Bragan announced that Tommie Aaron would start at first base in the season opener in Cincinnati, and "Santos" Alomar, as he was listed on the roster in the Opening Day scorecard, would be the second baseman. Hank Aaron was not expected to start because of his ankle problem. Carty had suffered a back injury during the Atlanta series, and Mack Jones had lost his center field spot after striking out three times in the final game in Atlanta. The team had finished the exhibition season 16-13, with utility infielder Mike de la Hoz assuring his roster spot with a team-best .371 average. Gene Oliver had batted .346 with 13 RBI, Mathews had hit .319 with two homers and 11 RBI, and Lee Maye had finished at .334. Nobody else hit better than .300, but the team ERA was 2.90, with none of the pitchers who made the Opening Day roster registering an ERA higher than 3.46. Bragan predicted that the NL pennant race would involve six teams, and named the Reds and the defending World Series champion Cardinals as the favorites. "We will be in the thick of it," he promised. Red Thisted wasn't so sure. "The Braves players are going to be affected by the assured move to Atlanta," he predicted. "The veterans think about it, mention guardedly they don't like it, but when the first ball is pitched, any given day or night, they become strictly professionals. They look askance at the whinnying and braying of club directors they can't miss. It could help immeasurably if these baseball-wise infants (in management) just shut up."

Players around the league apparently agreed with Thisted. In a players-only poll published by *Sport* magazine, the Braves were picked to finish sixth, behind, in order, the Phillies, Cardinals, Giants, Reds and Dodgers. American League players predicted that the order of finish would be: Yankees, Orioles, White Sox, Tigers and Twins. The players' fifth-place choices (the Dodgers and Twins) wound up facing each other in the World Series. Their first-place selections (the Phillies and the Yankees) both ended up sixth.

On April 12, the Braves opened their regular season at Cincinnati's Crosley Field against the Reds, and the Milwaukee County Board of Supervisors opened their legal campaign against the Braves and Organized Baseball, voting 20-3 to begin the process of filing an antitrust suit. The latter story rated larger headlines than the former in Milwaukee, which was preparing for the Milwaukee Braves' final home opener two days hence. In the game, Cloninger pitched a two-hit complete game as the Braves beat the Reds 4-2. The Braves, like the Brewers in the late 2000s and early 2010s, established a pattern that both sustained and subverted them: They won when they hit home runs, and lost when they didn't. Eddie Mathews and Joe Torre each hit two-run homers to account for all the Braves' runs. The game was played before a near-capacity crowd of 28,467. With Aaron still hurt, Bragan, who had been batting Mathews second throughout the exhibition season, switched him to the No. 3 spot in the season opener. He was preceded in the batting order by center fielder Lee Maye, and right fielder Felipe Alou. Torre, the catcher, batted cleanup, followed by Mack Jones in left field, Tommie Aaron at first base, Denis Menke at shortstop, Alomar at second, and Cloninger pitching.

The next night, only 4,286 showed up at Crosley Field to watch the Reds beat the Braves 8-3 as Sammy Ellis pitched a complete-game eight-hitter for Cincinnati. The second-day crowd represented a reminder that baseball was still in fiscal flux and that Milwaukee wasn't the only city that could soon find itself without major league baseball.

Then and a half-century later, Cincinnati fans had a de-served reputation for being among the most astute in baseball, and the city often trumpeted the fact that the 1869 Cincinnati Red Stockings has been baseball's first truly professional team. This prompted a long-standing tradition, abandoned by 2016, of scheduling the first game of every National League season in Cincinnati, one day before all the other openers. At the same time, Reds fans also have been known for showing their disdain for a sub-standard product by not showing up. The Reds had been rescued from a near-certain demise in 1934 when Powel Crosley bought the team from Sidney Weil, who had gone bank-rupt as the result of the Great Depression. Crosley, who retained ownership of the team until his death in 1961, immediately hired Larry MacPhail as team president, and in 1935, MacPhail in-stalled lights and the Reds became the first major league team to play night games. MacPhail also hired famed announcer Red Barber to broadcast the Reds' games, and attendance soared. The Reds led the league in attendance in 1939 when they won the NL pennant and again in 1940 when they won the World Series. But the team wobbled through the next two decades, and the Reds never again finished higher than third in NL attendance until they moved to Riverfront Stadium in 1970.

Although Crosley, who built financial empires both in radio production and in car manufacturing, was one of the wealthiest men in baseball, virtually nothing was done to improve Crosley Field after MacPhail left Cincinnati in 1938 to assume the presidency of the Brooklyn Dodgers. (Its primary distinguishing feature was the "goat hill" incline that tripped up many a left fielder trying to chase down fly balls.) The Reds finished last or next-to-last in NL attendance for 11 straight seasons (1945-55); as season-long pennant contenders in 1956, they moved up to third in attendance with 1,125,928 paying spectators, but by 1958, when they finished fourth, they atrracted only 788,582, last in the league, while the Milwaukee Braves led the league with 1,971,101. Even in 1961, when the Reds were surprise NL pennant winners, their attendance of 1,117,603 was only fourth in the eight-team league.

After the Dodgers and Giants left New York for California in 1958, rumors persisted that the NL was soliciting investors who would buy the Reds from Crosley and move them to New York as a replacement team. Those rumors, of course, dissipated after the NL announced plans to expand into New York and Houston in time for the 1962 season, but in 1965, the Reds' future in Cincinnati was far from assured unless a new ballpark could be built.

Reds management resorted to bizarre means to keep the franchise financially viable, both before and after Crosley's death. In 1954, the team's nickname had been changed to Redlegs in an attempt to distinguish the baseball team from the Communist

"Reds," the fear of whom created hysteria throughout the nation during much of the 1950s. Tom Swope, the sports editor of the *Cincinnati Post*, demurred. "We were the Reds before the Communists were," Swope wrote. "Let them change *their* name." Swope's protests notwithstanding, the team didn't change its nickname back to Reds until 1960. The Reds would finish seventh in the 10-team NL in attendance in 1965 despite a formidable lineup that, on Opening Day, featured Pete Rose at second base, Tommy Harper in left field, Vada Pinson in center field, Frank Robinson in right field, Gordie Coleman at first base, Deron Johnson at third, Johnny Edwards catching, Leo Cardenas at shortstop and former University of Wisconsin pitcher Jim O'Toole on the mound.

After an off-day on April 14, the Milwaukee Braves took the field for their last home opener. The hope was that the Teams Inc-sponsored game would result in an attendance figure of 30,000. The newspapers noted that this figure, if reached, would be higher than five of the earlier Opening Day crowds elsewhere in baseball - including the Cubs' opener at Wrigley Field, where only 19,751 had turned out two days before. About 18,000 tickets already had been sold, and Teams Inc said a 20,000 figure would enable it to recoup its buyout investment. Both Milwaukee papers, and all of its TV stations, were still on board with Teams Inc's premise that Milwaukee's baseball future would be best served by fans holding their collective noses and coming out to support the Braves. WTMJ aired a retrospective documentary called "Spirit of '53 - Milwaukee and Baseball." Although more than 200 people had been killed by a swarm of tornadoes that had hit the Upper Midwest a few days before, the weather forecast for the Braves' opener was favorable, by Milwaukee-in-April standards: Temperatures in the low 50s, cloudy but dry.

Major league baseball attendance, stagnant since the post-war boom era, continued to trend downward in the first days of the 1965 season, aside from the 48,546 who witnessed the regular-season debut of the Astrodome. In addition to the Cubs' turnstile count of just 19,751, the Twins' home opener had drawn only 15,388, although the weather was so bad that three Minnesota players had to be airlifted via helicopter to the ballpark because of widespread flooding. In Los Angeles, the Angels, bunking in with the Dodgers at Dodger Stadium for the fourth and last season, managed only a count of 11,278. The Boston Red Sox had only 18,018 spectators for their home opener; the Detroit Tigers, 32,658. In Kansas City, a crowd of only 18,109 saw the A's opener, during which owner Charles O. Finley rode the team's mascot mule, Charley O, onto the field from its regular grazing area behind the right-field wall. Finley, who fancied himself a master promoter, had established a pet-ting zoo beyond the wall at Kansas City Municipal Stadium, and had installed an automatic ball dispenser behind home plate. When home-plate umpire Bill McKinney stepped on a button, the dispenser, a wooden rabbit, emerged from the ground with the necessary baseballs. But Finley didn't have many players who could pitch, hit or field the balls in question. The A's never had a winning season in Kansas City after moving there from Philadelphia in 1955, and had sold only 2,602 season tickets for 1965. Finley, who had battled Kansas City officials over sta-dium lease terms since buying the team in 1960, was actively reconnoitering possible relocation sites - including, according to some reports, Milwaukee.

A national Harris Poll taken in 1965 reflected the fact baseball had a problem, both with its own lack of perception and the way it was perceived by the public. According to the Harris Poll, baseball was still America's favorite sport, but was favored by only 38 percent of the general population. Pro football, barely on the radar two decades before, was preferred by 34 percent of men aged 21-34, while baseball was favored by only 23 percent of those within that age group. Another question that was asked to everyone who participated in the poll was: Is your interest in baseball greater than, less than, or the same as it was a few years ago? Only 21 percent replied that they were more interested in baseball; 24 percent said less. Among males 21-34, 15 percent indicated they were more interested in baseball, while 32 said their interest had diminished. The corresponding numbers for football: 37 percent of the general population liked it more than previously, while only 9 percent liked it less. Among males 21-34, 60 percent had taken a greater interest in football, while only 6 percent hadn't. The poll didn't break down the numbers by state, but one can only imagine, in the midst of the Lombardi era in Green Bay, how lopsided the numbers probably were in Wisconsin in 1965 in favor of football.

But at least for one last day, the dreary offseason and Milwaukee's uncertain baseball future could be put aside. April 15 arrived, and the headline at the top of the *Sentinel* sports page read: "It's Opening Day At The Stadium - Let's Go!" The final advance sale stood at 21,000, and 1,352 season tickets had been sold - the lowest total in baseball, but a far cry from the 36 season packages the Braves had sold at the end of January. Hank Aaron had received medical clearance to play; the only downbeat note was that Billy Bruton had been forced to cancel his appearance at the last minute. Aside from the re-instituted carry-in ban, much was as it had been in 1953. Dick Emmons, the bugler who sounded "Charge!" when the Braves were rallying, was there. Myron "Tiny" Jansen, whose 380-pound presence had been a constant at County Stadium throughout the Braves' time there, was on hand as usual. So was "Chief Noc-A-Homa," the mascot who occupied a teepee beyond the outfield wall.

Hours before the first pitch, scheduled for 1 p.m., Eddie Mathews stood alone in street clothes in front of the Braves dugout, staring at the empty grandstand with a contemplative, reminiscent look on his face. Perhaps he was remembering 1953, the year he hit 47 home runs and the Braves were to Milwaukee what the Beatles became to Liverpool. Maybe he could feel the base under his foot as he had in 1957 when he touched the third-base bag at Yankee Stadium to clinch the 1957 World Series title for Milwaukee. Maybe he was thinking of the time he met his wife of 11 years, Virjene, in Milwaukee. He didn't say, but he was in a reflective and expansive mood - unusual for Mathews, a taciturn, sometimes-withdrawn man who accepted but never truly embraced his role as the voice and the face of the franchise.

As he put it that day: "I'm more of an introvert. I still find it difficult to adjust to the limelight. I never have learned to live with it. I'm still uncomfortable in crowds. It was worse when I was single and had to eat all my meals out. I couldn't go anywhere without being recognized. It was hard to relax. Nowadays, I spend most of my time at home with my family. I still can't get used to going out in public.

"It would be nice to leave the folks here with a pennant. I don't want to put the emphasis on the leaving but rather on the pennant. It has been a strange feeling, watching all my teammates peeling off one by one until I'm the only one left. Of course, it bothers you, because it was a great bunch of guys. Don't get me wrong. We've got a good bunch now. But the old gang ... was together for a long time. We had a real unique spirit, especially in '57. Those guys played beyond their potential. One thing that stands out in my mind ... there were 12,000 people at the airport, and there's no telling how many people lined the parade route (after the Braves beat the Yankees in New York in Game 7 of the 1957 World Series).

"It (the shift to Atlanta) could drastically affect me, for all I know. I've never had to go through that long a separation (from his family). I plan to keep my family in Brookfield; after all, we have all our friends here. So we'll play it by ear."

Later that day, the doomed Milwaukee Braves drew a paid crowd of 33,874 - the ninth-largest of the 20 home-opener crowds in 1965. It was more than the 32,678 partisans that the Cubs, who already had played three home games, had drawn in those three games combined. A few days later, Teams Inc indicated that the total attendance had been 35,098, with gross receipts of $67,918 - a $13,800 profit for Teams Inc.

In the *Journal*, Robert W. Wells wrote: "Considering all the harsh words that have been said since the hussy from Atlanta lured the Braves south with her southern gold, the crowd was surprisingly friendly. Some players feared they would be blamed for their owners' shenanigans. But not a boo was heard." The band that had been hired for the occasion underscored the underlying melancholy with some of its numbers: "I Found A New

Baby," "Love Me Or Leave Me," "They'll Be Some Changes Made," and, finally, "Heartache." A banner read: "Atlanta, you can have the rest. Leave us Eddie Mathews, our hero." The cloudy weather that had been forecast turned foreboding soon after the start of the game, and the stadium lights were turned on in the third inning. The introduction of the 1953 Braves by radio announcer Blaine Walsh seemed to set the tone for the game; Walsh introduced Andy Pafko, then Max Surkont, then Charlie Grimm, then Logan, then Sid Gordon. "Do I have to go beyond third base?" Walsh said after the crowd stood to give Mathews a three-minute ovation that reverberated throughout the Story Valley. It did the same for Warren Spahn, who was introduced after Mathews.

Then, almost anticlimactically, the 1965 Braves earned a 5-1 victory over the Cubs.

As with Mathews' pregame talk with reporters, the postgame discussion centered around mixed feelings. Doyle K. Getter wrote to the *Journal* in a letter published the next day: "The whole affair had an unreal quality about it. It was almost eerie. To this veteran Braves fan who has seen all 13 opening games here, the most striking absence from the premises was that of baseball's real excitement ... we doubt you could get 33,874 people to attend a wake anywhere but Milwaukee." Mayor Henry Maier and his wife sat a few rows behind the County Stadium owners box - which was, of course, empty. The box was rarely occupied by absentee owners Lou Perini and Bill Bartholomay, even during the halcyon years, and Maier sometimes used it when it was vacant. On this day, he remained in the stands. "I wouldn't sit there *this* year," he said. Elsewhere in the stands, Martha Schneider,

82, who lived on North 26th Street, said she was a friend of former mayor Frank Zeidler and his wife, and had attended every Braves and Brewers opener for 45 years. She even recalled attending games as a child at the Lloyd Street Grounds, the home of the American League's Milwaukee Brewers in 1901 before they moved to St. Louis and became the Browns. That park was built in 1895 at the intersection of North 16th and Lloyd streets, and torn down in 1904. She wore a lapel button that long had read "Back Our Braves." For this last opener, the "our" had been taped over, and on the tape, she had written "their." A vendor who was selling what later would be called "team gear" reported that only about 20 Braves pennants were purchased - "mostly by little kids."

Nevertheless, the players were energized by the turnout and by the support. In a *Journal* story headlined "Lame Duck Doesn't Limp," Mathews said: "It was incredible. Anyone who just walked into the ballpark would never know anything had happened. It seemed like any other Opening Day." Later, sharing drinks with some of his 1953 teammates at Jackson's, he added: "I can't agree with those who say it was just like the good old days. To me, this is something truly special on the part of some truly big-league fans."

Bob Sadowski responded to the occasion, giving up only a solo homer to Ernie Banks in the fifth inning. He retired the next 11 hitters and didn't give up another hit until the ninth, finishing with a four-hitter. Afterward, when it was mentioned that his wife was from Atlanta, he made it clear that he and his family lived in Pittsburgh fulltime and he had no ties to Atlanta other than those of his wife. Ty Cline, a surprise starter in center field in place of Lee Maye, got two hits, scored a run and drove in another, as did Mathews.

Conspicuously absent from the home opener were commissioner Ford Frick and NL president Warren Giles. Frick, reached by telephone by a reporter, had a one-word reaction to the high turnout: "Terrific." Giles' response was one word longer: "No comment." Nobody involved in the Bartholomay ownership group showed up either; Thomas Reynolds, the Braves' executive vice president, said Teams Inc member Ben Barkin, the advertising executive, had told them they would not be welcome. Governor Warren Knowles, who had thrown out the ceremonial first pitch, lingered in the stands after the game and signed autographs. One girl, 11, got Knowles to autograph her program, then confessed confusion as to Knowles' significance. "I think he's the umpire," she said.

Edmund Fitzgerald summed up the mood of the day when he said, "We don't look upon this season as the end, but as another chapter in the 'Miracle of Milwaukee.'"

If it was a miracle, it quickly turned into a mirage. The Braves, not Teams Inc, would be selling tickets for the remaining 80 home games, and the enmity that had been building against Bartholomay, McHale, Frick, Giles and baseball in general kicked in. The team could only settle in for the siege. It would be a lonely one.

The Braves had an off-day Friday - a built-in makeup day in case of a home-opener postponement - and by the time they resumed play on Saturday, April 17 against the Cubs at County

Stadium, the home-opener euphoria throughout southeastern Wisconsin had dissipated almost completely. The weather turned dour, and so did the pages of the Milwaukee newspapers. A fire on South 79th Street had killed two boys, ages 5 and 3. Icy floodwaters were threatening a number of Wisconsin cities, forcing the evacuation of 14,000 people in 16 counties and causing an estimated $10 million in damage. Anti-war and civil-rights demonstrations were raging more and more violently all over the country. And the Braves became lonesome pariahs, just as they had feared. On April 17, they played before only 3,362, and lost 9-4 to the Cubs. The next afternoon, 3,391 showed up in 43-degree weather to see the Braves beat the Cubs 9-6.

The Reds came to town on April 19. Cincinnati won 2-0; only 2,804 paid to watch, although the total crowd, including kids admitted for free as part of a Knothole Day promotion, was 6,792. During the final game of the Cubs series, a 42-year-old bartender brought and brandished a Confederate flag, prompting verbal confrontations with several of the handful of fans in his section. He was cited, and later fined $5 for violating County Stadium's carry-in ordinance. He told County Judge C. T. Saraphin that he brought the flag as a gag with the idea of mocking the soon-to-be Atlanta Braves. Replied Saraphin: "It makes my blood boil whenever I see that flag."

Eddie Mathews hit the 447th home run of his career and drove in three runs in that same game, during which the Braves pummeled former teammate Bob Buhl. Mathews said after the game that he was swinging freely for the first time since a series of shoulder problems began in 1963. He credited daily diathermy (a medical technique involving the production of heat in a part of the body by high-frequency electric currents) and a new stretching regimen for his rejuvenation. Billy O'Dell pitched four perfect innings after Hank Fischer and starter Denny Lemaster were hit hard; the latter was undermined by a poor first-inning decision by second baseman Sandy Alomar, who eschewed a sure out at first and began a double-play attempt on which both runners were safe.

In the game against the Reds, Cincinnati pitcher Jim Maloney took a no-hitter into the eighth before Denis Menke parachuted a single just over the infield. It was the third serious no-hit bid in a year for Maloney, who had thrown two one-hitters in 1964. In a game in 1963, he had struck out 16 Braves, including eight in succession to tie a major league record. Maloney was one of the most under-appreciated pitchers of the 1960s, winning 23 games in 1963 and 20 in 1965 and earning at least 15 wins every year from 1963-68. If he had pitched only against the Braves, he might have wound up in the Hall of Fame. He was to the Braves what Bob Buhl had been to the Dodgers in the late 1950s, finishing his career 22-7 with a 3.17 ERA against Milwaukee and Atlanta.

Wade Blasingame gave up a two-run homer to Deron Johnson - accounting for two of the league-leading 130 RBI Johnson was to accumulate that season - but otherwise pitched shutout ball over eight innings. Blasingame and Maloney both were from Fresno, Calif., and Maloney, who was three years older than Blasingame, recalled crossing town specifically to watch Blasingame pitch in Little League.

In the two decades following World War II, Fresno was as fertile athletically as the surrounding Central Valley - long one of the most productive farm regions in the world - was agriculturally. Fresno had a population of only 133,929 in 1960 (it was almost four times that size by 2010), but it had already produced an inordinate number of world-class athletes. The city first appeared in sports datelines throughout the world in 1940, when Cornelius "Dutch" Warmerdam, who had grown up in nearby Hanford and graduated from Fresno State College, became the first pole vaulter to clear the 15-foot mark - widely considered an impossibility in the bamboo-pole era. One of the first Fresno natives to make a national sports impact was Bill Vukovich, the race-car driver who won the Indianapolis 500s of 1953 and 1954 and was handily leading the 1955 race when he was killed in a one-car wreck. (As of 2016, no driver had ever won the Indy 500 three times in succession.) Bob Mathias, the 1948 and 1952 Olympic decathlon champion, was from Tulare, about 40 miles south of Fresno. Brothers Rafer and Jimmy Johnson were from Kingsburg, just outside Fresno; Rafer was the gold-medal decathlete at the 1960 Olympics, and Jimmy was a four-time All-Pro cornerback who played 16 seasons with the NFL's San Francisco 49ers and was named to the Pro Football Hall of Fame in 1994. Jerry Tarkanian, who coached UNLV's basketball team to the NCAA title in 1990 and as of 2016 had the seventh-highest winning percentage (.794) in college basketball history, played at Fresno State (graduating in 1955) and finished his coaching career there in 2002.

Fresno was even better known in the 1960s as a baseball incubator. Before Blasingame and Maloney, Dick Ellsworth had gone directly from Fresno High to the Chicago Cubs after he signed with them during the summer of 1958, and made his major league debut on June 22 of that year. Ellsworth went on to a 13-year major league career during which he won 115 games, including a 22-10 mark for the Cubs in 1963, although he also lost 137 games during his career, and was a 20-game loser twice while with Cubs teams that were only marginally better than the expansion Colt .45s/Astros and Mets. (Ellsworth's son Steve, who also grew up in Fresno, pitched briefly for the Red Sox in 1988.) One of Ellsworth's Fresno High teammates was Pat Corrales, the future major league catcher and manager. Dick Selma, who reached the major leagues with the Mets in 1965, was another highly-sought Fresno product. All five, though, were soon to be eclipsed by the most famous Fresno athlete of all - Tom Seaver, who in 1965 was still pitching for the University of Southern California. Seaver was signed to a $40,000 bonus contract by the Braves in February 1966, but commissioner William Eckert, who had replaced Ford Frick earlier that year, nullified the contract because it violated the amateur-signing rules that were in place at the time. Eckert in effect held a Tom Seaver lottery. Any team other than the Braves that was willing to match Atlanta's original offer could participate in a drawing for his services. The Indians, Phillies and Mets entered the drawing, and the Mets won. Seaver was in the majors with them a year later, beginning a career during which he won 311 games and a Hall of Fame plaque.

After the loss to Cincinnati, the Braves, because of three rainouts, played only two games in the next seven days, losing 6-3 at St. Louis on April 21 and 3-1 to the Cubs at Wrigley Field on April 24. This hiatus gave reporters their first extended opportunity to ask any and all people with longtime baseball ties a provincial-but-logical question that was to become a mantra as the 1965 season wore on: Is Milwaukee, even with the Braves poised to leave, a major league city?

As it happened, the Wisconsin Sports Hall of Fame that week inducted Clarence "Pants" Rowland, 86, a native of Platteville who had managed the Chicago White Sox to a World Series title in 1917. Rowland also had managed the minor-league Brewers, served as Pacific Coast League president during the time it was seeking major league status, and held varous executive posts with the Cubs. Rowland, asked The Question, replied: "Milwaukee will never be without baseball as long as it shows the spirit it has been showing." At a Rotary luncheon on April 20, Bill Veeck, ever a Milwaukee advocate, suggested that Milwaukee band with the other cities seeking major league teams "and act as a unit to force expansion." Veeck went on to say that "the rape of Milwaukee" was evidence of "the monstrous cynicism of baseball," and recommended that Teams Inc refrain from offering any future ballpark buyouts that would put money into the Braves' coffers. "Milwaukee's major league future won't depend on attendance in Milwaukee this year," he said. "You've already made your point on that score (with the opening-day attendance)."

In Los Angeles, Warren Spahn, two days short of his 44th birthday, continued to fly in the face of Bobby Bragan's reasoning, outdueling Claude Osteen and beating the Dodgers 3-2 with a complete-game eight-hitter. "I hope Bragan is reading the newspapers," Spahn said. Jim Lefebvre, the rookie second baseman whose arrival had enabled the Dodgers to field major league baseball's first-ever all-switch-hitting infield, struck out in the ninth with the Dodgers threatening. It was the 2,500th strikeout of Spahn's career. In Spahn's next start, against the Giants at Candlestick Park, Spahn retired the first 17 men he faced before Orlando Cepeda singled. Casey Stengel left Spahn in the game even though the Giants scored three subsequent runs against him, and Spahn popped up Jose Pagan with two on and two outs in the ninth to preserve a 4-3 win.

With the Braves off the field and the front pages, attention turned back to Wisconsin's real-life problems, the most pressing of which was the continued flooding on the banks of the Mississippi River. La Crosse was in danger of being inundated, but the dikes protecting the city barely held, largely because of the help of hundreds of college and high school students from Milwaukee who gave up their spring vacations to travel to La Crosse and assist with the sandbagging efforts there. They helped keep damage in La Crosse to a minimum, although 42 homes and 83 city blocks suffered some level of damage.

Milwaukee Mayor Henry Maier, as those who preceded him had done and those who succeeded him would do, blamed suburban governments and homeowners for Milwaukee's *de facto* segregation, accusing them of discriminating against blacks via building and subdivision red-lining, and calling for collective regional planning. "Current, subtle discrimination forces the central city to be the only island for the poor and for minorities," he said. "The problem of human relations does not stop at the city boundary." At the time, only 2 percent of the blacks in Milwaukee, Ozaukee and Waukesha counties lived outside the city of Milwaukee, where 10.2 percent of the residents were black. (In 1980, that figure had climbed to 22.9 percent; by 2010, it was 40 percent.) Whitefish Bay, one of Milwaukee's most affluent suburbs, in 1965 had a population of about 18,000. Of those, 16 were black, and almost all of them were domestic servants.

On the other (far-right) wing of the Wisconsin political spectrum, McCarthyism was being sustained in the state capitol building in Madison, even though Joe McCarthy himself had been dead for eight years. Three bills widening discrimination against suspected Communists were introduced, including one that would ban Communist Party members (or suspected members) from seeking or holding a teaching position at any Wisconsin public school, or speaking or debating on any campus. Talk-show host Bob Siegrist, the Rush Limbaugh of his state and his radio generation, subjected lawmakers to a 30-minute harangue against Communism and the threat it posed to the children of Wisconsin. (In May, speaking on the eighth anniversary of McCarthy's death, Siegrist said McCarthy had "the ability to penetrate the deep Red smog which confused and befuddled more complex and intellectual men ... to fathom the deadly Communist menace for precisely what it was." By 1965, though, McCarthy was marginalized in most minds, both within and beyond Wisconsin. Only 100 people showed up at the ceremony at which Siegrist spoke. One was Sen. Sam Roseleip (D-Darlington), who said he supported the 1965 Red Menace measures because his 82-year-old grandmother had urged him to do so to show he was on God's side, and because FBI director J. Edgar Hoover "is one of the greatest and grandest Americans we have today."

With his team at 3-5 entering a three-game home series with the Cardinals starting Tuesday, April 27, Bragan pondered line-up changes. Joe Torre had gone hitless in his first 14 at-bats, and Felipe Alou was 1 for 21 in the Braves' first eight games. The team batting average was .211, offsetting the better-than-expected work of the pitchers. Rico Carty was still out with a sore back, which he blamed on Bragan's experimentation with him at first base, but was set to rejoin the team for the Cardinals series. Most important, Hank Aaron was back at full strength. In a *Sport* magazine article in March, Sandy Koufax, ranking NL hitters, said Aaron was the best - even better than Willie Mays, who was beginning his second and final Most Valuable Player season, and Roberto Clemente, who had emerged as a superstar after a decade in the majors. But the highest average among NL hitters against Koufax belonged to Gene Oliver, who was batting .429 against Koufax at that point.

The Braves finally returned to action on Tuesday, April 27, winning 9-5 over the Cardinals before only 1,677 spectators - the smallest crowd ever for a Braves game at County Stadium. Those who showed up did so despite 40-degree weather; Eddie Mathews said he had never been in a colder ballpark environment, not even during his rookie year with the Boston Braves. (The previous attendance low had been 2,746 for a day game against the Pirates in 1962.) Hank Aaron, starting for the first time in 1965, singled in a run with his first hit of the season. "It's still a little stiff," Aaron said of his ankle, "but I can run alright. Nothing wrong with it that a little warm weather won't cure." The Braves amassed 13 hits, three by Frank Bolling, who had been reinstated at second base after Alomar's slow start. Mathews and Denis Menke homered off Ray Sadecki, a 20-game winner for the Cardinals the prevous season. Denny Lemaster gave up six hits and four runs in five innings, but got the win as Billy O'Dell held St. Louis to three hits and one run over the final four innings.

The next night, April 28, also brought about arctic conditions and another County Stadium attendance low. Bob Gibson pitched a three-hitter as the Cardinals beat the Braves 5-0 before 1,324. At least two of the fans, Ed Lang and Joe Kalsvada, were there exclusively to see their friend Bob Uecker, but Uecker, the Cardinals' second-string catcher, didn't play. Tim McCarver, the Cardinals' regular catcher, had two of St. Louis' seven hits, scored one run and drove in another. Wade Blasingame, the Braves' starter, was removed with one out in the second inning after issuing five walks. After three starts, his ERA stood at 6.97.

The weather, the crowd and the Braves all were slightly better the next night, as 2,812 watched the Braves dispatch the Cardinals 4-1. Aaron hit his first homer of the year; Bob Sadowski got the victory with six strong innings before coming out of the game because of a bruised knee, and O'Dell lowered his ERA to 0.68 as he continued to cement his position as the "stopper" with three more shutout innings. The homer gave the Aaron-Mathews combine 744 career homers, one fewer than the Dodgers' 1950s combo of Duke Snider and Gil Hodges, who held the NL record at the time. Aaron and Mathews would finish their careers with a total of 863 homers as teammates, breaking the record of 859 by Babe Ruth and Lou Gehrig of the Yankees from 1923-34. The only duo to come within 100 homers of the Aaron-Mathews total after Mathews was traded to the Astros in 1967 was the Giants' Willie Mays and Willie McCovey, who hit 801 homers as teammates from 1959-72.

The Braves concluded April with a 7-1 win over Philadelphia behind Tony Cloninger's five-hitter and Mathews' 450th career homer - a three-run blow that landed in the back row of the almost-empty bleachers and was reported to have traveled 485 feet. Jay Dallmann, a 16-year-old fan, retrieved the ball and returned it in exchange for a photo with Aaron and Mathews, now the co-holders of the NL record for most home runs by teammates. Jim Fanning, the Braves' assistant general manager, said it was the longest home run he had seen since Joe Adcock, notorious for squaring up down-the-middle fastballs and hitting them record-breaking distances, was zeroing in on the center-field trees that had provided a batters eye at County Stadium. Ty Cline played center field and was the leadoff hitter as Bragan continued to tinker with his outfield alignment, even with Aaron back in right field.

Attendance, despite a relatively warm evening, was 2,923 - now, obviously, the new normal for a spent franchise. "Chances are the Braves attendance won't reach 300,000," wrote Wells Twombly in the *Houston Chronicle*. "If it does, it will be 300,001 more than the club owners deserve. This is the saddest thing that happened to the game since the Chicago White Sox took a dive in the 1919 World Series."

'The Braves Salute the 913'

• • •

IF MILWAUKEE WAS GOING TO lose major league baseball, at least it was going to gain fountains.

That was the expectation of Mayor Henry Maier, who was jurisdictionally more of a spectator than a participant in the wrangling between the Braves, major league baseball and Milwaukee County, even though he made clear his hope that the Braves would stay or quickly be replaced. The Journal Company, which owned both the *Journal* and the *Sentinel*, on May 1 unveiled a new fountain that was one of the largest in the city, continuously circulating 5,600 gallons of water and featuring multi-colored lighting at night. This delighted Maier, who had a passion for fountains, often including them in various municipal projects during his 28-year tenure as mayor. One of his desires for Milwaukee was that the city become as synonymous with fountains as it was with beer, even though Cincinnati and Kansas City already were calling themselves "fountain cities." That didn't bother Maier, who said at the Journal Company's fountain dedication: "I hope it's followed by many, many more until we are at last a city of fountains."

An "avenue of fountains" already was planned. The proposal was to extend it from MacArthur Square to Lake Michigan, and feature a fountain that could project water 400 feet into the air. The cost of this fountain was estimated at $218,000, and projections were that it would cost $75,000 a year to operate. Many found this an inappropriate way to spend taxpayer money, especially considering the city's transportation problems. Construction of southeastern Wisconsin's ambitious freeway system was far behind schedule, and Milwaukee traffic seemingly was creeping along more slowly than Joe Torre on the basepaths. (Torre stole 23 bases and was caught 29 times during his 18-year career.) Less than two miles of the Stadium Freeway had been finished (the rest would never be built) and federal transportation officials said the entire system, begun in 1953, would not be completed until 1972 at the earliest, and would cost an additional $40 million, although 90 percent was to come from the federal government. Construction of the Airport Freeway, which was to become Interstate 894, was scheduled to begin in 1966, but that time frame was not etched in stone.

Given the outlook for major league baseball's future in Milwaukee in 1965, the choice of sites for the Journal Company fountain at the intersection of North Third Street (now Old World Third Street) and West Kilbourn Avenue represented a bitter irony. From 1836 until 1961, the lot (which by 2016 was a parking lot) had been the site of the Republican House, originally called the Washington House and renamed in the 1870s after the GOP became a dominant force in local and national politics. The Republican House, especially in its early years, had been one of the most luxurious hostelries in the city. As it name suggested, it had hosted many political functions. It also served as a gathering place for members of the extensive German-American community on the near north side. And on March 15, 1900, baseball's American League had been born in Room 185 of the Republican House.

Those present at that meeting included Connie Mack, who had been a major league catcher for 11 years before taking over as manager of the Milwaukee Brewers of the Western League in 1897. The Western League - and particularly president Byron Bancroft "Ban" Johnson, who had formed the league in 1894 - aspired to gain equal status with the National League, which was left as the only major league when the American Association went out of business after the 1891 season. The NL had dropped four of its 12 franchises after the 1899 season (including the Cleveland Spiders, at 20-134 the worst team in major league history) and the league had several instances of "syndicate" ownership, meaning an owner who had stock in more than one franchise could arbitrarily move players or an entire team to a preferred location. The NL also was notorious for drunkenness, game-fixing and rowdyism both on the field and in the stands, and the players had such a bad reputation that most of the better hotels in NL cities refused to accept them as guests. Umpires, who usually worked games alone, often had to halt games to ensure their own safety. The behavior of players, fans (then known, not affectionately, as "cranks") and management had endangered not only the National League but the National Pastime itself, and Johnson and his fellow American Leaguers saw themselves as crusaders for clean, wholesome baseball.

Johnson also was at the Republican House meeting in Room 185, along with Charles Comiskey, who owned the Western

League franchise in St. Paul, Minn. With the help of Milwaukee attorney Henry Killilea, who was an investor in the Western League's Milwaukee franchise, the group finalized and formalized plans to re-launch the Western League as the American League for the 1900 season. Johnson was chosen as the AL's first president. In 1901, which MLB and most baseball historians consider the AL's first year as a major league, its eight-team alignment included the Milwaukee Brewers, with Hugh Duffy, a Hall of Fame player who later served two terms as the manager of the minor-league Brewers, managing and patrolling center field. The Brewers, however, were a flop both on the field and at the gate at the Lloyd Street Grounds, their home park. They went 48-89 and finished in last place, 35 1/2 games behind the champion Chicago White Stockings and seven games behind the seventh-place Cleveland Bluebirds. After the season, the Brewers were sold and moved to St. Louis, where they played as the Browns from 1902 until their transfer to Baltimore in 1954. (A small tablet commemorating the 1901 Brewers is located down the right-field foul line at Helfaer Field, the Little League diamond that stands in the parking lot at Miller Park on the former site of County Stadium.) The American Association was re-formed as a minor league in 1902, and the re-constituted Brewers began play in the AA that year, using Borchert Field as their base. They remained there until the Braves arrived in 1953.

On May 1, 1965, Wade Blasingame beat Jim Bunning and the Phillies 6-1 at County Stadium before 2,486, with Lee Maye hitting a solo home run in the first and Felipe Alou driving in two runs with two hits. Both homers came after Phillies manager Gene Mauch ordered Joe Torre intentionally walked ahead of Alou. The strategy was surprising because Torre, after a lengthy spring-training holdout that had ended with his salary being increased from $25,000 to $35,000, had not yet found his equilibrium at the plate. He was batting only .200 after the May 1 game. The victory improved the Braves' record to 7-6, but their stay above .500 was a short one. An 86-degree day helped bring 8,630 to County Stadium for a Sunday doubleheader against Philadelphia, but the Phillies took both ends, 6-0 with Chris Short pitching a seven-hit shutout, and 10-7. Richie Allen had five hits in the doubleheader for the Phillies, who won despite the misadventures of Wes Covington in left field. Covington, essential to the Braves during their World Series seasons of 1957 and 1958, misplayed two routine fly balls that resulted in four Milwaukee runs.

Mathews hit a homer in the first game to give himself and Aaron the NL homers-by-teammates record, and Aaron cleared the outfield fence with another blow in the second game, but Mathews bristled when asked about the feat by reporters. "I'm not even thinking about records," Mathews said. "We lose a doubleheader and all anyone wants to talk about is that record." Mathews' homer was his fifth; in 1964, he had not hit his sixth homer until June 23. He set another NL record in the first game, playing in his 1,865th game at third base to break the record previously held by Hall of Famer Pie Traynor.

Elsewhere that day, the Astros, who had surprised everyone with a 10-game winning streak, were finally beaten 6-3 by the Cubs. The Reds held first place at 12-5, followed by the Dodgers (11-6) and Astros (12-7). The Braves were seventh. Denny Lemaster, who lost the first game of the doubleheader, was 1-2 with an 8.05 ERA after earning 17 wins in 1964. Billy O'Dell, a relief specialist for the first time in his career, was showing an affinity for his new role, but already had worked 19 innings in the Braves 15 games. Osinski, the right-handed member of Bragan's late-inning tandem, gave up two runs in two innings during the first game against the Phillies.

After an off-day, the Astros - who as the Colt .45s had unexpectedly tormented the Braves, winning 12 of the teams' 18 games against each other in 1964 - came to Milwaukee for a two-game series. Joe Morgan, who had been the MVP of the Double-A Texas League in 1964 and earned a September promotion to Houston, was hitting .323, but the Astros' 1965 success had been built around their starting rotation - Dave Giusti, Bob Bruce, Don Nottebart and Ken Johnson. The Braves, of course, were short on starting pitching, especially with Sadowski's status unknown because of his injured ankle, and already had made inquiries about Bruce's availability. Trade discussion between the Astros and Braves apparently continued during the series. But trade possibilities didn't represent the main story line in the Milwaukee papers on May 3 and 4. In the *Journal*, Oliver Kuechele again accused the Braves of creating a convenient poverty situation for themselves in Milwaukee by scheduling even fewer promotions than in previous seasons. County executive John Doyne was quoted as saying that the Braves had insisted, starting in 1964, on starting their Monday-through-Thursday night games at 7 p.m., instead of 8 p.m., as had been the norm. (Friday games continued to start at the later time.) In those days, when games rarely lasted as long as three hours and often were completed within two hours, it was the custom for a father to come home from work, eat a leisurely dinner while reading the evening paper, and then gather his family for the trip to the ballpark. The earlier starting time disrupted this routine, and more than occasionally resulted in fans staying home rather than fighting traffic and arriving at the game after it had started. "The Braves are using the lousiest possible times to have ballgames," Doyne said. "These starting times represent the picayunish and small-potato thinking of the Braves' owners."

In New York, Red Smith, writing for the *New York Herald-Tribune*, offered his readers his take on the Milwaukee situation. Smith, who was born and raised in Green Bay, in 1976 would become the first journalist to win a Pulitzer Prize for sports commentary, and more than three decades after his death in 1982, he was still making virtually all the top-10 lists of the best sportswriters of all time. On the Braves' actions in Milwaukee, he wrote, tongue almost penetrating cheek: "Next year, unless a court order prohibits it, the Braves will ship their carpetbags to Atlanta. Warren Giles will make a pious statement saluting once again the pioneering spirit of the National League, whose fearless missionaries are carrying gospel into the Deep South. He will be surprisingly eloquent."

During the Braves' off-day, the primary subject on the national baseball scene was the Dodgers' chances of contending despite the loss of left fielder Tommy Davis on May 1. Davis, a two-time NL batting titlist and the primary fulcrum of the Dodgers' offense after the off-season trading of Frank Howard, had broken his ankle and torn two ligaments in the ankle sliding into second base in a game against the Giants. Giants shortstop Jose Pagan, who signaled frantically to trainers to come immediately to Davis' aid even before the play was over, said the fracture sounded like a man breaking a large stick over his knee. Davis later said that when he looked down at his ankle, "I thought my ankle was in right field." He would undergo surgery during a five-day hospitalization and would be in a cast for eight weeks. Not only was he out for the season, but his career was thought to be in danger, and no replacement left fielder was readily at hand. First baseman Wes Parker could also play the outfield, but manager Walter Alston and general manager Buzzy Bavasi didn't want to weaken the Los Angeles defense at two positions by moving Parker, who won six Gold Gloves at first base during his career. Bavasi said the Dodgers were considering several options, including Al Ferrara, an outfielder who had such power that he was nicknamed the Baby Bull, but was much more baby than bull on defense. Wally Moon, a reserve outfielder best known for lofting opposite-field homers over the mammoth left-field screen when the Dodgers were still playing at the L.A. Coliseum, was another possibility. So was Derrell Griffith, a 21-year-old third baseman-outfielder who had hit .290 in 78 games for the Dodgers in 1964. Willie Crawford, an 18-year-old outfielder who already was considered the jewel of the Dodgers' farm system, had been with the parent club for 10 games at the end of the 1964 season, though it was understood in 1965 that he was far from ready for fulltime major league service.

Virtually unmentioned in the speculation was a 30-year-old outfielder named Lou Johnson, whose primary distinguishing physical feature was the fact he was missing the top half of his right ear after it was severed in an automobile accident. Johnson had originally signed with the Yankees organization in 1953 and had seen brief major league service with three clubs (including the Braves in 1962), but had spent most of his 13 pro seasons with 15 different minor league teams. The 15th team was the Spokane

Indians, the Dodgers' Triple-A affiliate. He had a good year with Spokane in 1964, batting .328 with 18 homers and 70 RBI, but by 1965 the "career minor leaguer" tag had been affixed to him, so it was a surprise to many that the Dodgers called him up after Davis' injury. He would become a longer-lasting equivalent of Bob "Hurricane" Hazle, a journeyman outfielder brought up by the Braves in 1957 after they were beset by a succession of outfield injuries. Hazle hit .403 in 41 games that season and was instrumental in the Milwaukee Braves' only World Series championship. He disappeared back into obscurity the following year, batting .211 in 63 games for the Braves and Tigers in 1958, his last major league season.

That 1957 title, of course, was the apex of the Milwaukee Braves' history. Their nadir, at least to that point, came on May 4, 1965, on a 45-degree night when the team played before its first three-figure crowd since coming to Milwaukee in 1953. The "Fan-a-Gram," a small electronic message board that had been attached to the main scoreboard, read at the end of the game, "The Braves salute the 913 fans here tonight." (The actual crowd count was 1,139, including senior citizens who had been admitted for free.) The paid crowd of 913 was the smallest to see any Braves home game since September 30, 1944, when the Boston Braves played the Dodgers before 666 at Braves Field, where lights weren't installed until 1946. The County Stadium silence was punctuated by two home runs by Hank Aaron and another by Mathews, and Tony Cloninger pitched a five-hitter as the Braves beat the Astros 9-3. Aaron's two homers moved his career total to 370 and enabled him to pass Ralph Kiner and tie Gil Hodges for 12th place on the all-time list.

Another witness to the dubious attendance record was John McHale, who had become to Milwaukee what Maris Crane was to the *Frasier* TV series three decades later: Both constantly were referenced, almost always disparagingly, but nobody actually saw either of them. McHale was making his first visit of the season to County Stadium even though he had said during spring training that he played to attend "90 percent" of the Braves' home games in 1965. Bill Bartholomay had been to an earlier game, but had sequestered himself in the team's mezzanine suite and had refused interview requests. McHale did grant interviews, but was terse. "I'll talk about the team and the players," he said, "but I have no comment on the attendance or any other aspects of the baseball situation in Milwaukee. Everything that should be said has been said on those subjects." Asked if the recurring rumors that the Braves might again try to move during the season, he said, "That's a loaded question, like 'have you quit beating your wife?' Anything I say (on that matter) is going to be misconstrued." On whether he planned to attend any more games in Milwaukee: "I'll be here just as often as I feel like coming. I have a right to change my mind."

He did, however, praise Teams Inc for its efforts to demonstrate that Milwaukee was major league worthy. "We think Teams Inc is doing a good job, and we respect their wishes," he said. But both parties had agreed that any level of continued partnership between the two would serve no purpose. Teams Inc was focusing on trying to get a new team for Milwaukee; the Braves management knew their team would be bled dry financially during their last year in Milwaukee, and Bartholomay and McHale were focused on trying to get to Atlanta financially solvent. "Milwaukee fans don't like the Braves or what they represent," Shirley Povich wrote in the *Washington Post*, "and will not be persuaded otherwise."

On Wednesday, May 5, the Braves gave their few remaining fans - 1,391 on this night - a flashback to fonder memories as Mathews hit a walk-off double off former Brave Claude Raymond in the bottom of the 14th inning to beat the Astros 2-1. Wade Blasingame, who said he hadn't pitched a complete extra-inning game since high school, doled out only five hits over the 14-inning distance, including a home run to fellow 21-year-old Rusty Staub in the seventh. Blasingame said after the game he was "a little tired," but was even more motivated than usual because his parents had traveled from Fresno to Milwaukee to see the game. His six-figure signing bonus had been based largely on his velocity, but he estimated that 75 percent of the pitches he threw this night were curveballs. "This kid right now has the best curveball in the league," Bragan gushed. "(He was pitching so well that) I didn't even ask him if he was tired until the 13th. He said he felt fine and could go another couple of innings." While Blasingame clearly, it seemed, would be central to the Braves' future, two paragons of their past revisited those pasts that night. Bob Buhl earned his 150th career win with a three-hitter as the Cubs beat the Pirates 3-1 before only 2,093 at Wrigley Field, and Warren Spahn pitched a four-hitter in defeat as Jim Bunning and the Phils blanked the Mets 1-0 at Shea Stadium. (Another pitching elder, Robin Roberts, earned his 275th career victory with a four-hitter the following night as the Baltimore Orioles beat Minnesota 5-1. Roberts would be released by the Orioles at the end of July, and signed by the Astros. He would end his 19-year career the following season, finishing with 286 victories and earning induction into the Hall of Fame in 1976.)

After the game, the Braves flew to New York for a three-game series against the Mets that would start a nine-game road trip. Nobody said so on the record, but the players undoubtedly welcomed the time away from Milwaukee after playing so many cold-weather games before so few fans. However, bad weather followed the Braves to New York. The series opener was rained out and rescheduled as part of a Sunday doubleheader, which would stretch an already-thin roster. Tommie Aaron, the opening-day first base starter, and pitcher Chi Chi Olivo had been sent to the minors. Bob Sadowski's ankle problem lingered. Rico Carty complained of renewed back problems, and Lee Maye was questionable for the Mets series with a sore ankle. Gene Oliver had played first base in both games against the Astros, leaving the catching almost exclusively to Joe Torre, who had registered eight hits in the previous four games.

The Braves were short-handed, but they weren't the only NL team with injury problems. The Dodgers, of course, had lost Tommy Davis for the season, and the Giants had lost Orlando Cepeda to a knee injury that would require knee surgery and keep him out for most of the remainder of the season. Cepeda, a future Hall of Famer, had finished second to Frank Robinson in the MVP balloting in 1961 after hitting .311 with 46 homers and 142 RBI, and he had hit 100 homers during the next three seasons. But his injury indirectly solved a long-standing problem for the Giants. Both Cepeda and Willie McCovey struck fear into virtually every pitcher they faced, and both were good first basemen, but both also were major defensive liabilities in left field and couldn't play any other positions. After Cepeda's injury, McCovey was planted at first base and remained there into the 1970s. In 1966, Cepeda was traded to the Cardinals for Ray Sadecki in what turned out to be one of the most lopsided trades in the Giants' San Francisco history. Sadecki went only 32-39 in four seasons with the Giants and led the NL with 18 losses in 1968, though he pitched 18 major league seasons for six clubs, including the Brewers in 1975. Cepeda went on to earn the MVP award in 1967 while leading St. Louis to the first of its two straight NL pennants and its second World Series title in four seasons.

In Queens, the Braves lost 4-2 to the Mets on Saturday, May 8, then split the Sunday doubleheader, winning the first game 8-2 with Tony Cloninger pitching a six-hitter, and losing the second 5-4 after squandering a 4-1 lead. Torre went 6 for 10 with three homers in the doubleheader, but committed a passed ball in the bottom of the ninth, on a knuckleball by Bob Tiefenauer, that allowed Charlie Smith to come home with the game-winning run. The Milwaukee papers carried only perfunctory stories on the Mets series. At a time when track was widely followed even in non-Olympic years, the lead sports story on May 10 was the first-ever 70-foot shotput (by Randy Matson), which was equated with Roger Bannister's breaking of the four-minute-mile barrier in 1954. The top news story was the disappearance of Carl Robert Disch in Antarctica. Disch, 26, of Monroe in south-central Wisconsin, was an ionospheric physicist on a National Science Foundation expedition. He vanished on May 8 while on a walk of slightly more than one mile from the expedition's radio substation to the main barracks - a route he had easily completed at least two dozen times during his stay in Antarctica - in minus-45 degree weather. His body was never found.

With the Braves off on May 10 before starting a three-game series in Pittsburgh the next day, editorial wrath continued to inundate baseball and the Braves management, and even, to a lesser degree, Teams Inc. Clearly, not only the Braves but also baseball itself had a public-relations catastrophe on their hands. *Sentinel* sports editor Lloyd Larson wrote: "None can say yet that Teams Inc and the county were wrong. Their efforts may yet prove fruitful. The very fact that leading writers around the country continue to hammer away at baseball for roughing up Milwaukee may encourage Congress and the courts to do something about it before the Braves take off officially." Larson, in comparison to some of his counterparts in Milwaukee and around the country, was a soothing voice. Even Jesse Outlar of the *Atlanta Constitution* weighed in with a scold. "If the issue were reversed and the Braves were spending a lame-duck season here, I am sure that Atlanta Stadium would be as empty as County Stadium. You can't fault Milwaukee fans. The most devout booster of the (soon-to-be) Atlanta Braves must admit that management mishandled the move. (But) what benefits do Eugene Grobschmidt and company expect to derive from the current situation? Plainly, there are no benefits. Milwaukee leaders have failed to view the loss of the Braves from a realistic standpoint. Doubtlessly they are deriving pleasure from the financial lashing the club is receiving. However, they are seriously damaging Milwaukee's chances of obtaining another franchise."

Meanwhile, the Braves' operational garrison in Milwaukee was thinned further when Bob Allen quit as Braves assistant director of public relations to take a job as an account executive at radio station WOKY. Allen, who had made more than 1,200 promotional speaking appearances in Wisconsin since joining the Braves in 1959, said of his departure: "As a Milwaukeean, I am naturally disappointed (that the Braves were leaving), and my feelings in this matter are so strong that I have decided to sever my relations with the organization."

While the Braves traveled from New York to Pittsburgh by air, May 10 was a somber day in Milwaukee rail history. Shareholders of Milwaukee Road approved a merger with its longtime competitor, North Western Road, creating a 15-state, 20,975-mile system that would extend from Chicago to Seattle. The two competing railroads were almost as old as Milwaukee itself, dating to the 1840s, and had long been large-scale employers in Milwaukee. Nationwide, the merger involved about 10,000 jobs, and rail unions predicted that 50 percent of those workers would be eliminated as the new company downsized. The combined railroad continued to founder, even after its passenger service was folded into the nationalized Amtrak network in 1972. In 1985, it was acquired by the Soo Line Corp., and was merged into that railroad the following year.

At Forbes Field, the last-place Pirates defeated the Braves 4-3 on May 11 as Eddie Mathews grounded into two double plays, the last, with the bases loaded and one out, ending the game. Former Braves catching citadel Del Crandall, playing the next-to-last of his 16 major league seasons, vaulted the Pirates ahead for good with a two-run single in the sixth. In New York, Yogi Berra - who, like Spahn, was a player-coach with the Mets - was taken off the roster after playing in four games, during which he had two hits in nine at-bats. Those two hits were the last of the 2,150 accumulated by Berra, a future Hall of Famer who had begun his career with the Yankees in 1946. Berra, who as a non-playing manager had been fired by the Yankees after the 1964 season despite getting his team into the World Series, in 1973 managed the Mets into their second World Series.

The Braves improved to 12-11 by winning the final two games of the Pittsburgh series. On May 12, Denny Lemaster took a 5-1 lead into the ninth, but the Pirates scored three times that inning and had the tying and winning runs on base before Billy O'Dell came in to quell the rally. The next day, the Braves won 5-4 despite a subpar outing by Cloninger, who gave up four runs before being relieved by Phil Niekro to start the fifth inning. Niekro, who had been relegated to mopup duty most of the season, shackled the Pirates while allowing only two hits the rest of the way to gain his first major league win. He would add 317 more over his remarkable 24-year career that landed him in the Hall of Fame in 1997. Torre continued his hitting resurgence, going 4 for 4 and singling in the winning run in the eighth. But shortstop Denis Menke suffered a sprained knee in the game, and was sent back to Milwaukee for treatment. Estimates were that he would be out a week to 10 days; as it turned out, Menke would not be completely healthy again that season. He and Frank Bolling had given the Braves their best double-play combination since the days of Johnny Logan and Red Schoendienst, and losing Menke further undermined a Braves defense that already was considered a liability.

Moving on to Philadelphia, the Braves lost 5-2 to the Phillies on May 14 as Bragan, still unhappy with his starting rotation, brought Billy O'Dell back from the bullpen. He pitched four perfect innings, then was cashiered in the fifth and wound up with the loss as Art Mahaffey completed a six-hitter. The next day, Dick Stuart - known much more for his "Doctor Strangeglove" nickname than for the 228 homers he accumulated during his 10-year major league career - hit a grand slam as the Phillies won 6-4. The Braves salvaged the final game of the series with an 8-6 win in 10 innings. They scored three runs in the top of the 10th, with two scoring on Gene Oliver's bases-loaded double, but O'Dell, moved back to the bullpen, gave up two runs before Bragan, with his entire staff exhausted, called on Denny Lemaster for his first relief appearance of the season. Lemaster responded with only the third save of his career. He would finish with eight saves over 11 years in the majors, during which he amassed 66 complete games and 14 shutouts.

The topic dominating postgame discussion, though, was the announcement by the Mets that Warren Spahn would pitch at County Stadium the following Thursday, in the final game of a three-game series against the Mets. Spahn would face Wade Blasingame, with whom Spahn had worked extensively during the 1964 season; in fact, Bragan had said at the time that Spahn was sold to the Mets largely because of Blasingame's development. Spahn, 44, had pitched in 41 professional games (including four major league games) and had served more than a year in the military by the time Blasingame, 21, was born in 1943. Blasingame was less than 2 years old when Spahn won his Purple Heart. Blasingame said he had been emulating Spahn since junior high in Fresno in 1957. "My admiration for him even grew when I got to know him (with the Braves) and roomed with him," Blasingame said. "Spahn is a pretty complicated guy when it comes to pitching. He regards it as a science and has made a deep study of pitching. I learned plenty just listening to him. We spent a great deal of time together, just discussing baseball."

The first two games of the series were little more than prelude - the Braves won both, 4-3 and 7-5 - except for the presence of Bill Bartholomay at the opener. This time, he granted interviews, primarily to try to quash rumors out of Atlanta that the Braves again were negotiating with Milwaukee County in an attempt to move the franchise to Atlanta immediately. He did not deny that talks along those lines had taken place, but tried to reassure all concerned that the Braves wanted to avoid the disruption of a midseason transfer.

"It seems quite obvious that we will have serious operational losses in Milwaukee," he said. "But at the same time, Milwaukee County as our landlord will suffer substantial losses in rental income. (The Braves' County Stadium rent was based in part on attendance, and the Braves to that point had drawn only 68,091 for 13 home dates, compared to 146,976 at the same juncture of the 1964 season.) In spite of all these factors, we've been led to believe that it is in the best interest of the city and county (for the Braves) to remain here this year. Therefore, our obligation is to provide the best baseball we can in this unprecedented year." Bartholomay also denied rumors that the Braves, in response to their financial woes, had made it known that they were willing to sell Eddie Mathews and/or Joe Torre. McHale confirmed that the Mets had offered $500,000 for Torre, "but Joe is unavailable, period." Meanwhile, a group of Congressmen, including Henry Reuss and Clement Zablocki from Wisconsin, urged commissioner Ford Frick to add four new major league teams in 1966, creating three eight-team leagues. Pressure from Congress had brought about expansion once before - in late 1960, after the Washington Senators had moved to Minnesota and become the Twins. Reacting to pressure from Congress, MLB, within two months, granted Washington and Los Angeles expansion teams to begin play in the American League in 1961.

Finally, May 20 arrived. Five thousand tickets had been sold in advance of Spahn's return to Milwaukee, and the upper deck at County Stadium was opened for the first time since the Teams Inc buyout of the first home game. Spahn joked before the game that, as a gag, he might go into the Braves dugout after pitching the bottom of the first inning. A sign in the ballpark read: "Spahn: Sink McHale's Navy" (a reference to the popular CBS comedy and the very unpopular Braves general manager). Spahn received a standing ovation from the 19,140 spectators (of whom 17,443 paid) as he walked to the mound to pitch the bottom of the first. But the night belonged to his young protege, as Wade Blasingame pitched the game of his 21-year life - and, as it turned out, his career - as the Braves beat the Mets 7-1 on Blasingame's one-hitter.

The Mets had only four baserunners against Blasingame, one on an error by Eddie Mathews, who more than atoned for that miscue wth a grand slam in the bottom of the fifth as the Braves scored all seven of their runs - all against Spahn, who had shut the Braves out over the first four innings and was lifted for a pinch-hitter after the fifth. The Mets, meanwhile, had no answers against Blasingame, who walked two and struck out eight. In the seventh, with the crowd starting to anticipate a possible no-hitter, Blasingame walked Billy Cowan with one out. He advanced to second on a wild pitch, and scored on Ron Swoboda's clean single to center, after which catcher Joe Torre went to the mound and asked Blasingame, in jest: "You're too young to be thinking about a no-hitter?" The final Mets baserunner was

Bobby Klaus, who led off the ninth with a walk before Blasingame finished off the final three hitters.

Interestingly, Blasingame's immediate postgame thoughts were of appreciation and wistfulness as he thought about the man who had done so much to get him to this point. "I really felt bad, deep down, after we got all those runs off him (Spahn)," Blasingame said. "I thought, too, about all the things we talked about last year, like changing speeds and getting the curve over when you're behind on the count."

"Tremendous," Spahn said of Blasingame's performance. "I kept thinking of the things we talked about in our room all last year, and here he was beating us with it." Spahn also was grateful for the reception he received from the Milwaukee fans. "Maybe I'm a little egotistical," he said, "but that (the fact he was pitching) obviously was why the people turned out. I'd like to think it was a tribute to me, and to the old days. Who knows? Maybe it inspired·him (Blasingame)."

Young as Blasingame was, though, his pitching presence was refined and defined long before he ever met Spahn. His father had first taught him how to throw a curveball at age 7, and by the time he signed for a six-figure bonus out of Roosevelt High in Fresno, he had been on no fewer than 10 youth baseball championship teams - four in Little League, three in Babe Ruth, and three at Roosevelt. He had also had the benefit of watching and competing against Jim Maloney and Dick Ellsworth, future major league standouts who were both two years ahead of him in the Fresno youth baseball system. Bragan said of Blasingame: "He was born knowing more about pitching than it's possible to teach some kids in a lifetime."

The Spahn-Bragan feud still hadn't been forgotten by either man. The 1965 Braves were a terrible bunting team, with only nine sacrifice bunts by non-pitchers all season, and Bragan almost never used that tactic except when his pitcher was at bat. But Alomar unsuccessfully tried to bunt his way on base early in the game, and Blasingame tried another bunt in a non-sacrifice situation. Spahn said he thought Bragan was trying to embarrass him by taking advantage of his limited range - the one element he lost somewhat in the latter stages of his career. Bragan said Spahn was right, but "we're just not a bunting club." Otherwise, though, he was relatively gracious in his remarks about Spahn, and Spahn didn't seem overly upset about his mound work, even the pitch that Mathews powered out of the park for his grand slam. "Pull up a chair and have some irony," he told reporters. Spahn said that early in Mathews' career, Spahn, Buhl and Burdette would try to get Mathews to sit on breaking balls because few pitchers would try to sneak a fastball by him. "Sometimes he'd walk away from us, he'd get so mad," Spahn said of Mathews. "But he knew we were right. So what did I do tonight (on the pitch that Mathews hit for the grand slam)? I threw him a fastball, right over the plate."

Mathews, for his part, would not talk at length about the return to Milwaukee of his teammate of 13 seasons (counting the 1952 Boston Braves), and clearly wasn't pleased by the fact most of the fans were rooting for Spahn and not for the Braves during the first four innings. Mathews, above all, believed strongly that any man wearing the other team's uniform was an enemy once the game started. "Feelings? I have no feelings," he said. "I don't care if it's Warren Spahn or anyone else. It's just a gray uniform."

Even with all the undercurrents that tugged at players and fans at County Stadium that night, Wade Blasingame was front and center. At only 21, he personified the possibilities of the present in Milwaukee and especially of the future in Atlanta. But he was never that good - or anywhere near that good - again.

More than one-third of Blasingame's career total of 46 wins (against 51 losses) came during that 1965 season. He pitched 224 innings that season, including the 14-inning complete game against Houston earlier in May, and although he stayed in the majors until 1972, he never again worked more than 158 innings in a season, and 10 of his 16 complete games came in 1965. Even that year, his fade in the final six weeks of the season paralleled that of the Braves. In his final seven starts, he earned only one win, and that was in the only start of those seven in which he got past the fifth inning. He never again pitched a complete game in which he gave up fewer than four hits, and that four-hitter came in 1970, after he had been traded to Houston. In the final start of his career, in 1972 for the Yankees against Detroit, he didn't retire a batter, giving up three hits and four earned runs before being taken out.

Whether his 1965 innings load at age 21 had anything to do with the fact Blasingame never blossomed as expected is, of course, impossible to ascertain. His problems first began the following spring, when he missed several weeks of spring training after accidentally slamming a car door on his hand. Even during spring training before the 1965 season, he had experienced shoulder tightness, and the tightness became pain in 1967. Blasingame, like most pitchers in the pre-free-agency era when all but the very best players were considered replaceable employees rather than investments, tried to work through the pain, sometimes with the aid of painkillers that also were *de rigueur* in major league clubhouses in the 1960s and beyond. Another element may have been the fact his go-to pitch was the overhand curveball, which is thrown across the body and thus stresses the shoulder, particularly the rotator cuff. By the 1980s, most pitching instructors were teaching away from the pitch, usually in favor of the changeup and later the split-fingered fastball, and only a few pitchers - Camilo Pascual and Bert Blyleven probably being the best-known - have based lengthy and successful careers on the overhand curve. In any case, Blasingame never completely regained the breaking ball about which Bragan and others spoke so glowingly in 1965. He was described by contemporaries - including Jim Bouton, who was Blasingame's teammate with the Astros late in the 1969 season when Bouton was writing *Ball Four* - as an individual who dressed, partied and handled himself with a high level of flamboyance. Of course, he was hardly unique in baseball in that respect at that time, but conditioning may have played a part in his rapid descent from stardom. He was out of baseball by age 30. Subsequently, he found financially-lucrative work during the construction of the Alaska Pipeline, and eventually settled in Anchorage.

While Blasingame enjoyed the aftermath of his one-hitter, the Braves followed their sweep of the Mets with a lost weekend against the Pirates, who had been having problems of a magnitude that seemed likely to cost first-year manager Harry Walker his job at any moment. Pittsburgh brought to Milwaukee an eight-game losing streak and a 9-24 record that had landed them in last place, 13 1/2 games behind the first-place Dodgers and - unforgivably in the early and mid-1960s - four games in arrears of the ninth-place

Mets. Pirates general manager Joe Brown apparently was willing to do just what the Braves sometimes had been accused of doing throughout the Bartholomay-McHale regime - dump salary and concede the season - and the Braves, their financial turmoil notwithstanding, apparently were to be the buyers.

McHale claimed, a month later, that he and Brown had met on May 20 when the Pirates arrived in Milwaukee, and before the game that night, they had agreed to what would have been a startling trade. The Pirates would send the Braves first baseman Donn Clendenon, pitcher Vern Law and pinch-hitting specialist Jerry Lynch in exchange for outfielder Lee Maye and cash. McHale and Brown apparently agreed to the deal before the game, but decided to hold off on making an announcement until afterward. The Pirates won the game, and for reasons never made clear, the deal was called off before the Pirates left Milwaukee.

If it had gone through, it almost certainly would have improved the Braves dramatically. Clendenon, 29, that year batted .308 with 14 homers and 98 RBI, and would have been a significant defensive upgrade over Gene Oliver, the Braves' most-frequently used first baseman in 1965. Law, 35, had gone 20-9 in 1960 for a Pirates team that won the World Series, and he finished 1965 at 17-9 with a 2.15 ERA - numbers that, if superimposed on the Milwaukee season, would have made Law the Braves' best starting pitcher. (Cloninger wound up with 24 wins, but his ERA of 3.29 was more than a run higher than Law's.) Law 10 years earlier, in 1955, had turned in one of the best pitching performances ever against a Milwaukee Braves team. He pitched 18 innings in a game at Forbes Field, giving up only two runs (one unearned) and nine hits and two walks while striking out 12. He left at the start of the 19th inning, and the Pirates won the game 4-3 in the bottom of the 19th. Lynch, 34, was considered in the same class as Smoky Burgess among the best pinch-hitters of the period. He retired with 116 career pinch-hits, and in 2016 still ranked 10th all-time in that category, though well behind Lenny Harris' record 212 from 1988-2005. The Braves never had a dependable bat off the bench in 1965 - their pinch-hitters collectively batted .166 - so Lynch could have been a difference-maker as well. Maye, conversely, had already been shopped by the Braves, and Milwaukee *did* deal him three days later after the trade with the Pirates was called off.

Why was the trade not consummated? Neither McHale nor Brown ever elaborated. It's possible that Bartholomay vetoed it on financial grounds; it's also possible that the Pirates' performance in the series against the Braves might have changed Brown's mind about whether his team could battle its way back into contention. The Pirates, despite their record prior to their arrival in Milwaukee, probably most resembled the eventual-champion Dodgers, although they had more power than the Dodgers, and neither the Pirates nor anyone else was nearly as intrepid as Los Angeles on the bases. Like the Dodgers, the Pirates were built around pitching and defense - a logical direction for them to take considering the dimensions of Forbes Field, where the 1965 distances from home plate were 365 feet to the left-field corner, 406 feet to the left-center power alley, 457 feet to dead center, 436 feet to right-center and 375 in right center before the surface angled inward to leave the right-field corner 300 feet away.

Even though they had finished seventh in 1964 and manager Danny Murtaugh, who had led Pittsburgh to a World Series title in 1960, had resigned for health reasons (and was replaced by Harry Walker), the Pirates still had high expectations going into 1965. Their pitching staff - led by Law, Bob Friend, Bob Veale and relief specialist Al McBean - appeared sound, and Walker said before the 1965 season that he had five Gold Glove candidates - first baseman Clendenon, second baseman Bill Mazeroski (who had just returned to the lineup after recovering from a broken foot), shortstop Gene Alley, right fielder Roberto Clemente and center fielder Bill Virdon. Clemente, Clendenon and left fielder Willie Stargell also provided power. But the Pirates simply hadn't hit during the first five weeks of the season; Law, the Pittsburgh starter on Friday night, May 21, brought a 2.98 ERA into the game, but his record was 0-5.

He was 1-5 after that night, even though he had to leave in the sixth inning because of a groin-muscle pull. Alvin McBean pitched 3 2/3 innings of scoreless ball and the Pirates, ignoring a chilly rain, won 6-1 as they knocked starter Denny Lemaster out of the game with a three-run seventh. Lemaster also was undermined by his defense. Sandy Alomar, installed at shortstop in Denis Menke's absence, made two errors that led to two Pittsburgh runs. He also failed to collaborate with left fielder Mack Jones on a fly to short left-center by Clendenon; the ball dropped between them, resulting in another Pittsburgh run. The next night, May 22, the Braves, leading 4-0 after five innings with Cloninger on the mound, lost 9-4 as Cloninger was dispatched in the sixth after giving up two-run homers to Stargell and Clendenon. Osinski was roughed up for five hits and four earned runs in two innings of relief. The Pirates completed the sweep the following day with a 10-1 rout as Bob Veale pitched a four-hitter and Andre Rodgers hit a grand slam. Alomar, still at shortstop, made another error, and Felipe Alou made two, though his full concentration couldn't have been on the field. Alou's family in the Dominican Republic was caught in the midst of the civil war there, and although he had gotten word that his family members were not in immediate danger, that war would be a burden for Dominican players throughout the 1965 season. It would play a role in August when one of the most volatile pennant races in NL history came to a flashpoint of unprecedented violence.

The attendance figure, 2,053, was the lowest ever for a Sunday game at County Stadium, and the three-game series had drawn a *total* of 7,394. Pittsburgh-area media members called attention to this because the Pirates' own future in Pittsburgh hardly was assured. Forbes Field, built in 1909, was a firetrap - it actually caught fire at least twice during the final few years before it was replaced by Three Rivers Stadium in 1970 - and the University of Pittsburgh had bought the ballpark in 1958 with the intention of tearing it down and using the land for other purposes as soon as the Pirates could be resettled elsewhere. (The football Steelers at the time played their home games at the university's Pitt Stadium.) As was the case in Cincinnati, Pittsburgh's political and business leadership in 1965 was confronted with the need to build a new stadium or risk losing major league baseball, and Pittsburgh writers and broadcasters called attention to the Milwaukee situation as an example of what could happen to a once-robust franchise in a worst-case scenario. A cartoon on the lead sports page of the *Pittsburgh Press* on May 21 depicted Pirates players staring into the virtually empty stands at County Stadium, with one of them saying, "Look at all the empty seats. Kinda makes you feel like you're back home, doesn't it?"

Perhaps playing before so many empty seats at County Stadium cured the Pirates of a collective case of enochlophobia (fear of crowds), though they weren't drawing that well at home (909,279, third-worst in the league, in 1965) themselves. Perhaps, also, the players needed time to get used to Walker, whose strength as a manager was his ability to teach the intricacies of the game and whose weakness as a manager was his inability to stop harping on his players about the intricacies of the game. Regardless, the three-game sweep of the Braves began a 12-game winning streak, and after two losses, the Pirates won seven more in succession to climb into the periphery of the NL race. After going 19-11 in June, they were only 13-18 in July, but went 38-19 the rest of the way, although they never got closer to the NL lead than 2 1/2 games on September 1 and finished third, seven games out.

As they boarded their airplane for San Francisco after the Pirates series, the Braves must have known that management, even in its murky financial state, would make changes in the aftermath of the Pittsburgh sweep. By the time they landed at San Francisco International Airport, the news came: The Braves had traded Lee Maye to the Astros for pitcher Ken Johnson and minor-league outfielder-first baseman Jim Beauchamp.

The Braves had been both tantalized and exasperated by Maye, who had grown up in Los Angeles, ever since signing him out of high school in 1954. He had reached the majors in 1959, batting .300 in 51 games, and periodically had shown indications that he could become the successor to Billy Bruton in center field. But injuries and illnesses - a shoulder problem in 1961, a respiratory infection in 1962, a back injury in 1963. and finally knee and ankle issues during the spring of 1965 - too often way-laid him. The one year he had stayed healthy, 1964, he had played 153 games (by far his career high) and led the NL in doubles with 44 while batting .300 with 10 homers, 74 RBI - a laudable total for a player who usually batted leadoff or No. 2 - and 96 runs scored. At 6-foot-2 and 190 pounds and with well-above-average straight-ahead speed, the Braves envisioned him as what would be called, several decades later, a "five-tool player." But while he had achieved a high overall level of play when healthy, he never excelled in any particular phase, and his speed and arm strength in the outfield were negated at times by the fact he had trouble getting a jump on the ball and didn't take a direct route to balls in the gaps - especially when the Braves played him in center field in 1964. The Braves also wondered whether he was devoting his full energy to baseball. He was a rhythm-and-blues singer of considerable talent - first demonstrated in his church's choir when he was a child - both during and after his baseball career. Maye led an R&B band called Arthur Lee Maye and the Crowns, and with that group and various other musical ensembles, he released 27 singles from 1954-85. Though none charted, he was well-known in the music community and made money touring throughout and after his baseball career, which ended in 1972.

With the acquisition of Felipe Alou, the emergence of Rico Carty and Mack Jones, and the increasing value of Ty Cline both as a leadoff man and as a bat off the bench, Maye became expendable. And with Hank Fischer and Bob Sadowski failing to prove themselves in the rotation and Denny Lemaster not yet approaching his 16-win form of 1964, there was no question that the Braves needed Johnson.

Johnson, 32, had originally been signed by the Philadelphia A's in 1952, and remained with that organization after its move to Kansas City in 1955. He had given the Reds a significant jolt in 1961 when they acquired him from the A's late in the season, pitching in 15 games (including 11 starts) for the Reds and compiling a 6-2 record and 3.25 ERA as the Reds won their first pennant in 21 years. But the Reds left Johnson unprotected in that winter's expansion draft, instead keeping Ken Hunt, who had earned nine wins as a spot starter and middle-inning reliever in 1961. Hunt never pitched again in the majors, and was out of baseball entirely by 1965. Johnson had gone to the Colt .45s in the expansion draft, and was 29-51 in his three full years in Houston, but with ERAs of 3.84, 2.65 and 3.63. Johnson was durable, having started 98 games and logged 639 innings despite the heat and humidity of the Colt .45's temporary outdoor ballpark. He had even pitched a no-hitter, against the Reds, in 1964 - but lost the game 1-0 as his teammates committed two errors in the ninth to allow Cincinnati to score the only run of the game. He was known as a knuckleballer, but like Phil Niekro early in his career, Johnson used the knuckler, by his estimation, about one-third of the time, and could throw his fastball for strikes from several different arm angles.

Bragan said Johnson would also give the Braves' rotation a "stabilizing" influence; with four starters ages 21 to 26 and O'Dell needed in the bullpen, adding a veteran arm was seen to be essential if the Braves were to mount any sort of pennant challenge. The Braves also needed Menke back to congeal their infield defense, and his return apparently was imminent; he had accompanied the team to San Francisco.

Fischer, who had pitched only 6 2/3 innings all season, was unhappy with his new spot starter/long relief role, and said so. "I hate the thought of going back to the bullpen," he said. "Nobody wants to go there." But Johnson was still en route to San Francisco, and Bragan, recalling that Fischer had pitched two shutouts against the Giants in 1964, sent him to the mound on Monday night, May 24, to oppose Bob Shaw, the former Brave whose ERA of 1.55 was the best in the NL entering the game. Fischer lasted into the ninth before leaving with a cramp in his pitching elbow, and got the victory, with the help of a three-run homer by Mathews and a lead-saving catch by Mack Jones - with the trade of Maye, now assured fulltime status in center field - as the Braves won 4-3 before 6,443 at Candlestick Park.

Fischer had to come out of the game after throwing two balls to Tom Haller. O'Dell came in against his former teammates and completed the walk to Haller, for whom Ken Henderson pinch-ran. This brought Harvey Kuenn to the plate, and first-year Giants manager Herman Franks followed a baseball adage - play for the tie at home and for the win on the road if you're one run down in the ninth inning or later - by having Kuenn sacrifice Henderson to second. However, Kuenn's successful bunt also meant that the Braves would have an open base at their disposal if Franks, who had given Willie Mays - who came into the game batting .379 and already had 17 home runs, by far the highest total in the majors - the day off as a starter, decided to use him as a pinch-hitter. Clay Carroll relieved O'Dell and got the No. 8 hitter, Jim Davenport, on a fly to center for the second out, with Henderson holding at second. This brought up the pitcher's spot, and Franks sent Mays up even though he knew Mays would be intentionally walked to bring newly-acquired shortstop Dick Schofield to the plate. (Bragan also defied a baseball adage - never intentionally put the winning run on base on the road in the ninth or later - but this, like many others, was a baseball adage that had to be ignored if following it meant pitching to Willie Mays.) Schofield, who finished as a .227 career hitter, grounded to second base to end the game.

Franks was an even-keel type who was far more popular with his players and the Bay Area media than Dark, known for his dark moods and periodic rages, had been. But Franks made two other moves during that game that cost the Giants. Franks had played for and coached under Durocher, who believed strongly - and had proved with Dusty Rhodes in the 1954 World Series - that game-deciding junctures could arrive early as well as late, and he had a chance to use Mays in the bottom of the sixth, with runners on first and second with two outs and Hal Lanier, a .226 hitter that year, at the plate. Instead of using Mays at that point, as Durocher probably would have done, Franks sent up Ed Bailey, who was batting .111 at the time. Fischer got out of the inning by retiring Bailey on a foul popup.

In the ninth, Davenport, with the tying run at second base and one out, worked the count to 3-and-1 against Carroll. In 1965, a No. 8 hitter in that situation usually would be instructed to take the next pitch, even if it was a strike, and a walk would have been even more beneficial in this game because Mays was lurking in the on-deck circle, and intentionally walking him then would have meant loading the bases. But Davenport swung at the 3-and-1 pitch, flying out to center.

Pitching around Mays under normal circumstances, of course, had become even more difficult with McCovey, now the fulltime first baseman with Cepeda hurt, batting in the cleanup spot. He hit 39 homers that year. The Giants still had the other two Alou brothers, Matty and Jesus, and many believed in 1965 that Jesus had the potential to become the best of the three Alou brothers. Third baseman Jim Ray Hart emerged as yet another menacing bat in 1965, with 23 homers that year, and even Haller, the catcher, was a 16-homer man in 1965. Having all this supportive weaponry enabled Franks - who was as close to Mays as Durocher had been, and helped him with many of his business investments - to provide more frequent respites for Mays, 34, who sometimes had finished seasons at less than his best because of the exhaustion factor. Mays played in all but five of the Giants' 162 games in 1965, but the May 24 game was one of nine in which he appeared only as a pinch-hitter, and Franks, unlike Alvin Dark and Bill Rigney, sometimes took him out of blowout games, including the contest the following night. Mays responded to Franks' approach with 52 home runs and the second MVP award of his career (and his first since 1954).

The next night, May 25, most of the country was attuned to the second fight between Muhammad Ali (still identified as Cassius Clay by most media outlets, including the two Milwaukee papers) and Sonny Liston, who was knocked out in the first round under still-dubious circumstances. Before 9,784 at Candlestick, the Braves delivered a first-round knockout of their own against Ron Herbel and three successors. They scored three runs in the first, accumulated 19 hits in the game, and won 14-1 behind a five-hitter by Blasingame, who didn't lose his shutout until Kuenn singled in the Giants' only run with a two-out single in the ninth. Mack Jones hit two home runs, both of which carried an estimated 450 feet into the swirling Candlestick winds. Jones had three hits, and so did Woody Woodward, who had been summoned from Triple-A Atlanta to replace Sandy Alomar at shortstop until Denis Menke was ready to return. Ken Johnson, who had joined his new team, was impressed, especially after pitching for so many poor teams in Houston and Kansas City. "It's been a long time since I saw my team hit like that," he said. Johnson also was happy about the trade for residency reasons. He lived in West Palm Beach, Fla., where the Braves trained, and his wife was from North Augusta, S.C., deep in what was to become Atlanta Braves territory.

The Braves also got their first-ever look at Masanori Murakami, a left-handed pitcher who had appeared in nine games for the Giants at the end of the 1964 season, thereby becoming the first Japanese native ever to play in the majors. Murakami was used sparingly by the Giants in 1964 and 1965 - though he was usually effective, finishing with a 4-1 record and a 3.75 ERA over 89 innings covering 54 games - before he returned home permanently, partly because of homesickness and partly because of a jurisdictional dispute between the Giants and the Nankai Hawks, for whom Murakami had pitched before coming to the U.S. Murakami knew no English, and some of his teammates hilariously took advantage of that. Before the only start of his American career in 1965, his teammates had told and taught him to greet home-plate Chris Pelekoudas in what Murakami presumed was a sportsmanlike manner. In keeping with Japanese baseball custom, Murakami bowed to Pelekoudas as he took the mound to begin the game. "Herro, you haily plick," Murakami said. "How you rike to piss up a lope?" Pelekoudas, astounded, bowed back. "I couldn't think of what else to do," he said later. On May 25, the beating the Braves gave Murakami during his three-inning stint didn't require translation. He gave up seven hits and six runs, all earned.

The Braves continued to confound, this time with the fury of their bats, as they moved past the Giants into third place with a 10-4 win on May 26 to sweep the series at Candlestick and run their three-game totals to 28 runs and 37 hits. Torre and Felipe Alou hit two home runs each as the Braves bludgeoned Giants ace Juan Marichal, who gave up 11 hits, three homers (including the two by Alou) and nine earned runs in 3 2/3 innings as his ERA ballooned from 1.40 to 2.33. After Torre's second homer, Marichal drilled two Braves in a row: Jones in the middle of the back, Oliver in the right elbow. Despite Marichal's obvious intent, Oliver didn't start a fight or even an argument. "I'm just glad you didn't have your good stuff today," he told Marichal. "Otherwise that one would have gone straight through me." Cloninger (6-3) gave up three unearned runs in the third, the result of two misplayed fly balls in center field by Mack Jones as he battled the Candlestick gales. Nevertheless, Cloninger crafted an eight-hitter.

Mays batted fourth instead of third in that game for one of the few times in his career to that point - he actually batted lead-off occasionally in 1971, his last full year with the Giants - and for one of the last times in his career, he heard boos at Candlestick after Cloninger snuck a called third strike past Mays with the score 10-3 in the bottom of the eighth. In one respect, the boos were inexplicable; Mays was batting .371 at the time, and he was ... well, *Willie Mays*. On the other hand, they also represented a reminder of his initial reception in San Francisco after the Giants moved there in 1958. This was at a time when major league baseball rarely was televised on the West Coast, and when many San Francisco fans - some of whom thought the team's nickname should have been changed to Seals after the Giants' arrival - were eager to identify with the Giants as their team rather than as a New York throwaway. Players like Davenport, Marichal, Gaylord Perry, Cepeda and McCovey - none of whom had been New York Giants - were embraced, while Mays was seen by some as the product of Madison Avenue and the New York mystique. Consequently, he heard occasional boos on the rare occasions when his performance was less than pristine, and as with Hank Aaron during his years with the Milwaukee Braves, some who didn't know baseball mistook Mays' grace for nonchalance. In 1959, Soviet Union premier Nikita Khrushchev visited San Francisco and received a surprisingly warm reception. At the same time, the Giants were playing a home series against the Dodgers at Seals Stadium. Frank Conniff, national editor of the Hearst newspaper chain, was there too. "This is the damnedest city I ever saw in my life," he wrote. "They cheer Khrushchev and they boo Willie Mays."

The Braves' sweep-clinching victory came before another smallish crowd - 6,538 - of the sort that made it apparent that Candlestick already had become a liability to the Giants, even though it was in only its sixth season of operation. Besides its notorious winds and gray-on-gray color scheme, Candlestick bordered on the Hunters Point neighborhood, one of the most impoverished and dangerous in the city. The park had been built by the company owned by Charles Harney, a developer who also had sold the city of San Francisco the land on which it reposed.

Harney had made it clear he thought the ballpark should be named after him. Herb Caen, the San Francisco man-about-town columnist who mastered the three-dot technique also employed by Milwaukee columnist Buck Herzog, suggested after seeing Candlestick for the first time that it would serve Harney right if the city *did* name the park after him. (The stadium, torn down in 2015, was named because it was located at Candlestick Point, which jutted into San Francisco Bay at the southernmost tip of the city.)

Of course, the Braves now were playing as if they *enjoyed* Candlestick, and they probably did, given their record-low attendance and the weather at their games at County Stadium, where the average first-pitch temperature (including day games) had been 53 degrees. Now they were off to Los Angeles for a three-game showdown with the Dodgers. At the same time, in Washington, D.C., the Congressional subcommittee that included Wisconsin's Clement Zablocki and Henry Reuss had its showdown with baseball commissioner Ford Frick.

Frick, who served as commissioner from 1951-65, arguably was demonized more often and with more venom than any other leader of a major professional sports organization, before or since. Much of that criticism came from sportswriters, and many found that ironic because Frick himself had been a sportswriter, serving as Babe Ruth's ghostwriter from 1924-34. Most of the criticism came not because of anything Frick did, or because they disliked Frick personally, but because, at least in the eyes of his detractors, he didn't do anything other than serve as a tool of the owners. He is best known, of course, for declaring in 1961 that if Roger Maris broke Ruth's single-season home run record of 60 in 1927, he would have to do it during the same 154-game schedule Ruth played for it to be considered an official record. If it was done in the 162-game schedule that was played in the American League for the first time in 1961, Frick decreed, an asterisk had to go alongside Maris' name in the record books. But it was under Frick's benign direction - "It's a league matter," he was known to say whenver a controversy came his way - that baseball lost its position as the most-followed and most-profitable American sport to football. And, of course, he did nothing to alleviate the danger of baseball losing its antitrust exemption and being thrown into operational and legal chaos as a result.

Frick accepted the criticism without much complaint, but he was hurt deeply by that criticism and by baseball's decline in popularity during his commissionership. He had held his previous job, that of National League president, for 17 years, and had served with distinction. In 1947, when Jackie Robinson made his major league debut and several teams threatened to go on strike rather than take the field against a black man, Frick made it clear that any players who followed up on that threat would face expulsion from baseball. "And I don't care if it wrecks the league for 10 years," he said. "This is the United States of America, and a black man has as much right to play major league baseball as anyone."

In 1973, at the age of 78, he was one of the former sportswriters interviewed by Jerome Holtzman for his book *No Cheering in the Press Box*. "Good Lord, I didn't want to become commissioner," he told Holtzman. "When my name was being bandied about as the next commissioner, I didn't want it ... any man who is doing something he likes to do in a profession he respects and enjoys can be happy. Writing was a wonderful job and I enjoyed it. Then, I was very happy as league president because I still had a lot of close personal contact with the ballplayers, the people I had known. The greatest change happened when I entered the commissioners office because then you're through with your close contacts. You are sitting up there in a position where you can't afford, and they don't want, the personal contact."

During the lengthy interview, Frick mentioned almost nothing about his tenure as commissioner, except to say the idea for the Maris asterisk came not from him, but from *New York Daily News* sportswriter Dick Young, one of Frick's harshest critics. He didn't disown his decision on that matter, though. "What the dickens," he said, "I tried to protect the Babe because his record should stand until it's honestly beaten ... now, Hank Aaron's going for Babe's lifetime record of 714 home runs. Well, if he breaks it (as he did in 1974), he breaks it. Hell, Hank Aaron's already had two thousand more times at bat than Ruth had in his whole career. And the seasons are longer, you know, more games. He gets more opportunities. But if Aaron breaks it, certainly it's a lifetime record. No question about it. It'll go into the books as a lifetime record (with no mitigating asterisks or other disclaimers).

"I got panned frequently. Oh, I don't think I was criticized any more than anybody else. The writers, many of them, always were insisting I didn't make enough decisions, enough rulings. They would get on me, insisting I was always saying this or that dispute 'is a league matter.' But I followed pretty good precedent. Judge Landis (Kennesaw Mountain Landis, the first commissioner, who served from 1920 until his death in 1944) would never step into a league controversy unless it had to do with the honesty and integrity of baseball ... But any man who says he doesn't pay attention to criticism is crazy. In your heart, there is a scar."

During his meeting with the Congressional delegation, Frick, as was his wont, opened himself up to criticism by saying he would not intervene in the Braves situation or the antitrust suit that was being prepared. "If and when expansion comes, the ultimate decision must rest with baseball," he told the Congressmen, some of whom took that as a mandate to eventually intervene. So did Oliver Kuechele, who wrote in the *Journal*: "Baseball can't be trusted, having screwed up everything and shirked its responsibilities where taxpayers built ballparks. It can't (handle expansion or franchise transfers). It needs more than the nudge six Congressmen sought to give it. It needs help." A few days later, the two league presidents, Warren Giles of the National League and Joe Cronin of the American League, affirmed that they too were not in favor of immediate expansion to replace the Braves in Milwaukee, and a few days after that, Reds president Bill DeWitt told Cincinnati reporters that if any teams were to be added in the next few years, he favored Dallas-Fort Worth and Buffalo as locations. It was now readily apparent that Teams Inc's effort to land a replacement team after the Braves left would not produce results at least until 1967, at the earliest.

The Braves had proved their offensive might in San Francisco, but during the opener of their three-game series with the Dodgers in Los Angeles on Thursday, May 27, they demonstrated again how maddening they could be in low-scoring games, especially against a Dodger team that had so little heavy artillery and so many swordsmen. Lemaster, on a 3-and-2 count with two outs and the bases loaded in the bottom of the ninth, walked pinch-hitter Al Ferrara on a pitch that the Braves thought scraped the strike zone. It was called a ball by home-plate umpire Jocko Conlan, forcing in the winning run in a 3-2 L.A. victory.

The Dodgers, who were led in homers that year by Jim Lefebvre and Lou Johnson with 12 each, got the winning run on a single by Willie Davis, a sacrifice bunt by cleanup man Ron Fairly, an intentional pass to Johnson, an infield hit by Lefebvre and then the walk to Ferrara, The Braves were leading 2-0 in the fourth when Davis was hit by a pitch and Fairly singled him to third. Johnson hit a comebacker to Lemaster, who threw home instead of trying for the 1-6-3 double play. Davis eventually was tagged out, but stayed in a rundown long enough to advance the runners to second and third, and both scored on Jeff Torborg's single. The Braves rebounded the next night, winning 5-4 even though Johnson managed to get through only three innings in his first outing for Milwaukee. O'Dell pitched the remaining six innings, giving up only three hits and no walks. But the Dodgers took the final game and the series on May 29, winning 5-3 behind Don Drysdale. Fischer pitched four strong innings, but was replaced in the fifth by Clay Carroll, who gave up four runs in four innings as Lou Johnson, who had only one home run previously in 1965, cleared the wall twice.

In Houston, the Braves beat the Astros 6-5 on Memorial Day (May 30) as Hank Aaron, who had only 16 RBI for the season going into the game, posted his first three-RBI game of the season. He homered and doubled off Houston starter Larry Dierker, 19, who was making the third start of a major league career that would cover 14 seasons and 139 wins, including a 20-13, 2.33

season in 1969. The Braves won despite the fact Menke was still injured - he would go on the disabled list the next day, rendering him unavailable until at least June 13 - and Frank Bolling had been excused to return to Alabama to visit his ailing wife.

This was the Braves' first visit to the Astrodome, where they played before 38,734 - the largest crowd before which they would play all year until the final three games of their existence. By this time, the roof panels had been painted over in an effort to reduce the glare, but apparently it did little good, especially with the daylight sunshine compounding the glare effect. "It's really bad," Aaron said. "I lost one ball and had to have (second baseman Sandy) Alomar take it. It's tough to pick up in the first place, and you lose it for a second when it gets in the lights. The dome glares like glistening gold. You take your eye off the ball, and you're in trouble." But this would be the only day game the Braves were to play in Houston in their final Milwaukee season, and most of the players were duly impressed by the Astrodome. "This is the coming thing," Mathews said. "Any park they build from now on will have a dome." The Braves concluded May, and their nine-game road trip with a 7-2 loss to the Astros. Tony Cloninger, despite walking four in seven innings, had a 2-1 lead in the eighth before issuing four more walks and leaving the game with one out and the bases loaded. The Astros pushed across six runs in the inning as Rico Carty misplayed a fly ball into a single, Clay Carroll gave up a double to .154 hitter Ron Brand, and Joe Torre threw wildly for an error on a pickoff attempt.

The Braves ended May with some deceptively-impressive offensive numbers. Torre led the team and was second in the National League with a .346 average, but that was down from a high of .383. The second-leading average on the team belonged to Bolling, at .300. Mathews had 10 home runs and 30 RBI, but his average was a pedestrian .260. The team average was a robust .271, but Alou and Mathews were the only players batting above .292 with runners on base. The pitching staff's ERA was 4.07, with only O'Dell (2.25) and Blasingame (2.73) chinning the 3.00 bar. Felipe Alou, who had ht 25 homers in 1962 and 20 in 1963 while playing his home games at power-hitter-unfriendly Candlestick Park, hit only five homers in the first two months of the 1965 season. He said the lingering effects from his knee surgery had contributed to his power shortage. "I had to start (his hitting stride) a different way to favor the right knee (the one on which surgery had been performed)," he said. "I'm lunging forward with my front foot and when the ball gets there, I have no power left." Alou said he believed he had diagnosed and fixed the problem. and predicted, correctly, that his numbers soon would reflect that. Another element of anxiety was alleviated on June 1 when Alou got his first letter in more than a month from his family, which was still caught in the midst of the civil war in the Dominican Republic. The letter indicated that nobody in Alou's family had been injured. On June 2, President Johnson, who had sent troops to the Dominican Republic to try to restore order, announced the situation there appeared under control and that most of the U.S. peacekeeping force would soon be withdrawn.

The Braves, with a 21-19 record entering June, were in a virtual fourth-place tie with the Cardinals for fourth place, 4 1/2 games behind the first-place Dodgers and only one game behind the second-place Giants. Despite a winning streak that now extended to 12 games, the sixth-place Pirates still were only 21-24, 2 1/2 games behind the Braves. Cincinnati first baseman Gordie

Coleman was leading the NL with a .375 average, and team-mate Pete Rose's 40 hits led the league in that category. Other NL leaders as May gave way to June were Don Drysdale with nine pitching victories, Willie Mays with 17 home runs, Ernie Banks with 44 RBI, and Maury Wills with 30 stolen bases. The degree to which the running game had been de-emphasized by 1965 - with the exception, of course, of the Dodgers - was illustrated by the fact that nobody in the entire league except Wills and Lou Brock (21) had reached double figures in steals. The 10 teams in the league combined for only 745 stolen bases in 1965, with the Braves finishing sixth in that category with 64. The lowly Mets only stole 28 bases that year.

The pitching-hitting paradigm in major league baseball also was undergoing a shift. In 1963, the strike zone had been enlarged, extending it upward to the top of the shoulder and downward to the bottom of the knee. The higher strike zone particularly helped high-velocity pitchers like Sandy Koufax, whose fastball literally defied gravity, veering upward as it neared the plate. It wasn't unusual for Koufax's two primary catchers, John Roseboro and Jeff Torborg, to have to reach up to stab a pitch at which a hitter, seeing the ball belt high, had swung and missed. Partly as a result of the new strike zone, major league teams in 1965 were averaging 3.99 runs per game, down from 4.49 in 1962. By 1968, the "Year of the Pitcher," teams were averaging only 3.42 runs per game, the lowest major league figure since 1908. This led, for the 1969 season, to a return to the old strike zone (extending from the armpit to the top of the knee) and a lowering of the mound from 15 inches to 10 inches.

Milestones and
a Millstone

• • •

THE BRAVES HEADED BACK TO Milwaukee after ending their nine-game road trip with a 2-1 victory over Houston as Aaron and Jones hit back-to-back homers and Billy O'Dell pitched three scoreless innings in relief of Denny Lemaster. During the championship-contending years, it was common for hundreds or even thousands of Braves fans to meet the team plane when it landed at Mitchell Field (and, before that, to welcome the team home at the Milwaukee Road rail station). But by 1965, this custom had long since been abandoned, and the Braves could get from the tarmac to their cars almost without notice. The hope of Teams Inc and others who hoped to get a replacement team for the Braves at County Stadium in time for the 1966 season virtually was extinguished by the end of May 1965, and so was the chance that the Braves' move to Atlanta in 1966 could be prevented or even forestalled.

Dodgers owner Walter O'Malley, considered by most insiders the most powerful man in baseball - and Ford Frick's puppeteer - at that time, spoke at a dinner in Milwaukee, and during a press conference at the Pabst brewery, he was asked about the city's baseball future. He said the best thing "the substantial and sincere men of Teams Inc" could do would be to let the Braves move to Atlanta immediately and drop the antitrust litigation. He also said that, in his estimation, expansion beyond the existing 20 teams was at least five years away and that Milwaukee's chances of getting a transplanted team in time for the 1966 season were "fairly poor." Added O'Malley: "There are many fine and sincere men in baseball, and Milwaukee may lose a little support if it persists in stiff-arming the situation and playing to empty seats ... I would have told the Braves to leave, because I am sure that certain people in baseball would have been impressed. It is not helping the image of baseball to put the Milwaukee situation in a political arena where it can be used as a soapbox for almost anyone." O'Malley also said the failure of Bartholomay's public stock offering had been a key factor in the owners' vote to allow the Braves to move once they fulfilled the terms of their County Stadium lease, and that the owners' sentiments were to keep the team in Milwaukee. "But that's a far different thing from telling an owner that he *has* to operate in Milwaukee."

His remarks drew derision from Eugene Grobschmidt (at whom they probably were aimed), John Doyne and Edmund Fitzgerald, among others who were trying to keep major league baseball in Milwaukee. "Our legal position is (airtight)," Doyne said. "So is our moral. The county is determined to make the Braves play out their contract." Added Grobschmidt: "They (the NL owners) forgot about the millions of dollars they once took out of here (as the visiting teams' cuts of ticket sales during the 1950s when the Braves led the major leagues in attendance for six straight years)." The *Chicago Tribune*, though, seemed to think O'Malley was bluffing. A *Tribune* story reported that "both leagues are set to go along with the demands of enraged Milwaukee fans to head off possible lawsuits - meaning a team to replace the Braves, even if it means expanding the leagues."

O'Malley's comments and the politicians' rejoinders elicited little more than a collective shrug after they were reported by the Milwaukee and Chicago papers. Most fans - or former fans - by now were spending their discretionary income outside baseball, and Wisconsinites had no lack of alternatives to the Braves as the summer of 1965 approached. The Milwaukee Polo Club's American Polo League opener drew 2,938 - more than the Braves had drawn for all but three of their home dates through the end of May. The Milwaukee Zoo was host to a single-day-record throng of 18,344 late in May, and the annual Memorial Day parade down Wisconsin Avenue drew an estimated throng of 70,000. The Milwaukee Mile on the Wisconsin State Fair grounds in West Allis had conducted auto racing since 1903 - making it, in 2016, the second-oldest continuously-used auto-racing plant in the world - and a near-capacity crowd of 35,938 turned out for the USAC's Rex Mays Memorial race on June 6. In 1965, the Milwaukee Mile was one of the most heavily-used one-mile oval tracks in the country, hosting eight races and many other car-related functions, and had long been a regular stop on both the USAC open-wheel and NASCAR stock-car circuits. The USAC event usually was held the week after the Indianapolis 500 and featured most of the same cars and drivers, and racing fans considered the Milwaukee race to be to the Indy 500 what the Preakness was to the Kentucky Derby.

Another indication that the Braves had become secondary in the Milwaukee sports hierarchy was signaled by the masthead of the *Sentinel* in its June 2 editions. Since the Braves' arrival in Milwaukee, the morning paper had always carried a caricature of an Indian after a Braves game the previous day. If the Braves had won, the Indian was shown dancing; after a loss, it was shown as bedraggled, and after a rainout, it was dripping wet. By June 1965, the Indian had been moved from the top of the front page to the bottom, although it was occasionally returned to the masthead as the season progressed.

On June 1, the Braves also were relegated to afterthought status by the death of former Packers coach Curly Lambeau, 67, who suffered a heart attack while mowing the lawn at his residence in Sturgeon Bay. Lambeau, a former teammate of George Gipp at Notre Dame, had coached the Packers for 31 years after founding them in 1919 - the year before the NFL was formed - with the $500 he had received from the Acme Packing Company for the naming rights. He left in 1950 with a record of 226-132-22 and six NFL championships. Most of the column inches in both Milwaukee sports pages were given over to remembrances and tributes to Lambeau; among those interviewed were former Packer stars Tony Canadeo, Ted Fritsch, Buckets Goldenberg and Don Hutson. NFL commissioner Pete Rozelle, Chicago Bears owner-coach George Halas and Packer president Dominic Olejniczak offered their tributes as well. Conspicuously missing from any of the next-day stories was any comment by Vince Lombardi, who had returned the Packers to greatness after taking the head-coaching job in 1959. Lombardi and Lambeau were not friendly, and after City Stadium was renamed Lambeau Field later in 1965, Lombardi told friends that the stadium should have been named after him instead. Lombardi, who was in New York at the time of Lambeau's death, a day later issued a terse condolence statement, which read: "Lambeau's death is a loss not only to Green Bay and Wisconsin, but also to pro football. He will be remembered always by those who played with and for him."

The next day, along with its Lambeau tributes, the *Sentinel* ran an editorial bemoaning the passage of another segment of President Johnson's Great Society program, providing federal housing subsidies for middle-income families. LBJ's Democratic Party held huge majorities both in the House (294-140) and Senate (68-32), and Republicans, the *Sentinel* claimed, had lost lawmaking relevance. "To oppose such socialistic programs is a futile exercise for the GOP ... in so doing, they maintain their self-respect, but not much else, unless one is to count a reputation for being reactionary and obstructionist as a political asset - which it definitely is not for the Republicans ... Republicans can only hope that the people will eventually wake up to the fact that Uncle Sam is only fooling when he says he will take care of all your wants and needs."

Meanwhile, Gemini 4 was being readied in Florida for its launch the next day. Its 98-hour, 62-earth-orbit voyage would be highlighted by man's first space walk, a 20-minute venture by Edward White. Jim Lovell was the backup pilot for the Gemini 4 flight. He had lived on the 700 block of North 35th Street, was a 1946 graduate of Milwaukee's Juneau High, had attended the University of Wisconsin before continuing on to the U.S. Naval Academy, and had married Milwaukee native Marilyn Gerlach. Lovell, for whom 7th Street in downtown Milwaukee would later be renamed, flew the Gemini 7 and 12 and Apollo 8 and 13 missions, guiding the latter spacecraft around the moon and back to

Earth after a malfunction put the three-man crew's lives in jeopardy. The other Gemini 4 astronaut, James McDivitt, also had a Milwaukee connection, albeit an indirect one. His first-grade teacher in Chicago had been Sister M. Charleen, who in 1965 was principal of Our Lady Queen of Peace, a Catholic school on West Euclid Avenue in Milwaukee. Sister Charleen said the two had stayed in touch. "I think it's real tremendous that someone would give himself to a program of this kind," she said.

At the University of Wisconsin-Milwaukee, the athletic department reached an agreement to play its home football games at the North Division High stadium, which then seated 11,000, starting in 1966. UWM's football history dated to 1899, when it was known as Milwaukee Normal School, and in 1913 it had been one of the founding members of what was to become the Wisconsin Intercollegiate Athletic Conference. UWM in 1965 planned to upgrade its football program from College Division to University Division (the equivalent of Division I at that time), and the Panthers - known before 1965 as the Cardinals and before that the Green Gulls - played some of their home games at County Stadium from 1968-71. But interest was minimal, and the program was terminated after the 1974 season and was never revived. (Marquette, a national power before World War II, had dropped football after the 1960 season.)

After a rainout of their scheduled home game against San Francisco on June 2, the Braves earned a 10-3 win over the Giants the next day before 3,336. Milwaukee ended former Braves pitcher Bob Shaw's day early with a nine-run outburst, climaxed by Mathews' two-run homer, in the third. Ken Johnson earned his first win as a Brave with a six-hitter, and contributed a two-run single. Willie Mays wasn't in the Giants lineup because of a sore hip, although he walked as a pinch-hitter in the ninth. The Braves, needing someone to make a spot start because of the doubleheader, summoned lefty Dick Kelley from Atlanta and optioned out Bob Tiefenauer, who had been used sparingly most of the season. The next night (June 4), the Braves, in the opener of a four-game series against Los Angeles, treated 5,760 to a heirloom win, 5-2 on Eddie Mathews' three-run walk-off homer in the ninth.

Blasingame, pitching despite a sore thumb that he had injured during batting practice in Houston earlier in the week, and Claude Osteen matched each other through seven innings, with Blasingame wriggling free of a bases-loaded situation in the top of the ninth after Bob Miller, in relief of Osteen, had done likewise in the bottom of the eighth. Bragan surprised the crowd by letting Blasingame hit for himself with one out in the top of the ninth; his hunch paid off, as Blasingame singled. Alou singled Blasingame to third. With Mathews up, most people at County Stadium thought Dodgers manager Walter Alston would bring in left-handed reliever Ron Perranoski, who finished that season with 17 saves, to face the lefty-hitting Mathews. Alston stayed with Miller, a right-hander, and overshifted his infield to the first-base side - but he couldn't station anyone in the right-field bleachers, where Mathews' homer landed. "We're in it to the end, the way this gang is playing," Bragan said in the jubilant Braves clubhouse. Blasingame said this victory was, in some ways, even more satisfying than his one-hitter or his 14-inning complete game earlier in ths season. "This team (the Dodgers) worries a pitcher more than any team in the league," he said. "A lot of people say they're not much on power. But they make up for it by running all the time. You can't afford to let any of those guys get on the bases, the way they fly. And if you give up two or three runs with the pitching they have, you're going to lose."

The next day's game - a Saturday afternoon contest played before 4,416 in 61-degree weather - involved far less suspense. The Braves won 9-1 for their ninth win in 12 games as Cloninger (7-4) spaced nine hits, giving up only a solo homer to John Roseboro, and got an early cushion when Mack Jones hit a grand slam off Johnny Podres in the first. Frank Bolling, continuing his offensive resurgence after his .199 season in 1964, raised his average to .312 with two hits. Bolling had made the American League All-Star team in 1961 and 1962 while with the Tigers, and was challenging the Reds' Pete Rose for the NL starting berth at second base. The Braves now were in second place, trailing the Dodgers by only three games (and by just one game in the loss column) with a doubleheader scheduled for Sunday, June 6.

The Dodgers had reshuffled their rotation to allow them to pitch Koufax and Don Drysdale, arguably baseball's two best pitchers that year, in the Sunday doubleheader, but Koufax was a last-minute scratch. Alston had planned to pitch Koufax against the Braves on only three days of rest because he had gone only two innings in his previous start, but changed his mind - understandably, considering doctors had told Koufax before the season that he might be limited to only one start a week. Howie Reed, who had made only four major league starts during a major league career that had started in 1959, was chosen to replace Koufax. Not having to face Koufax, of course, solved one problem for the Braves, but it also created another for Bragan:

Should he send Kelley, just up from the minors, to the mound for the first game against Drysdale, and use Lemaster, the Braves' other scheduled starter, against Reed in the second game? Bragan knew that Alston, playing on the road and wanting to assure at least a split in the doubleheader and avoid a four-game sweep in the series, would start Drysdale in the first game and that he wasn't likely to lose to Kelley (or, for that matter, Lemaster). But if Lemaster pitched the second game, he had a good chance of beating Reed. Bragan, like most managers in the days when doubleheaders were far more frequent than in the 21st-century game, opted to play, in effect, for the split - throwing Kelley up against Drysdale in a pitching matchup that heavily favored the Dodgers, and then using Lemaster in the second game against Reed in a game in which the Braves would seem to have the advantage.

If that was Bragan's plan - he didn't say - it worked. Drysdale became the major leagues' first 10-game winner with a six-hit shutout as the Dodgers won the first game 4-0, but the Braves earned the split and the series win with a 6-4 win in the second game with Lemaster going 6 2/3 innings and Gene Oliver, who came into the game with only one homer all season, connecting twice. Reed lasted only 1 1/3 innings, giving up six hits and three earned runs.

The outcomes of the games weren't the main subjects of conversation that day, though - either in the postgame clubhouses or in the stands. Bragan, in the second game, made scorecards look like hieroglyphics after the Dodgers had scored three runs to cut their deficit to 6-4 with two outs in the top of the seventh. O'Dell had replaced Lemaster and given up singles to Maury Wills and

Jim Gilliam. With Lou Johnson, a dangerous right-handed hitter, coming up, Bragan brought in righty Bob Sadowski. He also removed first baseman Oliver from the game and replaced him with *O'Dell*. It was the only time in O'Dell's 13-season, 499-game career that he played any position other than pitcher.

Sadowski gave up an RBI single to Johnson, making the score 6-4 - whereupon Bragan moved O'Dell back to the mound and inserted Ty Cline into the game in center field, with Alou moving from left field to first base and Mack Jones switching from center field to left field. This prong of Bragan's strategy worked. O'Dell got Ron Fairly, a left-handed hitter, to ground out to first base, ending the inning. O'Dell then got the final six outs to record a two-stage save of the sort few if any of the fans in the ballpark had ever seen before.

Bragan often was criticized by reporters and fans for over-managing and for his tendency to abandon decorum when he was dealing with umpires and the media. A few days before, in the loss to the Dodgers that had ended when Los Angeles' Al Ferrara had drawn a bases-loaded walk in the ninth, Bragan had gotten into an ugly row with umpire Jocko Conlan, who had retired after the 1964 season but was brought back in 1965 to replace an injured ump. Arthur Daley had written in the *New York Times* that Bragan should be fined heavily and perhaps suspended for questioning Conlan's integrity. But few managers at the time had a quicker, more adroit baseball mind than Bragan's. He'd always had a job in baseball - and would have jobs long after the Braves fired him during the 1966 season - because of the imagination and daring that Branch Rickey had first seen two decades earlier.

While Bragan's manuevering had entranced the crowd of 17,751 - the largest of the season to this point, other than the home opener - many of those fans left County Stadium vowing never to return even if the Braves somehow got into the World Series or were forced by the courts to stay beyond 1965. The Braves were down to a minimal game-operations crew because the bulk of the team's workforce already was in Atlanta, and advance sales for the Sunday doubleheader indicated that the attendance would be in the 5,000 range, especially with the Rex Mays race at the Milwaukee Mile being held on the same day only a few miles away. But a collective baseball impulse - not to mention an 81-degree day, the warmest of the year so far - seized the Milwaukee baseball community that day; 89 percent of the fans at County Stadium that day were walk-up buyers, constituting, according to the Braves, the largest game-day sales total in the franchise's Milwaukee history. But only six of County Stadium's 17 ticket windows were opened, and lines of up to 200 formed outside each of them. Many fans didn't get to their seats until well after the game had started, and some, after seeing the lines or waiting in them, simply spun their cars around and went home. "We just don't know what to expect these days," assistant general manager Jim Fanning said. "And things were complicated when five stand-by ticket sellers cancelled out on us." Though the situation wasn't entirely the Braves' fault - the county still was responsible for overall stadium operations, and it too had cut back its staffing - letters from outraged patrons lambasting the Braves pockmarked the newspapers' op-ed sections for two weeks afterward, and the Braves didn't draw another paid crowd exceeding 17,000 until early August.

The ticket-office snafu notwithstanding, the Braves were exhilarated after taking three of four games against the Dodgers.

"We've got a great shot," Gene Oliver said. "The Dodgers' pitching has got to tire out because of the daily pressure (placed on it by L.A.'s popgun offense). Blasingame looks like he's ready to be one of the great ones, Cloninger is going to win his 20, and we've got Sadowski and Lemaster as the other two stoppers. Ken Johnson is going to be a big help to us, and it looks like the bullpen is squared away." Even Aaron, rarely one to make pronouncements, was caught up in the enthusiasm. "In overall strength, I'd say we've got the best club I've ever played on - even better than the (pennant-winning) 1957 and 1958 teams," he said. "Of course, we had more consistent pitching then. But overall, (the 1965 team is) a better hitting team. The only thing we need to win this thing is more consistent pitching." Alston, though, pointed out that the Dodgers had played makeshift lineups throughout the series because of injuries. "We may be a little healthier the next time we play them - pitching and otherwise," he said.

It was clear by now that the Braves' hitters were an episodic group, both within the context of the season and within the framework of a game. On Tuesday, June 8, at Wrigley Field, they were tied 2-2 with the Cubs going into extra innings, and only two of their four hits were of the resounding variety. In the top of the 10th, they hit four home runs - by Alou, Torre, Oliver and Aaron - to come within one homer of the major league record in that category, and won 8-2. Only three teams - the 1939 New York Giants, the 1949 Philadelphia Phillies and the 1961 San Francisco Giants - had ever hit five home runs in one inning. Bragan, after the 10th-inning barrage, asserted that his team ranked with the most prolific long-ball-hitting teams in baseball history, "and that includes the 1927 Yankees." It was the second time in five seasons that the Braves had registered four homers in one inning; Mathews, Joe Adcock, Aaron and Frank Thomas had gone back-to-back-to-back-to-back against the Reds in 1961. The 1965 breakout gave the win to Bob Sadowski, who had come on in place of Johnson to start the seventh and had pitched three scoreless innings. Torre, whose homer had come while pinch-hitting for Sadowski, was left out of the starting lineup because of a hamstring twinge, and Mack Jones had left the game in the seventh with a groin-muscle pull. The game, of course, was a day contest, before 4,039 at Wrigley.

That night, the *Journal* broke a story that indicated Bill Bartholomay, for the second time in 1965, had offered to pay $500,000 - $400,000 to Milwaukee County and $100,000 to Teams Inc - to be allowed to move his team to Atlanta during the All-Star break in mid-July. This was a contradiction of what Bartholomay had said earlier in the season, after his first buy-out proposal had been summarily rejected by the county, and the idea made less even sense in June than it had made in April. Beyond the fact no major league team since 1890 had moved in the middle of a season, the injunction that had fused the Braves to Milwaukee for one last season was still in effect and would have to be set aside - a legal process that could take weeks. Schedules also would have to be reworked throughout the National League on almost no notice, and a temporary home would have to be found for the Atlanta Crackers, the Braves' Triple-A affiliate, who were playing their final season at Atlanta-Fulton County Stadium.

Some speculated that Walter O'Malley was behind the offer, given the fact he had said in Milwaukee earlier in the month that transferring the Braves out of Milwaukee immediately would be the best course of action for all concerned. The money offered may even have been O'Malley's, because the Braves were far from cash-rich. Ralph De Horge, the team's assistant treasurer and secretary, said the Braves' break-even attendance threshold was 1.2 million, and they were on pace to draw barely one-third that. He also said that by accepting the offer, the county could expect to make $300,000 more than it could by forcing the Braves to stay for the remainder of the 1965 season.

The next morning, the *Sentinel* carried the predictable response from Grobschmidt: "To hell with them." The Board of Supervisors president said he would meet with Edmund Fitzgerald and John Doyne before June 21, 11 days hence, and would not take any action until then. Fitzgerald said only that he didn't feel he could speak for Teams Inc until the group had time to study the offer. Aside from Grobschmidt, opinion on the county board regarding the offer appeared divided. Herbert C. Froemming, a county board member and a member of the commission that operated County Stadium, was angry at the idea that the county might be motivated by the money to accept the offer. "We didn't build the stadium to get some rental (income)," he said. "It was built for major league baseball, for entertainment. We don't make money on it. We don't build swimming pools or golf courses to make money either." But another board member, Donald F. Weber, said the buyout price should be much higher - he mentioned $1.5 million - and said none of that money should go to Teams Inc. "Teams Inc didn't get raped," he said. "It was the county of Milwaukee that got raped."

Ford Frick expressed some enthusiasm for the proposal, saying he had insisted all along that the Braves had to honor the final year of their County Stadium lease unless they were released from that lease by the county. But he also indicated, predictably, that he would not intercede in what he considered a National League matter. He also said he couldn't guarantee when or if Milwaukee would get a replacement team, "but I will say there would be a better spirit around the National League" to move quickly in that direction if the buyout offer were to be accepted. O'Malley and Bill DeWitt, owner of the Reds, said they would go along with whatever Milwaukee County decided. DeWitt had a further suggestion. "The only way Milwaukee is going to get a major league club (after the Braves' departure) would be to get Bill Veeck (to operate it). He's the only guy in the country who can put two million people in the Milwaukee park in a year."

Veeck was out of baseball in 1965, working for ABC's *Wide World of Sports* and completing his second book, *The Hustler's Handbook*, which was published in 1966. He harshly criticized the Milwaukee "Carpetbaggers" in the book, but did not express any interest in returning to the city where he had operated his first professional team. Asked later in the season if he would consider returning to Milwaukee, Veeck said: "I'm waiting to see who is going to be the new commissioner. If he turns out to be of the same homogenized pablum as Ford Frick, I'll remain at home and go into a respectable business such as running dope." *Sentinel* sports editor Lloyd Larson wrote: "They must take us for a bunch of rubes" and urged Teams Inc and the county "to keep 'em here and make 'em sweat."

That evening (June 10), the *Journal* reported that the Braves' offer would be addressed the following Wednesday, June 16, at the Board of Supervisors meeting that night. It was affirmed that the county, if it so chose, could ask Judge Robert Drechsler to vacate the 1964 order that he had issued to force the Braves to honor the last year of their lease. The *Journal* had a special polling department that it often used to gauge public opinion on controversial matters. It polled 160 people, 84 percent of whom said they had been to at least one Braves game and 41 percent of whom considered themselves strong fans of the team. Forty-two percent of those polled said the county should refuse the Braves' offer; 28 percent wanted the offer accepted, and 30 percent were not sure. Comments varied widely. "They should starve to death." one respondent said. "They're eventually going to go anyway. They might as well go now," replied another.

It was one of the most frenzied news days in Milwaukee's recent history, and not only because of the Braves' attempt to buy their way out of town. Muhammad Ali, the newly crowned heavyweight boxing champion, came with only a few hours notice to the Black Muslim mosque on North Third Street "to meet my Muslim brothers and sisters in Milwaukee." No whites were allowed inside the mosque for the meeting, during which Ali - still called Cassius Clay by the Milwaukee newspapers - was reported to be subdued, at least by his standards. He had heard of a spate of racially-charged incidents in Milwaukee since the start of 1965, and said he had decided to have himself driven the 90 miles from Chicago on the spur of the moment. If his manner was understated, his statements were not. Among other things, he called civil-rights leader Dr. Martin Luther King Jr. an "Uncle Tom," and called himself "the most hated man in America. They don't like me because I'm free and won't go downtown and pretend I'm not who I am."

Richard Nixon, the former Vice President and 1960 presidential candidate whose political career seemingly had been blunted by his defeat by Pat Brown in the California gubernatorial election in 1962, also was in town, for a fund-raising dinner at the Milwaukee Auditorium. The $100-per-plate dinner was attended by 2,000. Nixon urged general backing of President Johnson's Vietnam escalation - the U.S. troop strength in Southeast Asia was now up to 51,000, triple what it had been a year before, and would be increased to 75,000 by the end of June - but said nothing about his political future, if any. Little could anyone at that dinner have imagined that Nixon less than four years later would be sworn in as the 37th President of the United States. While the *Sentinel* continued to urge support of the war, the *Journal* ran an op-ed piece described the war as "a quagmire, literally and figuratively. The U.S. seems to be going steadily deeper into the Vietnam morass without meaningful public discussion and debate on official levels about where we are going."

Whether the news of the buyout offer had any impact on the Braves during the second game of their series in Chicago is unknown, but their cannonading bats fell silent during a 4-2 loss to the Cubs on June 8. The next day, though, Tony Cloninger earned his eighth pitching victory and Ken Johnson, making his first relief appearance as a Brave, struck out Ron Santo and Ernie Banks with two runners on to complete a 6-4 win. The team then proceeded to St. Louis to begin a four-game series against the defending World Series champion Cardinals and first-year manager Red Schoendienst, who had been the final piece in the Braves' World Series championship mosaic in 1957.

Cloninger, despite his 8-4 record, saw his ERA climb to 3.48 and was having trouble with his control, having walked 53 batters, including seven (two intentional) in seven innings against the Cubs. He had walked only 82 batters during the 1964 season. "It's a mystery to me," he said. "Maybe I'm thinking about it too much. My arm feels strong and I'm not going to worry about it. I'm just going out and pitch my game. But I'm not happy about the way I've been pitching."

Bragan, searching all season for a consistent leadoff hitter, had assigned Felipe Alou to that spot while shuttling him between first base and the outfield, depending on the pitching matchups. Gene Oliver filled in for Torre, still out with his hamstring issue, behind the plate. Mack Jones, who missed only one game because of his groin-muscle pull, was back in center field. Mathews had been batting second most of the season, but Bragan moved him back to the cleanup spot and moved Bolling up to the No. 2 hole.

The Braves continued to play efficiently the next day, beating the Cardinals 4-1 while scoring all of their runs in the seventh - three on a homer by Alou. Johnson, two days after finishing off the Cubs by striking out Santo and Banks, got the start and went the distance, retiring the first 11 and the last eight batters he faced while crafting a three-hitter. Jones and Aaron homered off Bob Gibson. On Sunday, June 13, Blasingame continued his masterful mound work, fashioning a four-hitter as the Braves won 4-2 in the first game of a doubleheader. The second game, though, was a reminder of the team's collective multiple-personality disorder. The Cardinals won 12-2 after scoring seven unearned runs in the fourth, during which the

Braves committed three errors and were hit with three ejections. Oliver was thrown out of the game after home-plate umpire Stan Landes - the same ump involved in the orange-juice argument that had led to Bragan's firing as Pirates manager in 1957 - called Dick Groat safe after he slid into Oliver on a suicide-squeeze attempt. After a fielders choice, Lou Brock doubled. Julian Javier attempted to score from first on the play. Jones made a pinpoint throw from center field to nail Javier at the plate, but third-base umpire Al Barlick called obstruction on Fischer after he bumped into Javier when the latter was rounding third. Bragan and Fischer were tossed during the ensuing argument. The Braves' bats were silenced by Bob Purkey, whose ERA was 7.38 entering the game.

The National League schedule listed the Braves as idle on Monday, June 14, before they began a 13-game homestand with a three-game home series against Philadelphia, but it wasn't an off-day for the Braves. The team traveled from St. Louis to Atlanta for another exhibition game in the new Atlanta-Fulton County Stadium. A crowd of 24,456 showed up to see the Braves beat the White Sox 5-1. Back in Milwaukee, the legal battle over the Braves intensified. Wisconsin Attorney General Blanton La Follette, whose office had stayed out of the jurisdictional dispute, said after meeting with Milwaukee County Chief Executive John Doyne he was considering joining the antitrust suit against the Braves. The question that had to be answered first, according to Doyne, was whether the plaintiffs in the case would seek financial compensation or specific performance - in this case, putting a complete stop to the Atlanta move and forcing the Braves to stay in Milwaukee not only through the 1965 season, but beyond. Meanwhile, Bill Bartholomay said he hasn't heard back from anyone in authority regarding his $500,000 buyout offer. "I can only say that I hope they will be willing to talk to us," he said. He also denied that the Braves had made previous attempts to buy their way out of Milwaukee during the season, even though McHale had already acknowledged that a similar offer had been made (and refused) in February.

June 14 was a busy day on other baseball fronts. The Reds' Jim Maloney pitched no-hit ball over 10 innings and tied an NL extra-inning-game record with 18 strikeouts, but lost 1-0 to the Mets when Johnny Lewis hit a homer in the 11th. The Cubs, in the last year of their five-season experimentation with a "college of coaches" who would split managerial responsibility and operate the team as a sort of co-op, kicked "head coach" Bob Kennedy upstairs into a front-office position. Lou Klein, one of the other coaches, became the nominal manager. The "College of Coaches" would be abandoned in 1966 when Leo Durocher took over the team. "I'm not the head coach here," he emphatically told reporters. "I'm the *manager*."

At its regular meeting on Tuesday, June 15, the Milwaukee Common Council, to nobody's surprise, voted to reject Bartholomay's buyout offer, calling it "unwarranted and unprincipled." The county Board of Supervisors, meanwhile, also rejected the offer, and Teams Inc did likewise. All three votes were unanimous; as far as all three bodies were concerned, there would be no buyout and no early Braves departure from Milwaukee, regardless of how much money it might involve and what it might mean to Milwaukee's chances of getting a replacement team. City and county officials, with the antitrust lawsuit pending, also discussed the possibility of serving representatives of the other nine NL teams with subpoenas when they arrived for games in Milwaukee.

At County Stadium that night before a gathering of 4,065, Eddie Mathews broke a 3-for-25 slump and banged out the 2,000th hit of his career - a home run - as the Braves punished the Phillies 12-7. "I'm glad I got it like I did, instead of on a blooper," Mathews said. "I was really struggling, believe me. I was beginning to wonder if I should try to beat out a bunt - anything to get it over with." He was the 111th major leaguer to attain the 2,000-hit milestone; Harvey Kuenn and Mickey Mantle had done so in 1964.

Mathews' mother, Eloise, with whom he had an extremely close relationship, had come in from Santa Barbara, Calif., for the homestand, and Mathews said getting to 2,000 with his mother present added even more meaning to the accomplishment. He also said he hoped to get to 2,500 hits before he retired (a goal he did not achieve, ending his career in 1968 with 2,315 hits). "But my biggest thrill will be when Hank and I break the Gehrig-Ruth record (for most home runs hit by teammates). If the two of us hit 30 homers apiece for the next two years - and I don't see any reason we can't - we'll have passed them." At the time, they had 762 homers between them as teammates. The Ruth-Gehrig record was listed at 870 in 1965, but later was adjusted to 859, the total recognized by MLB as official. (Gehrig spent most of the 1923 and 1924 seasons in the minors, and therefore wasn't Ruth's teammate throughout each of those two seasons.) Aaron and Mathews would combine to hit 863 homers as Braves teammates before Mathews was traded to Houston after the 1966 season.

Felipe Alou continued to thrive in the leadoff spot, but not in the conventional leadoff manner: He finished with two homers, a single and six RBI. He had been hitting .217 when Bragan elevated him to the leadoff spot; now, he was batting .302. Sandy Alomar, who had been dividing time at shortstop with Woody Woodward as Denis Menke remained on the disabled list, had four hits to raise his average from .225 to .263, and Carty had three. (Menke would play in only four games, all as a pinch-hitter, in June.) Cloninger staggered through 7 2/3 innings to get the victory despite giving up five more walks. Lew Burdette, 38, the three-victory Braves hero of the 1957 World Series, pitched two innings in relief for the Phillies and gave up eight hits and five earned runs. He would enjoy a brief revival as a relief pitcher for the California Angels in 1966, but retired after the 1967 season, with 203 career wins.

The Braves continued to hit the ball hard the following night - too hard, in fact. Milwaukee amassed nine hits against Jim Bunning, but hit six line drives directly at defenders as the Phillies beat the Braves 6-2. Denny Lemaster, the 17-game winner of 1964, took another backstep, lasting only 2 1/3 innings while giving up five hits - including Pat Corrales' first major league homer - and five earned runs to bloat his ERA to 5.60. Attendance was 3,479, but miniscule crowd counts had long since ceased to be a news story in Milwaukee, though out-of-town writers continued to bemoan baseball's mishandling of the situation. Dick Young, the best-known baseball beat writer of his generation, had covered the Brooklyn Dodgers through their death throes in 1957. He wrote in the *New York Daily News* that the men to whom he sardonically referred as the "Lords of Baseball" were treating Milwaukee as contemptuously as they had treated

Brooklyn. "Now all the world can see the pattern of the men running baseball," Young wrote after Bartholomay's attempt to buy out the last year of his Milwaukee lease. "It is the same kind of mind that bribes judges, DAs and cops. Everyone has a price. What's yours? A half-million? At first the people who run baseball tried blackmail. That didn't work, so now it's bribery."

The Braves weren't the only entity facing court action that summer. Lloyd Barbee, a Milwaukee attorney and civil-rights activist who also was a state Assemblyman, on June 17 filed a class-action lawsuit against Milwaukee Public Schools. The school district, in an effort to solve its segregation problem, had begun busing black children into schools in predominantly white areas. But the policy had been to keep the black children together in the same classes they had attended at their previous schools, and Barbee and other integrationists insisted that the MPS policy was intended to circumvent the actual mixing of white and black children within classrooms as well as schools. (Other cities, principally St. Louis, had tried the busing-en-masse approach, but had soon abandoned it, and were now splitting up all-black classes once they arrived at their assigned school.) Barbee, who had been president of the state NAACP chapter at the time the first anti-segregation legal actions had commenced in 1963, would continue to be a vocal and articulate advocate for underserved Milwaukee school children for many years.

The Braves won the series with the Phillies, prevailing 4-2 on June 17 as Torre broke a 2-2 tie in the eighth with an RBI single. They matched their season high by going 10 games over .500, at 33-23, and were still in second place, 3 1/2 games behind Los Angeles. And they appeared to be in a position to make up ground on the Dodgers during their next six series - against the Cardinals, Cubs, Reds, Mets, Phillies and Pirates. Other than Johnson and Blasingame, the starting pitching had been iffy, and O'Dell was showing some weardown signs. But the series-opening win against the Phillies had been the seventh time in the past 21 games that the Braves had scored at least eight runs in a game. Menke was due back soon from his injury, Alou and Mathews had broken out of their slumps, Aaron was Aaron, and the defense, though still erratic, was improved. If the Braves could win their next six series - all against teams trailing them - they could solidify their position as the primary challengers to the Dodgers and Giants.

Instead, they lost all six series while going 4-13 and dropping into sixth place by July 3.

The free-fall began with a 5-4, 10-inning loss to St. Louis on Friday, June 18, before a larger-than-usual crowd of 10,862 patrons, including 4,000 who were there on discounted tickets provided through a Cutler-Hammer Inc. buyout. Ironically, Edmund Fitzgerald - the president of Cutler-Hammer, a Milwaukee-based electronic-product manufacturer, at the time - said earlier in the day that the Braves had ignored a Teams Inc communication suggesting that Teams Inc buy out the ballpark for a game (as it had for Opening Day) and use the occasion to honor former Braves and Brewers. Bill White's solo homer in the top of the 10th provided the margin of victory after the Braves had frittered away a 4-1 lead by giving up three unearned runs in the sixth. Bragan, giving Eddie Mathews a day off, had started Mike de la Hoz at third base, and de la Hoz made the error that led to the three unearned runs.

The Braves came back the next night for a 6-5 win, but Lemaster didn't survive the second inning the next day in a 6-4 St. Louis victory on June 20, although Jones and Aaron hit solo homers and Denis Menke had a pinch-hit single in his first game since May 13. (In those days, teams weren't allowed to send players coming off injuries to the minors on rehabilitation assignments.) The Braves outhit the Cardinals 11-6, but were only 2 for 10 with runners in scoring position. Jones took a called third strike with the tying run at first to end the game. Alou strained a leg muscle running the bases in the ninth; earlier, after another round of positional shuffling by Bragan, Alou found himself playing shortstop for the first time as a major leaguer. (He played shortstop only one other time in his 2,006-game career.) He handled two popups and three ground balls without mishap.

Meanwhile, tensions between the warring off-field factions were heightening. Edmund Fitzgerald said he had written to Bartholomay accusing him of trying to drive attendance down to make the case that Milwaukee no longer was capable of supporting a major league team. Asked to comment, Bartholomay said: "I haven't seen the letter, but I imagine it was one of those things I wouldn't care to comment on." After the Braves' loss on June 20, assistant general manager Jim Fanning barred *Sentinel* beat writer Lou Chapman, who had covered the Braves since their arrival in 1953, from the clubhouse. Chapman said the ban was because of "recent stories I had written which the club considered 'of a negative nature.'" Later, Chapman said Fanning also told him: "You have had a disgusting effect on players, employees and throughout the stadium. Our people have a tingle whenever you come around them." Chapman, smiling, later said, "I might have replied that at my stage of life, to set anyone a-tingle is quite an accomplishment." The Milwaukee chapter of the Baseball Writers Association of America filed protests with Ford Frick and Joe McGuff, the *Kansas City Star* writer (and Marquette graduate) who was the BBWAA's president at the time. The Braves quickly lifted the banishment, Chapman returned to his normal duties the following day, and Frick apologized on behalf of MLB to Chapman, calling his ejection from the clubhouse "thoughtless, ill-considered and high-handed."

In Madison, the state Legislature unanimously passed a bill authorizing Milwaukee County to operate a team in County Stadium if the Braves were forced by the courts to stay or if baseball provided a replacement team by 1966. Governor Warren Knowles signed the bill, which, among other things, permitted the county to formally apply for a major league franchise for 1966 and begin the antitrust-suit process if the application was refused - which, of course, everyone knew it would be. In Washington, D.C., Wisconsin Sen. William Proxmire asked the federal Justice Department to investigate whether Bartholomay's $500,000 buyout offer "constitutes an element of conspiracy against Milwaukee County." Even the Braves' ownership group was in the midst of internal strife. The *Chicago Sun-Times* reported that Bartholomay was romantically involved with Marge Coleman, ex-wife of Del Coleman, the only Milwaukee-based member of the syndicate.

The NL schedule alloted the Braves an off-day on Monday, June 21, but again, it hardly was an off-day for the players. The Braves flew to Atlanta for another exhibition game, which it won 6-4 over Minnesota before 38,402. This would be the fifth of six exhibition games the Braves would play in Atlanta in 1965, drawing a total of 168,958. In Milwaukee, the Braves at this point had drawn 164,536 for 28 regular-season dates.

After their return to Milwaukee, the Braves lost 6-1 to the Cubs and were overtaken for second place by the Reds as Chicago's Doug Clemens - better known for his exploits as a football star at Syracuse University than for his baseball accomplishments - hit a three-run homer for the visitors off Ken Johnson in the fourth. It was Johnson's first loss since his acquisition by the Braves. Dan Osinski, who had received only token work for the past month, was brought in to pitch the eighth and gave up three game-clinching runs. Sadowski, who hadn't pitched in three weeks because of illness, turned in two scoreless innings. But Menke, whose injured knee seemingly had been healing, found himself unable to run again. It was finally determined that Menke had phlebitis, and no timetable for his return could be established.

On Wednesday, June 23, Blasingame improved to 8-3 with a 6-2, four-hit conquest of the Cubs before 7,440, becoming only the third left-handed starting pitcher out of 20 to beat the Cubs in 1965. (Spahn and Koufax were the others.) Blasingame, who in May had applied lessons learned from Warren Spahn while beating him in his return to Milwaukee, unveiled a screwball with which he said Spahn had helped him. The screwball, when thrown by a left-handed pitcher like Blasingame to a right-handed hitter, breaks away from the batter. In 21st-century baseball, it is usually described as a two-seam fastball and isn't generally thought to have any undue effects on a pitcher's arm. But managers and pitching coaches described it as an arm-killer in 1965, even though Spahn had used it as a primary weapon throughout his 363-win career and the Giants' Carl Hubbell had ridden it into the Hall of Fame. (Christy Mathewson, a right-hander who redefined pitching in the first 15 years of the 20th century, also used a screwball, but he called it a "fadeaway.") But in later life, Hubbell's arm was so twisted out of shape that his left palm faced straight out, and pitching coaches pointed this out to discourage their charges from using the screwball. Even when acknowledging in 1965 that he had adopted the screwball, Blasingame called it "a changeup with a scroogie effect." And he insisted he wasn't an off-speed "thumber," even though he threw non-fastballs about 30 percent of the time, by his own admission. Some of his teammates had taken to calling him "Stu," after soft-tossing late-inning reliever Stu Miller, and Blasingame made it clear that he liked the nickname not at all.

The Braves lost 3-1 to Dick Ellsworth the next night in the final game of the Cub series as Ellsworth beat Tony Cloninger with a six-hitter. Cloninger (10-5) seemed to have solved his recent problems with bases on balls, walking only one in 6 1/3 innings, but was wild in the strike zone, giving up nine hits.

This brought the second-place Reds, who had moved within 2 1/2 games of the Dodgers after winning eight of their past 10, into County Stadium for a four-game series. The Reds' upward progression had begun when Dick Sisler, in his first full year as Cincinnati manager, moved Tommy Harper into the leadoff spot and Pete Rose from No. 1 to No. 2, with Vada Pinson, Frank Robinson and eventual NL RBI champion Deron Johnson following. Those five, along with catcher Johnny Edwards, shortstop Leo Cardenas, and first basemen Gordie Coleman and Tony Perez, gave the Reds perhaps the most combustible combination of pitching and speed in the league. Sammy Ellis, a 24-year-old lefty who had won only 12 games in three previous seasons, was having a breakout year to complement Jim Maloney in the starting rotation, and Bill McCool, 21, had emerged as a viable closer. The Reds also seemed to be adjusting to Sisler, who had taken over the team the previous August when Fred Hutchinson had been forced to relinquish his position because of the lung cancer that would take his life in November.

The Reds and Braves hadn't met since the sixth game of the season; the Reds clearly were a better team than they had been in April, and the question entering this four-game series was whether the Braves had improved since then. The Reds were healthier than they had been in April, while the Braves were not expecting to have Lemaster, who had a sore arm, available to take his turn that weekend. Alou had suffered a thigh-muscle pull and was considered an unlikely participant in the Cincinnati series, and Menke remained out indefinitely.

Even though the teams hadn't reached the halfway point yet, the first three games involved postseason-type energy that belied the panorama of empty seats at County Stadium. Before 6,347 on Friday night, June 25, the Reds earned a 3-1, 11-inning victory on a two-run homer by a reserve catcher from Nathan Hale High in West Allis who once had dreamed of playing for the Braves - who hadn't been interested in signing him.

Don Pavletich, by 1965 a resident of Brookfield, was considered the second-string catcher behind Johnny Edwards, but as with Gene Oliver on the Braves' side, he was getting more starts because of his offensive numbers entering the game: .346 batting average, seven homers, 21 RBI. The first of only two graduates from Hale - which was opened in 1939 - to play in the majors as of 2016, Pavletich had signed a $40,000 bonus contract with the Reds after his graduation in 1956. A Braves fan as a student at Hale, he said he would have accepted a considerably smaller bonus from Milwaukee, but the Braves weren't interested in giving him any bonus at all. "After all, they had Del Crandall in his prime," said Pavletich, who did receive sizable bonus offers from the White Sox, Orioles and Yankees before signing with the then-Redlegs.

In accordance with the bonus-baby rules at the time he signed, Pavletich had to stay on the Reds roster instead of getting developmental time in the minors. He played in only one game in 1957 before missing the rest of that year and all of the 1958 season while in military service. He had returned to the Reds in 1959, but, again, he was limited to only one game appearance that year. Pavletich didn't get back to Cincinnati until 1962, and had played sparingly before earning part-time duty in 1965. Johnny Edwards had won the regular catching job as a rookie in 1961 and had been a three-time All-Star, but even though he remained the catching incumbent in 1965, the Reds organization regarded him as a placeholder after that. Cincinnati earlier in 1965 had chosen Johnny Bench in the second round of baseball's first amateur draft, and Bench made his major league debut in August 1967. Edwards was traded to the Cardinals after the 1967 season, giving the job permanently to Bench, who redefined both the mechanics and the standards of every major league catcher who came after him.

In the series opener against the Braves, Pavletich started at catcher and batted in the No. 6 position, and his rooting section was conspicuous in the sparse crowd. It included his parents, in-laws, two uncle-aunt sets, and about 20 employees from the Bucyrus-Erie plant at which he had worked during summer vacations while still in high school. They saw a taut game in which Dick Kelley, taking Lemaster's place and making only his second major league start, pitched Sammy Ellis to a 1-1 stalemate through nine innings, with Torre's fourth-inning homer accounting for the only Milwaukee run. Kelley was lifted for a pinch-hitter in the bottom of the ninth, but the Braves couldn't score, and O'Dell came on to start the 10th. In the top of the 11th, Pinson flied to center and Robinson walked before O'Dell gave up the game-deciding homer to Pavletich - the last HR Pavletich, who wound up with 46 homers at the end of a 12-year major league career, would hit that season. Ellis retired the Braves in order in the bottom of the 11th to wrap up his major-league-leading 12th win, which included 12 strikeouts. (Sandy Koufax that night beat the Pirates 4-1 on the West Coast for his own 12th victory.) In Houston, 44-year-old Warren Spahn and the Mets lost to 19-year-old Larry Dierker and the Astros, 6-2. It was the sixth straight loss for Spahn, whose next outing would be against his former teammates on June 29 in New York. Casey Stengel, 75, was still the Mets' nominal manager, but he had broken his hip in a fall a few weeks earlier. He also had broken with Spahn over how the pitching staff, including Spahn the pitcher, should be handled. Soon, both would be headed to California - Spahn to San Francisco to join the Giants, Stengel to Glendale (his longtime off-season home) as a retiree.

The Braves, who had fallen behind the streaking Giants and into fourth place, regrouped on Saturday, June 26, for a harrowing 2-1 victory before 5,002. Ken Johnson pitched a six-hitter for his sixth victory, getting each of the last five outs on ground-outs as he used his knuckleball as a changeup and had the long-ball-conscious Reds rolling over the ball on almost every swing. Bragan had scrambled his lineup again, moving Rico Carty, never known for his speed, to leadoff, with Mack Jones batting third and Eddie Mathews batting seventh - something he did only 72 times in his 2,391-game career. Mathews was 0 for 4 with two strikeouts, and the changes didn't achieve much for six innings against former Brave bonus baby Joey Jay. But in the seventh with the score tied 1-1, the Braves pushed across the go-ahead run against Bill McCool as Bolling drew a one-out walk, advanced to third on Aaron's single, and scored on a wild pitch. This set up the first real fork-in-the-road Sunday doubleheader of the season - one that, in the 1950s, likely would have sold out County Stadium. On June 28, 1965, 13,918 attended in 95-degree heat, and only a small fraction of that crowd was there at the end, though the spectators got more than their money's worth in the first game alone.

In the first game, the Reds unleashed their arsenal against Wade Blasingame, who had given up as many as four runs only twice in his 16 previous starts. Blasingame was gone after 2 1/3 innings, having surrendered six hits and six earned runs. The Reds led 7-1 after three innings and extended that advantage to 9-1 in the sixth as Tommy Harper hit a two-run homer against Dave Eilers, who had just been recalled from Atlanta. Eilers originally signed with the Braves organization in 1959 as a 22-year-old, and had pitched in six games for the Braves in 1964.

Improbably, almost impossibly, the first win of his major league career loomed after the Braves scored eight runs in the bottom of the sixth to earn a 9-9 tie. Tempers were almost as heated as the weather; Mathews, back in the No. 2 slot in the batting order, was ejected in the first inning by home-plate umpire Tony Venzon for arguing a called third strike from Reds pitcher John Tsitouris; Tsitouris, in turn, was tossed during the eight-run sixth after Torre tied the game with a three-run homer into the left-field corner that Tsitouris insisted was foul. The Braves already had lost first baseman Gene Oliver to a leg injury sustained when he slid into home plate early in the game, and Carty had been taken out in a double-switch. With Alou still out, this meant veteran utilityman Lou Klimchock, another callup from Atlanta, had to play first base for one of only 33 times in his 12-season career.

O'Dell, fighting through overwork-related fatigue, got the Braves through the seventh and eighth inning, but gave up a solo homer to Frank Robinson in the top of the ninth to give the Reds a 10-9 win. The second game was more epilogue than plot; the Reds won 10-2 with a six-run fourth - capped by Vada Pinson's grand slam - against Bob Sadowski, who was making his first start since May 23. Jim Maloney cruised through a seven-hitter for his eighth win.

To make matters worse, the Braves had to drag themselves onto a plane for New York for a 6 p.m. doubleheader against the Mets the following evening. (The teams had been rained out on May 7.) With his pitching staff trashed after the Reds series, Bragan needed not only a victory but a complete game from ace Tony Cloninger in the first game of the doubleheader against the Mets, who had lost 21 of 23. He got neither; although Cloninger, in his fifth try for his 11th victory, struck out 11, he gave up nine hits and five runs in 5 2/3 innings. The last two runs were unearned because of a two-out fly ball to right field that was misplayed by Hank Aaron - one of only four errors Aaron committed that season - and Jack Fisher pitched a nine-hitter in the Mets' 5-2 win. Roy McMillan, the former Braves shortstop who had been sold to the Mets during the previous off-season, singled home one run and tripled in another.

In the second game, New York ended Hank Fischer's start with a five-run fourth and the Mets went on to sweep the doubleheader with a 6-3 win. This meant the Braves had lost four games in the space of 34 hours. It also meant they were 36-32 and in fifth place, still only five games behind the Dodgers but now only one game ahead of the sixth-place Phillies. Bragan, whose latest lineup experiment featured Mack Jones batting leadoff, predictably got himself ejected during the second game in an attempt to jolt his team.

The Braves' predicament looked even more dire after the first inning of the game the next night (June 29) as Braves starter Dick Kelley was knocked out in the second after giving up four runs. But facing Warren Spahn for what turned out to the next-to-last time, the Braves tied the game 4-4 in the top of the third, scored four runs in the sixth through ninth innings, and survived a two-run Mets ninth to hang on for an 8-6 victory. The Braves, reverting to their long-ball-or-nothing DNA, hit three homers, by Bolling, Mathews and Oliver, off Spahn, who gave up eight hits and six runs (four earned) in six innings, and clearly had little left. Spahn's stay with the Mets would not last much longer; the tipping point would come against Houston on July 10, when Spahn lasted only one inning and gave up six hits and four earned runs to drop his final record with the Mets to 4-12 and pin him with his eighth straight loss.

In Philadelphia the next night, the Braves faced another future Hall of Famer - the Phillies' Jim Bunning, who had to come out of the game in the fifth inning because of an ankle injury. But the Braves could manage only one run - on a homer by Blasingame, his first of the season and the second of his career - off reliever Gary Wagner. The Braves had turned four double plays to allow Blasingame to skirt early- and middle-inning disaster, but in the seventh with the Braves leading 2-1, Tony Taylor singled home the tying run and Johnny Callison broke the tie with another single. The Braves lost 3-2 for their 11th defeat in 17 games ... and their June swoon would extend two weeks into July.

Power Outage

• • •

As a mental elixir, the annual Circus Parade couldn't have come at a better time for a city on the verge of change on so many fronts.

The first six months of the year had been punctuated by, among other things, the legal wrangling over the Braves, the increasingly strident voices of opponents of *de facto* segregation in Milwaukee, military draft calls that seemed to be multiplying every day, mounting frustration over the stop-and-go status of a freeway system that had been under construction or bureaucratic consideration for more than a decade, and ominous indications that the region's economic artery - the Menomonee River - was reaching an ecological crisis stage. So on July 1, when the Circus Train arrived in Milwaukee after its 120-mile journey from the circus' national headquarters in Baraboo, a crowd of 13,000 (larger than all but three of the Braves' home dates to that point in 1965) was there to greet it and perhaps harken back to days of simpler pleasures and less vexing problems.

Three days later, an estimated throng of 600,000, described by organizers as the largest Fourth of July crowd in the country and by far the largest ever to witness a Circus Parade in

Milwaukee, gathered to immerse themselves in a tradition that had begun in 1935, though it didn't become a full-on civic celebration until 1963. The spectators lined a 3 1/2-mile Circus Parade route along Wisconsin Avenue to see the animals, clowns, acrobats and colorfully-painted wagons as they made their way from the waterfront to the Milwaukee Arena for the start of a four-day, sold-out run. Commented Milwaukee County chief executive John Doyne: "We're going to lose the Braves, but at least we'll always have Baraboo." He was only partly right. The Circus Parade was still held in Milwaukee into the 21st century, but on a much smaller scale after 1968, when Summerfest emerged as a celebration that combined the best of previous events, including the Circus Parade and the Midsummer Festival, held from 1933-41. By 2016, Summerfest had become one of the largest and most diverse music events in the world. Attendance that year was 804,116. Headliners over the years have included Bob Hope (1968), Bon Jovi (1993 and 2009), Pearl Jam (1995), Rod Stewart (1989), the Doors (1972) and the Grateful Dead (1978).

The turnout gave Milwaukee another reason to crow about its ability to stage extravaganzas with record crowds. Besides the 1941 Tony Zale-Billy Pryor boxing match (with former heavyweight champion Jack Dempsey as referee) that set a still-standing record for that sport with 135,000 spectators, an estimated 225,000 had shoehorned themselves onto and around the streets for the parade that followed the Braves' 1957 World Series championship, and 200,000 had taken to Wisconsin Avenue to celebrate V-J Day in August 1945. The largest crowd ever in Milwaukee, though, was 900,000 for the parade that highlighted the American Legion's national convention in 1941. (The

Zale-Pryor fight was an adjunct to the national Legion convention.) Milwaukee was a first-run location for any entertainment genre as well; later in July 1965, a crowd of 8,800 showed up at the Washington Park amphitheater to see a production of the play *Music Man.*

In Philadelphia, the Braves began July as they had ended June, dropping a 3-2 decision that doomed Milwaukee to its fifth straight series loss and its sixth loss in its past seven games. Ray Culp's three-hitter gave the Phillies their 16th win in 22 games and moved them ahead of the Braves into sole possession of fourth place. Culp also scored his own winning run, in the eighth after beating out an infield hit against Ken Johnson. At that point, Bragan again turned his lineup card into a ransom note, with less-than-sterling results: Ty Cline went from center field to first base, Mack Jones switched from left fielder to center field, Gary Kolb went into the game in left field, and Felipe Alou - finally back from his leg injury - went to the bench. Johnny Briggs laid down a bunt that Cline fielded. Cline threw late to second instead of taking the sure out at first. After Cookie Rojas grounded into a fielders choice, advancing Culp to third, Callison grounded to Cline, who couldn't handle the ball cleanly (although Callison was credited with a hit) as Culp scored.

The loss wasted a complete-game effort by Johnson only two days after he had pitched and lost in relief in the second game of the doubleheader in New York. The only other positive of that day was the fact that with Alou starting at first and Menke starting at shortstop, the Braves, for the first time all season, had all their focal-point players healthy. It didn't make any difference in Pittsburgh the next night, though, as the Braves lost 8-3 to the

Pirates and dropped into sixth place, behind the Pittsburgh team that had spent virtually the entire first month of the season in last place.

Cloninger issued no walks, but was solved for nine hits and five runs (one unearned) in six innings. He would finish 16 of the 38 games he started that season, but this marked his sixth straight incomplete game, and in 1965 that was a problem, especially for the No. 1 pitcher on a staff. The mentality and the teaching methods of the time dictated that a starting pitcher approach his assignment from the standpoint of completing it - meaning a pitcher was expected to husband his energy and not show hitters his "kill" pitch until the game depended on that kill. By 1965 all teams had relief specialists, but few teams carried more than 10 pitchers (compared to the 12- and 13-man staffs that had become the norm 50 years later) and the "setup man" and "closer" concepts didn't come into vogue until the late 1980s when Oakland A's manager Tony La Russa applied those terms to eighth-inning men Gene Nelson and Rick Honeycutt and closer Dennis Eckersley. In 1965, the first impulse for almost every manager was to put his best pitchers in the rotation rather than in the bullpen. And staff aces finished what they started unless their stuff (or lack of it) determined otherwise. In 1965, the five top starting pitchers in the National League - Sandy Koufax, Juan Marichal, Don Drysdale, Bob Gibson and Cloninger - had 107 complete games between them. Fifty years later, in 2015, the 30 major league pitching staffs had a *total* of 104 complete games.

After Cloninger was lifted for a pinch-hitter in the seventh in the July 1 game, Dave Eilers replaced him and faced three batters, giving up a double and two triples before Dick Kelley relieved him. The next day represented more of the same, as the Pirates beat the Braves 9-5 to assure the Braves their sixth straight series loss and run the Pirates' winning streak to six games.

Less than a month before, Bragan was comparing his stable of sluggers to the 1927 Yankees. Now, he said: "The way we're going, we couldn't beat our (Double-A) Austin farm club." The Braves had scored more than three runs only three times in their past 14 games, 11 of which they had lost. The Pirates, conversely, found no mystery in the offerings of Sadowski and Phil Niekro. Willie Stargell had a single, double and triple, and Roberto Clemente finished with a homer, triple and single. The return of Denis Menke to his shortstop post didn't last long; he came out of the game with what was described as a "slight" aggravation of the knee problem that had sidelined him for almost the entire month of June.

Presumably it was of some solace to Aaron and Torre that they were named as National League starters in the All-Star Game, scheduled for July 13 at Metropolitan Stadium in Bloomington, Minn. (Milwaukee had hosted one All-Star Game, in 1955, when Stan Musial's walk-off homer in the 12th inning gave the NL a 6-5 victory after the Braves' Gene Conley had struck out the side in the top of the 12th.) After a farcical ballot-box-stuffing episode in 1957 that had resulted in seven of the eight position-player slots given to members of the fourth-place Redlegs, the All-Star vote had been taken away from the fans, and player balloting determined the All-Star starters until fan voting was reinstated in 1971. Aaron earned his right-field position by a 204-28 margin over the Phillies' Johnny Callison, and Torre beat out Johnny Edwards by 246-24 for the start at catcher. Frank Bolling fell just short of becoming a third Braves starter, losing 110-100 at second base to Cincinnati's Pete Rose. The NL's starting lineup would consist of Willie Mays, Aaron and Willie Stargell in the outfield, Torre catching, Ernie Banks at first, Pete Rose at second, Maury Wills at shortstop and Richie Allen at third. Juan Marichal would draw the starting pitching assignment. Indicative of the NL's talent level in 1965, during which 29 future Hall of Famers would play for NL teams, Billy Williams didn't make the starting lineup, nor did Roberto Clemente, Frank Robinson or Ron Santo, although all four were added to the team as reserves. Torre and Aaron were the only Braves on the team; only four seasons before, they had six All-Stars. Mathews, a nine-time All-Star, was left off the NL team for the third straight year.

The American League's starting lineup didn't include a single New York Yankee. It was only the second time in the history of the All-Star Game, which was first played in 1933, that this had occurred. (The first time was in 1943, when American League manager Joe McCarthy, showing his disdain for the quality of National League play, kept all of the All-Stars on his Yankee team on the bench.) The Yankees finished sixth in 1965, one year after winning their fifth straight pennant and ninth in 10 seasons. The AL did have a former Milwaukee Brave in its starting lineup - Boston Red Sox second baseman Felix Mantilla, who had been so valuable for his versatility during the 1957 World Series championship drive. Mantilla, 30, was in his next-to-last major league season in 1965. This would be the only All-Star appearance of his career. His fellow AL All-Star starters were Detroit's Dick McAuliffe at shortstop, Baltimore's Brooks Robinson at third, Minnesota's Harmon Killebrew at first base, Cleveland's Rocky Colavito in right field, Detroit's Willie Horton in left field, Cleveland's Vic Davalillo in center field, Minnesota's Earl Battey catching and Baltimore's Milt Pappas pitching.

On July 4, the Braves salvaged the final game of their series in Pittsburgh, 5-2, with another peculiar-looking lineup - Bragan's 66th different position-player alignment in 74 games - featuring Gary Kolb as the leadoff man and Hank Aaron batting fifth. Kolb, 25, had played football as well as baseball at the University of Illinois before signing with the St. Louis Cardinals in 1960. He had been acquired by the Braves before the 1964 season in a trade that sent Bob Uecker to St. Louis. His main asset was his versatility; during his seven-season, 501-game, four-team career, Kolb played every position except shortstop and pitcher. He was a .209 career hitter, and batted leadoff only five times. In this 1965 holiday game, batting him first was one hunch that paid off for Bragan; Kolb went 2 for 4, drew a walk and scored a run. Hank Fischer gave the bullpen a much-needed hiatus, completing a six-hitter that was marred only by solo homers by Jim Pagliaroni and Bob Bailey.

The Braves' return home to face Houston on Monday night, July 5, had an anticlimactic feel after the huge Circus Parade and mammoth turnouts for fireworks displays elsewhere - including 150,000 at Juneau Park, 90,000 at Lake Park and 60,000 at McKinley Beach - the previous night. Of course, the Braves' entire season was an anticlimax in many if not most minds in Milwaukee, and only 7,775 turned out to watch the Braves lose to the Astros 5-4 on a suicide-squeeze bunt in the top of the ninth inning by Walter Bond - one of the least likely suicide-squeeze candidates in the league. Bond, a 6-foot-7, 228-pounder who had originally signed with the Cleveland Indians organization in 1960, was one of the most menacing-looking hitters in all of baseball even though his major league home-run high had been 20 with the Colt .45s in 1964. That same year, he had been diagnosed with leukemia, and though he was in remission in 1965, the disease returned in 1967. Bond played his last major league game, for the Twins, on May 7, 1967, and died that November at age 29.

The Braves' return to near-total player availability had not lasted long. Denny Lemaster, finally acknowledging that he had been trying to pitch through tendinitis in his left (pitching) shoulder since spring training, was scratched from his scheduled start after two cortisone shots and cobalt X-ray treatment hadn't helped. A 17-game winner the previous season, Lemaster was 4-7 with a 6.13 ERA. Mack Jones also was questionable after Bob Friend hit him in the elbow with a pitch during the Pittsburgh series. Sandy Alomar was sent back to the minors, meaning that if Menke continued to have problems with his knee, Woody Woodward and Mike de la Hoz were the only options there. The Braves, fearing that Jones' absence might be long-term, were reported to be considering signing Frank Thomas, a veteran outfielder who had been released by the Phillies after getting into a fight with teammate Richie Allen before a game. Thomas had just turned 36 and had a reputation as a "clubhouse lawyer" who wasn't well-liked by his teammates or by management, but he had been with the Braves previously (in 1961), had power (286 career homers) and could play first base and third base as well as the outfield. This would mean, among other things, that Bragan could use Thomas, a right-handed hitter, at third while resting Mathews against tough left-handers. Houston, however, put in a $20,000 waiver claim on Thomas, and although the Astros later traded Thomas to the Braves, they did so in September, too late for him to make any appreciable difference in Milwaukee.

None of this mattered to county Board of Supervisors president Eugene Grobschmidt, who had been saying all season that the Braves deliberately were operating at a bare-minimum level to ensure that Milwaukee's last team wouldn't achieve any level of championship martyrdom. Grobschmidt also had pushed through a county-board resolution condemning the Braves for their allegedly-deliberate mishandling of the ticket situation during the doubleheader against the Dodgers in June. The *Journal* quoted Grobschmidt, who was putting together a committee to work with state and federal officials on the antitrust legislation against baseball and the Braves, as saying the Braves were not playing to their capabilities "because it would look silly for them to play the World Series here and then move to Atlanta the following year." Rejoined Bragan, speaking for his employers and more than a few people who were eager to get a replacement team for Milwaukee after the Braves left: "(Grobschmidt) is a dim-witted politician who wouldn't know a baseball from a softball if it hit him on his bald head ... Charging ballplayers with not trying to win is a serious thing. I wouldn't blamed them if they sued."

The Braves and Astros were rained out on Tuesday, July 6, giving the Braves' beleaguered pitching staff a welcome respite. The Braves (38-37) were in sixth place and the clamor for Bragan's firing was intensifying, but assistant general manager Jim Fanning said no managerial change was contemplated and that Bragan had done well "managing around obstacles." The rainout was rescheduled as a day game on Thursday, July 8, and Fanning announced that discount prices would be available for seniors and ladies. More important to more people in Milwaukee, Lloyd Barbee, who had already pressed legal action against Milwaukee Public Schools on segregation grounds, said on July 7 that he would ask the federal government to cut all aid to the Milwaukee district because of non-compliance with civil-rights laws. Several Southern cities had already been threatened with loss of federal funds for the same reason, and the U.S. Department of Health, Education and Welfare (which later changed its name to the Department of Health and Human Services) had sent investigators to several cities - including San Francisco, Boston and Chicago - that were accused of violating or circumventing the new civil-rights mandates.

Barbee and his supporters knew that even with federal intervention, the attitudes of a bigoted but vocal few would be difficult, if not impossible, to alter. Milwaukee long had a reputation, from a political standpoint, for progressivism, and its Socialist mayors had been advocates of equal opportunity in workplaces and in law enforcement. But the Ku Klux Klan had 25,000 registered members in 1925, and although the KKK virtually had disappeared from southeastern Wisconsin by the mid-1930s and lost its charter in 1946, a few splinter groups were still operating in 1965. The German-American Bund (a group of *emigres* from Germany who supported Adolf Hitler's Nazi regime) in the 1920s and 1930s had a strong presence in parts of Wisconsin, even after Germany's invasion of Poland in 1939. The Milwaukee-area Bund bought a tract of land outside Grafton, and often had Nazi-style rallies there on weekends until just before the U.S. entered World War II after the Japanese bombing of Pearl Harbor. By 1965, with Milwaukee's black population increasing markedly, racial tension was simmering. In July, in a letter to the editor of the *Sentinel*, a man claimed four "Negro hoodlums" had beaten his 4-year-old son while the child sat in his father's car. "These same people want to be equal, and be treated like all other Americans, (but) while civil rights leaders and clergy condemn (segregation in) schools and other aspects of Milwaukee life, not once have I read (of them) condemning these types of brutal acts." The newspapers also reported that a new Ku Klux Klan branch had been started in Wisconsin, and had signed up 48 members, most of them from south Milwaukee, Waukesha and Wauwatosa. It later turned out that the organizer had served time in jail in 1964 for burning a cross on the front lawn of a home in Waukesha, and had been charged with making racist threats to a black man in his neighborhood.

The Braves returned to action on Wednesday, July 7, and salved their wounds even if they didn't solve their overriding problems. Ken Johnson, now perhaps the most reliable pitcher on the staff, survived solo homers by Bond and Jim Wynn and six walks over 6 2/3 innings as the Braves beat the Astros 5-2. O'Dell got the last seven outs in order, Aaron hit a home run, and Carty went 3 for 3 with another homer.

The next day, before 2,522 paying spectators and 2,399 kids who were admitted for free, second-year Astros second baseman Joe Morgan unleashed an offensive barrage that foretold his subsequent emergence as a Hall of Famer and arguably the best second baseman in the sport's history. Morgan, 21, went 6 for 6 at the plate to tie a post-1900 National League record. He hit two home runs, doubled, scored four runs and drove in three more. No other Astro even reached base six times in a single game (let alone register hits in all six at-bats) until Josh Anderson in 2007, and as of 2016, Morgan remained the only Astro ever to collect six hits in a game.

Braves second baseman Frank Bolling, conversely, was retired in each of his first five plate appearances, but in his sixth at-bat, he singled home Mike de la Hoz with the winning run in the 12th for a 9-8 Milwaukee victory that gave the Braves their first series win in the past seven. The 3-hour, 50-minute game (at a time when games of three hours or more were rare) seemed even longer because of the 90-degree heat at game time. Thirty-six players, including 20 Braves, participated. Bragan used a season-high seven pitchers, including Wade Blasingame, who was working in relief for the second of two occasions that season and got the final four outs. Cloninger again pitched poorly, leaving in the fifth after surrendering eight hits - including both of Morgan's home runs - but the Braves hit five homers of their own, including two by Alou, who played the entire game and even finished at third base after Bragan had removed Mathews for a pinch-runner earlier in the game. Alou played third base only four other times, totaling 14 innings there, during his 17-year major league career that ended with three unsuccessful at-bats in three games with the 1974 Milwaukee Brewers. Menke also started at shortstop, although he played only until the fifth when Bragan took him out as part of a double switch.

Next stop was Cincinnati, where the Reds took over sole possession of first place for the first time since May 2 with a 6-2 victory at Crosley Field. Jim Maloney, who had been named to the NL All-Star pitching staff (as had teammate Sammy Ellis), beat the Braves for the third time in 1965, even though he had to navigate through constant danger as Milwaukee got at least one baserunner in eight of the nine innings. The only damage was inflicted by Eddie Mathews, who came into the game batting only .223 and had been dropped back to seventh in the batting order, even though Maloney was a right-hander. Mathews had never batted seventh before 1965. Hank Fischer kept the Braves in the game through the sixth inning, but an error at first by Alou, who dropped a routine throw to first after a comebacker to O'Dell, gifted the Reds three unearned runs in the eighth.

Mathews had been left off the All-Star Game roster for the third straight year after making the team during nine of his first 10 Milwaukee Braves seasons. (Cloninger didn't make the All-Star team either, even though he was on his way to a 24-win season.) But Mathews had three hits in this game, including his 16th homer of the season - underscoring the fact the Braves, for all their other inconsistencies and shortcomings, were on pace to tie the National League record with five hitters with 20 or more home runs in a season. Torre had 17, Aaron and Mathews 16, Mack Jones 14 and Alou 12 through the July 9 game, which was the Braves' 78th of 162. Gene Oliver, dividing time between first base and catcher and even taking an occasional turn in the outfield, hadn't hit his first homer of 1965 until May 5 and had only five as of July 9. Yet Oliver would help make the 1965 Braves only the third major league team (the 1964 Twins and 1961 Yankees were the others) to include six men with 20 or more homers.

Bragan renewed his ongoing feud with National League umpires after the July 9 loss. Frank Secory, one of the umpires on the crew that had ejected Bragan during the orange-juice incident at County Stadium that led to Bragan's dismissal as Pirates manager in 1957, had home-plate duties on July 9, and Bragan called Secory's work "the worst game of umpiring, on balls and strikes, I've ever seen." Bragan also called on management to add pitching help. "We've got to add some pitching," he said, "and how much pitching we add depends on Blasingame."

Blasingame, not yet 22, had carried more than his share of the pitching burden throughout the season, including his two relief appearances and his 14-inning complete game in May. But when he took the mound in Cincinnati July 10, he was coming off three underwhelming starts during which he was branded for 20 hits, 13 earned runs and 11 walks in 17 innings. He was even worse in this start, leaving with no outs after pitching to three batters in the fourth, and taking the loss as the Reds won 9-8 despite a five-run rally by the Braves in the eighth.

Blasingame gave up seven hits and five earned runs, and his successors, Bob Sadowski and Phil Niekro, fared little better. Joe Nuxhall, who 21 years earlier had become the youngest major leaguer ever when he pitched in a game for the Reds at age 15, had a three-hitter through seven innings and hadn't given up a hit since Alou's homer in the third. But after Woodward and Bolling singled, Hank Aaron doubled both of them home and Torre scored Aaron with a single to bring the Braves within 9-6. Nuxhall was lifted in favor of Bill McCool, off whom Mack Jones hit a two-run homer to narrow the deficit to 9-8. That's where it stayed, as McCool retired the last five hitters in order without allowing a ball to be hit out of the infield.

The Braves were 40-39 and in fifth place, 6 1/2 games behind the Reds, after that July 10 game, and had lost seven of their eight most recent series. At the same time, they had been swept in a series of three games or more only once - by the Pirates in mid-May. They won another salvage game July 11, 2-1, on Hank Aaron's two-run homer in the seventh off Sammy Ellis, who had retired 18 straight after Alou began the game with a home run. Ken Johnson pitched a seven-hitter over eight innings.

The previous day, with two outs and first base open in the fourth and Frank Robinson up, Bragan had elected to walk Robinson intentionally to get to Deron Johnson, who responded with a two-run single. Johnson was having a career year, finishing with 130 RBI that year - the second-highest total of his 16-year career was 95 with the Phillies in 1971 - and intentionally walking anyone, even Robinson, and pitching to Johnson with first base open was hazardous at best in 1965. A similar situation came up in the bottom of the eighth on July 11, with runners on second and third, two outs and Robinson at the plate and Gordie Coleman, who came into the game batting .337, on deck. This time, Bragan decided to have Ken Johnson pitch to Robinson, who flied out to center to end the inning.

Ken Johnson started the ninth, but gave up a leadoff double to Coleman and clearly was spent. With the two-day All-Star break coming up - it was usually three days then, but the Braves had a makeup doubleheader scheduled in Chicago July 14, the only major league games scheduled that day - and his bullpen overworked, Bragan summoned Cloninger, who made only two relief appearances in 1965 while starting 38 games. Cloninger had returned to Milwaukee after his previous start to be present at the birth of his third child, but came back to Cincinnati after the birth.

A wild pitch sent pinch-runner Marty Keough to third, but Cloninger struck out Deron Johnson before walking Johnny Edwards to put the winning run on base. Leo Cardenas tapped back to the mound; Cloninger first set himself to throw to second to start a double play that would end the game, but knowing that Cardenas ran well enough to make a double play unlikely, Cloninger looked Keough back to third and threw to first for the second out, with Edwards advancing to second. That brought up pinch-hitter Tony Perez, another future Hall of Famer who was a rookie platoon partner with Coleman at first base in 1965. Cloninger, never a finesse pitcher, cranked up nothing but hit-me-if-you-can fastballs to Perez, and struck him out to end the game. It was the only save of the 1965 season for Cloninger, and the fourth of six he was to record during his 12-year career.

Despite their deficiencies in pitching, defense and overall team speed, and the fact they were playing in a league that included 29 future Hall of Famers, the Braves had reached the All-Star break with a winning record (41-39) and, though in fifth place, were only 5 1/2 games behind co-leaders Los Angeles and Cincinnati. The Giants lingered three games back, followed by the Phillies (3 1/2), the Braves, and the Pirates (6). Houston (8 1/2, Chicago (9) and St. Louis (9 1/2) were also marginally in the race; only the Mets, 20 games behind, were not. The All-Star break was much needed by all the teams, and none more so than the Braves. Lemaster's post-break status remained uncertain, Menke's knee and Aaron's ankle continued to trouble them, Jones had hurt his shoulder in a collision with the outfield wall at Crosley Field in the final game of the Reds series, and O'Dell, for the first time, was pitching virtually every other day in relief after serving as a starter throughout his career.

With no game results to fill their pages during the All-Star break, papers in Milwaukee and elsewhere returned to the Braves' move and the antitrust threat surrounding it. Giants owner Horace Stoneham, who had been quiet on the situation since it unfolded, indicated that he regretted having voted to allow the franchise shift. "If I had to vote on this thing again," Stoneham said, "I'd vote for Milwaukee being in the league." Frank Lane, the former GM of four teams and in July 1965 a special assistant to Baltimore general manager Lee MacPhail, also expressed sympathy for Milwaukee. He suggested that a shotgun marriage between Kansas City A's owner Charles O. Finley (who had been looking to move his franchise ever since buying it in 1960) and Milwaukee might be the best way out of a bad situation. "Not that I want to wish Finley on the good people of Milwaukee," said Lane, who had sued Finley after the latter had fired him as the A's GM, "but he and the A's would be better than nothing. I don't think (the antitrust suit) will solve anything. It looks like (Teams Inc) is still trying to bargain with the (Bartholomay) carpetbaggers. So you draw 500,000 and (Teams Inc) gets $25,000. That won't go far ... maybe the county will find a way to keep the club. I hope so, but I think expansion is at least five years away, maybe 10." (Lane was to serve as Brewers GM in 1971 and 1972, their second and third years in Milwaukee after moving from Seattle.)

Amid the uncertainty, county executive John Doyne put together a package to offer prospective County Stadium tenants starting with the 1966 season. Under Doyne's plan, a team would have to pay $1 per paid admission up to 1 million, and would be given concession rights and revenues if the team failed to draw 1 million. If the attendance total exceeded 1 million, the county would be owed 10 percent of revenues from both sources. The new team also would be allowed to keep 90 percent of outside concession revenues, particularly those from Packers games. Under the terms of the Braves' lease that was to expire at the end of the 1965 season, the team paid the county 5 percent of all revenues up to the 1 million attendance mark (which the Braves reached for the last time in 1961) and the county kept 90 percent of the concession revenues up to $800,000. The *Sentinel* reported that Milwaukee County netted $125,000 in 1964 from its contract with the Braves. Eugene Grobschmidt, though, followed his usual pattern and took issue with Doyne, saying he would vote against such a rental arrangement - calling it a $1-a-year token deal - and vowed that the county Board of Supervistors, of which Grobschmidt was president, would kill the proposal if it came before the board for a final vote.

Also during the All-Star break, Milwaukee broke with a part of its past while breaking ground on what it envisioned as its future. Plans were to tear down the Milwaukee Road train depot, built in 1880, and the Chicago and North Western depot, through which passenger service began in 1889. They would both be replaced by a state-of-the-art transportation depot on West St. Paul Street that opened on August 2 and remained in operation 50 years later as the Milwaukee Intermodal Station. Meanwhile, the plan to build the Northridge Mall at the intersection of Brown Deer Road and North 76th Street in the northwestern part of Milwaukee was unveiled. The mall, which was to be enclosed, was expected to cost $50 million and include a hotel, a bank, theaters and restaurants. Most of those plans never were completely fulfilled. It took until 1972, four years after the original target date, to complete a scaled-down mall, which was closed in 2003. (Construction on another new mega-mall, in Brookfield, began later in 1965.) Another building project was the expansion of Frenchy's, on 1827 E. North Ave. Franchy's was perhaps the best-known restaurant in Milwaukee, at least among tourists, and it unquestionably had Milwaukee's most eclectic menu. On a given night, diners had their choice of entrees such as buffalo steak, elk steak, roasted quail, venizen, chukar, partridge, raccoon, African hippopotomus, and European wild boar. (The restaurant was closed in 1980, and never reopened.)

In Minnesota, Joe Torre went 1 for 4 and Hank Aaron went 1 for 5 in the National League's 6-5 win in the All-Star Game. Torre said he hurt his left hand catching NL starter Juan Marichal, but would not be forced to miss the regular-season doubleheader at Wrigley Field the next day. Because of weather impediments, the Braves - who had another makeup doubleheader scheduled for July 18 at home against the Mets - had played only 80 games, fewest in the majors; the Dodgers had played 89 games, the Pirates 87, and the Giants (who had the second-lowest total) had completed 83 contests. The Braves' pennant hopes had been sabotaged in the past by late-season doubleheaders forced by early-season postponements, and Bragan worried that this might happen again if his pitching staff didn't attain a higher level of consistency.

Warren Spahn's short tenure as Mets pitcher and pitching coach ended the day after the All-Star Game, when New York placed him on waivers. Spahn had lost eight straight decisions after starting the season 4-4, but still insisted he could win on the major league level even though he was 44 and was operating on a knee that had been surgically repaired three times. "Sure,

I'm dismayed," he said. "But the world hasn't come to an end. I feel I can still pitch winning ball. My arm feels fine. I feel fine physically. I lost 1-0, 2-1 twice, and 3-0 ... when you pitch for this (Mets) team, you're really in trouble if you fall behind. They don't pick up any runs for you, so you lose." Spahn said he would return to his ranch in Oklahoma and try to get back into baseball in 1966 "in some capacity." As it turned out, he wouldn't have to wait nearly that long. Two days later, on July 19, the Giants signed him for the remainder of the season. McHale scoffed at the idea of the Braves bringing Spahn back to augment a pitching staff that looked flimsier than that of the Giants. "See our attendance?" he asked rhetorically. "We aren't offering anybody anything. How about Teams Inc? Maybe they have a job for him." Commented Casey Stengel: "He (Spahn) helped us, except when he pitched."

In Chicago, the Cubs' Bob Buhl beat his former teammates 5-2 at Wrigley Field in the first game of the doubleheader. Cloninger took the loss, his fourth straight, and failed to register a complete game for the eighth consecutive start. Even with the All-Star break, he was pitching on only two days of rest after his relief stint in the final game before the break. In the second game, the Braves were victims of a triple play, the first against them since 1955. It happened in the second inning, with two runs already in, Mack Jones at first and Rico Carty at third. Woodward hit a foul popup that catcher Ed Bailey tracked down even though Woodward had caught Bailey in the head with his backswing. Carty, noting that Bailey was recoiling and off-balance, tagged up and tried to score, but was tagged out at the plate by pitcher Bill Faul. Jones, seeing the confusion, broke for second, and Faul threw to second baseman Glenn Beckert for the third out.

Shrugging off that calamity, the Braves won the second game 6-3 as Hank Fischer continued his upswing, completing a five-hitter during which he allowed only one Cub to advance past first base over the final seven innings. Gene Oliver hit two home runs, and scored four of the Braves' six runs. He said afterward that he had never scored four runs in a game, at any level.

Back home the following night (July 15), the Braves beat the Pirates 9-6 after knocking Vern Law out of the game with a four-run first inning. Law, who had come into the game with a 1.70 ERA, retired Felipe Alou to begin the bottom of the first, but then gave up five straight hits - a single by Bolling, a double by Aaron, a two-run single by Oliver, a two-run homer by Mathews and a single by Carty - to give the Braves a 4-0 lead that reached 9-0 in the fourth, but Ken Johnson had to be rescued by Dan Osinski, who held the Pirates scoreless over the final 3 1/3 innings. Before the game, the Braves recalled journeyman outfielder Don Dillard from Syracuse, where he had been playing on loan to the Detroit organization. Dillard, 28, had first reached the majors with the Indians in 1959, but had done little to distinguish himself with Cleveland, or in the Braves' organization after Milwaukee had acquired him from the Indians in the trade that sent Joe Adcock to Cleveland after the 1962 season. Denis Menke had suffered yet another setback in his recovery from his knee injury, so the Braves were looking for infield help as well.

The Braves on July 16 followed their bombardment of Law with a similar outburst against Bob Veale, whose velocity was thought to be on a par with that of any pitcher in baseball. Veale exited with no outs in the third after surrendering six hits, two walks and seven runs (two unearned), and although Blasingame labored while giving up 10 hits, he got through the full nine innings without any late-game suspense as the Braves won 12-2. He would have had a shutout had it not been for a two-run single by Robert Clemente in the seventh. Oddly, the Braves at that point were the only team in baseball that didn't have a complete-game shutout by any of its pitchers. Only two teams in baseball history had gone through an entire season without achieving that feat; one was the 1899 Cleveland Spiders, whose 20-134 record was the worst in the history of baseball (and remained so 50 years later).

Milwaukee completed the sweep the next night in far more dramatic fashion, winning 6-5 with two runs in the bottom of the ninth. The Braves, leading 4-1, had fallen behind 5-4 as the result of a four-run Pittsburgh rally capped by Bob Bailey's two-run double off Sadowski. In the bottom of the ninth, Pirates reliever Frank Carpin walked Woody Woodward, and pinch-hitter Mike de la Hoz hit a potential double-play grounder to third that was fumbled by Jose Pagan for an error. Alou then hit a grounder to Pirates shortstop Andre Rodgers, who had remained in the game after an earlier pinch-running assignment. If Gene Alley, the Pirates' regular shortstop, had been in the game, the Pirates might have been able to turn a double play. But Alou beat the throw to first, with Woodward taking third. Frank Bolling then lined a double into the left field corner, scoring the tying run and sending Alou to third. The Pirates then went to Veale, whose wild pitch brought home Alou with the winning run.

It was the fourth time in 1965 that the Braves had won four straight games, but they had not stretched any of those streaks past that point - nor had they won both ends of any doubleheader.

Those blanks in their portfolio were eliminated the following day, when they swept a Sunday doubleheader from the Mets 5-1 and 5-4 before 12,127 - a heady attendance level by 1965 Braves standards, but barely half the total of 22,659 who spent the day at the Milwaukee Zoo. Tony Cloninger finally regained his top-of-the-rotation stuff and stature in the first game, shutting out the Mets on five hits after giving up a game-starting homer to Chuck Hiller. Mathews, who was 10 for 23 since the All-Star break, hit two solo home runs for all the runs Cloninger would need. In the second game, Dick Kelley earned his first major league win, giving up only a single run in seven innings after taking over for starter Hank Fischer to start the third. Kelley, used early because the Mets started a predominantly left-handed hitting lineup, used a screwball to neutralize the Mets. "I didn't even know he had one," catcher Gene Oliver - himself on a 10-for-21 breakout - said after the game. The next night, the Braves forcefully removed themselves from the realm of the 1899 Cleveland Spiders; Ken Johnson pitched a seven-hit shut-out and the Braves won 6-0 behind solo homers by Alou, Aaron, Mathews and Torre. "That was the best knuckleball I've had all year," said Johnson, who ran his record with the Braves to 7-2. "I must have thrown it 60-65 percent of the time (instead of about one-third of the time, as he had done most of his career). I guess the secret was that I didn't throw it as hard as I had been. When I throw it hard, it doesn't do much."

Even in the midst of the Braves' seven-game winning streak, or maybe because of it, ownership and management hadn't given up on the idea of fleeing to Atlanta before the end of the season. For the third (and final) time since the start of the 1965 season, Bartholomay and his group put a proposal before Milwaukee

County and the other 19 owners: Let us leave for Atlanta immediately, and we'll formally propose a 1966 expansion that would include a new Milwaukee team.

The proposal was made at a secret meeting in Washington, D.C., attended by Teams Inc representatives Ben Barkin, Bud Selig and Edmund Fitzgerald. Several Congressmen, from both Georgia and Wisconsin, also attended, as did baseball commissioner Ford Frick, County Stadium manager William Anderson, and multiple attorneys representing both sides. Although little was decided, the tone of all parties' rhetoric seemed to soften, albeit incrementally, during and after this meeting.

From Milwaukee County's perspective, the meeting changed nothing. County executive John Doyne, who wasn't present, said it was his understanding that the county remained committed to the antitrust suit, and he indicated that the county's stance wouldn't change "based only on a promise." At the same time, Teams Inc had formalized itself as the group that would represent Milwaukee in its quest to regain major league baseball, with Schlitz president Robert Uihlein - a newcomer to the discussions - and Selig at its head. Bill Bartholomay, meanwhile, had told owners that "responsible" people in Milwaukee were "genuinely intrested in a (new) franchise." This was taken to mean that Bartholomay and his group would not try to block Milwaukee in its efforts to secure a franchise as soon as possible. Commissioner Ford Frick urged Milwaukee to "stay in there swinging for a franchise," but added that expansion in time for the 1966 season was "physically impossible," conveniently forgetting the 1961 AL expansion that had created a new franchise for

Washington only three months after the original Senators had moved to Minnesota.

Frick also shot down the idea of the Braves moving to Atlanta before the end of the 1965 season, saying: "I don't see how in the devil the Braves are going to move at this late date." It also was hard to see how the Braves would be able to operate during their final 2 1/2 months in Milwaukee. Ralph Del Forge quit as the team's secretary and assistant treasurer on July 19; with the front office essentially operating out of Atlanta, that left three Braves officials as the Milwaukee garrison: assistant general manager Jim Fanning, traveling secretary Donald Davidson, and ticket director Austin Brown. The *Journal's* Oliver Kuechele wrote that, based on the figures released by the team and the county and the Braves' projected income had they been able to consummate the move to Atlanta the previous winter, playing in Milwaukee in 1965 would cost the Braves anywhere from $2.5 million to $3.5 million, including out-of-pocket taxes and debt service. (The exact amount the Braves lost in '65 is unknown for certain, but is generally placed in the $1.5 million range.)

While officials deliberated and wrangled, the Braves kept playing - and winning. They finished their four-game series sweep of the Mets, 7-1, on July 20, to stretch their winning streak to eight and move into third place. Milwaukee scored all seven of its runs in the seventh, with Hank Aaron notarizing the inning with a three-run homer, and Hank Fischer - working seven innings after his two-inning stint two days before - and Billy O'Dell teaming for a five-hitter. The Braves were within five games of the first-place Dodgers, and would next play Los Angeles - which was on a six-game winning jag of its own - in a two-game series at Dodger Stadium starting Wednesday, July 21. The schedule had been tormenting the Braves since the start of July; even with the two-day All-Star break, they had played 19 games in 20 days during the month. But the Dodgers' rotation worked in the Braves' favor in this series; they would not have to face Sandy Koufax or Don Drysdale, both of whom had worked in the prior series against Houston. (Koufax had beaten the Astros 3-2 the previous day for his 17th victory of the season.)

While the Mets were in Milwaukee, the teams agreed on a trade: Gary Kolb, whose playing time had evaporated almost completely, to the Mets for Jesse Gonder, who would serve primarily as a pinch-hitter and third-string catcher. Gonder would join the Braves in San Francisco, where they would play the Giants in a three-game series after leaving Los Angeles. "That's one plane I'm not going to miss," said Gonder, 29, who had been in the vanguard of the Oakland talent armada that had enriched the major leagues with Frank Robinson, Joe Morgan, Curt Flood, Vada Pinson and many others, but Gonder had been a disappointment as a major leaguer. He batted just .151 in his 31 games with the Braves, though he did contribute several pinch-hits, including a three-run double in a critical win over the Giants in August.

The Dodgers started Claude Osteen in the first game of the series against the Braves' Wade Blasingame. Osteen had pitched for Cincinnati from 1957-61 before being traded to Washington, but had only appeared in 26 games and totalled 60 innings as a National Leaguer, so most of the Braves' hitters were unfamiliar with him. But the Braves' scouting reports indicated that Osteen, a 5-foot-10, 160-pound lefthander who was more guile than style, liked to "pitch backward" - that is, use his breaking ball to set up his fastball, while most other pitchers took a vice-versa approach. Consequently, Felipe Alou, Frank Bolling and Hank Aaron all were hunting for off-speed stuff on Osteen's first pitches to each of them. Alou singled, Bolling doubled, Aaron hit a three-run homer, and the Braves had a 3-0 lead three pitches into the game. They went on to win 6-4, stretching their win streak to nine and pulling within one-half game of second-place Cincinnati.

Osteen came out after walking Aaron to start the third. Blasingame (11-7) had a shutout after five innings and a 5-1 lead through six, but gave up three runs in the seventh - the first scoring on a pinch single by Don Drysdale, whose .300 batting average that year was higher than that of any of Los Angeles' most frequently-used position players. After Jim Gilliam's RBI single carved Milwaukee's edge to 5-4, Bragan brought in lefty Billy O'Dell to face the left-handed-hitting Ron Fairly, who popped up to catcher Joe Torre to end the inning and preserve the Braves' lead. The Braves tacked on an insurance run in the eighth on singles by Woodward, Jones and Alou, who got his fourth hit of the game.

In the bottom of the ninth, with O'Dell remaining on the mound, pinch-hitter Dick Tracewski led off with a single. This brought up Maury Wills, one of the best bunters in the history of the sport. But Wills, a switch-hitter, was batting right-handed against O'Dell, somewhat nullifying the possibility that Wills would drag-bunt for a hit or, at worst, a sacrifice to move the tying run into scoring position. The Braves' infielders crept in anyway, prompting Dodgers manager Walt Alston to let Wills hit away, and he hit a line drive - directly at left fielder Ty Cline, who had been brought in for defensive purposes at the same time

O'Dell came into the game. O'Dell then struck out Wes Parker and Gilliam, the latter on a called third strike, to end the game.

The next night (July 22), the Braves went for the sweep with Tony Cloninger working against Bob Miller, a relief pitcher who was making his first start of the season. Cloninger, who had gone 0-4 in six starts before beating the Mets four days earlier, still hadn't completely alleviated his command issues; against the Dodgers, he issued three walks for the third straight start. (He would lead the NL in walks with 119 and wild pitches with 22 in 1965.) But he stifled the Dodgers on four hits over 7 2/3 innings as the Braves extended their win streak to 10 with a 5-2 victory that left Milwaukee tied in the loss column with the first-place Dodgers, though Los Angeles had played and won six more games than the Braves).

As had been the case the previous night, the Braves' first three hitters put three runs on the board in the first inning, with Alou and Mack Jones singling and Aaron homering. Carty added a solo homer - the Braves' 17th during their winning streak - later in the inning, and O'Dell got the final four outs, retiring Willie Davis on a popup with two on and two outs in the eighth.

The win gave the Braves their seventh double-figure victory streak since their arrival in Milwaukee in 1953, and three of those - all 10-gamers - had come during the 1954 season. In 1956, the Braves had won 11 straight immediately following Charlie Grimm's resignation as manager and the appointment of Fred Haney to replace him, and they had won 10 straight during the World Series championship season of 1957. A 10-0 burst in 1961 hadn't mattered much. When it began on August 11, the Braves were in fourth place, 12 1/2 games out of first place; they were within eight games, but still in fourth place, when it ended on August 20. (As of 2016, the longest win streak by the franchise, a charter member of the National League when it was founded in 1876, was 18 by the 1891 Boston Beaneaters.)

The Braves' attempt to match the longest win streak in their Milwaukee history would come on Friday, July 23, in San Francisco. The Braves had swept a three-game series at Candlestick Park earlier in the season, but the Giants hadn't lost as many as four straight all year. Like the Braves earlier in the season, they were in a one-step-forward, one-step-back mode, and as with the Braves, their power suggested they weren't going to stay dormant indefinitely. Frank Linzy, a right-hander with a submarine delivery so extreme that he sometimes would scrape his hand against the pitching rubber as he released the ball, seemed to have given the Giants the late-inning bulwark they had lacked since trading Stu Miller after their pennant-winning 1962 season. While they were in fourth place, they trailed the first-place Dodgers by only 4 1/2 games entering the series against Milwaukee. And the Giants now had Warren Spahn, albeit a diminished, 44-year-old Warren Spahn. In his first start with San Francisco, he had lasted only 2 1/3 innings, giving up three hits and three unearned runs. As a measure of respect, Giants outfielder Len Gabrielson gave up his No. 21 to Spahn and subsequently wore No. 7.

While the Braves were in Los Angeles, they had heard news that would affect many major league baseball players over the next few years: On the same night that the House of Representatives passed the bill that would create Medicare, President Johnson acknowledged what most Americans already knew: The U.S. was now engaged in a full-scale war in Vietnam, and troop strength, which had been 75,000 at the end of June, would be increased accordingly. By the end of 1965, 184,300 Americans were engaged in Southeast Asia, and by 1968, that total would reach a peak of 536,100. More than 58,000 U.S. servicemen and women would die in the war.

Major league baseball players knew in 1965 that hundreds of their counterparts a generation earlier had seen their careers interrupted or shortened by World War II military service. Two former major leaguers, Elmer Gedeon and Harry O'Neill, had died in combat during the war. Ted Williams, after losing three full seasons (1943-45) during World War II, missed most of the 1952 and 1953 seasons while serving in the Korean War. The Phillies' loss of pitcher Curt Simmons to the military during the Korean conflict almost cost them the NL pennant in 1950, and Willie Mays missed most of 1952 and all of 1953 after being drafted and inducted into the Army, although he was never sent overseas. In 1965, some players already were in National Guard units that could be deployed at any moment, either to Vietnam or to American cities where racial strife was turning violent (as had already happened in several U.S. cities, including Cleveland and the East New York section of Brooklyn). And this state of readiness and anxiety was, in 1965, indefinite. Sen. Mike Mansfield (D-Mont.) said projections were that the war might last 10 years, and added that the war "is an ordeal of indefinite duration and increasing sacrifice which will persist until the problem can be resolved at the conference table."

The conflict did last almost as long as Mansfield had predicted, but its impact on major league baseball was not as profound as had been the case during World War II, or even Korea. Draft quotas were not as broad as in the previous two wars, especially among men 25 or older. The average age of combat infantrymen in World War II was 26; in Vietnam, it was 22. A few days after President Johnson's announcement, the Pentagon said immediate callups might not be as extensive and immediate as had originally been planned. This was a relief for at least six of the Braves; Torre, Menke, Woodward, Cline and Niekro all were in various reserve units, and Wade Blasingame was a senior clerk-typist with the Army's 32nd Infantry Division and already was obliged to participate in 48 drills per year. In August, however, LBJ increased the draft quotas, making married men ages 19-26 eligible, and the casualty tolls were beginning to rise exponentially. During the first week of September, 68 Americans lost their lives in Southeast Asia, with 326 wounded and 11 missing.

Although doubts about the wisdom of the pending involvement were increasing, a *Sentinel* poll in August found that 60 percent of respondents were in support of the buildup, though 48 percent expressed concerns that it might bring Communist China into the war, as had happened in Korea.

While LBJ and the military braced for the total-war commitment in Vietnam, major league owners were at a meeting in Dearborn, Mich., trying to knit together their tattered tapestry. While overall attendance was up from 1964, it was still well below the heights it had attained in the postwar years, and the opening of the Astrodome had offset the fact that attendance was down in seven of the other nine NL cities, including, of course, Milwaukee. Kansas City A's owner Charles O. Finley still was in the midst of a five-year hunt for a new home for his team; having already had proposed moves to Dallas, Atlanta and Louisville nixed by Frick and AL owners, he was now casting eyes on Oakland - and the Cleveland Indians and Cincinnati Reds also had made it clear they would consider relocating if the offer and the circumstances were right.

Both, of course, stayed put; the Reds were assured they would have a new ballpark by 1971 (a mandate that was completed one year early), and Indians president Gabe Paul said he was encouraged enough by a 85,000-patron increase in attendance to stay in Cleveland. This made it even less likely that the Braves would be replaced in Milwaukee. Lloyd Larson wrote: "Every day ... it becomes more apparent that nobody in baseball is even slightly interested in keeping Milwaukee in the picture." At the same time, baseball had attendance problems that it could not ignore. In September, the AL pennant-winning Minnesota Twins would draw only 537 for a game against Kansas City, and the Los Angeles Angels - tenants of the Dodgers at Dodger Stadium for the fourth and final year - had a "crowd" of just 945 against Baltimore. (In 1966, the once-mighty Yankees, sixth-place finishers in 1965 and a last-place team the following year, had their smallest Yankee Stadium crowd ever - 413 - and drew just 1,440 for a game against the "rival" Red Sox.) With so many ballparks around the major leagues in need of overhaul or replacement, with benign-at-best leadership from a soon-to-retire commissioner, and with all of the potential expansion or transfer sites being flawed in some way, it seems counterintuitive in retrospect that it was so widely thought that Milwaukee was permanently out of the major league picture. But that was the way it appeared to stand as the owners ended their Dearborn meeting.

More sad news unfolded in Milwaukee, where Harry L. Bradley, chairman of the board of Allen-Bradley Co., died of heart disease at age 80. Allen-Bradley, which made many types of electrical equipment, employed 6,000 in Milwaukee in 1965. (It was purchased and absorbed by Rockwell Automation in 1985.) Bradley had one of the largest art collections in the Midwest, and he was known for his municipal philanthropy. One of his largest gifts during his lifetime was $2 million to St. Luke's Medical Center (later renamed Aurora St. Luke's Medical Center), and two decades after his death, his family donated the money that was used to build the Bradley Center (home of the NBA's Milwaukee Bucks and the Marquette men's basketball team) in 1988.

The Braves on July 23 probably had fewer complaints than usual about the wind and cold at Candlestick Park, if for no other reason that the high temperature in Milwaukee that day was 99 degrees with hail, rain, tornado sightings, and gale-force winds that toppled a 600-foot-high television transmitter in Marshfield. Conditions at Candlestick, of course, were far less treacherous, but the wind and Ron Herbel conspired to keep every batted ball (except for Mathews' 21st home run of the year) in the ballpark. The Giants ended the Braves' 10-game win streak with a 5-1 victory; San Francisco managed only five hits, but two, by Willie McCovey and Jesus Alou, were home runs. Ken Johnson, who got the loss, lasted only four innings before giving way to Denny Lemaster, who completed two scoreless innings in his first outing since June 20. Jesse Gonder, making his Braves debut and playing across San Francisco Bay from his home town of Oakland, pinch-hit in the seventh and grounded into a double play.

The next day, the Giants prevailed again, 4-2, even though San Francisco starter Bob Shaw lasted only long enough - three pitches - to drill Felipe Alou, one of the players for whom Shaw was traded after the 1963 season in the transaction that sent longtime Braves catcher Del Crandall to the Giants. Shaw, notorious for his temper and his memory of long-ago slights - and the fact he taught Gaylord Perry how to throw the spitball that helped get Perry into the Hall of Fame - apparently had a verbal exchange with several of his ex-teammates before the game. In those days, beanball-related ejections were rare as umpires generally did not try to gauge intent, but this time, plate umpire Bill Jackowski had no doubt as to Shaw's purpose when he hit Alou. It was the first first-batter ejection of a pitcher in the major leagues in at least 40 years, and no others would occur until 2001, when the Astros' Scott Elarton was tossed for hitting Kansas City's Rey Sanchez. Surprisingly, there was no fight after the incident, but it was an indication that the pennant race was beginning to simmer. The 22,812 fans at Candlestick Park couldn't have imagined that it would reach the incineration level at the same site less than a month later.

The Shaw ejection worked to the Giants' advantage, as Bob Bolin replaced Shaw and doled out only six hits over the next six innings. Willie Mays, enjoying one of the best seasons of his career at age 34, added another memento to his personal Louvre. After Hank Fischer picked him off first base, he eluded three different rundowns while causing two errors and scoring a run standing up. Tom Haller then hit a home run to put the Giants ahead for good, 3-2.

Making matters worse for the Braves, Rico Carty re-injured his back and was unavailable for the series finale, which the

Giants won 2-1 behind - of all people - Bob Shaw. NL president Warren Giles had not deemed Shaw's ejection the previous day as grounds for suspension, so Giants manager Herman Franks simply pushed his rotation back a day, and Shaw, though pitching almost constantly from the stretch, scattered nine hits over eight innings as the Braves stranded 12 runners in the game. Bob Sadowski pitched almost as well, giving up only seven hits and two earned runs in his eight-inning complete-game effort. But former Brave Len Gabrielson was involved in both of San Francisco's scoring sequences. The Giants took a 1-0 lead in the second when Gabrielson hit into a bases-loaded, no-out double play. In the eighth, with the score tied 1-1, he singled off Sadowski's bare hand, and after a fielders choice and a walk to Ken Henderson, Sadowski got Willie Mays, pinch-hitting for Shaw, to pop up for the second out. But he gave up the go-ahead single to Dick Schofield, a .215 hitter.

The Giants started a makeshift lineup in this game because Mays was hampered by a sore hip and Jim Ray Hart, who had become a dangerous No. 5 hitter while providing Mays and McCovey with protection in the lineup, was suspended for the game by Franks for "training violations." That Franks considered this game and the sweep of paramount importance was signaled by the fact he sent Gaylord Perry to the mound to start the ninth. He faced one batter, pinch-hitter Jesse Gonder, who singled. Franks then brought Linzy into the game. Felipe Alou bunted pinch-runner Phil Niekro to second. Mack Jones grounded out to shortstop as Niekro had to hold at second. Aaron beat out an infield single as Niekro advanced to third, but Torre grounded to second to end the game. The sweep moved the Giants within 2 1/2 games of first place and dropped the Braves to fourth, four games back.

Despite the three successive losses to the Giants, the Braves' situation was far from dire, at least numerically. After three games in Houston, the Braves would play their next 15 games at home, and their next seven games after that were in St. Louis and Chicago - virtual commutes to play out-of-contention teams. But the Braves were as banged up as they had been all season. Besides Carty, Gene Oliver was out with a badly infected toe, and Mack Jones had suffered a hamstring injury running out his ground ball in the ninth inning of the July 25 game. Additionally, Frank Bolling was in the midst of a 3-for-33 slump and Bragan had already sat him in favor of Mike de la Hoz at second, and Menke could barely run because of his continued knee problems. So Bragan started Ty Cline in center field and Menke at first base, a position he had played only three times in his first three major league seasons.

It worked, mainly because of Blasingame, who was at his best for the first time since his one-hit shutout nearly three months before. Despite needing 133 pitches, he beat the Astros 6-0 with a five-hitter, with two of the hits coming off the bat of ex-teammate Lee Maye. Joe Torre's three-run homer in the eighth sealed the deal. The next night, with the same lineup except for Bolling's return to second base, Cloninger picked up his 13th win and O'Dell his 12th save as the Braves won 7-1, and they ended the road trip with a 6-4 win on July 28, with O'Dell - who had come to Cloninger's rescue in the seventh the night before - toiling another 2 1/3 innings to save the win for Lemaster. Bragan, like most managers in the 1960s and before, didn't hesitate to use starting pitchers in relief if the situation called for it, and Ken Johnson, whose knuckleball drained comparatively little vitality from his arm, had replaced Lemaster in the seventh. He gave up a two-run single to pinch-hitter Joe Gaines, pulling Houston within 5-4, and a walk to Jim Wynn before O'Dell shut the Astros down. Denis Menke, still playing first base, hit a home run. Only 24 homers had been hit in the Astrodome by visiting teams during its first four months as a baseball venue, and the Braves had hit 10 of them.

The Braves already were exhausted and gimpy, but Braves management had scheduled yet another exhibition game in Atlanta on the team's first off-day since the All-Star break - which, of course, had been only a two-day layoff, instead of the usual three- or four-day break, because of the makeup doubleheader in Chicago. Some have since pointed to the scheduling of the six in-season exhibition games in Atlanta in 1965 as evidence that management was undermining its own team, and while it's not likely that was directly true, the fact the team badly needed the additional income from the Atlanta games was no secret, then or later.

Aside from the break, it was only the Braves' second sched-uled off-day since June 21. The Braves had played 37 games in 38 days, and had won 20 of them despite an almost-continuous succession of injuries. Eddie Mathews, at 33 the oldest of the position-player regulars, played a team-high 156 of 162 games that season, and he did so despite a nagging shoulder problem that had bothered him since 1963. Aaron, despite ongoing ankle soreness, played in 150 games; nobody else on the team played more than 148. Denis Menke, the team's defensive talisman at shortstop, participated in only 71 games, and Rico Carty, second in the NL batting race in 1964, got into only 83. Ken Johnson had been an epiphany since joining Cloninger and Blasingame in the starting rotation, and Billy O'Dell had congealed the bullpen during his first season with the team and in that role, but all four had been overworked out of necessity because of the schedule and the fact no other pitcher had assumed a go-to role.

At least the '65 Braves by the end of July no longer had to worry about the franchise moving to Atlanta during the season; that question already had been settled earlier in the month, after the third and final attempt by management to escape the final year of its County Stadium lease. But their once-imposing home-crowd advantage had become a liability. As of July 29, the Braves were dead last among the 20 major league teams in attendance with only 262,809 for 43 dates, an average of 6,112. The Braves were far behind the Cubs, whose total of 451,615 was the second-worst in the NL. Milwaukee even trailed the Kansas City A's (276,600), who had never come close to a winning season since arriving from Philadelphia in 1954. The Braves, of course, had never come close to a *losing* season since their transfer from Boston in 1953. Often after that - most notably when the Braves picked up Red Schoendienst from the Giants midway through the 1957 season - they had upgraded their roster late in seasons even if it meant expanding the payroll. Because the franchise was hemorrhaging money, the players knew that wouldn't happen in 1965, although Johnson had been a valuable acquisition earlier in the season. They would have to try to win with what they had.

Yet despite all those obstacles and distractions, the Braves were 54-43, in third place, and were only three games removed from the NL lead entering their 15-game homestand, which would begin with a five-game series against the Giants starting Friday, July 30.

The Dodgers, who were in first place, on July 27 had signed manager Walter Alston to a one-year contract for the 1966 season - the 13th of 23 one-year deals under which Alston would work while winning four World Series and seven NL pennants. This was the first time since Alston took over in 1954 that he had been re-upped in the midst of a season, and Walter O'Malley said Alston was being rewarded because "I feel this is the best job Alston's ever done and the best job the players have ever done."

Bobby Bragan was, in about every way imaginable, the antithesis of Alston, who praised in public and prompted and persuaded in private. Most of Bragan's players disliked him, for various reasons ranging from his constant tinkering with lineups and his proclivity for over-managing to his using the media to motivate (or degrade) players rather than settling problems behind the closed doors of the manager's office. The fans booed him virtually every time he stuck his head out of the dugout at County Stadium; not only did they find his demeanor distasteful and his tactics and lineups moonstruck, they would not let him forget the 1957 orange-juice ejection, his "crooked creek" remark, or his other not-so-subtle insinuations that he thought Atlanta deserved major league baseball more than Milwaukee did. And yet, as the end of July approached, had Bragan, under the circumstances, not done at least as much as Alston to keep his team in contention? His bosses obviously didn't think so; Bragan's status for 1966 remained uncertain as the Braves trudged off to Atlanta to play the International League All-Star team. (The all-star team, which included several Atlanta Crackers, won the game 6-2 before only 16,626, the smallest of the six exhibition-game crowds the Braves drew in Atlanta in 1965.) Carty played most of the game; Torre, Menke and Aaron made cameo appearances.

For their six exhibition games in Atlanta, the Braves had drawn 185,582 - an average of 30,930, almost six times the Braves' attendance average to that point.

The Braves got home from Atlanta in the early-morning hours of July 30, 1965 - the same day that the Milwaukee Brewers were born as a corporate entity. Members of Teams Inc went to Madison that morning to officially incorporate as "Milwaukee Brewers Baseball Club, Inc." Selig, Uihlein, Jack Winter and Fitzgerald were among the board members of the new corporation. They announced that as the corporation's first act, it would formally apply to major league baseball for a franchise to begin play in 1966. During the four years that Milwaukee was without a major league team, the Brewers corporation would remain the legal instrument by which baseball's return would be sought. July 30 was an historical day in another, far broader, sense; in Independence, Mo., President Johnson signed the bill that created Medicare. Johnson signed the bill in Harry Truman's hometown because the idea had originated during and because of his administration.

Hoping for a short-term revival of the enthusiasm and success they had enjoyed at County Stadium in the 1950s, the 1965 Braves on July 30 instead ran into two obstacles, both involving moisture, on their way to a 9-2 loss to the Giants. The high temperature in Milwaukee was 51 degrees, a record low for that date, and rain forced an 18-minute delay at the start of the game and another 24-minute halt after the first inning. Only 6,787 braved the elements - about twice that number attended a concert in South Milwaukee that was part of that weekend's Wisconsin Spectacle of Music - and most of them left unhappy after Bob

Shaw pitched a seven-hitter and Giants catcher Tom Haller drove in five runs with a three-run homer and a two-run double. Braves starter Hank Fischer didn't survive the second inning, and the Giants led 9-1 after six innings. Willie Mays, who hadn't driven in a run since July 8, broke an 0-for-24 downturn with his 24th homer of the season and the 477th homer of his career, sixth on the all-time list. (At the time, Aaron had 21 homers for the season and 387 for his career.)

After the game, Bragan engaged in another of his superfluous rants, complaining that Shaw was throwing spitballs and that the umpires knew it but didn't intervene. In response, Bragan said, he had his four relievers - Osinski, Kelley, Sadowski and Niekro - throw a total of 83 spitballs themselves. Sadowski said his hands were chapped because his expectorations exceeded his expectations, and Osinski said he loaded every single pitch he threw. "The spitter is Shaw's best pitch," Bragan complained, "and he's got one of the best ones in the league." John Kibler was the home-plate umpire, and the arbiter at first base was Bragan's familiar target, Frank Secory, who said: "The only reason they claim Shaw is throwing a spitter is because they can't hit his stuff. I don't believe he throws one. He goes to his mouth and then to the resin bag, and according to our instructions, that's OK." Shaw, for his part, proclaimed his innocence. "I never threw a spitball," he said. "I wouldn't even know how to do it." Besides his spitball reputation, his temper - which played a role in the 1963 game in which Shaw had set a major league record with five balks in one inning - and his unquestioned talent (he won 108 big-league games, including 16 for the Giants in 1965), Shaw had a reputation for his off-the-field predilections. With the White Sox earlier in his career, his manager had been Al Lopez. In Jim

Bouton's book *Ball Four*, he recounted a conversation that supposedly took place between Shaw and Lopez. "I see you with a different broad every night," Lopez said to Shaw. "You must be a lousy lay."

From the Braves' point of view, the question that would seem to supersede the clamor over Shaw's spitball was whether the side trip to Atlanta for the exhibition game had left the Braves unnecessarily road-weary going into this vital series. If that question was asked by any reporters in the Milwaukee clubhouse, it went unanswered. The next night, the crowd count was down to 5,796 and the Braves virtually were down to zero visibility against Juan Marichal in a 3-1 loss. Marichal (16-8) pitched his 17th complete game in 24 starts. He retired the first 12 hitters he faced and had a two-hit shutout before giving up another hit and an unearned run in the ninth, and the Braves managed only four baserunners. Denny Lemaster, from whom the Braves would need a return to 1964 form if they were to stay in contention, pitched well but not nearly well enough, giving up three runs in six innings, including a home run by Jim Ray Hart. The Giants, considered by most the league's most talented team, now had beaten the Braves five times in nine days and had allowed only seven runs in those games.

Clearly, the Braves were on the precipice as the month ended. In less than three weeks, they would briefly rise to the National League pinnacle for the last time as the Milwaukee Braves.

The Summit Summons

• • •

IT WAS A SUMMER DURING which many time lines intersected in Milwaukee, and perhaps many of the 14,864 people who passed through the turnstiles at County Stadium on August 1, 1965 had that in mind.

A decade before, the 1955 Braves, on their way to drawing more than 2 million people for the second straight year, played a three-game weekend series at County Stadium on July 29-31 against the defending World Series champion New York Giants. It drew 108,121 fans, an average of 36,040 per game, even though the Braves finished the weekend (and the season) 13 1/2 games behind the eventual World Series champion Brooklyn Dodgers. In 1955, if you lived in or around Milwaukee, a night of self-indulgence might involve a trip to the Blatz Temple of Music amphitheater at Washington Park, where you might have seen performances by the likes of Jeanette MacDonald and other stars of the stage and screen. MacDonald, who died in 1965, often included Milwaukee on her stage tours between movie gigs. She was one of many entertainers with Milwaukee ties, including Liberace, the piano maestro, and Fredric March, a Racine native and University of Wisconsin graduate who won two Best Actor Oscars. March had worked his way through college by waiting on tables at the Alpha Delta Phi fraternity, and had sold apples and Hershey bars on campus to earn spending money.

If you went to the State Fair in West Allis, you saw and heard the top Big Band, country and polka acts of the postwar era. If you had even heard of rock 'n roll, which got little airplay on Top 40 radio in 1955, you might have referred to it as "race music" because of its rhythm-and-blues and jazz origins and overtones. If you traveled out of town and you weren't taking the Milwaukee Road or North Western railroads or driving your brand-new Chevrolet "mighty mouse," you might have flown North Central Airlines Flight 728, on the DC-3 - N21728 - that had been headquartered in Milwaukee's Mitchell Field since 1952 and had been in passenger service since 1939 without a single accident. It linked Milwaukee to Chicago, New York, Detroit, Cincinnati, Minneapolis and many smaller cities in the Great Lakes region. The nation was at peace and still in the midst of postwar prosperity. And, of course, you had the Braves, the franchise that in 1955 led major league baseball in attendance for the third of six straight years.

Now, in August 1965, the San Francisco Giants - whose move from New York was prompted in large part by the Braves' spectacular success in the 1950s after they departed Boston - were in town, and while Milwaukee was still much the same as it had been in 1955, in 1965 the times, as Bob Dylan sang that year, they were a-changin'. In one important respect, they were better; President Johnson on August 6 signed the Voting Rights Act of 1965, eliminating many of the obstacles that kept minority voters away from the ballot box, especially in the Deep South. The Washington Park amphitheater was still there, and Al Hirt and

Andy Williams played the State Fair that August. North Central still flew Flight No. 728 with the same DC-3. But N21728 was taken out of passenger service in August 1965 after logging more air miles than any other passenger plane in America at the time, while using 136 different engines. (It was later restored to its original condition and sold to the Henry Ford Museum in Dearborn, Mich. North Central, which had begun passenger service in 1948 as Wisconsin Central Airlines and served more than 90 cities at its peak, ceased to exist in 1979 when it merged with Southern Airlines and Hughes Air West to form Republic Airlines.)

Both of the old rail terminals, the backdrops for untold thousands of tearful welcomes and farewells, were closed in 1965. The nation was at war again, for the fifth time (counting the Spanish-American War in 1898) within the lifetimes of some Milwaukee residents. Rock 'n roll clearly was here to stay, at least among teenagers who by 1965 were doing most of the record-buying in Milwaukee and throughout the country. The Rolling Stones had played the Milwaukee Auditorium in 1964 and the Milwaukee Arena in 1965, though neither concert came close to drawing a capacity crowd. On September 4, 1964, the Beatles had taken the stage at the Arena, to the obligatory screams of thousands of teenaged girls. In 1955, TV viewers looking for laughter were watching *I Love Lucy* and *The Honeymooners* and *Father Knows Best*, on black-and-white sets. In 1965, the comedies of choice included *The Addams Family* (one episode in August 1965 revealed that Cousin Itt had trouble properly expressing himself because he drank too much formaldehyde too often) and *Mister Ed*, which once featured the talking horse, in an effort to become the first equine to play major league baseball, sliding into Dodgers catcher John Roseboro and sending him hurtling over the upper deck of Dodger Stadium. If you were a young baseball fan and you watched *The Flintstones*, you believed the San Francisco Granites played their home games at Candlestone Park (of course, that belief wasn't that far from the truth).

Some of those changes were landmarks, some were un-nerving; some were incremental, and some weren't even widely noticed. But not many Milwaukeeans, especially those with a baseball bent, could have imagined in 1955 that one decade later, the Milwaukee Braves were about to become the Atlanta Braves.

In fact, the Braves' legal and corporate name became "Atanta Braves" on August 9 after the team's board of directors so voted late in July. By the start of August 1965, the search for a replace-ment franchise was well under way, but because of existing and pending litigation against major league baseball, Milwaukee fans and most of Wisconsin's political leaders knew their city would be last in line, if in line at all. The Milwaukee Braves, with two months left in their existence, were already past tense in the minds of those who were angry with the Braves, with the investment group that was about to dislocate them, and with major league baseball in general. But the Milwaukee Braves were in a pennant race for the first time since 1959, so at least for this Sunday double-header against the Giants and for at least some of their fans of long standing, reality was suspended and the Braves' past became their present again. And after losing the first two games of their series against the Giants, they needed two wins on this Sunday.

In front of those 14,864 people, they got them both. The Braves won the first game 4-2 as Mack Jones gave the Braves a

2-0 lead with a first-inning homer and Tony Cloninger never relinquished that lead. He finished with a seven-hitter and retired the final seven hitters - the last of whom was Willie Mays, who fouled out to end the ninth after the Giants had scored a run. Warren Spahn came on to pitch the final two innings for San Francisco, and the Braves scored an unearned run - made so by Spahn's own error - off him in the seventh. The Giants would return to Milwaukee in September, so it wasn't certain that this would be Spahn's last game at County Stadium. Assuming it might be, the audience gave him a standing ovation as he left the mound. But the cheers were much louder during the first inning of the second game. Mathews, the only man who had been with the Milwaukee Braves when they arrived from Boston and would leave with them for Atlanta, hit a three-run homer in that first inning, and Wade Blasingame held that lead with last-out help from Billy O'Dell as the Braves won 6-3. O'Dell relieved Blasingame with two on, two outs and a 3-and-0 count against Jim Davenport, who, after taking a strike, flied out to center to end the game. The doubleheader sweep propelled the Braves past the Giants and into third place, 3 1/2 games behind the Dodgers.

The next night, before 6,293, the Braves won the five-game series and took their 16th win in 21 games with a 4-2 victory as Jesse Gonder got only his second hit as a Brave - a three-run double in the fourth - and Ken Johnson ran his record as a Brave to 9-3 with a six-hitter. The Braves managed seven hits in seven innings against Giants starter Gaylord Perry (7-9), and claimed they caught him doctoring the ball. In a reprise of the incident involving Bob Shaw - Perry's alleged mucus mentor - in the first game of the series, Braves third base coach JoJo White claimed he picked up a ball after the Braves were retired in the sixth, only to have it stick to his fingers as he tried to flip it to Johnson. During the bottom of the seventh, Aaron asked home-plate umpire Frank Secory to examine Perry's glove and the ball. Secory did so, and found nothing incriminating. "Well, at least they (the umpires) got worked up enough to go out there," Bragan said afterward. For all his accusations about spit skulduggery by the Giants, Bragan never made a formal complaint to the league. "I asked Bragan to substantiate his charges or tell me he could not substantiate them," NL president Warren Giles said. "I heard nothing."

While the Braves were preparing for that evening's game, Milwaukee County made official its intention to fight major league baseball in the courts, even if it meant losing a chance to get a new or recycled franchise in the immediate future.

The county filed its antitrust suit in federal court in Milwaukee, naming the National League and all of its member clubs as defendants and asking for specific performance (meaning a ruling forcing major league baseball to provide Milwaukee with a team in 1966) along with undisclosed financial damages and an injunction prohibiting the Braves from playing games at any home site other than County Stadium. It also claimed the agreement to move the franchise to Atlanta constituted "conspiracy and agreement to monopolize by major league baseball, the Braves, Atlanta, and Fulton County" and had eliminated the ability of Milwaukee Brewers Baseball Club, Inc., to operate a major league team out of Milwaukee. As in the Federal League case that was decided in baseball's favor in 1922 (and as would be the case when Curt Flood unsuccessfully sued baseball in 1971), the plaintiffs argued that regardless of whether baseball was a sport or a business in legal terms, it was interstate commerce and therefore not immune from antitrust laws.

The wording of the suit became important at the time it was filed because it gave county officials the right to subpoena all visiting NL clubs for the remainder of the 1965 season, and they dutifully served every manager as soon as he arrived at County Stadium for a series opener. It became even more important in 1966, when the plaintiffs obtained a favorable circuit-court ruling that the Wisconsin Supreme Court subsequently overturned by only a single vote. If that vote had gone in favor of the plaintiffs, the specific-performance element would have returned the franchise to Milwaukee - which, of course, by then didn't want it back. Meanwhile, in Madison, state officials were preparing a similar suit that they filed the next day, alleging that baseball had violated Wisconsin statutes at the same time it was violating federal law. This, however, was less urgent. The federal district court in Madison already had a backlog of 479 cases, and this meant it was unlikely that any action against MLB would be heard for at least a year. But the case was immediately assigned to Judge Elmer W. Roller.

Frick and Giles said they weren't concerned about the litigation, although Walter Alston was taken by surprise the next night (August 3) when the Dodgers came to town for a three-game series. When the team arrived at County Stadium, Alston was slapped with a subpoena based on the county's court filing earlier in the day. The Fan-O-Gram on the scoreboard at County Stadium read: "Welcome, Walt Alston. Glad you were able to meet the Marshal." Alston, unruffled as usual, filed the subpoena away, and rain washed the scheduled series opener away after the Dodgers had taken a 1-0 lead in the first on a double by Jim Gilliam and a single by Jim Lefebvre off Denny Lemaster. This forced the Braves' 10th doubleheader of the season, and they would play three more before the season was over.

Though their leave-no-entrails rivals always had been and always would be the Giants, both in New York City and in California, the Dodgers-Braves rivalry also was at least at smolder stage throughout the Braves' stay in Milwaukee. This was partly because the Braves' main NL obstacle during the 1950s had been the *Boys of Summer* Brooklyn Dodgers, but it ran deeper than that. The Dodgers, both in Brooklyn and in Los Angeles, were seen as the darlings of the national media, which then were concentrated in and on New York and Los Angeles to a much greater degree than was the case 50 years later. Meanwhile, teams from smaller markets like Milwaukee felt ignored. Jim Brosnan referred to the Dodgers' sense of self-entitlement in both of his best-selling first-person books, *The Long Season* and *Pennant Race*, written about the 1959 and 1961 seasons respectively. And there was the Jackie Robinson incident on June 2, 1954 at County Stadium. Robinson, who was perhaps baseball's most feared and intimidating player after Branch Rickey lifted his mandate that Robinson take any and all slights without complaint, glared at a fan who had been heckling him from a box seat. Robinson "swung" at the next pitch and lost his grip on the bat, which sailed into the stands, just missing the offending fan. Robinson later apologized and said the incident was an accident, and he wasn't disciplined by the league or by major league baseball. But few in Milwaukee believed his claim that he didn't throw the bat with malice in mind.

After the Brewers switched from the American League to the National League for the 1998 season, their principal rival became the Cubs, and during seasons when the Cubs were contenders, it wasn't unusual to see thousands of Cubs fans in the stands at Miller Park when the teams met there. But the opposite was true during most of the Braves' time in Milwaukee, where they drew many fans from the northern Chicago suburbs and more than a few from Chicago itself. The Cubs did not finish in the first division in any season from 1947 through 1966, while the Braves, of course, never had a losing season in Milwaukee. So that rivalry was geographic and nothing more, but even with the Milwaukee Braves less than two months from extinction, their rivalry with the Dodgers was still intact. That had a lot to do with the fact 19,950 - the Braves' largest crowd since Opening Day - showed up for the two games against the Dodgers on August 4 after a pre-sale of only 2,700. A sweep would bring the Braves within one-half game of first-place Los Angeles.

The Braves almost got it.

In 21st-century baseball, most managers simply skip a pitcher's turn in the rotation if he starts a game that is stopped because of weather before it becomes an official game. That was far less often the case in 1965, but Bragan decided to lead with left-hander Dick Kelley in the first game of the doubleheader instead of bringing back Lemaster. Kelley lasted only one-third of an inning and gave up two runs, but Hank Fischer, relegated to spot starter-long relief duty during the Braves' surge, rationed the Dodgers only an unearned run over the next 4 2/3 innings, and Dan Osinski and Billy O'Dell blanked L.A. the rest of the way as the Braves won 4-3. They managed only five hits off 15-game winner Don Drysdale, but two of the hits, by Oliver and Aaron, were home runs. Another, an infield hit by Felipe Alou, brought home what turned out to be the decisive run.

If Bragan had originally decided to start Kelley instead of Lemaster in the first game - both were lefties - because he didn't want Lemaster starting the day after he'd worked an inning in a rained-out game, he changed his mind between games. Lemaster started Game 2, and although the Dodgers could scrounge only three runs from the 10 hits they amassed against Lemaster in 7 2/3 innings, it was enough for a 3-2 victory and a split. After beating Drysdale, the Braves lost to left-hander Claude Osteen, who was proving to be the best No. 3 starting pitcher in the league even though his record was only 9-11.

The Dodgers took a 3-2 lead in the eighth as Bragan defied managerial dogma with Willie Davis on third base with two outs after Lemaster retired Ron Fairly in a matchup of lefty hitter against lefty pitcher. Bragan had right-hander Bob Sadowski warming up in the bullpen, but he let Lemaster pitch to right-handed hitting Lou Johnson, who singled home the deciding run. In the bottom of the ninth after Osteen had retired the first two Braves, Aaron doubled. Alston took Osteen out and brought in right-hander Bob Miller to face Torre, who struck out to end the game.

The Dodgers won the series with a 6-3 victory the next night before another surprisingly large turnout - 18,368 - although this time Sandy Koufax, the best pitcher of his generation, certainly was an added attraction. Braves fans didn't know if this would be Koufax's last appearance in Milwaukee, and Koufax couldn't be sure from game to game whether his next outing would be his last, period. Koufax had missed a starting turn against the Reds late in July, and it was reported that the circulatory problem in his pitching arm had worsened to the point where he might not be able to complete the season - as had been the case in 1962 and 1964. Koufax strongly denied those reports, saying he had sat out against the Reds because he had trouble getting loose while warming up. He wasn't at his best on August 5 against the Braves, giving up seven hits - including homers by Mack Jones and Joe Torre, who hit his HR one pitch after Koufax decked him with a high-inside fastball of the sort that only Koufax could throw. But Koufax struck out 12, and the Dodgers dispatched Blasingame with four runs in the third, two on a homer by Lefebvre.

The Astros were in next, for a four-game series featuring still another doubleheader. It loomed as a "trap" series given the emotion and energy that had been expended against the Dodgers and Giants. But the Braves held serve with three wins in the four games. Cloninger wobbled through a seven-hit, four-walk complete game for his 15th victory as the Braves opened the series with an 8-4 win in a drizzle as Gene Oliver drove in four runs. The Astros came back with a 4-0 victory on August 7 as Turk Farrell shackled Milwaukee with a five-hit, zero-walk shutout, but the Braves swept the Sunday doubleheader 8-5 and 8-4 to creep within two games of first place. Eddie Mathews had two homers, a double and six RBI in the doubleheader. Crowds of only 2,805 and 3,778 (the latter in 71-degree weather) turned out for the first two games, but Bat Day on Sunday coaxed a paid crowd of 20,882 into the stands. The Braves, who had done virtually no advertising all year - except, of course, in and around Atlanta - took out a one-column, 6-inch ad in both Milwaukee papers to "promote" the bat giveaway. The Braves, doubtless remembering the fiasco earlier in the season when only six gates were open for a doubleheader against the Dodgers, added game-day personnel to bring in and man temporary ticket booths and entry gates. This time, 33 gates and ticket booths were open; 14,000 bats were given away. The team sold 15,116 tickets on game day, and the total crowd, including 4,107 kids who were admitted for 50 cents, was 24,899.

The Braves had a much-needed off-day on Monday, August 9, and management used the time to counter-attack against its opponents in the antitrust action. This was the day that the Milwaukee Braves began operation as the Atlanta Braves, although they were incorporated in Connecticut for tax purposes and therefore, under federal law, could still do business under their former business name. Bartholomay claimed in a statement that the Braves had lost $1.5 million in 1965 because they had been forced to operate in Milwaukee instead of Atlanta. "The integrity of our players has been challenged," Bartholomay said in the statement. "Our contending team has been boycotted, and litigation intended to harass our operation has been instituted during the height of the pennant race." County executive John Doyne strongly denied the claims. "I don't know that anyone has challenged the integrity of the players," Doyne said, perhaps forgetting that Grobschmidt, a longtime political and personal rival, had done just that on more than one occasion. "I don't know of anyone who has boycotted them at all. Sure, a lot of people are angry at Mr. Bartholomay, but no one has organized a boycott. This (litigation by the county) is the only remedy the Braves left open to Milwaukee. Was their lawsuit an harassment of county government?"

The Sporting News, the self-proclaimed "bible of baseball" at a time when it covered all levels of professional baseball and nothing else, had long been a mouthpiece for ownership and management. Predictably, TSN scolded Milwaukee for taking its case to the courts. While acknowledging that the litigation "might force expansion," as the threat of a Continental League that had never existed except in the fertile mind of Branch Rickey had done in the late 1950s, C.C. Johnson Spink, TSN's owner and publisher, warned that "baseball people who want to move do not regard Milwaukee as a greener pasture." In September, though, *The Sporting News*, citing what it considered a preponderance of evidence that leaving Milwaukee without a team would do baseball more harm than good, abruptly reversed editorial course. It declared that "there are ominous signs that a legal struggle over the Braves' desertion of Milwaukee will do baseball no good regardless of the decision rendered ... (a legal victory) probably would do little to dissipate the moral indignation which the move to Atlanta engendered ... at worst, a court antitrust ruling favorable to Milwaukee could rip the reserve clause and create utter chaos ... Most of baseball's headaches have originated because of footloose management which feels not the slightest obligation to remain in a city where it has no roots. The Braves' case for abandoning Milwaukee without so much as a fare-thee-well is not enhanced by what happened in Washington five years ago (when the original Senators left Washington for Minnesota and, within months, were replaced by an expansion team that began play in D.C. in 1961). It was deemed poor public policy to leave the national's capital without big league representation. Do you think the Braves and the NL will be allowed to forget this in the upcoming court battle? Neither do we."

Spink nevertheless maintained that if Milwaukee ever got another team, it would subsist from the attendance standpoint and never revisit the Braves' record-breaking levels of the 1950s. He turned out to be right, but only temporarily. After the Seattle Pilots became the Milwaukee Brewers in 1970, the Brewers' first-year attendance was 933,690, and their highest total during their first eight seasons in Milwaukee (all of which ended with sub-.500 records) was 1,213,357 in 1975, the first of Hank Aaron's two farewell seasons in the Cream City. But attendance jumped to 1,601,406 in 1978 when the Brewers won 93 games. In 1982, when they won their only American League pennant and took the Cardinals to seven games in the World Series, they drew 1,978,896, and that total leaped to 2,397,131 - more than the Braves drew during their 1957 World Series championship season - in 1983. The Atlanta Braves didn't exceed the Brewers' 1983 mark until 1992, when they drew 3,077,400.

Bragan and his players, though, had other worries, specifically the defending World Series champion St. Louis Cardinals, against whom the Braves would open a three-game series on Tuesday, August 10, to complete the vital 15-game homestand during which Milwaukee so far had gone 7-5. But they had held steady in the NL race as the four leading contenders continued to slipstream each other. The Reds and Giants had played a contentious series the previous week that had featured a bench-clearing incident. Frank Robinson was suspended two games and fined $150 for his role in the fracas, and Reds manager Dick Sisler and pitcher Bill McCool had been fined $50 each. In those days, suspensions were rare and large fines even rarer because "purpose pitches" and retaliation was considered part of the game. This view was to change over the next 50 years, and one of the catalysts was a blot on baseball's history that would occur less than two weeks later.

As the Braves enjoyed their R&R day, they were in a virtual tie with the Reds for third place, two games behind the Dodgers and one game behind the Giants, who had won six straight (including a win by Warren Spahn to end his personal nine-game losing streak). Spahn in that game had broken the National League record for most innings pitched with 5,192. The record had been held by Grover Cleveland Alexander, who had worked 5,189 innings in the NL from 1911-30.

Bragan reiterated his previously-stated belief that the Braves would have to find a reliable fourth starting pitcher (behind Cloninger, Blasingame and Ken Johnson) if they were to have any chance, especially against the pitching-rich Dodgers. "I don't particularly care who it is," he said. "If Denny Lemaster gets untracked, he could do it. But somebody has to take the bull by the horns." Bragan, for the first time, also wondered aloud whether he had pushed his only reliable late-inning relief pitcher, Billy O'Dell, to his limit. But the Braves, for all their deficiencies on the mound and in the field, still hit home runs. They had gone deep in 23 of their past 29 games, and hit 40 homers in those 23 games. As long as the long-ball spree continued, the Braves were a team with which the other contenders had to reckon.

The Braves opened their series with the Cardinals with a 5-3 win on Tuesday, August 10, with Cloninger earning his sixth straight win and 16th of the season. Mathews hit yet another home run and singled in another run, and Oliver - getting a relatively rare start behind the plate as Torre rested - hit a homer off Bob Gibson. He even threw Lou Brock out when the latter tried to steal second base. Before the game, Cardinals manager Red Schoendienst - who was still a ranking deity in Wisconsin because of his role in bringing two pennants and a World Series championship to Milwaukee while with the Braves - was served with what would become the obligatory visiting-manager's subpoenas (one by the state, one by the county) before the game. Told of the fact his team's opponent was now the Atlanta Braves for all legal intents and purposes, he frowned. "Some son of a gun is out there on the field throwing the ball for the Milwaukee Braves," Schoendienst said. "He exists."

Sandy Koufax, with his arm back in working order, had beaten the Mets while striking out 14 for his 20th victory, and the Giants' Juan Marichal and the Reds' Sammy Ellis notched their 18th and 15th wins respectively that same night. With 52 games remaining for the Braves, who were still plowing through their backlog of makeup games, Cloninger figured to get at least 12 more starts in which to achieve the four wins he needed to become a 20-game winner at the age of 24. Other than Spahn, who had earned 20 or more wins during nine of his 12 seasons as a Milwaukee Brave (and in four other seasons with the Boston Braves), only one other Milwaukee Braves pitcher - Lew Burdette in 1958 and 1959 - had reached the 20-win plateau. No other Braves pitcher had won 20 since Johnny Sain did it for the Boston Braves in 1950. Cloninger, of course, had been a 19-game winner for the Braves in 1964, and he said Bragan, on the last day of the season, had offered to put him in as a reliever if doing so would help get him a 20th win. Cloninger said he declined the offer. "I didn't want to do it that way," he said. "I want to do it the right way." For his part, Bragan had utter faith in Cloninger. Leading

5-2 In the ninth, after getting the first two outs, he had given up two singles, a walk and a wild pitch to bring in one run. With Lou Brock at the plate representing the potential go-ahead run, Bragan had Billy O'Dell ready in the bullpen and could have gone lefty-on-lefty against Brock. But after a mound conference, Bragan stuck with Cloninger, who fell behind 2-and-0, then threw three straight strikes to end the game. Bragan said afterward that he came out to talk not to Cloninger, but to Oliver. "He's still fogging them in there, right?" he asked. "He sure is," Oliver replied. "That's all I want to hear," said Bragan, who then walked back to the dugout.

The Braves' victory the day before notwithstanding, August 11, 1965 was the first day of a cataclysm that gripped the entire country, including Milwaukee. In Los Angeles' predominantly-black Watts district, white police officers got into a scuffle with a black motorist who had been pulled over at the intersection of Avalon Boulevard and 116th Street on suspicion of drunken driving. Los Angeles had been a racial cauldron for many years, largely because of alleged mistreatment of minorities by the Los Angeles Police Department. A crowd gathered, weapons were brandished, and the Watts riot was underway. It lasted five days, left 34 dead, 1,032 injured and more than 4,000 arrested before police and National Guardsmen finally restored order. Amazingly, the Dodgers played all four of their scheduled home games during the riot, but several players, including catcher John Roseboro, had homes that were dangerously adjacent to the violence. After the riots had subsided, attempts to effect reconciliation among the warring factions in L.A. included a commitment by the city to tear down blighted buildings and create more parks and other open space. As a result, it was decided to convert Wrigley Field - located 5 1/2 miles away from the riot's flashpoint - into a facility better suited to serve the entire community. The ballpark, which served the PCL's Los Angeles Angels from 1925-57 and was the home of the AL's Los Angeles Angels in 1961, was still used occasionally for other sports events after 1961. But in 1966, most of the main structure was torn down, and the remainder of the structure was leveled in 1969.

Neither of the Milwaukee papers devoted much space to the Watts riots in their August 12 editions, largely because only sketchy wire-service news stories emerged from L.A. during the previous night and early morning. Coincidentally, though, the *Journal* had undertaken a unique journalistic exchange. The Milwaukee paper had sent a reporter to Spartanburg, S.C., and the South Carolina paper had sent a reporter to Milwaukee. The subject, for both, was segregation in the cities they were visiting *vis a vis* segregation in the cities in which they worked. Fred Rigsbee of the *Spartanburg Herald*, noting that about 78,000 of Wisconsin's 90,000 black residents at the time lived in Milwaukee, wrote: "The integrationist may integrate all he wants in the Badger State, and the segregationist will not be affected." Rigsbee also noted that Milwaukee's black population had tripled from 1950 to 1960, and described the area locals called the "inner core" (the near north side, roughly bordered by Third and 12th streets and Juneau and North avenues) as a "black island." He elaborated: "Whether through design or preference or a combination of both, Milwaukee's Negroes are segregated. The Negroes say they are prohibited by the unwritten law from renting property outside the core area. Some core schools are 95 percent Negro, whereas several schools in other parts of the city have no Negro enrollment. A federal suit (filed by Lloyd Barbee) is pending which seeks to break the school segregation situation and to promote racial balance. The (Milwaukee Public Schools) board argues that there is no intentional segregation policy." Rigsbee also noted that MPS had 4,053 white teachers and only 452 black teachers, that only one black was on the 15-member school board, and that only 40 of Milwaukee's 1,800-member police department were black. His stories, coming as they did from a neutral party and not somebody with a stake in the racial-balance question in Milwaukee, can be seen in retrospect as a harbinger of the strife that would manifest itself in 1967 when a riot was averted only because martial law - virtually clearing all city streets - was declared before isolated violence became widespread.

For the Braves and Milwaukee baseball fans who were now counting down the final weeks and days of the Milwaukee Braves, the last season and the last pennant race went on despite all that was taking place in the all-too-real world. On the night that the Watts riots broke out, the Braves beat the Cardinals 5-2 before 9,580 as Ken Johnson veered around trouble while completing a nine-hitter, and Milwaukee's home-run fusillade continued. Alou and Aaron put the Braves on top with solo homers off Ray Washburn in the fourth, and Aaron added a three-run blow in the fifth. The Braves now had a major-league high 148 homers, and stayed within two games of first place after the Dodgers' Don Drysdale beat the Mets 1-0. There was a discordant note in the Braves' clubhouse, as Carty complained to reporters about the fact he had played sparingly even though his sore back felt better. "If you're playing for a man and he doesn't have confidence in you, then you can't play baseball, and you may be the best outfielder there is." Bragan's retort: "Any move I make is designed to win. The fact remains that he can't play left field with Alou and he can't play center field with any of our center fielders (usually Jones, sometimes Cline)." Even though the Braves were playing their best baseball of the season, the relationship between Bragan and his players was as it had been since Bragan had taken over the team in 1963 - one that played out in the media and not in the manager's office or the clubhouse.

The 15-game homestand concluded with a getaway-day afternoon contest against the Cardinals on Thursday, August 12. If former Brooklyn Dodgers catcher Mickey Owen was watching on TV or listening on radio - he was sheriff of Greene County, Mo., at the time - he must have cringed even if he was rooting for the Cardinals, for whom he played from 1937-40.

Owen was the Dodgers' catcher in Game 4 of the 1941 World Series when he committed perhaps baseball's most infamous passed ball, on a third strike to Tommy Henrich with two outs in the ninth inning and the Dodgers leading the Yankees 4-3. The Yankees pushed across four runs, won 7-4 and locked up the World Series the next day. On August 12, 1965, the Braves and Cardinals were locked in a 4-4 tie after 12 innings with Phil Niekro on the mound for Milwaukee. He struck out Ken Boyer to lead off the 13th inning with the pitch - the knuckleball - that wound up being his ticket to the Hall of Fame. This time, though, it got past catcher Gene Oliver, allowing Boyer to reach first. Dal Maxvill bunted Boyer to second, Bill White was intentionally walked, and Dave Ricketts fouled out. But Mike Shannon singled Boyer home, and Bob Purkey, a Cardinals rotation member who had entered in the 12th, finished off the 5-4 St. Louis win with a 1-2-3 13th. (Purkey won 129 big-league games during his 13-year career, and he had more wins, 21, against the Braves than against any other team.) Ironically, Purkey also threw a knuckleball, and Shannon, normally a third baseman, caught until Ricketts relieved him in the bottom of the 13th. Shannon played in 882 games as a major leaguer, but caught in only five of them.

Niekro in 1965 was still struggling both with command and with commitment to his knuckleball, even though it had helped him reach the majors after the Braves signed him for only a $500 outlay in 1959. Bragan used Niekro primarily as a long reliever during the first four months of that season, and he was in this game only because the Braves had gone through five other pitchers, including recently-recalled Clay Carroll. But even though this was the first time that Niekro had been beaten while relying exclusively on the knuckleball, it also helped him decide to commit exclusively to it instead of trying to nurse along other nondescript pitches to complement the knuckler. "I threw 30 knucklers in a row," he said later, "and the one that got away was the one that hurt. I threw him (Boyer, the National League's MVP the season before) two strikes with it, too." It also didn't help that Oliver, not known for his expertise defensively, had caught the entire game; Torre was playing first but was unable to catch because of bruised and bandaged hands. The Braves' third catcher, Jesse Gonder, had already been used as a pinch-hitter.

Bragan's overmanaging also cost the Braves in this game. With one out in the eighth, after Mack Jones had hit a homer to bring the Braves within 4-3 and Aaron had doubled, Cardinals manager Red Schoendienst baited Bragan by replacing right-hander Tracy Stallard (best known for giving up Roger Maris' 61st home run four years earlier) with left-hander Hal Woodeshick. Bragan countered by lifting Eddie Mathews - probably the most locked-in hitter the Braves had at this point of the season - in favor of right-handed hitting Mike de la Hoz. de la Hoz flied out, and although Aaron advanced to third on the fly and scored on a wild pitch by Woodeshick to tie the game 4-4, Mathews' bat was now out of the lineup. With no other position players available on the bench, de la Hoz stayed in the game. He flied out in the 10th, and popped out in the 12th after Aaron had doubled with two outs.

Despite the loss, the Braves had won nine of the final 13 games of the homestand after losing twice to the Giants, and remained only 3 1/2 games out of first. They cut that margin to 2 1/2 games and moved past the Reds into second place the following afternoon at Wrigley Field with an 8-3 win against the Cubs and former teammate Bob Buhl. Oliver, who had hit only five home runs before the All-Star break, hit his 13th and 14th of the season, and Lemaster won his first game since June 11, striking out 13 while spacing eight hits, four of them in the ninth inning. The Braves also won without Hank Aaron, who was given a rest day in favor of Billy Cowan, who was seeing his first action since being acquired from the Mets on August 5 for a player to be named later. Cowan, an outfielder-first baseman who wound up playing eight major league seasons for six teams, went 1 for 4 and played left field, with Felipe Alou moving to right.

The Watts riots were now in their third day, and Los Angeles was under 24-hour curfew as President Johnson offered to send in federal troops to help quell the violence. While the *Sentinel* had played the story on Page 2 the previous two days, its front-page, 72-point headline screamed: "Jungle Law." The *Sentinel* throughout the Braves' time in Milwaukee also had another constant besides its right-wing extremism - a stereotypical Indian either celebrating, brooding or weathering raindrops, depending on how the Braves had done the previous day. After the Braves beat the Cubs, the dancing Indian was dutifully printed - right next to the "Jungle Law" headline, making an unfortunate headline an even more distasteful juxtaposition.

The *Journal* had localized the story as soon as its urgency became apparent, reporting in detail how some of the same combustion elements that had triggered the Los Angeles riots existed in Milwaukee as well, but the *Sentinel* focused on the carnage while figuratively wringing its hands, calling the riots nothing more than "tragic examples of what can happen when flagrant disrepect and defiance of law supplants reason and tolerance." Meanwhile, Robert F. Kennedy, who had resigned as LBJ's attorney general the previous year, was in Milwaukee for a fund-raising dinner at the Pfister Hotel. Kennedy, after serving as U.S. Attorney General, had been elected to the Senate in 1964 and was a supporter of numerous Wisconsin Democrats who were running for office that November. He said, though, that he was in Milwaukee "as a Kennedy and not as an endorser." He had been a staunch advocate of the civil rights movement - and particularly the Voting Rights Act of 1965 that LBJ had signed into law on August 6 - as attorney general, but had not yet set forth the omnibus agenda or fully projected the charisma and unifying persona that were to make him the frontrunner for the 1968 Democratic presidential nomination before he was assassinated in June 1968.

Civil unrest also was festering in Chicago. The Illinois National Guard had been put on alert, and would soon be called in to break up a riot that resulted in 67 injuries and 123 arrests. But at Wrigley Field, the Braves and Cubs went about their business as usual on August 14, with the Braves winning again, 8-2. Tony Cloninger won his seventh straight decision and ran his win total to 17, although he was lifted after six innings with his uniform completely drenched after his labor in 88-degree heat and 70 percent humidity. Gene Oliver, atoning for his passed ball two days earlier, hit two more homers, his 15th and 16th of the season (and his sixth and seventh of the year at Wrigley Field) and discussion began in earnest about the Braves becoming the first National League team ever to have six players hit 20 or more homers in a season. Four players already had reached and passed the 20-homer threshold: Aaron would hit his 27th on August 17, Mathews connected for his 27th the day before, Mack Jones hit his 22nd in this game against the Cubs, and Joe Torre would launch his 24th on August 18. Alou also hit a homer, his 22nd, in this win over the Cubs. And four of the six had been virtually powerless during the early stages of the season. Alou hadn't hit his first homer until May 2, Oliver was at zero HRs until May 15, Torre only had two before May 5, and Jones was held to three before May 25.

Mathews and Aaron had two doubles each as the Braves belabored Cubs pitcher Bill Faul, who was one of the first major league players to use self-hypnosis in an effort to maximize his concentration and minimize outside distractions. The Braves also stayed with Woody Woodward at shortstop, even though Menke's knee injury had healed enough for him to play. "Woodward makes the double play as well as anyone in the league," Bragan said. "He has good range and good hands and he has a real good arm. He's been looking better with the bat, too."

In Washington, a bill by Sen. Philip Hart (D-Mich.) to over-turn baseball's antitrust exemption appeared doomed almost from the moment it was introduced. Sen. Sam Ervin (D-N.C.) attached a rider to the bill that would strip teams of exclusive rights to players taken in the draft, which had been held for the first time in 1965. With this provision, Ervin knew, the bill would die in committee, and that was fine with Ervin, who had been among Atlanta's most ardent supporters as Bartholomay and his group sought to claim the Braves from Milwaukee and provide the Deep South with its first professional sports franchise.

Thirty-two deaths had been reported in Southern California as the Watts rioting extended into a fifth day and well beyond the Los Angeles city limits. Two police officers in Long Beach had been shot, and in San Diego, two black men were reported to have stabbed a white man with no provocation. The con-flict in Southeast Asia, meanwhile, was beginning to be seen, through media coverage and interpretation, as far more sin-ister and far less manageable than anyone without first-hand knowledge of the situation could have imagined at the start of the year. Milwaukee, though, generally went on as before. Al Hirt drew 6,429 - more than most of the Braves' 1965 home games - at the State Fair, which was attended by 109,688 over its seven-day run. Van Cliburn and Henry Mancini performed with the Milwaukee Symphony Orchestra. *Sound of Music* would be performed at the Melody Top for 13 days starting August 17. Fats Domino was scheduled to come to Devine's Million Dollar Ballroom in September, and County Stadium was booked for a country-and-western concert - featuring Buck Owens, Ferlin Husky, Claude King and an obscure convict-turned-twanger named Merle Haggard - for September 24, two days after the Braves' last home game.

The Braves continued to play as if they expected to extend their County Stadium occupancy into October, sweeping the series in Chicago with a 4-3, 12-inning victory to pull within a game and a half of first place. The Braves, leading 3-2 going to the ninth, gave up an unearned run on Mathews' error to tie the game, but Denis Menke - in the game because Carty had pinch-hit for Woodward earlier - singled with one out in the 12th against Cubs relief specialist Ted Abernathy, and Ty Cline and Felipe Alou legged out infield hits. Newly acquired Don Dillard, pinch-hitting for Billy O'Dell after the latter had pitched four scoreless innings in relief, dribbled a potential double-play grounder to shortstop Don Kessinger, who flipped to second baseman Glenn Beckert. But Dillard outran the relay, scoring Menke with the go-ahead run. It was only the eighth game in which Dillard, the outfielder acquired in 1962 as an afterthought in the Joe Adcock-for-Ty Cline trade, had appeared since his recall on July 23. He had been used only as a pinch-hitter, with one hit in his previous seven tries, and the fielders-choice groundout gave him his first RBI as a Brave. Three days later, his last two RBI as a Brave - and as a major leaguer - would send the Braves into first place and Milwaukee into a brief base-ball tizzy of the sort Braves fans never thought they would see again.

The Braves' bullpen, considered the team's weakest link at the start of the season, continued to flourish. O'Dell took the "point lead" on Abernathy for the Fireman of the Year award, awarded in those days to the top relief pitcher in each league.

O'Dell now had eight wins and 13 saves for 21 "points," and had not given up an earned run since July 8, appearing in 16 games and completing 28 innings during that span. Osinski came on in the bottom of the 12th to get the save, working around two singles and ending the game by striking out Billy Williams on a 3-and-2 curveball that the future Hall of Famer wasn't expecting. "It was low," Osinski said. "He could have taken it, and it would have been ball four." The scoreless inning gave Osinski, who had not given up an earned run since June 27, his third save and lowered his ERA to 2.78, the lowest it had been since May 2. He would continue to pitch well for the remainder of the year, finishing with a 2.82 ERA and six saves while absorbing more of the workload that had been O'Dell's by default.

The win over the Cubs boosted the Braves' August record to 11-4, and they made it 12-4 by outlasting the Cardinals 10-8 at Busch Stadium, which had been known as Sportsman's Park when the woeful St. Louis Browns had owned the decaying facility and leased it out to the far wealthier and more popular Cardinals. Phil Ball, who had bought the Browns and the ballpark in 1925, had spent $100,000 on improvements that wound up benefitting his rival far more than his own team, and no more upgrading of significance was done until the Browns sold the park to the Cardinals just before the Browns left for Baltimore in 1954. A new Busch Stadium, of the now-fashionable monolithic, multi-purpose design, was under construction in 1965, but wasn't completed and ready for occupancy until May 1966. The new Busch Stadium would be the haven of sprinters and gap hitters. The soon-to-be-demolished Busch Stadium, with its temptingly-adjacent right-field pavilion, was far more friendly to long-ball hitters, and Eddie Mathews had one of the best games of his career in the opening game of the Braves-Cardinals series. He went 4 for 5 and drove in six runs with two homers, a double and a single, giving him 26 homers and 82 RBI for the season. Since August 8, Mathews had whacked 18 hits in 33 at-bats, raising his average from .233 to .259, and had collected five homers and 20 RBI during that span. His two-run single in the eighth extracted the Braves from an 8-8 tie. O'Dell's stretch of scoreless innings came to an end when he gave up a grand slam to Tim McCarver to forge the 8-8 tie, but Bragan stuck with him in the ninth, and he retired Curt Flood, Ken Boyer and Bill White to record his ninth win.

In Los Angeles, the Phillies beat the Dodgers 6-1, leaving L.A.'s National League lead over the second-place Braves at one-half game, with the third-place Giants lurking a game and a half off the pace. Said Red Schoendienst: "I thought we had a power-hitting team (in 1957 and 1958, when he helped the Braves reach two World Series) but this club has even more," he said. "I've said all along that they should run away with this thing (the NL pennant), and I still say it." The Braves to this point had 156 homers and were on pace to break the franchise record of 199, set during the World Series championship season of 1957. The Braves also had a chance to become only the eighth team in major league history to have three players (Aaron, Mathews and Mack Jones) with 30 or more homers.

On Wednesday, August 17, the Braves landed in first place for the first time since Opening Day, though they remained there for only about three hours after beating the Cardinals 4-1 and before the Dodgers reclaimed the top spot by beating Philadelphia 4-1 at Dodger Stadium. Lemaster continued to reprise his 1964 form, finishing with a seven-hitter and striking out seven. In five starts after his return from tendinitis, Lemaster had given up only nine earned runs and 25 hits in 34 innings. In this win over the Cardinals, he gave up a lead-off single to Lou Brock in the first, picked him off, and then retired 17 of the next 18 hitters. Afterward, he talked about his reluctance to reveal his earlier arm trouble. "I couldn't even lift my arm (after a start in an exhibition game in Atlanta on June 21)," he said. "If I had done it earlier, I might have had a decent season. But actually, I'm just happy to be out there winning again when every game means so much. I feel like (as a pitcher) I'm smarter (than he had been during his 17-win breakout in 1964). I think more than I used to. I try to work on the hitters instead of just throwing the ball down the middle and hoping for the best." (Unfortunately for Lemaster and the Braves, his comeback turned out to be an illusion. The win was his sixth of the season, but he would earn only one more, leaving him at 7-13 for the season.)

Aaron his a two-run homer and Alou continued his batting splurge with four hits, raising his average to .315. He had 10 hits in 16 at bats, and 23 in his past 47 plate appearances. "I'm finally back in the groove," he said. "My knee doesn't bother me at all, and I know what I'm doing at the plate. When I wasn't pulling the ball, I was hitting a lot of long flies to center field." Because of his offseason knee surgery and because he didn't fit the leadoff-hitter prototype, Bragan had hesitated before installing Alou in the No. 1 spot. Now, he would not be dislodged, and the Braves' every-day lineup finally seemed cemented: Alou in left field, Mack Jones in center, Aaron in right, Mathews at third, Torre and Oliver either behind the plate or at first base, Bolling at second, and Woody Woodward at short. With Lemaster seemingly back to his 1964 level of excellence, the Braves thought they had four dependable starting pitchers - Cloninger, Blasingame, Lemaster and Johnson - and Osinski was giving the Braves a late-inning alternative as O'Dell's innings count mounted.

By this time, at least some Milwaukee fans - even the ones who had sworn off the team and baseball entirely - were envisioning a final, rousing encore to this season of angst and apathy. The third game of the Cardinal series would be on TV in Milwaukee, and if VCRs had existed in 1965, sons and grandsons would still be pulling this August 18 tape off the shelf to evoke memories or get a sense of what it had been like to be a baseball fan in Milwaukee during the 1950s. The Braves moved into first place with a 5-3 victory that was first the Chris Pelekoudas Game before it became the Don Dillard Game.

In 21st-century baseball with its 12- and 13-man pitching staffs, Dillard almost certainly wouldn't have been on the active roster at this stage of the season, especially considering the Braves' outfield talent glut. A 28-year-old who had been a throw-in acquisition by the Braves when they sent Joe Adcock to the Indians following the 1962 season, Dillard had spent all of 1964 with Toronto of the International League on loan from the Braves. Originally signed by the Indians out of high school in 1955, he had reached the majors with Cleveland in 1959, but had played only 16 games for the Indians in 1959 and 1960. He had spent all of the 1961 and 1962 seasons with Cleveland, getting into 74 games in '61 and 94 in '62, but had hit only 12 home runs in those two seasons while batting .272 and .230.

After being traded to the Braves, Dillard had played 67 games for Milwaukee in 1963, but his numbers again were desultory - .235-1-12 - and at age 26, he appeared finished as a major leaguer. After his 1964 season in Toronto, Dillard began 1965 with Syracuse in another loanout, this time to the Detroit organization, and then was moved to the Braves' Triple-A affiliate in Atlanta. (Loan arrangements of this type were common in the late 1950s and into the 1960s as the minor leagues continued to shrink and major league organizations sometimes found themselves with too many players and not enough affiliates.) The Braves recalled Dillard to serve as an additional left-handed bat off the bench, and he had been used exclusively as a pinch-hitter, producing one hit in eight at-bats entering the August 18 game in St. Louis.

He was sent up to pinch-hit for Woody Woodward against right-hander Ray Washburn with two outs in the top of the ninth of a 3-3 game that the Braves believed should have been a 4-3 game in their favor. During the top of the eighth with one out and the bases empty, Aaron had hit a solo home run off Curt Simmons that apparently had put the Braves ahead - but even before the ball disappeared over the left-field wall, plate umpire Chris Pelekoudas raised his hands, pointed at Aaron and called him out for being outside of the batters box at the time he made contact. The Braves, of course, mounted a loud and long protest that resulted in Bragan's ejection. The play was officially scored as an unassisted putout by the catcher, and Torre flied out to left to retire the side.

The score remained 3-3 as the Braves came to bat in the top of the ninth against Washburn, who had replaced Simmons. Gene Oliver lined a sharp single off the glove of Cardinals third baseman Ken Boyer, Menke sacrificed him to second and Bolling went down on strikes for the second out. That brought Dillard to the plate as a pinch-hitter for Woodward, and under normal circumstances, Schoendienst either would have walked Dillard intentionally to get to the pitcher's spot, or brought in a lefty like Hal Woodeshick to face the left-handed hitting Dillard. But Bragan had left Eddie Mathews out of the starting lineup (playing Menke at third) for rest-and-recuperation purposes, and now he was lurking in the on-deck circle. Schoendienst wanted no part of Mathews, regardless of the pitcher, and even though Dillard was never more than a platoon player - a left-handed hitter, he finished his career with only three hits in 17 at-bats against left-handed pitching - Schoendienst left Washburn in to face Dillard, probably because Washburn (9-11 in 28 games that season) was a long relief-spot starter type and might be needed to go multiple extra innings if the score remained tied.

It didn't, although the umpires became involved again in the immediate aftermath of Dillard's homer. The Cardinals claimed the ball should have been ruled a ground-rule double because the ball had nicked the wall in right-center before leaving the ballpark, but even a ground-rule double would have scored Oliver from second. The home run stood, the Braves led 5-3, and at least for this one night - and for the only time in his major league career - Don Dillard was to the Braves as Dusty Rhodes had been to the New York Giants in the 1954 World Series when his three pinch hits, two of them homers, sparked the Giants' stunning sweep of the 111-win Cleveland Indians.

As with Rhodes, Dillard's time as a team and municipal luminary would be fleeting. He would disappear from the major leagues after the 1965 season, though he lingered on in the minor leagues for two more years. He was a .244 hitter with 14 homers over his major league career, and he batted only 10 more times in 1965, all as a pinch-hitter, and managed only one more hit. The day after his pinch homer, the achievement was pushed off the sports pages by the Reds' Jim Maloney, who won with a 10-inning no-hitter - the first time since 1917 that had been done in a major league game - against the Cubs the same day even though he walked 10 batters. But this night, after Cloninger (18-8) finished off his six-hitter with the help of a bottom-of-the-ninth double play, Dillard had lifted the Braves back into a tie for first place, and later that night, after the Phillies beat the Dodgers 6-3 in 12 innings in Los Angeles, the Braves were alone in first place for the first time all season.

They would drop back to second the next afternoon when the Cardinals beat them 5-4 to end their six-game winning streak. Defense was the Braves' undoing as they committed four errors after being guilty of only four miscues during their past 11 games. After the game, Bragan acted as if he had expected his team's defensive largesse. "We were long overdue for a game like this," he said. "Ken Johnson pitched as good a game as he has pitched since we got him (allowing seven hits and four runs, two of them unearned, in six innings). He should have won 4-1." Alou hit his 20th homer, making him the fifth Brave to reach that mark in 1965, but Bragan was as displeased by his team's offense as he was with its defense. The Braves managed only three runs and seven hits in 6 2/3 innings against Ray Sadecki, who had helped pitch the Cardinals to a World Series title with a 20-win season in 1964, but entered this game only 2-11 and ended it with a 5.92 ERA. "He's the worst-looking 20-game winner I've ever seen," Bragan said. "He's a thrower, not a pitcher."

Sadecki never again approached his 20-victory from of 1964, and was traded to the Giants in 1966 for Orlando Cepeda, who became the NL MVP in 1967 while Sadecki led the NL with 18 losses for San Francisco in 1968. But Sadecki did last 18 seasons while playing for six teams, including the Brewers in 1976. The Giants in 1965 had played virtually their entire season without Cepeda because of his knee injury, but he was activated on August 18, with the Giants selling one-time 24-game winner Jack Sanford to the Angels to make room for him on the roster. San Francisco was only 1 1/2 games behind the Dodgers and one game behind the Braves, and the return of Cepeda loomed as a difference maker, even though he was still too gimpy to play regularly in the outfield and Willie McCovey had long since established himself as the first baseman.

From St. Louis, the Braves traveled to Pittsburgh for a three-game weekend series with the Pirates, who had leveled off after the 12-game winning streak in late May that had thrust them back into the NL race. Entering the series opener August 20, Pittsburgh was in sixth place, 8 1/2 games behind the Dodgers, and a sweep of the Braves appeared to be a virtual necessity if the Pirates were to remain a factor in the pennant race. The Braves eliminated that possibility with a 4-3 victory that, combined with Los Angeles' 5-1 loss to host San Francisco later that night, returned the Braves to the top spot in the NL standings. It would be the last time the Milwaukee Braves would ever occupy that niche, and the fact they were locked in a pennant race, though far more germane than it had been during the first four months of the season, was obscured by other events that Friday night.

The Wisconsin State Fair attracted 123,912 patrons, its largest single-day turnout since 1956. Gemini 5 was orbiting the planet, although fuel-cell problems forced cancellation of some of its planned experiments and maneuvers. And the Beatles were playing at Chicago's Comiskey Park before 56,000, including about 800 teenagers who had made the trip via chartered buses from Milwaukee. Some of those teens had transistor-radio earplugs; not so many years before, their radios would have been tuned to WTMJ's broadcast of the Braves' game. But every Wisconsin concert-goer who was questioned on the subject said the earplugs were being used to listen to pre-concert broadcasts by Chicago-area stations. Nobody interviewed was listening to the Braves game. For their tickets, priced between $2.50 and $5.50, the concert-goers got only 35 minutes and 12 songs from the Fab Four. The Beatles, who had played the Milwaukee Arena in September 1964, would never appear in Milwaukee again. Their last concert together would be on August 29, 1966, at Candlestick Park in San Francisco.

In the game against the Pirates, Torre hit a home run in the seventh to tie the game at 2-2 and Mathews followed suit in the eighth with a two-run blast to put the Braves up 4-2. Blasingame, who had given up a two-run homer to Roberto Clemente in the sixth, gave up a third run in the ninth on an RBI single by Andre Rodgers, but ended the game by knocking down Bob Bailey's comebacker smash, scrambling to his feet and throwing Bailey out at first. Blasingame said after the game that he had felt fresher in games because he had eliminated his previous practice of throwing between starts. His win this night was his 15th; he would earn only one more in 1965.

The next night (August 21), the Braves found themselves up against Bob Friend, who was closing out the last of his 15 seasons in a Pirates uniform. For much of that time, especially in the early part of his career, the Pirates were even worse than they were during their record-setting succession of 20 straight losing seasons from 1993-2012. Branch Rickey had taken over as president of the Pirates in November 1950, after Walter O'Malley had wrested operational control of the Dodgers from him, and his five full seasons in Pittsburgh - he resigned after the 1955 season - constituted an almost-total purge of veterans who were replaced by a succession of Ron Necciais. Necciai, while pitching for Bristol in the Class D Appalachian League in 1952 as an 18-year-old, won a game in which he got all 27 outs via strikeouts. After striking out 109 in 43 innings, Necciai was promoted to Burlington of the Class B Carolina League, where he was 7-9 but had a 1.57 ERA and struck out 172 in 136 innings. Branch Rickey said at the time of Necciai: "There have only been two young pitchers I was certain (were headed) for greatness, simply because they had the meanest fastball a batter can face. One of these boys was Dizzy Dean. The other was Ron Necciai. And Necciai is harder to hit." That didn't prove true after Necciai was promoted to the Pirates in early August. In 12 games, he went 1-6 with a 7.08 ERA with only 34 strikeouts in 54 2/3 innings. He went into the Army soon after that, and after his discharge, ulcers and arm problems soon ended his career. He never returned to the majors, and retired after a comeback attempt in 1955.

Friend had first made the Pirates roster amid far less furor in 1951, when they went 64-90. They went 42-112 in 1953, and didn't win more than 66 games again until 1957. Through that time, Friend endured. He won an ERA title with a 2.83 mark in 1955. His total of 1,375 innings pitched from 1956 to 1960 was the highest in baseball during that span, and in a "secret" *Sport* magazine poll of NL scouts and front-office personnel late in 1957, he was ranked as one of the three best pitchers in the NL, with Don Newcombe and Johnny Antonelli. Friend's only 20-win season came in 1958, when he went 22-14, and during most of his career with the Pirates, his last name was a proper noun but rarely an adjective at Forbes Field. Fans, frustrated by the Pirates' downward spiral, booed him lustily and complained he was good enough to keep his team in games but not good enough to win them. He lost 218 games in a Pittsburgh uniform, but he also won 191 with a very presentable 3.55 ERA, was a three-time All-Star, and went 18-12 in 1960 as the Pirates expunged their misadventures of the previous decade and won the World Series for the first time since 1925. Even in 1965, when Friend was 34 and operating on guile and subterfuge rather than velocity, the Braves knew better than to under-estimate him. Besides the Cubs, Colt .45/Astros and Mets, all dregs during most of Friend's career, the Braves were the only team against which Friend had a winning record, at 31-30. And on August 21, Friend dropped the Milwaukee Braves out of first place permanently with a five-hitter (three by Aaron) as Pittsburgh won 3-0 after knocking Lemaster out of the game in the fourth inning. The Braves had been 70-50 entering the game; they would finish 16-26, while the Pirates would win 27 of their last 38 games, including a 5-4, 11-inning decision in the series rubber game on Sunday, August 22. Dan Osinski walked Bill Virdon with the bases loaded to force in the winning run.

Despite the two losses in Pittsburgh, the Braves still had put together a respectable 7-3 road trip, and for the first time in several years, their supporters resurrected a tradition that had been *de rigueur* during the championship years: Welcoming the team back from a road trip at Mitchell Field. About 1,000 people crowded the terminal to show their support for the Milwaukee Braves as they entered the final six weeks of their existence. It was a modest turnout compared to those in the 1950s, and less than one-quarter the size of the throng of 4,167 who saw the Milwaukee Polo Club lose 7-2 that day to Santa Barbara, Calif. (The MPC had won three national championships and finished second three other times since 1945.) At the Milwaukee Mile, 30,905 saw Gordon Johncock win a USAC race. But for the relatively few fans who had resolved to support the Milwaukee Braves until they were no longer the Milwaukee Braves, the excitement of a final pennant race temporarily trumped their disgust with the team's ownership, the politicians' bickering and indecision, and the stammering from baseball's "leadership." The pennant race still included six of the 10 clubs, with the Dodgers leading the Giants and Braves by one-half game, with Cincinnati 2 1/2 games behind and the sixth-place Pirates still loitering on the periphery, 6 1/2 games behind.

Anything could happen ... and while the Braves were airborne following their loss to the Pirates in the final game of the road trip, something that 50 years later remained unfathomable did happen at sold-out Candlestick Park as the Giants and Juan Marichal (19-9) met Sandy Koufax (21-4) and the Dodgers. *Time* magazine reported it thusly:

Most so-called U.S. sports rivalries are frauds, preserved only by tradition. The feud between the Giants and Dodgers is real. It was bad enough when it involved Manhattan and Brooklyn, two boroughs of the same city. Now the principals are San Francisco and Los Angeles, two cities 325 miles apart whose partisans hate each other's guts. In ordinary times, Giants-Dodgers games are still games. August 22, 1965 was no ordinary time. Dodger catcher Johnny Roseboro was deeply concerned about race riots in the Watts section of Los Angeles near his home. Giants pitcher Juan Marichal had been brooding over the bloody civil war in the Dominican Republic. For tinder, there was the tension of the tightest National League race in history; for fire, a provocative trading of beanballs, curses and threats.

In the third inning, with the Dodgers leading 2-1, Marichal came to bat. The second pitch was low-inside; Roseboro dropped the ball, then picked it up and deliberately fired it as hard as he could back to the mound - right past Juan's right ear. Marichal later claimed that the ball had ticked his ear. He spun around, bat in hand. "Why did you do that? Why did you do that?" he screamed. Roseboro did not answer. He charged at Marichal and in front of 42,807 at Candlestick Park, Juan clubbed him three times on the head with the bat, sending blood streaming down the catcher's face from a deep wound in his scalp.

Shag Crawford, the home-plate umpire, gave this account of what happened next: "The whole thing happened three feet in front of me. Everybody ... was completely flabbergasted. Naturally both dugouts emptied ... we finally got Roseboro away, but then Marichal went crazy. He went down the first-base line, swinging the bat like a wild man. The Giants were in front of him, and the Dodgers were in back of him, but nobody would make a move on him because of the bat. I came up on the home-plate side, trying to get a shot at him. I waited until he raised the bat to swing again; then I dove at him. I hit him around the neck, grabbed the bat, and we both went down. That's when both teams dove on him. And me too ... I got cut up and bruised pretty good."

While Marichal and Roseboro were entangled, on-deck hitter Tito Fuentes - who had made his major league debut four days before - charged into the fracas swinging *his* bat, which soon was pulled away from him in the pileup along the first-base line. Mike Kekich and Nick Willhite, two young pitchers who had just been promoted from the minor leagues, sprinted from the Dodgers' bullpen (which at Candlestick was on the field of play and not within a separate enclosure) and both got in several blows on Marichal before the pileup engulfed them. Play was halted for about 20 minutes, and the San Francisco Police Department stationed mounted officers along the warning track that ringed the playing surface. They remained there for the rest of the game. Marichal, of course, was ejected, and Roseboro went to the clubhouse and then a local hospital to undergo treatment for his head wounds, which turned out to be relatively superficial. He would miss three games before returning to the lineup on August 26 against the Mets at Shea Stadium, though he had to leave that game after a foul tip split the middle finger of his throwing hand. He and Jeff Torborg would share catching duties for the remainder of the regular season.

When play finally resumed, Mays - his uniform jersey stained with Roseboro's blood after he tried to separate Roseboro and Marichal - hit a three-run homer off a shaken Koufax and the Giants went on to a 4-3 victory that lifted them into a virtual tie with the Braves, one-half game behind Los Angeles.

The game was televised only in Los Angeles, but NBC, ABC and CBS all interrupted their national programming to show what little footage was available. This was the first time the networks had ever broken into non-sports programming to show an incident involving sports, and the fight was the lead story on each network's evening news - another dubious baseball first. Surprisingly, the cataclysm at Candlestick, though extensively recounted, was not the lead sports story in either Milwaukee newspaper - possibly because of the seven-game homestand that would begin the following night, August 23, against the Reds. Beyond the obvious fact that the outcomes would be central to the NL pennant race, the attendance totals seemed likely to figure into the equally-important question of whether Milwaukee would regain major league baseball after the Braves left. The headline atop Oliver Kuechele's column in the *Journal* put it bluntly: "Do We Want Big League Baseball?"

That afternoon, National League president Warren Giles issued a ruling on the Marichal matter that was almost as shocking as the incident itself. Marichal would be suspended for nine games - in effect, two starts - and would be fined $1,750. It was the largest fine ever levied against a major league player for an on-field incident, far exceeding the $1,000 Yankees catcher Bill Dickey had been assessed, along with a 30-day suspension, for breaking the jaw of Washington's Carl Reynolds during a fight in 1932. Giles, in a statement, labeled Marichal's actions "unprovoked, repugnant and obnoxious," but the Dodgers and many others in the baseball realm were vehement in their insistence that Marichal's suspension should have been much longer. "They got the numbers mixed up," Ron Fairly was to say years later. "They should have fined him $9 and suspended him for 1,750 games." No disciplinary action was taken against any of the other participants in the brawl. In Milwaukee, Reds manager Dick Sisler said that a slap on the wrist for a blow to the head was due to Giles' not wanting to alter the pennant race with a lengthy suspension of one of the best pitchers in the league - and Giles admitted as much in his statement announcing the suspension and fine.

"But this was a case of assault and battery," Sisler said. "One of our players in the minor leagues was involved in a similar incident early in the (1965) season, and he was banned for the rest of the year. What's more, he was banished from the league. I would say (Marichal) should have been given at least 30 days." Said Bragan: "If Marichal had been banned for the rest of the year, that would have been surprising - but justified. Marichal will be lucky if he doesn't have to settle with Roseboro in court." (Litigation was instituted by Roseboro later that year, but he and Marichal later became close friends; Roseboro attended Marichal's induction into the Dominican Republic's baseball Hall of Fame, and Marichal was a pallbearer at Roseboro's funeral after he died in 2002.)

New York Journal American columnist Jimmy Cannon, who had frequently assailed the NL and commissioner Ford Frick's office for their roles in the Braves' pending exit from Milwaukee, tied the Milwaukee situation into the Roseboro-Marichal incident. "The lies told to the people of Milwaukee by the owners of the Braves brought no protest from Giles," Cannon wrote. "The Braves come under Giles' jurisdiction. But the illegal move obviously was sanctioned by the man who admits that Marichal was leniently handled because he is with a pennant contender. Giles explained what a glorious feat the NL had accomplished when it planted the Braves in Atlanta. He didn't mention baseball forfeited even the illusion of integrity by abandoning Milwaukee."

Roseboro was to acknowledge in later years that he wasn't completely blameless for the outbreak of the violence, though he never admitted to throwing at Marichal's ear. He said at the time: "I don't care what they do to him. I don't have any feelings about it. As far as I'm concerned, it's over and done with." A few days later, though, Roseboro was far less conciliatory. Asked about what he thought Marichal's punishment should have been, he said: "Just him and me in a room for 10 minutes." Roseboro had been with the Dodgers since their Brooklyn years, and was known throughout the league as both a gentleman and a gentle man (as, for the matter, Marichal had been). Roseboro was known to smoke a pipe in the clubhouse, and he spoke on matters other than baseball so seldom that his team nickname was "Gabby." But he was also known as a man who could take care of himself in any argument that came to blows.

Light as Marichal's punishment seemed to most people, it may have cost the Giants the 1965 pennant. Ron Herbel started the first game that Marichal would have pitched, in a doubleheader in Pittsburgh on August 26, and the Giants lost both games. The second fill-in was Warren Spahn, who on August 31 hooked up with Lew Burdette in a senior pitchers seminar in Philadelphia that was reminiscent of the days when they anchored the Braves' staff. Spahn (6-16) pitched a three-hitter, but Burdette crafted a six-hit shutout and the Phils won 2-0. Marichal didn't pitch again until two days later, on September 2 in the first game of another doubleheader at Connie Mack Stadium, and was off his game, giving up seven hits and four earned runs in seven innings as Philadelphia won 4-3. The Giants finished two games behind the Dodgers; if Marichal had not been suspended and the Giants had won two of those three games, they would have tied the Dodgers for the pennant for the second time in four seasons. If they had won all three, of course, they would have reached the World Series.

Amid the latest swirl of controversy, there was base-ball to be played in Milwaukee that evening, and a crowd of 12,565 - supportive in voice but inconclusive in numbers from the standpoint of Milwaukee's baseball future - showed up in support of their estranged team. They were rewarded with a harrowing 7-6 victory that kept the Braves within a half-game of first place. It was a game that was at once a microcosm of what they had been during the first five months of the season, and what they were about to become during the final six weeks of their stay in Milwaukee.

Reds manager Dick Sisler gave Jim Maloney an extra day of rest after his 10-inning, 10-walk no-hitter against the Cubs, and the Braves teed off on Joey Jay, who was excused for the evening during the fifth inning as the Braves scored four runs to take a 7-1 lead. Gene Oliver hit his 17th homer, a two-run blow, and Felipe Alou contributed a two-run single. Denis Menke, back as the regular shortstop barely a week after Bragan had strongly suggested that Woody Woodward had done more than enough to earn starter status, had two hits and drove in a run. But Ken Johnson ran into trouble in the seventh, coming out of the game in favor of Billy O'Dell after surrendering a single to Art Shamsky, a home run to Johnny Edwards, and singles to pinch-hitter Marty Keough and Tommy Harper. Pete Rose greeted O'Dell with a triple to bring in two more runs and narrow the Reds' deficit to 7-5, and Rose scored on Vada Pinson's infield out to make it 7-6. Don Pavletich and Deron Johnson singled and pinch-hitter Frank Robinson, who had not started because of a swollen hand, was hit by a pitch to load the bases, but O'Dell got Edwards to hit into a forceout to end the inning.

O'Dell got a second wind after that, retiring the Reds in order in the eighth and ninth for his 17th save - only three fewer than he had collected during the first 10 years of his major league career. In his first full season as a short reliever, O'Dell had been a revelation for the Braves, and had been well worth the modest price - a well-past-his-prime Ed Bailey - that the Braves had sent to San Francisco. But his workload was beginning to manifest itself by the end of August. He would record only two more saves over the final 40 games of the 1965 season, during which he pitched in 11 games and gave up at least one hit in all but two of them. His numbers during that time were far from terrible - 17 1/3 innings, 20 hits, seven earned runs, 15 strikeouts and only one walk - but because of the fatigue factor, Bragan was able to use O'Dell only twice between September 1 and September 17.

No day in the final year of the Milwaukee Braves would have been complete without a serve and volley in the courtroom, and on August 23 the Braves asked the circuit court to dismiss Milwaukee County's antitrust lawsuit. The team claimed that the attendance figures since 1961 proved that Milwaukee couldn't or wouldn't support major league baseball, and maintained that forcing the Braves to stay there constituted "involuntary servitude" and denied them property (meaning the Atlanta market) without due process of law. It also reiterated baseball's long-standing claim that the industry did not engage in interstate commerce as defined by the antitrust laws.

That same day, it became apparent why the Braves were so eager to plant their flag in virgin television territory in Atlanta. ABC's Roone Arledge said it was unlikely that the network's Game of the Week package would be extended after its expiration at the end of the 1965 season. In 1964, MLB had sought to put together a Monday night package - much like the Monday Night Football deal to which the NFL and ABC agreed in 1970 - but none of the three major networks wanted any part of it, and the Saturday package for 1965 was only a one-year extension of the previous agreement. The total payout for 1965 was only $5.4 million, including $300,000 that went to the Braves. This payment was of relatively little help to a franchise that was in the midst of costly litigation, was trying to operate in two locations at once, owed hundreds of thousands of dollars in bank-loan service dating to the Bartholomay group's original purchase of the team in 1962, had lost almost all of its Milwaukee advertising base, and had been last among the 20 teams in attendance most of the season. When Bill Bartholomay and his group bought the Braves late in 1962, they wanted to move the team to Atlanta. Now, at least financially, they had no choice; if the courts were to force Bartholomay and his group to stay in Milwaukee another year, they almost certainly would have been bankrupted.

The next night (August 24), Bragan paid for playing the Billy O'Dell card again after he had worked 2 2/3 innings the previous night, and the Reds scored two runs in the top of the ninth for a 3-2 win before 12,413. Milwaukee had taken a 2-1 lead into the ninth even though Maloney, with his extra day of rest, held them to four hits over eight innings. Wade Blasingame gave up only four hits and one run through 7 1/3 innings, but his command - an issue throughout a season during which he walked 116 and struck out 117 in 225 innings - deserted him as he walked eight. He was lifted in favor of Dan Osinski after Pinson singled and Robinson walked with one out in the eighth. Osinski struck out Deron Johnson, and the next scheduled hitter was Don Pavletich, a right-handed batter. Cincinnati manager Dick Sisler sent lefty swinger Gordie Coleman up as a pinch-hitter; Bragan countered with O'Dell, and Sisler counter-countered with right-handed Charlie James. Bragan's maneuvering gave him the pitcher-hitter matchup he wanted - O'Dell against James, who batted .205 in 26 games for the Reds in 1965. From the Braves' standpoint, this was far more viable than Osinski against Pavletich, the West Allis native who had already hit a game-winning homer against the Braves earlier in the season, or even O'Dell against Coleman. O'Dell got James on an infield popup, and Milwaukee had averted crisis - but only for the moment.

After O'Dell struck out Leo Cardenas to begin the ninth, Jim Coker, the Reds' third-string catcher, trickled a ground ball into the shortstop hole on which Menke had no play. Chico Ruiz batted for Maloney and grounded out to first, with Coker moving to second. This brought up Tommy Harper, a right-handed hitter, with switch-hitting Pete Rose on deck.

Harper, 24, another of the cache of star players from Oakland, had emerged as a quality leadoff man during his third full major league season. He had both power and speed, leading the NL in runs scored in 1965 with 126 while stealing 35 bases and hitting 18 home runs. Rose, also in his third season, was in the midst of the first of his seven 200-hit years and the first of his 17 All-Star campaigns. But in 1965, he batted .354 as a right-handed hitter against southpaws and .288 swinging lefty against righthanders.

Bragan, understandably, also was intent on staying with his most dependable relief pitcher. So, given all those circumstances, he had little choice but to have O'Dell pitch to Harper instead of walking him to get to Rose.

Harper swung through O'Dell's first pitch, a fastball. The next pitch was a slider that landed in the almost-empty left-field County Stadium bleachers. The Reds led 3-2. Bill McCool gave up a two-out single to Gene Oliver in the bottom of the ninth, but pinch-hitter Billy Cowan struck out to end the game.

A win would have moved the Braves back into first place and dropped Cincinnati four games out. Instead, O'Dell had lost to the Reds for the third time in 1965, and in each case the winning blow was a home run at County Stadium. (The others were by Pavletich on June 25 and Robinson on June 27.) Sisler, who had convened a rare clubhouse meeting before the game, called it the most important win of his team's season to date. "We have to beat the Braves," he said. "If we, or anyone else, can finish ahead of the Braves, they'll have a real good chance of finishing ahead of everyone else, too." *Journal* beat writer Bob Wolf, though, described the loss as "unquestionably the toughest of the year" after making his rounds in the silent Braves clubhouse. Even Bragan, for one of the few times in his managerial career, could think of little to say.

Harper would remain with Cincinnati through the 1967 season, after which he was traded to Cleveland, where he batted only .217 in 1968. The Seattle Pilots chose him in the expansion draft after that season, and in 1969, even though he batted only .235, he stole 73 bases to lead the American League and set a franchise record that still stood as of 2016. After the Pilots moved to Milwaukee,

Harper proved he was more than a basepath sprinter, becoming the Brewers' first All-Star selection in 1970 while batting .296 with 31 homers and 82 RBI - all highs for his 15-year career. On April 7, 1970, when the erstwhile Pilots returned major league baseball to Milwaukee, Harper was the Brewers' leadoff man in a 12-0 loss to the California Angels at County Stadium. (The year before, he also had been the first Pilot to take the batter's box, against the Angels in Anaheim in a game Seattle won 4-3.)

The Braves, of course, were still part of the NL standings pileup, remaining one-half game behind the Dodgers, who had lost 7-4 to the Mets in New York, and 1 1/2 games ahead of the fourth-place Reds. But Harper's homer had been a negative catalyst from which the Braves never recovered, and on August 25, the weather seemed to turn against them too. Rain limited the crowd to 7,773 spectators who saw a 7-4 defeat that was a virtual reprise of the previous night.

The Braves' bullpen didn't get the respite for which Bragan had been hoping; Lemaster lasted only into the sixth inning while giving up six hits and three earned runs. He also got himself in trouble in the third by failing to cover first base on a grounder to first baseman Torre; Frank Robinson followed with a homer. The Reds scored another run in the fifth when Lemaster, with the bases loaded and one out, picked up a safety-squeeze bunt by Sammy Ellis. Seeing he had no play at the plate, Lemaster looked at second, then at first, and wound up holding the ball helplessly as the tying run crossed the plate.

Denis Menke, back in the lineup at shortstop but clearly limited by his season-long knee problem, committed three errors and Oliver added another while catching as Torre played first. Nevertheless, the Braves had forged a 4-4 tie going to the top of the ninth as Mack Jones, who was to hit nine home runs in August but only five thereafter, wafted a three-run homer and Mathews singled home the tying run in the bottom of the eighth.

Osinski had wriggled out of an eighth-inning predicament by striking out Vada Pinson and getting Frank Robinson to fly out with two on in the eighth, and with O'Dell available only as a last resort, Osinski took the mound to start the ninth. Deron Johnson singled. Pavletich grounded out to shortstop, with pinch-runner Matt Keough advancing to second, where he stayed as Cardenas grounded to third for the second out.

At this point, rain intervened, and play was stopped for 15 minutes. When the game resumed, Bragan had Osinski intentionally walk Johnny Edwards, anticipating that the Reds would send Gordie Coleman up to bat for pitcher Sammy Ellis. Sisler obliged, whereupon Bragan brought in O'Dell. Sisler pulled Coleman back and sent up Tony Perez, who hadn't played in a week because of a hamstring injury. Perez said after the game that if he had hit a ground ball, he would have had to limp to first base. He didn't have to run fast or hard to complete this at-bat. He pounded O'Dell's second pitch into the same left-field bleachers into which Harper's homer had disappeared the night before. McCool struck out the side in the ninth to cement the Reds' 7-4 victory. Afterward, Bragan shifted blame away from O'Dell. "We got beat on fundamentals. Fundamentals. That's what you learn in spring training. If he (Lemaster) plays fundamental baseball, he probably pitches a shutout." Lemaster was even more succinct. "I fouled up," he was quoted as saying, presumably using another word as the verb. Throughout the 1965 season, the Braves' diminished cadre of patrons had earned kudos from players who said the fans had never taken out their frustrations on the team itself. This night was an exception; Bob Wolf wrote in the next day's *Journal* that Lemaster's misadventures "gave him the dubious distinction of being the first Brave, other than Bragan, to be booed (during the 1965 season) at County Stadium."

The Braves had missed out on two chances to catch the Dodgers and move ahead of the Giants; neither team had won since the Marichal-Roseboro bloodletting. At the conclusion of action on August 25, the Dodgers were one-half game ahead of the Braves, one game ahead of the Giants and 1 1/2 games up on the Reds, and despite the wrenching nature of the previous two losses, the Braves were confident that they could gain a split by winning the final game of the four-game series on August 26. The Braves were sending Tony Cloninger and his eight-game winning streak to the mound against Joe Nuxhall. Nuxhall finished his career with a 6-14 record and a 4.58 ERA against the Braves, and he left this game after facing one batter in the bottom of the fourth, with the Reds up 2-1 on a two-run homer by Deron Johnson, after complaining of elbow pain.

But the Braves felt their own kind of pain because of reliever Ted Davidson, a 25-year-old rookie lefthander against whom the Braves managed only three baserunners - on a single by Bolling in the sixth and walks to Jones and Aaron in the fifth - over the final six innings. Davidson, who was reputed to be a knuckleball specialist, threw not a single "bug" while shutting down the Braves, retiring the final 10 Milwaukee batters as the Reds won 3-1 and moved into a second-place tie with the Braves, a half-game behind the Dodgers, who'd lost in New York. It was the Reds' 10th win in 14 games against the Braves, and Cloninger (18-9) saw his win streak ended despite pitching well, aside from the homer to Johnson, over seven innings. Alou and Oliver each went 0 for 4, dropping their averages to .300 and .273 respectively, and Bragan said after the game he would rest both players the following night when the Braves opened a three-game home series against Chicago. Mathews denied that panic had set in among the players after five losses in six games. "We're not panicking. All I know is we're a half-game out. Is that good or bad? We're not hitting. I'd feel a whole lot worse if we had just lost three straight to the Mets (as the Dodgers had). It's just that I hate to see us getting into the habit of losing in the ninth inning."

Instead, the Braves lost the next night in the fifth inning, during which the Cubs scored all five of their runs and Bob Buhl evoked memories of his excellence in the Braves' rotation. In what would turn out to be his last-ever outing at County Stadium, he went 7 1/3 innings in a 5-3 Chicago win. A crowd of 20,723, the Braves' third-largest of the year, saw Billy Williams hit a grand slam off Ken Johnson in the fifth inning; Williams later said it was the first home run he ever had hit off a knuckleball, at any level. As promised, Bragan reshuffled his lineup, moving Mack Jones into the leadoff spot, starting Ty Cline in left in place of Alou, and using Jesse Gonder as the cleanup man and catcher. Alou's pinch-hit, two-run homer in the eighth ended Buhl's shutout bid, and Jones followed with another homer to end Buhl's night. But Ted Abernathy submarined the Braves into submission by retiring the final five hitters on only 10 pitches for his 26th save. (He would finish with 31, most in the major leagues in 1965.) Elsewhere, Willie Mays tied Mel Ott's National League record with his 493rd career homer, and equaled Ralph Kiner's 1949 record of 16 home runs in a month, as the Giants won 9-2 at New York before a Shea Stadium record crowd of 56,167. (Mays would break both the Kiner and Ott records the next day as the Giants beat the Mets again.) Don Drysdale beat the Phillies for his first win in Philadelphia in three years, and the Pirates continued their late-season charge with a win over the Astros.

The 70-degree weather for the opening game of the Cubs series was seasonal by Upper Midwest standards, but as the Braves had done, it went cold quickly. Game-time temperature for the August 28 game was 57 degrees, and it descended to 40 by the end of the game. The crowd of 9,241 was less than half the size of the turnout the previous night, and the Braves' offensive freeze continued as they lost 3-1 while managing only five hits off Larry Jackson and Abernathy, who again finished the game with 1 2/3 scoreless innings. Again, future Hall of Famer Billy Williams put the Braves into an immediate predicament with a two-run homer in the first off Wade Blasingame, who was taken out for Bob Sadowski with the bases loaded and no outs in the sixth. Sadowski kept the score at 2-1 with two strikeouts and a groundout, and he, Osinski and O'Dell silenced the Chicago bats through the next two innings. But with one out in the ninth, O'Dell gave up a single to Abernathy - a .138 hitter over his 14-year major league career - and after O'Dell walked Joey Amalfitano, he was obliged to pitch to Williams, who lined a single to center to score Abernathy. It was the only run Abernathy would score in 1965.

The denouement of the 1-6 homestand was a 10-2 loss during which the Braves ran afoul of Bill Faul, the self-styled self-hynotist (and divinity student at the University of Cincinnati). Faul pitched a seven-hitter, and Hank Fischer, given an emergency start because Lemaster was sidelined by back problems, gave up five earned runs in 5 1/3 innings. Fischer and four successors gave up five home runs to the Cubs' three future Hall of Famers; Ron Santo and Ernie Banks hit two each, and Williams hit his third in the three-game series. The Braves, after six straight losses (during which they had scored only 13 runs) and nine defeats in 11 games, were in fourth place, still within 2 1/2 games of the first-place Dodgers but now only two games ahead of the onrushing Pirates.

To Bartholomay's credit, the Braves had been kept virtually intact through their final season in Milwaukee despite the financial beating ownership was taking. At the same time, the only in-season roster move they had made that had turned out to be significant was the acquisition of Ken Johnson from the Astros for Lee Maye, a player the Braves no longer needed. There would be no repeat, from that standpoint, of 1957, when the Braves knew they were one component - a second baseman - short of having a true World Series title contender. The '57 Braves had the money to spend for a final piece. Then-GM John Quinn got that player, Red Schoendienst, and the Braves had won the 1957 World Series and were up 3-1 on the Yankees in '58 before New York came back to win the final three games. The Braves' financial situation, of course, was far different in 1965 than it had been in 1957 and 1958. But the Braves did make three moves that would take effect on September 1, when active rosters could be expanded from 25 to 40 players. Sandy Alomar and Chi Chi Olivo, both of whom had been on the season-opening roster but had been sent down shortly thereafter, would be recalled from Triple-A. They also purchased Harvey Haddix, 39, from Baltimore, in hopes that he would give the Braves another veteran left-hander to augment O'Dell in the bullpen.

Haddix, of course, in 1959 had been the central figure in the most memorable game in County Stadium history. Then with the Pirates, Haddix had pitched 12 perfect innings against the Braves, only to lose 1-0 on an unearned run in the 13th. He had pitched passably (3-2, 3.48 in 33 2/3 innings) for the Orioles in 1965. But he already had decided to retire at the end of the season, partly because of lingering injuries, and made that known to Braves general manager John McHale after the sale had been consummated. Haddix told McHale that he didn't want to relocate to Milwaukee for only the month of September, and two days later, the sale was cancelled. And even with Alomar and Olivo back on the team, the Braves were still short-handed going into their series in Cincinnati, which was set to begin with a doubleheader on Tuesday, August 31. Menke and Carty were questionable with recurring knee and back injuries respectively.

Also on August 30, Casey Stengel, 75, announced his retirement as Mets manager effective at the end of the season - a move that was little more than a formality because Wes Westrum had been in charge since July 25, when Stengel broke his hip in a fall. "They won't let me take my pitchers out with a cane," he said, "so I have to quit." Stengel, who had first come to the major leagues as a player in 1910 and had managed the Yankees to 10 pennants and seven World Series titles from 1949-60, had produced four of the worst teams in major league history since becoming the

Mets' first manager in 1962. By then, he was known to fall asleep in the dugouts during games, and having carefully cultivated relationships with "his" writers during his Yankee days, he thought nothing of getting laughs by ridiculing his Mets for public consumption. "We got a player here named (Greg) Goossen," he said in 1965. "He's 20 years old (actually Goossen, briefly a Brewer in 1970, was 19 at the time), and in 10 years he's got a chance to be 30." Roger Craig, the former Dodger who was probably the Mets' best pitcher during their subterranean years, was asked later how it felt to take the mound for such poor teams. "I could stand the losing," he said. "It was the not winning that hurt." As manager of the Giants in the late 1980s and early 1990s, Craig often said his experience with Stengel served as an enduring reminder to him to treat his players with respect and understanding rather than contempt.

In Cincinnati, the Reds' presence in the pennant race was almost a secondary story, just as had been the case all season in Milwaukee because of the Braves' imminent departure. Frank Robinson had been a franchise cornerstone since joining the team in 1956, and had been the NL MVP when the Reds won the pennant in 1961. He was an All-Star for the sixth time in 1965, and in his 10 seasons with the Reds, he hit fewer than 29 homers only once, and had 122 or more RBI four times. Yet fans at Crosley Field had taken to booing him during the 1965 season, first intermittently and then, after he lapsed into a slump that lasted through most of August, almost every time he made an out. There was talk, never squelched by management, that he had become a "clubhouse lawyer" whose unquestioned leadership skills had become counterproductive because they were dividing the club rather than uniting it.

The Reds were one of the most racially and ethnically diverse teams in the majors, and in a city that is across the Ohio River from onetime slave state Kentucky, no black or Latino player in 1965 could expect the benefit of the doubt on any issue with racial overtones. Manager Dick Sisler was quoted in an *Associated Press* story that the verbal abuse of Robinson was affecting his play, and therefore the Reds' chances of winning the pennant. "If they want to boo someone, let them boo me," Sisler said. "If we can get him going, just think how much it'll perk up this whole club. He's trying desperately. If they want to boo Robby, there's no way I can stop them. But I sure wish they'd give him encouragement instead of the treatment he has been getting." Robinson, for his part, didn't blame the booing for his slump, but did say it made him try "a little too hard. A fellow can try too hard, you know. It doesn't matter to them how the game is going. We could be 10 runs ahead, but if I fail to hit, some of them boo. Then the fans will come through with cheers in the same way when I come through."

After the season, the Reds traded Robinson to the Orioles for pitcher Milt Pappas in a deal that reeked of a lot of things, not the least of which was bad judgment; Reds general manager Bob Howsam meekly defended it by saying Robinson was "an old 30." He was a young 31 in Baltimore in 1966, winning the American League MVP award and leading the Orioles to a World Series championship, and he played on for 10 more productive seasons. In 1974, when he was named player-manager of the Cleveland Indians, he became the first black to hold a managerial position in the majors, and he was a first-ballot Hall of Famer in 1982. Pappas, meanwhile, went only 30-29 during his three seasons with Cincinnati, and although he finished his career with 209 wins, he never won more than 17 games in a season, and appeared in only one postseason game - pitching two innings for the Atlanta Braves in 1969 when the Mets swept them in the first National League Championship Series.

Craig had been liberated from the Mets after the 1963 season - he had helped pitch the Cardinals to a World Series title in 1964 - and was on the Reds' pitching staff for the scheduled August 31 doubleheader against the Braves. In the first game, he gave up the Braves' third and final home run - by his longtime adversary Eddie Mathews in the eighth inning - as the Braves took a 4-1 lead and held on to win 5-3. It was the 475th homer of Mathews' career, leaving him tied with Stan Musial (who had retired after the 1963 season) for seventh place on the MLB career list, and his 30th of the season. Tony Cloninger earned his 19th win despite shoulder pain that forced him to leave the game after five innings, and Aaron and Oliver homered earlier against Joey Jay.

Paradoxically, the Braves were fortunate to have gained one win on this night, and yet were also unfortunate to have not gained a sweep. And both teams were lucky that nobody was injured, considering the field conditions. Crosley Field was pelted by rain throughout the first game of the scheduled doubleheader, forcing a 25-minute delay before the first pitch and a 2 hour, 5-minute stoppage during the fifth inning. The rain intensified after the end of the first game, and the second game didn't get underway until 11:39 p.m. This game was halted during the third inning, with Cincinnati leading 4-1. After another hour-long delay, the game was postponed at 1:15 a.m., with almost everyone in the original crowd of 19,645 gone, and rescheduled as part of a twi-night doubleheader the next day. The Braves' only run in the second game came on a homer by Aaron, but because the game had not gone the required five innings to be considered an official game, the postponement wiped all the statistics from the books. It was the second time in August 1965 that Aaron had hit a home run for which he was not given credit - the first being the game in which he was called out for stepping out of the batters box - and so, to baseball purists, Aaron's hallowed career home run mark should be 757, not 755.

Despite their recent tribulations, the Braves had gone 18-13 in August, and at the close of business August 31, they were one of four teams within one game of each other in the loss column. Their position going into September was the best it had been since 1958, the year they won their second straight pennant, when they ended August 7 1/2 games ahead of the second-place Pirates. Even in 1959, when the Dodgers and Braves finished the regular season tied and the Dodgers went on to sweep a best-of-three playoff for the pennant, the Braves had gone into September in third place, down 2 1/2 games to San Francisco and 1 1/2 to the Dodgers.

In every season from 1960-64, Milwaukee had entered September with miniscule hope, at best, of getting to the World Series, trailing by seven games in 1960, 6 1/2 in 1961, 16 1/2 in 1962, 7 1/2 games in 1963 and 12 1/2 (in fifth place) in 1964. At the end of August 1965, the Dodgers (75-57) were 1 1/2 games up on the Giants (72-57) and two games up on the Reds and Braves, both 72-58, with the Pirates (71-62) 4 1/2 games back. The Braves still had six games left against both the Giants and Dodgers, the two teams Milwaukee trailed. They also had five games remaining against the unconscionable Mets, and three others against the ninth-place Astros.

The Milwaukee Braves entered the final month of the season and of their existence with no small supply of collateral. Unfortunately, as it turned out, they were already spent.

Gone for Good

• • •

THE RAINOUT OF THE SECOND game of the August 31 double-header appeared to be a godsend to the Reds, even though they had been ahead by three runs in the third inning at the time the game was called.

With Jim O'Toole, who had won 69 games for the Reds over the previous four seasons, on his way to a 3-10 season and the performance charts of Joey Jay and Joe Nuxhall wavering like approval polls during Lyndon Johnson's presidency, the Reds knew their pennant chances depended primarily on their two 20-game winners, Sammy Ellis and Jim Maloney. Both had pitched in Cincinnati's previous series, against St. Louis, with Ellis lasting only two innings on August 29 and Maloney going 5 1/3 the previous day. The combination of the two relatively low pitch counts and the rainout the previous day convinced Cincinnati manager Dick Sisler to push his two largest stacks of chips to the middle of the table. Ellis would start with only two days rest, Maloney with three. Milwaukee would counter with Blasingame, working on three days rest, in the first game, and Lemaster, who had missed his most recent turn because of back problems, in the nightcap.

As it turned out, the starting-pitching matchup meant little in the first game, which came down to a bullpen affair won 7-6 by the Reds.

Ellis exited after giving up six hits and six earned runs in 4 1/3 innings, but Blasingame's stint was even shorter and stormier. He gave up a solo homer to Deron Johnson leading off the second, and in the third, with one out, he issued his fourth walk of the game - to Pete Rose, who then moved to second on a passed ball by catcher Gene Oliver. First baseman Joe Torre then committed an error on a ground ball by Vada Pinson, enabling Rose to score and narrowing the Braves' lead to 3-2. Blasingame, still two months short of his 22nd birthday, did not react well to the two miscues, staring at Torre as he returned to his position. Bragan, interpreting this as an attempt to show up a teammate, came to the mound and yanked Blasingame, who stomped off the mound and into the clubhouse instead of waiting for his replacement to come in from the bullpen, as was the custom at the time. The replacement was Clay Carroll, whose second pitch was lofted out of Crosley Field by Deron Johnson to put the Reds up 4-3.

The Braves dispatched Ellis and took a 6-4 lead in the fifth with a three-run rally started by Rico Carty, whose outfield playing time had dwindled to virtually nothing as Alou, Jones and Aaron played almost every day. Carty, pinch-hitting for Woodward, led off the fifth with a single, and was replaced by pinch-runner Sandy Alomar, who promptly stole second. Jesse Gonder, batting for Carroll, drew a walk, and after Alou hit into a fielders choice and Jones walked, Ted Davidson came on to pitch to Hank Aaron, whose two-run single finished Ellis and gave the Braves a 5-4 lead that was extended to 6-4 when Mathews grounded to second and beat the double-play relay.

Bob Sadowski clung to the lead through the next 4 1/3 innings, though the Reds narrowed the deficit to 6-5 with a run in the seventh. But Sadowski, who had been a starter earlier in the season, had pitched 3 1/3 innings the night before, and his outing on this night had been his longest since July 25, so Bragan turned the game over to his short relievers after Jim Coker nubbed a single off Sadowski's bare hand to lead off the ninth and Marty Keough hit into a force play. After Gordie Coleman was announced as a pinch-hitter for Leo Cardenas, Bragan signaled for Billy O'Dell, and Sisler countered with right-handed hitter Lee May. O'Dell got the ground ball he wanted (to third) but not the double play he needed, as Mathews' only play was at first. With Keough now at second, the Reds turned to Tommy Helms, a 24-year-old rookie infielder who had been a life preserver for Cincinnati: In 21 late-season games after being recalled from Triple-A San Diego, Helms was 16 for 42 (.381), and at the time he was sent to the plate in this game, he was 4 for 4 since joining the Reds. Bragan left O'Dell in to pitch to Helms, a right-handed hitter, and Helms slashed a triple to tie the game. Bragan brought in Dan Osinski to face Tommy Harper, whose single was his second walk-off hit against the Braves in a week. It also gave O'Dell his fourth loss in as many 1965 decisions against Cincinnati. His ERA in eight games against the Reds was 5.14; against the rest of the league, it was 1.76.

The Braves had not seen Ellis at his best in the first game, but they saw prime-time Jim Maloney in the second as he improved to 17-6 with a five-hitter as the Reds completed the sweep with a

2-0 win. Mack Jones, the second hitter of the game, was ejected by home-plate umpire Ed Sudol for arguing a called third strike, and the situation deteriorated from there. Lemaster could get through only three innings, giving up a home run to Perez in the second and a sacrifice fly to Pinson in the third. The Braves, meanwhile, got more than one runner on base against Maloney in only one inning - the fifth, when Oliver walked and Bolling singled with one out. Bragan went to two of his in-season acquisitions as pinch-hitters, but Gonder flied out and Frank Thomas took a called third strike to end the inning.

Thomas had just been re-acquired from the Astros for a player to be named later. He hit 286 home runs during his 15-season career, including 25 during a 124-game stint with the Braves in 1961. He could play first base, third base and the outfield. But he had turned 36 on June 11, and would bat only .212 with no homers and one RBI in 15 games for the Braves. Invariably, the media brought up Thomas' fight with Richie Allen that had led to Philadelphia's decision to release Thomas earlier in the season. Thomas said: "I've been unfairly blamed. I was told that's what happens when you're 36 and the other fellow is 23 and leading the league in hitting." Thomas said the incident started during batting practice when Allen got on him about a strikeout the previous night. "I shouted back that he was running off at the mouth like Cassius Clay," Thomas said. Thomas claimed that Allen hit him first, in the chest, and that he hit Allen with a bat "in a reflex measure." Ryne Duren, the veteran pitcher who had been with the Phillies at the time of the fight, didn't buy the idea that Allen and not Thomas was the instigator. "Everybody in baseball knows Thomas is an obnoxious needler," Duren said. "When he gets on a guy, he doesn't know when to stop."

Cincinnati's sweep, coupled with the Pirates' sweep of a home doubleheader against the Dodgers, vaulted the Reds into a first-place tie with L.A., with the idle Giants one-half game back. The Braves still were only two games out of the lead, but they now led Pittsburgh by only half a game, and even the sixth-place Phillies were just 3 1/2 games behind Milwaukee. Given the fact the Braves hadn't won back-to-back games since August 18, and the state of their pitching staff in the aftermath of so many short starts in long games, their situation looked desperate going into the final game of the four-game series in Cincinnati, on Thursday night, September 2.

Bragan had only two pitchers who were even reasonably rested - Hank Fischer and Phil Niekro, both of whom had spent most of the 1965 season clinging to the lower rungs of Bragan's preference ladder. Fischer, who was best known as a basketball player at Seton Hall University at the time he signed with the Braves in 1959, was a 30-39, 4.23 pitcher during his six-year major league career, and while this contest wasn't one of the 14 complete games he recorded during his career, it may have been the pinnacle of his baseball life. He gutted and wormed his way through the dangerous Cincinnati order for 10 innings, circumventing six hits and five walks, and even though he couldn't hold an early 3-0 Braves lead, he got eight of nine outs with runners in scoring position. In the top of the 11th, Mathews led off with a single and Ted Davidson, the fourth Reds pitcher, fielded Bolling's bunt and threw wide of first, with Mathews taking third and Bolling second. Pinch-hitter Billy Cowan popped out, but Mike de la Hoz, batting for Fischer, lofted a sacrifice fly to bring home the go-ahead run. Niekro retired the side in the bottom of the 11th, and the Braves escaped Cincinnati with a 4-3 win and a series split. But there would be no escape from baseball on the precipice as the Braves returned home for a three-game series with Pittsburgh starting Friday, September 3.

Even with a month left in the season, the Pirates-Braves series loomed as an eliminaton proposition for both clubs. The Pirates, of course, had started the season 9-24 before trampolining their way back into contention with a 12-game winning streak. They were still below .500 (52-53) on July 9, but had gone 21-10 since then, and had won two out of three against the visiting Dodgers in the series before they came to Milwaukee.

The Braves had gifted several wins to the Reds over the past two weeks, but this time they were the beneficiaries of three Pirate errors that led to three unearned Milwaukee runs, and Ken Johnson limited Pittsburgh to seven hits and three runs over eight innings to gain his 15th victory (and his 12th since being acquired from Houston) as the Braves prevailed 4-3.

The tinge of farewell enthusiasm that had permeated County Stadium in August was gone, possibly because of the combination of Labor Day weekend travel, the threat of rain in the weather forecast, and the fact the Packers were into their exhibition season and would begin their regular season on September 19. After 1959, when the Braves' decline began and Vince Lombardi arrived in Green Bay, September meant - and means - football in Wisconsin, and only 5,349 baseball fans turned out at County Stadium this night. They weren't disappointed, as the Braves, trailing 3-2 going to the bottom of the eighth, began the inning with a pinch-hit single by Felipe Alou, who was being rested in favor of Rico Carty. Carty promptly singled Alou to third.

Wilbur Wood, later a knuckleballing inning-gnawer with the White Sox but in 1965 a lefty reliever with conventional stuff, replaced starter Don Cardwell. Mack Jones hit a liner to medium-deep right field that was caught by Roberto Clemente, on whose throwing arm baserunners rarely dared to tread. But Alou dared, and Clemente's throw hit him as he slid into home plate, tying the game. Pinch-runner Billy Cowan advanced to third on Clemente's error. Aaron was walked intentionally, and with the corner infielders playing in, Mathews hit a ground ball to first baseman Donn Clendenon, who might have had an inning-ending double play had he thrown to second. Instead, he threw home, and his throw went awry for an error and the Braves' go-ahead run.

Phil Niekro, who had begun the season as a mop-up man but now was drawing important assignments, got Bill Mazeroski on a groundout and Manny Mota on a strikeout, but a third-strike knuckleball to pinch-hitter-extraordinare Jerry Lynch that should have ended the game eluded catcher Joe Torre and went to the backstop for a wild pitch that allowed Lynch to reach first. It was the second time in less than a month that a third-strike knuckleball by Niekro that should have ended a game had been misplayed.

Lynch was replaced by pinch-runner Jose Pagan. Niekro then gave up a single to another pinch-hitter, Andre Rodgers, sending Pagan to third. Niekro, facing Bob Bailey, threw a ball on the first pitch before Bragan, not wanting to risk another way-ward knuckleball with the tying run at third and the winning run on first, called on Dan Osinski. He got Bailey to ground into a second-base forceout to end the game.

After the game, Bragan, pungent as ever in an attempt at sarcasm and earful as ever of the boos that cascaded on him every time he left the Milwaukee dugout, harped on the attendance figure rather than the essential victory. "We didn't want to disappoint all those fans ... I actually thought that the closer we came to the end of the season, the more fans would come out. You know ... the last opportunity to see the club and with the chance to sit in on a pennant. We're 10 games over .500 at home, and who knows how many more we'd be if we were getting, say, 20,000 people." The players, too, had been disappointed by the size of the crowd. Mathews said he thought the crowd count would be at least 10,000. Oliver and Sadowski both said they guessed 15,000 or more would show up. All season, the Braves had buffeted a continuum of confusion and conflict and consternation - none of which had been of the players' making - and at least some of them thought that a significant segment of their former fan base would rally to the last-but-not-lost cause. After this game, the Braves must have known they were strictly on their own, and that feeling was confirmed the following evening (Saturday, September 4) when only 2,471 saw an 8-3 Braves victory that was called during the eighth inning because of rain.

Cloninger became the major leagues' second 20-game winner, after Koufax; and his line in the box score is pedestrian: Six innings pitched, 10 hits, two earned runs, one walk, three strikeouts. It was the 11th and last time that season that Cloninger had given up nine or more hits in a start - that he went 5-6 in those starts testified to his survival skills - and the reality this night was that, as Joe Torre put it, "It was like he pitched a doubleheader." The rain was constant, and because Cloninger couldn't get loose after his first warmup session, he decided to take another - and then a third one after a 2-hour, 11-minute rain delay. Cloninger, who had endured a similar multi-warmup ordeal in Cincinnati during his previous start and had been forced out of that game after five innings by shoulder tightness, acknowledged his discomfort. "My arm was really tight when I went back out there the last time," he said. "I felt better in the fourth and fifth innings, but it tightened up again (before the seventh)." Eddie Mathews was critical of the decision to even attempt to play the game, especially after the rain intensified to the point where the glare of the lights reflected the standing water on the infield. He slipped twice going after ground balls, and said that he had never lost his footing under those or any other circumstances since he was 10 years old.

No 21st-century manager would have even started Cloninger under those circumstances, let alone allow him to resume after a rain delay of more than two hours, but in the pre-free agency era, when even the best pitchers were considered replaceable commodities, such a practice was more the rule than the exception. Cloninger's Pittsburgh counterpart, Bob Friend, didn't fare nearly as well under the adverse conditions, failing to survive the first inning as the Braves carded five runs and Mack Jones and Felipe Alou hit home runs. O'Dell, who had appeared in only two games since being used four times in four days from August 22-25, got through the seventh inning without undue difficulty, but was rescued by another cloudburst in the eighth after the Pirates scored one run and had runners on first and third with one out. The umpires waited 42 minutes before calling the game, which had been scheduled to start at 2 p.m., at 8:06 p.m. The Braves' franchise limbo entered into the decision to try to play the game at all; the weather forecast for the next day (Sunday,

September 5) was ominous, this was the Pirates' last scheduled trip into Milwaukee in 1965, and nobody wanted to risk having to play an all-or-nothing makeup game in an empty stadium after the end of the regular season. The ground crew, directed by chief groundskeeper Wally Higgins, used so much sawdust on the skin portion of the infield that it resembled a high-jump pit (in the days before foam rubber was used for that purpose), according to *Journal* reporter Cleon Walfoort. The crowd was so small that all the fans who remained after the first delay could fit comfortably under the upper-deck overhang.

The win notwithstanding - and it kept the Braves in a third-place tie with San Francisco, two games behind the Dodgers and one game behind the Reds - it was a day that in many ways encapsulated the final year of the Milwaukee Braves. Ironically, it was also the day Edmund Fitzgerald - one of the four men who had incorporated the former Teams Inc into Milwaukee Brewers Baseball Club, Inc. - received a letter from a man who wanted to become the first Milwaukee Brewer. Walter C. Yerger Jr., an 18-year-old from Simi, Calif., wrote that he had played one winter season for a Los Angeles-area team managed by Phillies scout Ralph Sutherland, and another season for the semipro Compton Phillies. He also said he had spent a week at the camp of former Dodger catcher Mickey Owen. "If at all possible, I would like to become a member of your organization," Yerger wrote. Fitzgerald said he would keep the application on file while Milwaukee Brewers Baseball Club, Inc., searched for a franchise. It was never recorded whether or not the letter was in the Brewers' file when they actually began play in 1970, nor is there any record of the remainder of Yerger's life, other than Social Security documents that show he died in 2003 at the age of 56. Meanwhile, a softball team from Grafton entered a state tournament under the name of Atlanta Braves. Milwaukee attorney Dominic Frinzi, representing Milwaukee County, had previously filed papers to gain legal title to the Atlanta Braves name - a detail curiously overlooked by Bartholomay and his group - as part of the ongoing litigatory battle. But he gave the Grafton team permission to use the name in the tournament, perhaps because it was sponsored by the *Journal.*

The Braves went after a series sweep against the Pirates on Sunday, September 5, before a crowd that was swelled to 20,409 by a Ball Day promotion - the last formal Milwaukee promotion by a franchise that had done little under the Bartholomay regime to augment attendance. (The actual attendance was 26,590, including 4,801 children admitted for 50 cents and 1,380 rain checks issued Saturday to the fans who remained through the rain delays.) Bob Sadowski pitched well for seven innings before being lifted for a pinch-hitter, but Tommie Sisk, who started only 12 games in 1965, was even better in his spot-start assignment, shutting the Braves out on seven hits and taking a 2-0 lead into the ninth. But his energy tank hit E at that point, and he gave up singles to Felipe Alou and Frank Bolling. Lefthander Wilbur Wood and right-handed closer Al McBean were up in the Pittsburgh bullpen as Sandy Alomar stepped to the plate. Bragan could have stuck with him given the fact it was a sacrifice situation and Alomar was one of the team's few proficient bunters. Instead, Bragan sent lefty-swinging Jesse Gonder up as a pinch-hitter, whereupon Pittsburgh manager Harry Walker countered with Wood. Bragan parried with right-handed hitter Mike de la Hoz, but he had lost Gonder's bat before being able to deploy it. de la Hoz grounded to shortstop

Gene Alley, who got a forceout at second, leaving runners on first and third with one out. McBean then came on and gave up a single to Gene Oliver, making the score 2-1 and advancing the tying run to second and the winning run to first. Bragan then played his last card - Don Dillard, who had vaulted the Braves into first place for what turned out to be the next-to-last time with a pinch-hit homer against St. Louis on August 18. Could Dillard come through similarly this time? He could not. He hit a bouncer to Alley, who started a game-ending double play as the Pirates salvaged the final game of the series.

For one of many times during Bragan's tenure as Braves manager, he came under media scrutiny for his ninth-inning tactics. He said he took Alomar out of the game in a bunting situation because he wanted to get Sisk out of the game, which made little sense to reporters because Sisk had not thrown a complete game all season and had only two in his previous two seasons with the Pirates. Bragan also said he deliberately wasted Gonder's bat so that he could get the matchup he wanted - de la Hoz against Wood. He said he didn't use Alomar to bunt because "we haven't had any success bunting all year. I would guess that about six of our players (including de la Hoz) haven't bunted all year." Pirates manager Harry Walker defended Bragan's order of battle, noting that "bunting is getting to be the toughest part of the game" (an opinion that was still being echoed by managers a half-century later) and that part of managing is putting players in position to do what they do best. "Each individual situation changes 'the book,'" Walker said. "Percentages - that's what managing is. He has got a hitting ballclub. The only thing he had to worry about was the double play (which, of course, was what happened)."

The loss left the Braves three games out of first for the first time since August 8 as the Dodgers, Giants and Reds all won. Tommy Helms, still on his rookie rampage, got the game-winning walk-off hit that gave Cincinnati a 10-9 victory over Philadelphia. Marichal got his 20th victory, and his first since his suspension, by beating the Cubs 4-2, and Jim Gilliam's pinch-hit, two-run triple in the ninth gave Los Angeles a 4-2 victory over Houston. Next for the Braves: the Mets and their 45-94 record, in a doubleheader at County Stadium on Labor Day (September 6). The Braves had won the teams' 13 most recent meetings in Milwaukee, and given the way the three teams ahead of them were playing, the Braves simply couldn't afford to lose either of the Labor Day games to a team like the Mets.

They didn't, even though only 7,213 fans showed up to watch. Bragan had declared that Niekro henceforth would be the finisher out of the bullpen, and he saved both games - working 2 1/3 innings in relief of Hank Fischer in a 4-2 victory in the first game, then going two innings to preserve Wade Blasingame's 16th (and final) win of the season as Milwaukee prevailed 3-1 in the second game. The saves were Niekro's fourth and fifth of the season. "He's the hottest thing we've got going right now," Bragan said. "He's mixing a good fastball with his knuckler and he's getting the hitters out." Bragan even said that because of Niekro's emergence, he was considering using O'Dell, who had started only one game all season, as a fifth man in the rotation. The Braves were idle on Tuesday, September 7, but would have only two more scheduled off-days - the second coming on September 23, the day after their last scheduled home game as the Milwaukee Braves - and Bragan was hoping to avoid having to use his four arm-weary starters on three days rest instead of four any more than was necessary. He also noted that the Braves still had six games left against the Dodgers, and he wanted to be able to use as many lefthanders as possible to control the Dodgers' running game and minimize the impact of left-handed-hitting outfielders Willie Davis and Ron Fairly. Moreover, the Braves looked as if they might be one left-handed pitcher short going into the series. Wade Blasingame had told Bragan after the games Sunday that his arm had deadened, and that he had taken his warmup tosses before the eighth inning just to give Niekro enough time to get loose. Blasingame started four games after that, and didn't get past the fifth inning in any of them.

Most of the baseball world's attention was focused on Dodger Stadium that Labor Day, as the Giants and Dodgers played before 53,581 - many of whom probably expected to see a resumption of the violence at Candlestick Park on August 22 - in the opener of a two-game showdown between the California rivals. As a precaution, NL president Warren Giles had ordered the Giants not to bring Juan Marichal on the trip to L.A. - he wasn't scheduled to pitch anyway - and nothing untoward occurred as the Giants won 7-6 in 12 innings, tying the game on a ninth-inning homer by Tom Haller and winning it in the 12th on an RBI single by Jim Davenport. It was the third victory in what became a 14-game winning streak that would give the Giants a 4 1/2 game lead on September 17 - the day they began their last-ever road series against the Milwaukee Braves.

The Braves' off-day on Tuesday, September 7 gave fans and media a chance to catch up on the boardroom and courtroom proceedings that would decide Milwaukee's baseball future, and take stock of the frantic NL race and the Braves' chances of making Milwaukee a World Series venue in their final season there.

The Braves, in response to the pending antitrust suit, had countersued the state of Wisconsin, and State Attorney General Bronson La Follette had found himself as a specified defendant. La Follette, the son and grandson of U.S. Senators, and an unsuccessful candidate for governor in 1968, asked the circuit court to dismiss the suit, saying the Braves could not sue him personally because, as attorney general, he was only fulfilling his duties when he filed the suit on the state level. Meanwhile, federal Judge Robert E. Tehan set a hearing for October 4 on the state's motion to send the antitrust suit against the Braves to federal court.

In the *Sentinel*, Lloyd Larson, as was his wont, crunched numbers. He wrote that at the start of the season, he had thought the Braves, given circumstances past and pending, would be fortunate even to surpass the 281,278 attendance figure for 1952, their final year in Boston. Instead, Larson wrote, the Braves were on pace to more than double that total, and if the Braves stayed in the race, they might even approach the New York Giants' postwar low of 629,179 in 1956, their next-to-last year in Manhattan. Larson also conjectured that if this had been a "normal" season - i.e., one without the virtual certainty of the move to Atlanta - the Braves would have drawn at least 1.25 million and perhaps even 1.5 million. The latter total would have been the team's highest since 1959, when they drew 1,749,112 to finish second in the NL in attendance after leading the major leagues in that category for six straight years. As it was, though, Larson felt breaking the 500,000 barrier in 1965 was "an amazing achievement" during "the most trying season in all baseball history."

After the September 7 results, the NL standings were more jumbled than they had been at any time this late in the season since 1908, with the Giants and Dodgers tied for the lead, the Reds one-half game back, the Braves a game in arrears, and the Pirates four games behind and closing fast. The Pirates actually were seven games behind the Giants in the loss column, and five behind the Dodgers, Braves and Reds, yet Bragan said he thought the Pirates had the advantage, given the fact their final 10 games were against the eighth-place Cubs and the last-place Mets, and that 15 of their final 20 games would be at Forbes Field. But only two of the five contending teams, the Giants and Dodgers, could say they were being carried by immortals who were ascending to heights even they had never attained.

In an informal poll by *The Associated Press* of all 50 of the writers and broadcasters who would vote at the end of the season to decide the NL's Most Valuable Player, all 50 said they would vote for Willie Mays if that vote were taken that day. Mays, at 34, had a worksheet that surpassed his only MVP season to that point, in 1954. In August, he had set an NL record with 17 home runs and had accumulated 29 RBI in 31 games, and he had moved past Lou Gehrig into fifth place on the MLB career list with his 494th homer. Mays' average after games of September 7 was .318, third in the NL behind Roberto Clemente (.342) and Aaron (.325). But Mays, the Giants and everyone else were up against the Dodgers' starting pitching, particularly that of Sandy Koufax. Despite his ongoing arm trouble and the fact the Dodgers without Tommy Davis were among the league's most anemic hitting teams - they finished seventh in team average at .245 and were dead last in homers with 78 - Koufax was 21-7, with a 2.20 ERA and a strikeout total of 318 - 85 more than second-place Bob Veale of the

Pirates. He was on pace to break Bob Feller's major league strikeout record of 348 in 1946, and would finish with 382, an MLB high until Nolan Ryan fanned 383 for the California Angels in 1973. Since then, only one other pitcher - Randy Johnson with 372 Ks for the Arizona Diamondbacks in 2001 - has approached Koufax's 1965 strikeout total.

Koufax's next start, on September 9 against the Cubs at Dodger Stadium, would do more than any other game of his career to notarize his status as a yardstick by which all past and future lefthanders would be measured.

The Milwaukee newspapers also dutifully reported the latest utterings of Eugene Grobschmidt, whose voice and actions remained the most strident of those who wanted to punish the Braves to the maximum, even if it meant Milwaukee losing major league baseball forever. During a speech at the Exchange Club of Milwaukee during the Braves' off-day, Grobschmidt tried to dispel the notion that the county and state lawsuits that had been filed against the Braves would prevent another team from moving to Milwaukee. Grobschmidt claimed that he had met with Kansas City Athletics owner Charles O. Finley, who had told him that the A's were free to leave after the 1965 season - despite the fact their lease at Kansas City Municipal Stadium didn't expire until the end of the 1967 season - and that he, Finley, would be interested in moving the A's to Milwaukee. Finley immediately denied that anyone representing Milwaukee interests had even asked him for a meeting, and that even if the subject had been discussed at any meaningful level, Finley was not free to leave Kansas City without negotiating his way out of his lease. (The A's didn't move to Oakland until 1968, after the Kansas

City lease expired.) Grobschmidt also said the Cubs had inquired informally about the possibility of playing 20 of their 81 home games in Milwaukee in 1966 - a claim that the Cubs quickly denied - and that when he had said that the Braves weren't putting forth their best effort during their last year in Milwaukee, he had been talking about the owners, not the players. Finally, he said he had information that the Braves' black players had expressed to management strong objections to the move to Atlanta. This was never corroborated by any of the players, although Aaron had said, before visiting Atlanta and apparently finding the environment and racial climate to his satisfaction, that he had concerns about the housing and segregation factors in the Deep South.

School was back in session, and with the new school year came a renewed effort by integrationists to address the separate-and-unequal reality in the Milwaukee public schools. Lloyd Barbee, the Milwaukee attorney and state Assemblyman who had emerged as the primary force in the integration efforts, said: "Milwaukee is afflicted by a sleeping sickness. The tendency is to say that we all get along here, that nothing violent could occur here and that Milwaukee is superior to other cities (in terms of race relations). But the Negroes here are just as angry as in Harlem or Watts. They just haven't expressed themselves in terms which anyone but an astute observer could see." A one-day citywide boycott by black students had been organized in 1964, and Barbee predicted, correctly, that a broader, longer boycott would occur before 1965 was over. (It took place in October and lasted three days.)

Barbee, 40, was a native of Tennessee and a Navy veteran who had graduated from law school at the University of Wisconsin and started his own practice. Although Father James Groppi was to achieve wider notoriety in 1966 and 1967 with his more confrontational and militant desegregation efforts, Barbee would be remembered as a more temperate, behind-the-scenes mainstay in the Milwaukee civil-rights movement. He had helped organize MUSIC (Milwaukee United School Integration Committee) to coordinate reform efforts. In June, he had filed a federal lawsuit, *Amos et al. v. Board of School Directors of the City of Milwaukee*, which challenged the long-standing MPS argument that it could do little about *de facto* segregation because the neighborhoods MPS served had developed along distinct racial and ethnic lines that were so entrenched by 1965 that they would be impossible for the district (or the city) to alter. This was particularly true, the district and its attorneys maintained, on the near north side, euphemistically called Milwaukee's "inner core area."

The case wound its way through the courts until finally being decided in MUSIC's favor in 1976, leading to widespread busing in an effort to achieve better racial balance. Four decades later, it was considered one of the most important American civil-rights proceedings on the state level. Barbee always considered it a hollow victory, though, because *de facto* segregation remained entrenched in Milwaukee long after 1976. In fact, it got worse, to the point where urban-development experts had taken to calling Milwaukee's situation - both in its schools and in its neighborhoods - "hypersegregation." In 2011, the four-county Milwaukee region was deemed by the federal government as the country's most segregated metropolitan area. Ninety percent of the region's African-American residents lived in the city of Milwaukee, while Waukesha County, immediately to the west, was 93 percent white. And the hypersegregation, by the

21st century, no longer was confined to the "inner core area." Milwaukee, which had been 91 percent white in 1960, was 40 percent black by 2014, yet the racial separation was virtually unchanged in most of Milwaukee's schools and neighborhoods.

Despite the daunting task before Barbee and his supporters, he continued to work toward unification of Milwaukee's racial factions and pluralism for most of the rest of his life (he died in 2002). Barbee served in the Assembly until 1977 and later accepted a position as a professor and guest lecturer at the University of Wisconsin-Milwaukee. A street and an elementary school in Milwaukee were named for him.

Amid the off-diamond cacophony, the Milwaukee Braves' history at County Stadium was down to its last seven games, and whatever sentiment for them that remained in Milwaukee apparently had been only a summer romance. The events during the off-day had crowded the Braves off the front pages of the city's newspapers, and on a day (September 8) when 1.65 inches of rain fell in downtown Milwaukee, only 3,417 turned out to see the Braves' game against the Phillies. Philadelphia, though eight games off the lead and mired in sixth place, exacted a small measure of revenge for the Braves' four-game sweep during Philadelphia's epic collapse the year before. The Braves had been errorless in each of their previous six games, winning five of them, but on this night the Phillies cashiered Ken Johnson while scoring three runs - two of them unearned because of errors by Mathews and first baseman Felipe Alou - during a three-run seventh that gave them a 6-2 lead. They held on to win 6-5 despite a three-run rally by Milwaukee in the eighth. Phils manager Gene Mauch went to a starting pitcher, Chris Short, after Torre and

Aaron had hit home runs in the eighth, and Short finished up to get the save on behalf of starter Ray Culp. It was a pratfall that became a plunge because the leaders were at such close quarters. The Giants took over the NL lead and dropped the Braves two games out by blowing out the Astros 12-3 in San Francisco as Willie Mays hit his 44th and 45th homers of the season. The Reds, meanwhile, beat the Mets 11-2 as Jim O'Toole got only his second win of the season against nine defeats.

The weather went from dismal to dangerous overnight, with a tornado touching down in Waukesha County and trees and power lines toppling throughout southeastern Wisconsin. The Braves were able to get in one inning that night at County Stadium, with Cloninger and Phillies starter Jim Bunning each retiring the other side in order, before the game was postponed, and rescheduled for Monday, September 20. This eliminated one of the Braves' two remaining off-days, and Bragan knew that would complicate an already fragile pitching equation. Bragan had taken Lemaster out of the rotation, using him in relief of Johnson the game before, and it seemed almost certain that Billy O'Dell, at some point, would be moved from the bull-pen into the starting rotation. This was also the third straight time, and the fourth time in five weeks, that a start by Tony Cloninger had been impacted by weather. "The rainmaker, that's me," Cloninger said. "And I had good stuff, too." Despite this, Cloninger had won 10 of his past 11 starts, after having won his final seven starts of 1964. Bragan said his next start would be two days hence, on Saturday, September 11, against the Mets at Shea Stadium. Blasingame would open the Mets series Friday night, and Hank Fischer was tabbed as the starter for Sunday. The Braves' roster also would be modestly augmented for the

Mets series. With the roster limit having been expanded from 25 to 40 players at the start of the month, the Braves bought Johnny Blanchard, the longtime Yankees reserve catcher, from Kansas City to give Bragan another left-handed bat off the bench. They also brought up first baseman outfielder Jim Beauchamp, who had been obtained from Houston in the Ken Johnson deal, from Triple-A Atlanta.

Even if the Braves hadn't been rained out on September 9, it was a day that would have belonged to Sandy Koufax under any circumstances. He pitched his record fourth no-hitter - a perfect game at Dodger Stadium against the Cubs. West Allis native Harvey Kuenn, pinch-hitting in the bottom of the ninth, became the 27th and last out when Koufax fanned him on a signature Koufax fastball that leaped like a startled gazelle as Kuenn focused in on a belt-high contact point. It was the last of Koufax's 14 strikeouts, including the final six hitters. Only one ball was hit sharply - a line drive by Byron Browne that centerfielder Willie Davis, probably the fastest man in the National League at the time, flagged down in right-center for the third out in the second inning.

Before 29,139 in a game that required only 1:43 to play, the Cubs' Bob Hendley was close to perfect in defeat. Hendley, 26, had signed with the Braves out of high school in 1957, and from 1961-63 had taken regular turns in the Braves' rotation, going 25-29 with a 3.78 ERA. After the 1963 season, he had been traded along with Del Crandall to the Giants in the deal that brought Felipe Alou to Milwaukee, and earlier in 1965, the Giants had sent him to Chicago with Kuenn for Len Gabrielson.

Against Koufax, Hendley kept eight of the nine Dodger starters off the basepaths, though he struck out only three. The only player on either team to reach base in that game was Lou Johnson, also an ex-Brave. Johnson, a well-traveled 30-year-old who was mired in Triple-A until Tommy Davis suffered a broken ankle on May 1, led off the fifth with a walk, and was sacrificed to second by Ron Fairly. With Jim Lefebvre at the plate, Johnson attempted to steal third. Catcher Chris Krug's throw sailed wide of the bag; Johnson got up and trotted home with the only run of the game. Johnson also had a bloop double in the seventh to break up Hendley's bid for a no-hitter. *Sentinel* sports editor Lloyd Larson, who had covered Warren Spahn throughout Spahn's 12 seasons with the Braves in Milwaukee, paid grudging tribute to Koufax in his column the next day. "(Koufax) probably won't last as long as some of the famous pitchers who preceded him ... (but) although it is impossible to make comparisons, Sandy might even wind up as the No. 1 pitcher in all of baseball history. (The perfect game) added to the personal feeling that (Koufax) would be so acclaimed some day."

To Braves fans, Hendley's cruel fate in this game must have been reminiscent of the game at County Stadium in 1959 when Harvey Haddix of the Pirates pitched 12 perfect innings against the Braves, only to lose in the 13th on an unearned run. Afterward in the Pirates clubhouse, Haddix was talking with commiserating reporters when a telegram was handed to him. The telegram, from a friend of Haddix's in his native state of Ohio, read simply: "Dear Harvey: Tough shit." Haddix showed reporters the telegram, then shrugged. "I guess that's about all it is," he said. (In a little-remembered quirk that was a corollary to Koufax' prefect game, Hendley matched up against Koufax and the Dodgers again five days later, at Wrigley Field. This time, Hendley pitched a complete-game four-hitter, and the Cubs won 2-1.)

The way the Dodgers' rotation lined up, the Braves would have to face Koufax at least twice more - on September 22 in the Milwaukee Braves' last-ever home game, and then again in Los Angeles on October 2, the next-to-last day of the regular season. They could also expect to see eventual 23-game winner Don Drysdale in each of those series, and they still had two series left with the Giants and their future Hall of Famers, Juan Marichal and Gaylord Perry. Still, Bragan, as he had all season, said his main concern remained the Reds, who led Milwaukee by two games going into the Mets-Braves series. "If we get above Cincinnati, we'll win it," Bragan predicted.

Even to put themselves in such a position, though, the Braves knew they had to sweep the Mets at Shea Stadium, and they won the first game of the series 3-1 on a two-run, pinch-hit homer by Felipe Alou, who had been benched after enduring a 3-for-31 slump. Blasingame, weakened by a fever, could get through only five innings, but conceded only a solo homer in the fourth by Jim Hickman - the Mets' only hit of the game. O'Dell worked a 1-2-3 sixth, and was followed by Niekro, who finished with three hitless innings for his sixth save and his fourth in eight days since being installed as the closer.

The Mets' Jack Fisher pitched well, but became the major leagues' first 20-game loser. During the four years of their shabby existence to this point, the Mets "boasted" no less than six 20-game losers - Roger Craig and Al Jackson in 1962, Craig in

1963, Tracy Stallard in 1964, and Fisher (and later Jackson) in 1965. The only pitchers on any other NL teams to lose 20 during that time were Larry Jackson of the Cubs in 1965, and Turk Farrell of the Colt .45s and Dick Ellsworth of the Cubs in 1962.

Wes Westrum had been given the full-time Mets managerial job after being named interim manager upon Casey Stengel's retirement. While much of the baseball world would miss Stengel, his Mets players certainly would not. It had been clear from the time the Mets began play in 1962 that they had hired Stengel strictly as a drawing card and reference point for the new franchise, especially during the first two years when it had to play in the ramshackle Polo Grounds. Most of his players thought of him as an embittered, diminished old man who had no interest in improving them collectively or individually, was prone to dozing off in the dugout during games, and more than willing to get laugh lines at his players' expense. One of the few early Mets who considered Stengel a paragon was Wayne Graham, an infielder who played 20 games for the Mets in 1964. Graham would go on to become one of the most successful coaches in college baseball history, taking his Rice team to the College World Series championship in 2003 and reaching Omaha with the Owls six other times. He earned his 1,100th win as Rice coach in 2016. Graham, who turned 80 on April 6, 2016, always credited Stengel as the main influence in his baseball life, and throughout his coaching career, he wore No. 37, Stengel's number when he managed the Yankees and Mets.

The Braves, despite their win, made up no ground on the Giants or Dodgers, but did pick up a game on the Reds, who lost to Bob Veale and the Pirates 7-0. The Giants were now one-half game up on the Dodgers, 1 1/2 games ahead of the Reds, 2 1/2 ahead of the Braves and 4 1/2 in front of the Pirates. The Braves kept pace on Saturday, September 11, winning 9-0 as Cloninger, coming back on only one day of rest after pitching one inning before the rainout against the Phillies, crafted a one-hitter that was marred only by Cleon Jones' pinch-hit single in the fourth. The Braves eliminated any suspense by scoring three runs in the first and three more in the second against Al Jackson, who fell to 7-19 as the Mets committed five errors and sustained their 100th loss of 1965. (They would finish the season 50-112, giving them 452 defeats in their first four seasons.) Bragan moved Carty to the leadoff spot, followed by Alou. Mike de la Hoz played third base in place of Mathews, who got a rare rest day, and with Menke still hobbled and Woodward contributing little offensively, Sandy Alomar started at shortstop.

Carlton Willey, periodically a starting-rotation member while with the Braves from 1958-62, pitched two scoreless innings for the Mets in what would turn out to be the fourth-to-last appearance of his major league career. The Braves scored their final three runs off Jim Bethke, an 18-year-old who was the youngest player in the league in 1965. Bethke had begun his pro career in the rookie-classification Gulf Coast League in 1964 after signing with the Mets, and was 1-5 with a 5.70 at Triple-A Buffalo during the 1965 season in addition to his 25 games with the Mets, for whom he went 2-0 with a 4.28 ERA. This September 11 outing, during which he walked four in one-plus inning, was the final major league appearance for Bethke, who spent 10 weeks in Army boot camp after the end of the 1965 season. He was sent back to the minors in 1966 and would not advance higher than Double-A again before his retirement in 1971 at the age of

24. Bethke did have one distinction during his abortive career: He was the third Met player to wear No. 41. The fourth and last was Tom Seaver, who joined the Mets in 1967. The franchise, of course, retired No. 41 in honor of Seaver soon after the end of his Hall of Fame career.

The top of the NL standings remained unchanged; the Giants won their eighth straight, 6-4 over the Cubs; the Dodgers prevailed 8-3 over the Astros, and the Reds edged the Pirates 3-2. With only 21 games to go, the Braves, despite their relative proximity to the top of the standings, were still in fourth place, and had almost no wriggle room if they were to keep pace with the Giants. As it turned out, they would win only seven of those 21 games. They would be four games back of San Francisco by the end of play on Sunday, September 12 - and by the time they got out of Philadelphia four days later, they were seven games behind and knew with virtual certainty that there would be much more pathos than passion during their final homestand as the Milwaukee Braves.

The Braves' spiral out of the NL race began despite Bob Sadowski pitching perhaps the best game of his major league career.

Sadowski, 27, was the youngest member of major league baseball's least-known three-brother combination; Ed Sadowski had been a catcher for the Red Sox and Angels from 1960-63, and Ted had pitched for the Senators/Twins from 1960-62. The best-known brother trio, of course, consisted of Joe, Dom and Vince DiMaggio. The three Alou brothers - Felipe, Jesus and Matty - had played together in the same outfield with the Giants in 1963, and all three had lengthy major league careers. Much later, J.D., Stephen and Tim Drew all made the majors. Much earlier, in the late 1890s and early 1900s, *five* Delahanty brothers made the big leagues, and one, Ed, was a Hall of Famer.

Bob Sadowski was acquired from the Cardinals, with whom he had signed in 1958, in the mid-1963 deal that sent Lew Burdette to St. Louis. The Braves immediately inserted Sadowski into Burdette's spot in the rotation, but he was a "swing" pitcher throughout most of his three seasons in Milwaukee. In 1964, when he went 9-10 with a 4.10 ERA, he pitched in 51 games, but started only 18. His start against the Mets on September 12, 1965, represented the 31st game in which he had appeared, and only his 10th start. He shackled the Mets through nine full innings, allowing only three hits and one walk and permitting only one runner past first base.

But the Braves - without Hank Aaron, who had to sit out after fouling a ball off his instep the day before - were no better against Mets rookie Dick Selma, Wade Blasingame's onetime Fresno high school pitching adversary. Selma, 21, making his second major league start after beginning the season in the Class A Western Carolinas League, set a franchise record with 13 strikeouts (including six straight Ks in the ninth and 10th innings) while alloting four hits and a walk, and New York finally broke through against Sadowski in the 10th. Joe Christopher singled, advanced to second on a sacrifice by Ron Hunt (another Braves farm-system discard, though he never played for the parent club) and after Ron Swoboda struck out, Charlie Smith lined a single through the box and into center field to hand Milwaukee its 17th one-run defeat of the season. In San Francisco, the Giants ran their winning streak to 10 with a 4-3, 9-2 sweep of Chicago, with Warren Spahn going the distance for his 363rd and last major league win in the second game and Willie Mays hitting his 499th career homer on Spahn's behalf. This left the Braves four games - their largest first-place deficit since July 31 - behind the Giants, although the two teams still had six games left against each other.

Another kick in the teeth awaited the Braves in Philadelphia, where they lost 4-3 to the Phillies on Monday night, September 13. Ken Johnson, though unsuccessful for the seventh straight time in his quest for a bullpen-saving complete game, got the Braves through the sixth inning with a 3-3 deadlock despite having walked catcher Clay Dalrymple with the bases loaded in the fifth for the Phils' second run that inning. But Johnson's elbow began to throb during that inning. Niekro relieved Johnson and retired Dick Stuart and Tony Gonzalez to start the inning - whereupon Dalrymple, another former Brave farm-system player (the Phillies had obtained him in the Rule 5 draft in 1959) and a .213 hitter in 1965, took Niekro over the right-field wall for only his third home run of the season.

"Braves Beaten by Feat of Clay," was the clever headline in the next day's *Journal*, but an equally critical play, also involving Dalrymple, went against the Braves in the bottom of the third. After Rico Carty began the inning with a double on which he advanced to third on an outfield error, Mathews - back in the No. 2 spot in the batting order - was retired on a foul popup. Aaron grounded to shortstop Bobby Wine, and Carty took off for the plate. Wine's throw was accurate, and home-plate umpire Tony Venzon signaled Carty out - only to change his call to safe when the ball squirted out of Dalrymple's glove. Philadelphia manager Gene Mauch asked Venzon to consult with first-base umpire Doug Harvey. Venzon did so, and changed the call to out after Harvey told him Dalrymple had gloved the ball and had transferred it to his throwing hand by the time he dropped the ball. Bragan, who had had his difficulties with Venzon throughout his managerial career, surprisingly didn't argue the reversal, and said after the game that Harvey had made the correct call. "It's when an umpire obviously doesn't see a play and still won't ask for help, that's when I get upset," he said. Adding to the Braves' misery was their injury-illness list. In addition to Johnson's elbow problem, Alou had to leave the game in the fourth inning after Ray Culp hit him on the elbow with a pitch, and Gene Oliver, his replacement, made an error in the fifth that led to the Philllies' two runs in that inning. Mack Jones' wife was ill in Atlanta, and while he played in the first two games of the Philadelphia series, he would have to leave the team for at least one game after that.

The next night belonged to Phillies ace Jim Bunning, who retired 27 of the 29 batters he faced for his 17th win, a 2-0 triumph during which he allowed only two hits. Both were leadoff doubles, by Gonder in the second and Mathews in the seventh, and Bunning marooned both runners. Hank Fischer limited the Phils to five hits over five innings, but one of those hits was a two-run homer in the first by Johnny Callison - the 16th homer Fischer had given up in 100 innings in 1965. It was the sixth straight win for the Phillies as they continued to wreak revenge for the Braves' role in their 1964 collapse. The Braves were so weakened that their lineup included Jesse Gonder batting cleanup and Johnny Blanchard batting fifth. The Giants, meanwhile, widened their lead and extended their winning streak to 12 with a 7-5 win over the Astros in which Mays hit his 500th career homer, off Don Nottebart. The Giants were now 3 1/2 games ahead of Cincinnati and Los Angeles, with the Braves six games behind. "The only thing we have going for us now is the schedule," Bragan said. "Sweeping these six home games (beginning Friday, September 17, against the Giants) is our only hope. We've lost our karate (long-ball hitting). It's not the pitching ... we're a free-swinging club. When the home run is not forthcoming, we die. It's been all or nothing. Lately, it's been nothing."

That fact didn't affect the courage or resolve of pain-wracked Tony Cloninger, who on Wednesday (September 15) pitched with three or fewer days rest for the 18th of 22 times that season and earned his 22nd win as the Braves beat the Phillies 4-2. Cloninger managed to get through only six innings, but would not complain about, or even discuss, how his arm felt. "He hasn't been any better all season, not even during the one-hitter," catcher Joe Torre said. It was Cloninger's 12th win in his past 13 starts, but the Braves gave it back with an 8-6 loss in the final game of the series as Sadowski gave up eight hits and four earned runs in 5 1/3 innings and Denny Lemaster, now relegated to relief duties, got the loss after giving up two of the three runs the Phillies scored to go ahead in the bottom of the eighth. Future Hall of Famer Ferguson Jenkins, a rookie with the Phillies that year, pitched the ninth for his first career save. He would have only seven saves during his 19-year career, but his 284 wins were more than sufficient to merit his induction into the Hall of Fame in 1991.

The Giants won their 14th straight, 5-1 at Houston, and led the Reds and Dodgers by 4 1/2 games with only 16 games remaining.

The Dodgers looked all but done after dropping two of three in Chicago and losing Don Drysdale in the second inning of the second game when a line drive off his foot forced him to leave the game. The injury was not serious and Drysdale was soon cleared to make his next start, but the Giants looked uncatchable.

By this time, many in Milwaukee, especially media members, were benumbed by the imminent reality of the franchise's departure, though the litigation would drone on even after they began play in Atlanta in 1966. The story, and the Milwaukee Braves themselves, was slowly grinding to a halt.

Lloyd Larson wrote in a column that Houston, with the Astros playing their first year in the Astrodome, had become the fifth city ever to clear 2 million paid admissions in a season. (Milwaukee, of course, had done so every season from 1954-57.) The Phillies had *never* drawn 1.5 million, Larson noted, and the recent Reds-Pirates series in Cincinnati had drawn three crowds of under 7,200. Pittsburgh's home attendance likely would be in the 900,000 range even though the Pirates had recovered from a 9-24 start to lurk on the periphery of the NL pennant race. Meanwhile, Atlanta had shown its big-league baseball "readiness" by drawing 532, 859 and 607 for its three International League playoff games. "Yet Milwaukee was picked as the first city to be abandoned (since the Baltimore Orioles had moved to New York in 1903)," Larson wrote. "Not Cincinnati or Pittsburgh or Philly, or any other. Only Milwaukee, which dared to show the way in stadium building and gave baseball its greatest shot in the arm in all history."

John Quinn, the Phillies general manager who had built the 1950s Braves colossus before being forced out as GM after the

1958 season, had this to say: "There is the money to swing a deal for an estabished team. (Schlitz president) Bob Uihlein and associates can do it. And do it well. (But) an expansion team in Milwaukee is a long ways off, and I'm not sure the fans there will support one."

The football season was to start in earnest that weekend, with the Packers opening in Pittsburgh against the Steelers and the Wisconsin Badgers playing Colorado in Madison. A 250-mile USAC event was scheduled at the Milwaukee Mile, and hundreds of high school football seasons around the state would get underway as well. The Milwaukee baseball garrison was a modest one during that final homestand, and most of the talk within that group was not of the Braves - they were seven games out with 16 to play - but of the Giants. Not surprisingly, the San Francisco entourage was in a celebratory mood when the Giants arrived in Milwaukee to begin a three-game series that would constitute the first half of the last home stand in Milwaukee Braves history. Even if the Giants went only 8-8 the rest of the way, the Dodgers would have to go 12-3 to force a tie, and the question was raised as to how Los Angeles' unimposing batting order could accomplish that, even with the Dodgers' pitching. Warren Spahn, in the final month of a major league career that had begun in 1942, called the Giants "the happiest team in baseball."

Even if Spahn made his comment as a cosmetic gesture of solidarity, the fact in 1965 was that the Giants were unified under Franks' command to an extent that had not existed within the team since Leo Durocher had taken them to a surprising World Series conquest of the Cleveland Indians in 1954, and would not exist again in San Francisco until Bruce Bochy brought the

Giants their next World Series title, in 2010. Even though Franks' Giants finished second in each of his four seasons (1965-68) under his direction, he created a modicum of unity in a clubhouse that had been deeply divided under Alvin Dark - who, of course, had been fired after the 1964 season largely because he said black and Latino players didn't respond as well as white players to the pressures of a pennant race - and before him Bill Rigney. "Franks was far and away the one who stood closest to owner Horace Stoneham," Charles Einstein wrote in his book, *Willie's Time.* "And he had one other advantage: He didn't need baseball for a living. A successful real estate developer in his native Utah, Franks wanted to manage a baseball team because he wanted to manage a baseball team. ... In truth, Franks never had to manage like a man wth an overdue mortgage payment, and so he had the better of a Durocher or a Dark. Paper it over though they would, Durocher and Dark never left any doubt but that they were the smartest men on the team. The more relaxed Franks would give full rein to his coaches and team captain (Mays). The blame would be his, but the credit - victory has a hundred fathers, defeat is an orphan - he would happily assign to others ... Unlike Dark (a self-proclaimed born-again Christian who tended to use his position as a pulpit), Franks smoked, drank, chewed tobacco and never said 'Son of a buck' (Dark's favorite and supposedly most off-color expression) in his life."

Mays was friendly with Dark and Rigney, both of whom had been his teammates when the franchise was in New York, but both maintained a player-manager distance from Mays, and he sometimes felt neither of them fully appreciated the extent of his greatness. Franks, on the other hand, worked with Mays the same way Durocher had at the time of Mays' promotion to the major leagues in 1951. In effect, he said that the team would have two sets of rules - one for Mays, the other for everyone else - and he deferred to Mays to a far greater degree than was the norm in player-manager relationships at that time. Mays was a player-coach without portfolio during Franks' four seasons in San Francisco, and Franks' financial counsel was largely responsible for the fact that Mays, who had financial problems throughout much of his playing career, was able to live comfortably after his retirement as a player in 1973. In 1975, when the Giants were bankrupt and on the verge of being sold to interests who planned to move them to Toronto, Franks put together a consortium that tried unsuccessfully to purchase the team and keep it in San Francisco. (Horace Stoneham eventually sold the club to Bob Lurie, under whom the team stayed at Candlestick Park.) If that transaction had been completed, Franks later said, the plan was to make Mays manager.

In 1965, Mays was having probably the best overall season of his career, and he had carried the Giants to 14 straight wins and into first place by 4 1/2 games as the team arrived in Milwaukee on September 17. The Giants looked and felt invincible. "Four or five more wins ought to just about do it," Franks said before the series opener on Friday, September 17. Little could he have known then that the Dodgers, who had squandered seemingly-sure pennants because of five-alarm finishes by the Giants in 1951 and 1962, would become the hunters in 1965 as they won 13 straight and 15 of their last 16 games.

The Dodgers had begun their pursuit of the Giants by salvaging the final game of their series in Chicago on September 17 - before only 550 paying witnesses at Wrigley Field - and

Drysdale beat the Cardinals 3-2 in St. Louis while the Braves administered one of the few bombardments of Juan Marichal's season and clipped a game from the Giants' lead with a 9-1 victory. With Ken Johnson's elbow still bothering him, and Wade Blasingame still not fully recovered from the virus that had weakened him in his previous start, Phil Niekro made his first major league start after 46 relief appearances (many of them in mopup roles) and transfixed the free-swinging Giants with his knuckleball as he allowed only five hits and one run over five innings. Only 6,924 saw Niekro's outing, which would be the Braves' first true investment in a pitch and in a career that would land Niekro in the Hall of Fame.

In fact, Niekro was one of *eight* Hall of Famers to play in this game, along with Aaron, Mathews, Mays, McCovey, Marichal, Gaylord Perry (who gave up four runs in two innings in relief of Marichal) and Orlando Cepeda. Two other future Cooperstown inductees, Joe Torre of the Braves and Warren Spahn of the Giants, were in uniform that night, but didn't play. Another uniformed non-participant was the Braves' Sandy Alomar, whose son Roberto - who wasn't born until more than two years later - became a Hall of Famer in 2011. Russ Hodges and Lon Simmons, who called this game for San Francisco radio station KSFO, later were recipients of the Hall of Fame's Ford C. Frick Award for broadcast excellence, and *San Francisco Chronicle* beat writer Bob Stevens, who covered this game, in 1998 would win the J.G. Taylor Spink Award, enshrining him in the equivalent of the sportwriting Hall of Fame.

Billy O'Dell, rejuvenated by his reduced workload during the previous few weeks, squirmed out of a bases-loaded, no-out situation in the sixth and shut his former teammates out the rest of the way for his 19th save (and only his second since August 23). It would be his last save of the season. Marichal was taken out in the fourth after giving up seven hits - including two homers by Hank Aaron - and five earned runs. While the Braves were on the road, county executive John Doyne had announced that $200,000 would be allotted to sand-blast the exterior steelwork at County Stadium. Doyne, like almost everyone else in Wisconsin, knew for a virtual certainty that County Stadium would not host major league baseball in 1966; a few days earlier, Indians president Gabe Paul had announced that the team would stay in Cleveland at least one more season, ending Milwaukee's last faint hope of landing a transplanted franchise for 1966. Even so, Doyne wanted the ballpark to be ready just in case a needy team should happen to land on its doorstep in 1967.

The Braves moved within six games of the Giants with the victory, but the Giants eliminated the Braves last wisp of hope by winning the final two games of the series - 2-0 on September 18 on a combined three-hitter by Ron Herbel and Frank Linzy and home runs by McCovey and Tom Haller, and 4-2 on September 19 despite a complete-game effort by Tony Cloninger. The last two weekend games in Milwaukee Braves history were played amid silence and indifference. Only 8,563 turned out for the Saturday game, and while the vast majority of Wisconsin's sports fans watched on TV as the Packers opened their season with a win at Pittsburgh, and 21,350 saw Jim Hurtubise win the 250-mile USAC auto race at the Milwaukee Mile, just 12,084 were present at County Stadium the next day. The only hint that the game mattered much to the Braves - and of course, it mattered a lot to the Giants - came in the eighth with the game tied

2-2. Hal Lanier led off with a single, and Jim Davenport bunted along the first-base line. First baseman Joe Torre picked it up just as he thought it had rolled foul, about 10 feet short of first base, but first-base umpire Billy Williams ruled the bunt fair.

Torre went berserk, arguing nose-to-nose with Williams as Lanier made it to third without Torre even noticing or calling timeout. Finally, Torre slammed the ball to the ground in disgust and frustration, and Lanier scored what turned out to be the winning run. As it turned out, Torre's outburst didn't matter, other than the fact it got him ejected: Catcher Gene Oliver had followed the play up the first-base line, so nobody was covering home on the play. Lanier could have trotted home, even if Torre hadn't spiked the ball in his fit of pique. "That confounded ball was foul," Torre said afterward. "Sure, I pulled a bush play, but that ball was foul. The ball kept hitting the chalk as it rolled along. It lost speed and finally started going foul. When (Williams) called the ball fair, I lost all connection with Earth."

Only three home games remained - a Monday-afternoon makeup game against the Phillies, and then two final night games against the Dodgers. Monday, September 20 would have been a dismal afternoon at County Stadium even if the weather had cooperated. Tornadoes touched down in Neenah the previous day, and the forecast was for thunderstorms, some of them severe. The Phillies, like the Braves, were playing for nothing more than first-division World Series money; in those days, players on the fifth-place team would get a few hundred dollars each from the World Series receipts, while the sixth-place team would get nothing. Most of the baseball action that day took place at the county courthouse, where Braves attorneys served subpoenas to obtain all of the county's records pertaining to the Braves' time at County Stadium, going all the way back to 1950 when work had begun on the Braves' future home. Bud Selig, Edmund Fitzgerald, Ben Barkin and others who had been involved with Teams Inc were required to appear for depositions. Elsewhere, the city was preparing for a visit by Lady Bird Johnson, the First Lady, to dedicate the three new Mitchell Park domes, all of which were self-contained natural environements. (The Mitchell Domes, each 140 feet in diameter, were closed for repairs in 2016, and although two of them reopened before the end of the year, it was estimated that $70 million would be needed to perform necessary upgrades on all three domes. The National Trust for Historic Preservation added the Domes to its list of the country's 11 most-endangered historic places.)

At County Stadium, John Pinter, 30, and his two sons, 4 and 2, had traveled from their home in Mequon to buy tickets for the Milwaukee Braves' last-ever home game, two days hence. Pinter, a candy-company sales manager who was a graduate of Marquette University High School (less than a mile east of County Stadium), had attended the Braves' first-ever home game in Milwaukee as a high school student in 1953, and was able to do without repercussions because Marquette, like every school in the area, was shut down that day in celebration of Milwaukee's arrival as a true major-league city. On August 11, 1961, Pinter had seen Warren Spahn earn the 300th win of his career, and Pinter had been at all seven of the World Series games played at County Stadium in 1957 and 1958. He said he was still a Braves fan, even after all that had happened in the seven years since that last World Series. On this day in 1965, upon reaching the ticket office, he asked for the same seat he had occupied on Opening

Day in 1953 - Section 2, Row 30, Seat 4 - along with the adjoining seats for his sons. He had no trouble getting them. "They looked at me like I was out of my mind," Pinter said after purchasing the tickets. "The people at the ticket window told me they had no reservations for lower grandstand seats that far back. They couldn't understand why I wanted it when there were much better seats available." The price per ticket was $2.30, compared to the $1.85 he had paid to see the Braves make their debut in Milwaukee.

If Pinter and his sons had stuck around to attend the Phillies-Braves game, they probably would have had Section 2 entirely to themselves. The Phillies won, 4-1, after waiting out a storm that delayed the start of the game by 45 minutes and another cloudburst that interrupted the game for 1 hour, 45 minutes in the third inning. Ray Culp, who finished 14-10 that year, went the distance for his fourth win against the Braves since July 1. Given the weather and the fact the game was virtually meaningless, a few of the fans who sat through all or part of that dreary afternoon and early evening (the game started at 1 p.m. and ended at 5:45) likely did so because they wanted to be part of a dubious Milwaukee Braves postscript. If so, they weren't disappointed: The paid attendance was 812 - 101 fewer than had attended the only other triple-digit game of the Braves' County Stadium history, on May 4. The exposed seating areas in both the upper and lower decks were completely unoccupied as fans easily found shelter in covered seating sections.

That same day, the AL pennant-winning Twins played before 537 in Minnesota in conditions similar to those at County Stadium, and the Cubs had played the Dodgers before 550 at

Wrigley Field the previous week. And it wasn't the last time the Braves would play at home before a triple-digit crowd. Ten years later, on September 8, 1975, the Atlanta Braves and Astros played before 737 at Atlanta-Fulton County Stadium - the Braves' smallest home crowd since 1944 when they were still in Boston.

Damning as the 812 attendance figure looked in 1965, triple-figure crowd counts had not been uncommon in the majors in the years before World War II, especially during the Great Depression, which the Browns, Reds, Braves, Dodgers and Phillies barely survived. All five of those teams were either in foreclosure or at the mercy of lien holders at least once during the 1930s.

Long before that, in 1901, the American League's original version of the Milwaukee Brewers had drawn only 139,034 during its only season of operation. The Brewers moved to St. Louis and became the Browns in 1902, and routinely outdrew the Cardinals for most of the next quarter-century - with first baseman George Sisler, one of the sport's most luminous and most-admired stars of the 1920s, as their headliner - before the Cardinals won four pennants and two World Series in the six seasons from 1926-31. This made the Browns permanent paupers, even though they owned Sportsman's Park, where both teams played. In 1933, the Browns drew only 88,113 for the entire season, and that included a home-opener crowd of 12,000. Paid attendance at one game, in September, was 34. In 1935, their attendance dropped to 80,992, and the AL, knowing that traveling to St. Louis in September would cost the other seven teams far more than they could possibly make as their share of the gate receipts, realigned the schedule so that the Browns' last home game would be played on August 31. The Browns finished the year with a 29-game road trip during which they made stops at all seven of the other AL cities. In Detroit, where the Tigers were on their way to their second straight pennant and first-ever World Series championship, a total of 96,000 saw a three-game series against the Browns in late September - almost 16,000 more than the Browns drew at home that entire season.

It was seen as symbolic as well as saddening that two days before the Milwaukee Braves endured their single-game attendance nadir, Ray Jackson's steakhouse-bar on West Blue Mound Road was badly damaged by fire. Jackson's had opened in 1953, the same year the Braves came to Milwaukee, and during the Braves' time in Milwaukee, it was known as Jackson's House of Hits. It had been a gathering place for many Braves players, opponents and fans during the 1950s and early 1960s; athletes found it particularly appealing because it kept its kitchen open until after midnight, affording the players the opportunity to have a good meal (and, if they wished, a few drinks) after a night game, and because Jackson and his staff did not allow patrons to bother players and other dignitaries while they ate. Even Vince Lombardi, whose favorite place in Milwaukee was the departure concourse at Mitchell Field, was a regular visitor.

Jackson's establishment had been where Casey Stengel and several of his victorious Yankees had drank deep into the night with more than a few Braves players after the Yankees had beaten the Braves at County Stadium in Game 7 of the 1958 World Series. The bar bulged with momentos, particularly autographed chalkboards from that night and so many others; some were lost in the fire, but Jackson recovered many of the artifacts and rebuilt his restaurant, renaming it the House of Prime. After the Brewers' arrival in 1970, many players - and team officials, including George Bamberger, who managed the Brewers from 1978-80 and in 1985 and 1986 - became frequent guests. Jackson kept his place until 1986, when he sold it to new owners, who renamed it O'Donoghues's. After Ray Jackson died in 1989, his son Jimmy opened a new Jackson's, at the intersection of 38th and Mitchell streets. It was still in operation, as the Jackson Grill, in 2016, and had much of the same sports-related decor and memorabilia that had characterized the original Jackson's.

The Brooklyn Dodgers, of course, had been the Braves' main obstacle during the 1950s, and if the Braves' move from Boston to Milwaukee had not redefined baseball finance and geography as it did, the Dodgers might well have stayed in Brooklyn instead of moving to Los Angeles for the 1958 season. So it was symbolic, also, that the Milwaukee Braves' final two home games would be against the Dodgers. But if they felt any sentiment or sympathy as they came to Milwaukee, they spoke little of it. They had begun the 15-1 stretch that would push them past the Giants and into the World Series, but few outside their clubhouse thought they could erase their four-game deficit, even with Koufax, Drysdale and Osteen ready to pitch in a three-man rotation the rest of the way if needed. "Anyone who wouldn't pick the Giants," Phillies manager Gene Mauch said during his team's one-day stopover in Milwaukee, "has got to be crazy."

The Dodgers, though, didn't concur, and even though they had no games remaining with the Giants, they had six left with the Braves, who by now were bruised and battered, and more than ready to begin their impending rebirth in Atlanta. Los Angeles won its fifth straight and pulled within three games of the Giants, who lost 7-4 in Cincinnati, with a 3-1 victory over Milwaukee before 5,169 who showed up despite the forecast of possible rain, which had fallen in measurable amounts in Milwaukee during 30 of the previous 53 days and each of the past six.

Don Drysdale pitched a six-hitter for his 21st victory. Denny Lemaster, who hadn't won since August 17, fell to 6-13 (after going 17-11 in 1964) despite pitching seven strong innings, giving up two runs and six hits while striking out eight. Jim Lefebvre, the second baseman who would be named NL Rookie of the Year, hit a home run in the second. It was the 12th and final homer that season for Lefebvre, who wound up tying Lou Johnson for the team HR lead. (Lefebvre would later manage the Seattle Mariners to their first-ever winning season, in 1991, and in 1999 would direct the Brewers for the final 49 games of the season on an interim basis after Phil Garner was fired.) Later that inning, Wes Parker, Jeff Torborg and Drysdale singled to bring in a second run. The Braves scored an unearned run in the fourth on a sacrifice fly by Frank Thomas, but the Dodgers reciprocated in the top of the ninth with a run of their own, set up by an error by Mathews at third.

The final home game in Milwaukee Braves history would be the next night, September 22, and perhaps the final tinges of emotion were being husbanded for that last game. Little was made of the penultimate game, other than its impact on the NL pennant race. "All we can do now," wrote Lloyd Larson in the *Sentinel*, "is hope for a favorable decision, by the courts and/or baseball. The Braves' sudden nosedive eliminated that (World Series in Milwaukee) possibility. Maybe it's just as well this way, because a World Series (in Milwaukee) might have made an uncomfortable situation even worse."

The *Journal* that evening ran an op-ed piece that turned out to be prophetic, albeit a bit Pollyannaish. Headlined "Great While It Lasted," it opined that the Braves' final game in Milwaukee the next day "ends Chapter One in the history of Milwaukee's big league status as measured by professional baseball ... meanwhile, Milwaukee does not cease to be 'big league' in every other sense, and will continue to be ever more so. It is setting a dynamic pace of enterprise, growth and renewal. It has no apology to make to the Braves' owners, no cause to rebuke itself. One way or another, baseball will return another day; it will have to. Thus, continued resentment in the community against the greed, ingratitude, deception and betrayal by the absentee Braves owners can afford to give way in our thoughts at this time. It was great while it lasted. And the apparent end for the moment is at best a disappointment, not a calamity."

Interviews after the next-to-last Milwaukee Braves home game indicated that the players and other *dramatis personæ* of 1965 had not given The Last Game much forethought, and wouldn't until the next day. Instead, questions focused primarily on Bobby Bragan, whose relationship with the Milwaukee media had been spiky from the start and became even more so as the Braves fell out of contention. On this occasion, though, Bragan spoke more openly about his 1965 experience and his 1966 status than he had all season.

He had not yet been offered a 1966 contract, even though Bragan probably had the Braves as high in the standings as his bosses had any right to expect, given the team's pitching and defensive shortcomings and its over-dependence on the long ball. "I have every reason to feel confident (about returning in 1966)," Bragan said. At the same time, he called the Braves' late-season play "the most disappointing finish" of his career. Bragan also spoke to the fact he had become the verbal target for frustrated fans. "It's like having your choice of eating spinach or cake. Naturally, I'd rather eat cake. (But I) spent three enjoyable years in Milwaukee (and he) never enjoyed working as much as I have here." On the team's disappointing finish: "Five other clubs (including the Braves) could be where the Giants are right now if the ball had bounced differently and they hadn't incurred injuries." On decisions he made or helped make on personnel and procedure: "We depended too much on power. In order to win a pennant, you have to spend more time bunting and hitting behind the runner. If there aren't any changes made on the ballclub next year, there will be a lot more concentration on those two fundamentals."

Bragan would be rehired for 1966, but was fired the following August with the Atlanta Braves at 52-59. It was his third major league dismissal, and he would never manage in the major leagues again, though he remained in baseball in various capacities (including seven years as president of the Texas League, starting in 1969) until he died in 2010 at age 92. The *Sentinel's* Red Thisted wrote at the time the Braves announced that Bragan was being re-upped: "They (the Braves) started with the best team in the NL in the opinion of many baseball buffs, and finished in contention for the flop of the year. Injuries took (their toll), but the Dodgers went ... without Tommy Davis, twice the league's batting champ, and the Giants lost Orlando Cepeda. (The Braves') field direction left a great deal to be desired and there, probably, was the most important key to the club's collapse. (Bragan) again managed by whim and caprice, and it wasn't often an observer could see much logic or consistency in the way the club was handled." The Braves would lead the league with 196 homers, and they won 25 of 39 games that had been decided by five or more runs. But while they were 27-9 against the two worst teams in the league (the Astros and Mets), they went 59-67 against the other seven teams, including 6-12 marks against both the Reds and Phillies.

Wednesday, September 22, dawned rainy and shrouded in shades of gray that matched most moods in Milwaukee, now that the last of the crates and baseball paraphernalia and personal belongings in the home clubhouse at County Stadium were fully ready for removal with the 1965 Milwaukee Braves' 81st and final home game at hand. Virtually all of the Braves' non-baseball personnel, of course, had long since made the move to Atlanta. It was a day of anger, but it also was a day of reflection and sadness. Red Smith, the nationally-syndicated New York columnist and a Green Bay native, had come to Milwaukee for the final homestand. Much of his column on September 22 focused on the taxicab ride he had taken to the ballpark for the last game. Like a lot of people in service industries in Milwaukee, the cabbie stood to be hurt financially by the absence of major league baseball at County Stadium, and his mood matched the weather. "(Several days before) was the first break the Braves have gotten all year from the weather," he told Smith. "So on top of everything else, they didn't figure to draw any crowds. Everybody knows how the town feels about them quitting. And for what? Can you imagine anybody quitting on a city that put over 900,000 in the park for a second-division team (as the Braves had done in 1964)? Sure, they used to draw 2 million, but any town would fall off if they got rid of all the stars. Where's Joe Adcock? Where's Johnny Logan? Where's Lew Burdette?"

Smith wrote on: "He paused to gun the car through an amber light, swerving away from a driver tryng to jump the green. 'Just the same,' he said, 'this team woulda won the pennant without Bragan.' Bragan is the visible symbol of the carpetbaggers, the earthly vicar of management whom the fans see on the field. So he's a rat fink. 'You can't have a bad day with this Bragan, or you're outta here,' the driver continued. 'You notice when Hank Fischer was pitching yesterday and then (the Giants' Tom) Haller hit a home run off him? He throws two balls to the next hitter and Bragan's got him out of there. Two balls, and he wasn't even trying to throw strikes. One of 'em was a (high-inside) duster. I hope they fill the park (for the final home game), just to show these boobs what kind of town they're quitting.'"

Of the 33 players who were Los Angeles Dodgers in 1965, only five - Sandy Koufax, Don Drysdale, Johnny Podres, John Roseboro and Jim Gilliam - had been Brooklyn Dodgers in 1957. Although none of them mentioned it to anyone outside their clubhouse - after all, they were in the midst of a pennant race with the hated Giants - perhaps they fleetingly remembered the last game the Brooklyn Dodgers ever played at Ebbets Field, on September 24, 1957, when Danny McDevitt pitched the Dodgers to a 2-0 win over Pittsburgh.

A turnout of 6,702 watched the funeral game of the Brooklyn Dodgers, the subjects of more books and folklore than any other major league team except the Yankees. For the Milwaukee Braves' last home game, almost twice that number - 12,577 - showed up to remember the delirium of 1957 and 1958 and hear the final dirge of 1965. It came from the bugle of Dick Emmons, a mail carrier who lived on South 35th Street. Emmons had been a fixture at County Stadium throughout the Braves' tenure there, with his wide-brimmed straw hat and his denim jacket, which had "CHARGE!" stitched across the back. Three hours, 38 minutes and 11 innings after the start of the game, Emmons played "Taps" after the Dodgers moved within two games of the Giants, overcoming a 6-1 third-inning deficit to beat the Braves 7-6.

Koufax, who came into the game 23-8 with a 2.05 ERA, had given up more than three earned runs in only one outing since July 7, and that had been in the August 22 game in San Francisco that had been so violently abridged by Juan Marichal's attack on John Roseboro. Four days before the September 22 game in Milwaukee, Koufax had shut out the Cardinals on four hits. Despite the unrelenting pain in his elbow, he was the best at his best throughout the Dodgers' pennant drive. Yet on this night, unaccountably, the Braves belabored him, ending his evening after he faced two batters in the bottom of the third. Koufax's final, almost unfathomable pitching line for that evening: Two innings, six hits, five earned runs, no walks, three strikeouts and the first grand-slam homer of Frank Bolling's 12-year career. It came in the second after Koufax surrendered singles to Torre, Oliver and Mathews, and put the Braves ahead 4-1. "He was off that night; he was wild," Bolling recalled. "It wasn't one of his better days. I played 12 years in the big leagues and did a few other things (including all-star years in '61 and '62), but I guess that was my claim to fame."

In the third, Mack Jones led off with another homer, and after Aaron singled, Koufax was removed and replaced by Howie Reed, who got Torre to hit into a double play. Oliver followed with his 19th homer of the season - an inside-the-park job that put him within one HR of joining Aaron, Mathews, Torre, Jones and Felipe Alou as part of the first sextet on one NL team to reach the 20-homer mark in the same season. (Oliver would get his 20th homer four days later in San Francisco, and would finish with 21. The distinction of having six 20-plus home run hitters on one team remained unmatched in the National League until 2003, when the Atlanta Braves did it with Javy Lopez, Marcus Giles, Vinny Castilla, Chipper Jones, Andruw Jones and Gary Sheffield. Seventeen American League teams, including the 2016 Baltimore Orioles, had reached that plateau as of the end of the 2016 season - aided, of course, by the designated-hitter rule that the AL had adopted in 1973.)

But Braves starter Wade Blasingame couldn't protect the 6-1 lead, failing to get through the fifth inning after giving up two runs in the fourth and three more in the fifth as the Dodgers tied the game 6-6. The Braves managed seven hits but no runs against Reed, Ron Perranoski and Bob Miller. In the 11th, Bragan - having already used O'Dell, Osinski and Niekro in relief - turned to Chi Chi Olivo, 37, who had pitched in only four major league games that season and had spent most of 1965 with Triple-A Atlanta. Dodgers manager Walter Alston sent up Don Drysdale, the best-hitting pitcher in the major leagues, as a pinch-hitter to lead off the 11th, and Drysdale grounded out to shortstop. But Maury Wills beat out a bunt single, and stole the 88th of his 94 SBs he amassed that season. Jim Gilliam was intentionally walked, and lefty Dick Kelley was brought in to face left-handed hitting Willie Davis, who flied out to left. This brought up right-handed hitter Lou Johnson.

Like many managers of that era, Bragan occasionally used starters to get critical outs late in close games, but he didn't do so this time, leaving Kelley in to face Johnson. The former Brave lined a single to center field to put the Dodgers up 7-6. Miller took the mound for the 11th. Jesse Gonder grounded out to shortstop. Mack Jones singled to earn himself the distinction of being the right-side trivia bracket mate of Joe Adcock, who in 1953 had become the first Milwaukee Brave ever to record a base hit at County Stadium. Appropriately, Hank Aaron smoked a line drive on his final home at-bat as a Milwaukee Brave. Appropriately, in terms of the Braves' decline and demise in Wisconsin, the ball was hit directly at Davis in center field. Jones, running on the pitch, was easily doubled off first to end the game and send the Milwaukee Braves off the County Stadium diamond for the final time.

While it had been a night of melancholy, the anger that had permeated 1965 - and had been so pointedly voiced by the cab driver with whom Red Smith spoke - generally was nudged aside for one night in favor of gratitude for all that the Braves' players had brought to Milwaukee: Two pennants and a tie for another, a World Series title, a total of 47 seasons from five Hall of Famers (13 from Mathews, 12 each from Aaron and Spahn, six from Joe Torre, and four from Red Schoendienst), and no fewer than 83 wins in any one season. Those who had been at County Stadium from the beginning weren't about to let all of that go, even if the Braves themselves were going and soon would be gone.

The *Sentinel's* Lou Chapman, who had covered the team throughout its time in Milwaukee, got his paper's last editorial word after the final home game. Wrote Chapman: "Major league baseball hereabouts is dead - at least temporarily, unless and until it can be reincarnated through expansion. It was the end of an era - those dizzy, daffy days of the cowbells (often heard at County Stadium during the 1950s), the beer carry-ins, the loud cheer of (even) the foul balls, the Warren Spahn kick, the Andy Pafko belly-flop ... Even the elements conspired (to) spread the gloom of the day. Dark clouds hung like a shroud over the Stadium as the Atlanta-bound Braves took the field for their final appearance before the home folks. Ode to Aaron, Mathews, Hazle, Logan, *et al* continues, then to the spirit of the team ... the time Spahn and Burdette burned Wes Covington's straw hat on the team bus, the time they tied (together) the shoes of a sodden sportswriter on a train from Philadelphia to New York, Walker Cooper (an eight-time All-Star catcher who spent 53 games with the Braves in 1953) lighting newspapers on fire in the clubhouse as they were read. Spahn burying his cap in the outfield at (Pittsburgh's) Forbes Field and digging it up the next year ... Del Crandall, whose strongest drink was ice-cream soda, and the devil-may-care youngsters like Mathews and Buhl; Joe Adcock, the silent strong man from Louisiana; Johnny Logan, the master of the malaprop; Burdette, who learned to throw by heaving rocks at a deserted World War I munitions plant in Nitro, W.Va. ... it was a kaleidoscopic cavalcade that may never again be equaled in Milwaukee's sports history - or anywhere else."

Robert R. Wells wrote the Page 1 summation for the *Journal*: "Old habits returned, and watching the game began to be fun instead of duty. It was a minor historical occasion, this apparent end of what was once a strangely emotional era in a very sort of practical community, so some had come simply to be in on the death ... but a fan knows that a willing suspension of disbelief is as necessary to the enjoyment of a game as a novel ... and so the fine old illusion came back in spite of everything." But after the game, Wells wrote, "The crowd stood around. It seemed to be waiting for something more. But there was nothing more. There was nothing left to do but put aside the pleasant illusion that baseball matters, and go home."

The lists of lasts were dutifully recorded: Dick Kelley as the last Milwaukee Braves pitcher at County Stadium, Mack Jones as the last Brave to record a base hit at County Stadium (until 1998, when the Brewers moved from the American League Central to the NL West), Gene Oliver as the last Milwaukee Brave to hit a home run at the stadium, Chi Chi Olivo as the last pitcher of record in a Milwaukee Braves home game. The last of 19,551,909 turnstile clicks (an average of 21,091 per game) over 13 seasons at Braves games at County Stadium may have been registered upon the arrival of Mrs. George Riordan, who joined her husband at the park in the fifth inning after attending an American Legion auxiliary meeting.

It was a last for Red Thisted, who had covered professional baseball in Milwaukee for the *Sentinel* since 1926, and saw his last game after being at Borchert Field and then County Stadium for 3,282 games in succession. The last of the many bedsheet banners that had been draped over the bleacher barriers throughout the stadium read, "Hello Braves, Goodbye Carpetbaggers." (One that had been displayed earlier read, "See You Next Year Milwaukee Braves," with Milwaukee crossed out.) There was a last forlorn-fan photo, taken of John Franzen as he draped his chin over the railing as the last outs were recorded. Franzen, another start-to-finish Milwaukee Braves fan, had been to all 81 home games the Braves had played in 1965, along with 21 road games. It was the last time Earl Gillespie ever broadcast a Milwaukee Braves game; Gillespie, who had been the Braves' lead broadcaster since they had arrived in Milwaukee, had left the Braves' radio team to take a television job after the 1964 season, but he was brought back this night to join his longtime sidekick Blaine Walsh in the broadcast booth. There were the last of the pregame fan-to-player gifts, an everyday occurrence throughout the team's time in Milwaukee. Five teenage girls presented Eddie Mathews with a cake, with tiny players on a sugar-frosted diamond. He also was given a scrapbook, covering his entire career, by a young admirer. It was the last chance Braves fans would have to boo Bobby Bragan, and they availed themselves of that opportunity each time Bragan walked to the mound to make a pitching change. But none of the Braves players heard anything except cheers, as had been the case all season except for the one chorus of catcalls Denny Lemaster had heard after a bad outing in August.

This, of course, was the night the snapshot by photographer Ernie Anheuser that crystalized and symbolized all that had happened in Milwaukee baseball over 13 years was taken as Mathews and Hank Aaron walked for the last time through the narrow tunnel that led from the clubhouse to the playing field.

Mathews and Aaron, though friendly and respectful of each others' passion and skills, were not close friends during or after their time in Milwaukee, and that wasn't because Mathews was white and Aaron was black. They were as different and distinct as Santa Barbara, Calif., and Mobile, Ala., their respective childhood hometowns. They had different backgrounds, different temperaments, different friends within the club, and different types of fan admiration. Though Aaron a half-century later had far more visible testimonials in Milwaukee to his greatness than did Mathews, Aaron during much of his career was underappreciated in Milwaukee - and throughout baseball - because many fans mistook his grace and fluidity for effortlessness. Mathews, on the other hand, was seen as Everyman Eddie, the personification of the labor and industry that his fans tried to bring to their own lives. He played third base almost as if he were a hockey goalie, getting glove or foot or chest in front of even the most sinister ground balls and live drives, regardless of the pain and danger factors. Except for the swing about which Ty Cobb had raved when Mathews was a rookie, he was never elegant, never demonstrative, and tended to keep his emotions to himself and go about his job. He rarely started fights, but his style of play was combative, and once he was provoked, so was his on-field persona. As Johnny Logan was to say years later: "I started a lot of fights, and Eddie finished most of them."

Milwaukeeans had loved Eddie for being Everyman Eddie, and they came to love Aaron for the elegance and quiet efficiency and unfailing instincts with which he had played the game. The fans would love both of the two franchise citadels one last time this night, and the two of them seemed to realize that night that they would be forever bonded in time. Both got standing ovations before all of their turns at bat; Mathews' final one lasted a full three minutes. Afterward, Mathews said: "I was nervous before the game ... after all, this may be the end of the 13 best years of my life. I'm ordinarily not a sentimental guy, but this really shook me up. I haven't felt this way since we got back to Milwaukee from winning the 1957 World Series and that crowd greeted us at the airport. But I'm unhappy too. I'm sorry that the Braves are leaving, if that's the way it's going to be."

Aaron didn't say much after the game about his ovations - talking about himself wasn't his way - but he was seen wiping tears from his eyes after he stepped out of the batters box during his last at-bat. "This I've never seen before," he said after the game. "Words can't describe the way I felt. It was the greatest thrill of my baseball career." Torre had participated in the ovations to his two extraordinary teammates while awaiting his turns at bat; he was stunned when he was greeted with similarly emphatic cascades of cheer when *he* batted for the last time. "I never expected a tribute like that," he said. "I wish I would have done something about it. Naturally, there's a little nostalgia, but I suppose it'll really hit me when I realize we're actually gone."

The Teepee Room, the hospitality suite underneath the stands at County Stadium, was the site of a "raucous wake" after the game, according to *Sentinel* columnist Buck Herzog, who was present. "Johnny Logan, with heavy heart, took over the bartending chores and was lavish in his servings of the Braves' liquor," Herzog wrote. "Several drinks were tossed down for Al Cissa, the scoreboard (operator), who was ill. Al is probably closest to Red Thisted in continuous attendance of Brewers and Braves games." The last man to leave the Teepee Room that evening was Dodgers broadcaster Vin Scully, who locked the door behind him. "Don't give up the fight, boys," Scully told his Milwaukee brethren. "This is a great town. A great bunch of people. And I don't want to give up those delightful walks around your lakefront."

Scully would visit the lakefront and County Stadium again, starting in 1982 when he and Sparky Anderson announced the Brewers-Cardinals World Series for CBS Radio, and from 1998-2000 after the Brewers switched from the American League to the National League. He also graced Miller Park, working Brewers-Dodgers games there from 2001 until 2007, when he reduced his work schedule and stopped traveling with the Dodgers for road games other than those on the West Coast and within the Natioanl League West. He retired at the end of the 2016 regular season after 67 years with the Dodgers in Brooklyn and Los Angeles. Having started his Dodger broadcasting career as Red Barber's sidekick in 1950, Scully had called games from Braves Field during the Braves' final three seasons in Boston. At the time of his retirement, he was thought to be the only living individual who had witnessed Braves games at Braves Field and County Stadium and Brewers games at County Stadium and Miller Park.

Finally, as the last of the kids - including future Milwaukee mayor Tom Barrett - who had wandered onto the field after the game were shooed off by stadium personnel, and all the player-fan thank-yous had been expressed, there was the last song. Janis Malone, the ballpark organist, squeezed off "Till We Meet Again," and then, of course, "Auld Lang Syne."

The handful of fans who had lingered on in the stands stood up and disappeared into the night. It was the last of the lasts. The Milwaukee Braves had buttressed baseball in its years of need, and had been the entity that made Milwaukee as famous for its baseball as for its beer. Now, reality had arrived. The Braves never would be seen again as the home team at County Stadium. The three years of turmoil, starting with the day that the Bill Bartholomay group had bought the Braves and started them on their way to Atlanta, had been, in some ways, abstract, because the Braves were still in Milwaukee. Now, it was real. The Milwaukee Braves really *were* gone.

"If the song is over, though, the melody lingers on," Oliver Kuechele wrote in the *Journal*, "and who knows? Maybe the song itself will return."

Last Tangles, New Beginnings

• • •

ONE MONTH AFTER LODGING IN first place for the last time on August 20 with a 70-50 record, the Braves were in fifth place, nine games out, after the loss to the Dodgers in the County Stadium finale. They had gone 11-21 in the interim, and they had only three sources of motivation as they headed off on their final road trip as the Milwaukee Braves: Beating out the Phillies for fifth place and thus earning modest World Series gate-receipt money for finishing in the first division; enhancing individual portfolios, always a consideration once a team falls out of post-season contention; and serving as obstacles to the Giants and Dodgers as they fought through the final days of the season.

The latter objective was achieved during the weekend of September 24-26, with the Braves winning two of three games at Candlestick Park to drop the Giants into a first-place tie with the Dodgers, who were in the midst of the 15-1 finish that earned them their third NL pennant in their eight seasons in Los Angeles and their fifth in 11 seasons. The Dodgers had been the antithesis of the Giants and Braves, hitting an NL-low 78 home runs - only 26 more than Willie Mays hit by himself - with

Jim Lefebvre and Lou Johnson leading the team with 12 each. Their slugging percentage of .335 was lower than any other team in the league except the 112-loss Mets. But they stole 172 bases, 72 more than anyone else in the league, and their pitching staff - with Don Drysdale at his best and Sandy Koufax beyond anyone's best - had a team ERA of 2.81 with 23 shutouts and led the NL with 58 complete games.

The Braves handed Los Angeles its only loss during that 15-1 binge, with season-long disappointment Denny Lemaster flinging a five-hitter in a 2-0 win at Dodger Stadium on October 1 for his seventh win of the year and the last victory in Milwaukee Braves history. The Dodgers clinched the pennant as Koufax outpitched Cloninger in a 3-1 Los Angeles victory the following day in the next-to-last game of the season and of the Milwaukee Braves' existence. The Dodgers finished with a 97-65 record, two games ahead of the Giants (95-67) and seven games ahead of the Pirates, who had overtaken the Reds for third by posting a league-best 81-48 record after beginning the season 9-24. The Braves (86-76) finished fifth, one-half game ahead of the Phillies and 11 games behind the Dodgers, who went on to win the World Series from the Minnesota Twins, four games to three.

Bud Selig attended the Series games in Minnesota in an attempt to press Milwaukee's case for a new team, but NL president Warren Giles said that his league hadn't even discussed additional expansion since the Colt .45s and Mets had been added in 1962, and AL president Joe Cronin said his league wasn't looking to expand either. In Milwaukee, once the site of municipal baseball obsession at World Series time even if the Braves weren't participating, few paid attention. The *Journal* canvassed some downtown bars during World Series games - all of which were played in the afternoon then - and found virtually no baseball interest in the telecasts among patrons. "We used to pile them in 10 deep, from the TV all the way to that wall back there," one barkeep said, pointing to a wall about 30 feet away. "The smoke was so thick, you could barely see the game." At another bar about a block away, 20 patrons were sipping their beverages, but only two were watching the game, even though the bar had a color-TV set, still relatively rare in 1965. Another patron was asked if he was paying any attention to the game. "What game?" he replied.

● ● ●

While losing 3-0 to the Dodgers on October 3 in the 2,050th and last Milwaukee Braves game, the last of the list of lasts was completed. In an attempt to get Tony Cloninger a 25th victory, Bragan had inserted him into the game in the eighth in place of starting and losing pitcher Bob Sadowski, and Cloninger retired the side in order. The Braves didn't rally on Cloninger's behalf, but Bragan's gesture made Cloninger the last man to take the mound for the Milwaukee Braves. Cloninger also was the last Milwaukee Brave to record a strikeout, fanning Al Ferrara. Mike de la Hoz, as noted at the beginning of this book, made the last Milwaukee Braves out; playing third base with Eddie Mathews given the day off, de la Hoz also made the final Milwaukee Braves error. Sadowski, in addition to being the last Milwaukee Braves starting pitcher and losing pitcher, contributed the Milwaukee Braves' final pickoff and their final wild pitch. Denis Menke was the last Milwaukee Brave to reach base, drawing a walk against

Bill Singer in the eighth, which Woody Woodward led off with the last Milwaukee Braves hit, an infield single.

Cloninger had earned his 23rd win in San Francisco two days after the Braves' home finale, and his 24th in Houston on September 28. As of the end of 2016, only one of the franchise's pitchers had earned more wins in a season since the start of the 20th century - Dick Rudolph, who had gone 26-10 for the World Series-winning "Miracle Braves" in 1914. Johnny Sain in 1948 and John Smoltz in 1996 were, as of 2016, the only other Braves pitchers to have won 24 games in a season since 1900. Warren Spahn's career high was 23 wins, as was Phil Niekro's; Tom Glavine never won more than 22, and Greg Maddux's career best was 20. Cloninger was only 25 years old at the end of the 1965 season - he turned 25 on August 13 - and seemed destined to become to the Atlanta Braves what Spahn had been for so long with the Boston and Milwaukee Braves. But Cloninger, who pitched through arm fatigue and pain so often in 1965, never fully recovered from his 279-inning workload. He was 14-11 in 1966, and then went 32-45 over the next six seasons with the Braves, Reds and Cardinals before retiring after the 1971 season. He is best known to 21st-century fans as the only pitcher to have hit two grand slams in one game, against the Giants at Candlestick Park in 1966.

The Braves at the start of 1965 thought they had a young-rotation base - Cloninger, Wade Blasingame and Denny Lemaster-thatwouldbeaconstantjustastheSpahn-Burdette-Buhl trio had been throughout the 1950s. That didn't work out as planned either. Aside from his 17-win campaign as a 24-year-old in 1964, Lemaster's single-season victory best was 13 for the Astros in 1969, and his final career record was 90-105, though his career ERA was a more-than-respectable 3.58. Of Blasingame's 46 career wins, more than one-third - 16 - came in 1965. Among the pitchers who spent significant time on the Braves' 1965 roster, only the two knuckleballers - Ken Johnson and Phil Niekro - maintained or improved upon their 1965 performance levels. Johnson, who was 13-8 with the Braves and 16-10 overall in 1965, went 14-8 with a 3.21 ERA in 1966 and followed with a 13-9, 2.74 worksheet in '67. After that, he had brief stints with the Yankees, Cubs and Expos before ending his 13-year career after the 1970 season. Niekro, of course, completed his 24-year Hall of Fame career in 1987 with 318 wins. Of those, 268 came in a Braves uniform, but only two came while he was a member of the Milwaukee Braves.

Other than Billy O'Dell, who had 19 saves while closing for the first time in his career, and Sadowski, the Braves' bullpen was marginal at best in 1965. The Braves were in 43 one-run games in 1965 and lost 22 of them - far too many for a team with such offensive firepower. Having another late-inning rescuer like Ted Abernathy might have made a significant difference, especially after O'Dell's output diminished late in the year. On the eve of the 1965 season, the Cleveland Indians had decided to part with Abernathy, a 32-year-old right-handed submariner who originally had signed with the Washington Senators in 1952 and had been in the Braves minor-league system for parts of the 1960 and 1961 seasons. The Indians sold Abernathy to the Cubs, for whom he appeared in 64 games and saved 31 (five against the Braves) in 1965 to lead the league in both categories. Aside from O'Dell, who recorded only three saves after August 8, the Braves bullpen accounted for only 19 saves - four by starting pitchers thrown into emergency breaches, and six by Phil Niekro, who was rarely used in crucial situations until the final two months of the season. (The Braves did trade for Abernathy in May 1966, but Abernathy was minimally effective with Atlanta; he was traded that winter to the Reds, and led the NL in saves with 28 in 1967.)

The Braves also came into the 1965 season thinking their defense would enhance rather than diminish their pitching, but that rarely happened, especially when shortstop Denis Menke was out with injuries. While their 140-error total was fourth-lowest in the league, second baseman Frank Bolling and third baseman Eddie Mathews (both 33 that year) had lost range, and the three most frequently-used first basemen - Joe Torre, Gene Oliver and Felipe Alou - were all out of their natural positions when they played there. The Braves had been forced to trade Maye, an erratic but speedy and lithe outfielder, to get Ken Johnson as a much-needed fourth starting pitcher, and Rico Carty was a liability when he was asked to play left field (and was reluctant when asked to play first base). Most days, the Braves were above average defensively at only two positions - at shortstop with Menke or Woody Woodward, and in right field with Hank Aaron.

Despite the fact they had become the first team in National League history - and only the third in major league history - to have six players on the same team with 20 or more home runs, the 1965 Braves had only four players among the top 30 vote-getters in the Most Valuable Player balloting won by Willie Mays. Aaron, with a .318 average, 32 homers and 82 RBI, finished seventh. Torre (.291-27-80) was 11th, Mathews (.251-32-95) was 20th, and Cloninger was 28th. The Cy Young Award voting was done on a first-place-vote-only basis, and unsurprisingly and deservedly, all 20 votes went to Koufax. One 21st-century statistical-ranking system had Cloninger. despite his 24 wins, as the 16th-best pitcher in baseball in 1965, just behind White Sox knuckleballer Hoyt Wilhelm and just ahead of Claude Osteen, the Dodgers' No. 3 starter.

• • •

The 1965 Braves would wind up with a final attendance count of 555,584 - worst in the NL, but not as bad as the Kansas City A's, who drew 528,344 in what turned out to be their third-to-last season in Kansas City. As of 2016, 11 teams had changed addresses since the Braves' move from Boston to Milwaukee in 1953, and only one - the 1957 Brooklyn Dodgers - had broken the 1 million mark, with 1,028,258. The list of swan-song attendance figures:

1. **957 Brooklyn Dodgers - 1,028,258**. Owner Walter O'Malley didn't formally announce until October that the Dodgers would be moving to Los Angeles for the 1958 season, and throughout the 1957 season, he cynically encouraged the ongoing efforts to keep them in Brooklyn. (He even wore a "Keep The Dodgers in Brooklyn" pin on his lapel.) Although most Dodgers fans understood that the move was a *fait accompli* before the start of the 1957 season, some continued to turn out in the hope that O'Malley and New York City might yet agree to a deal that would keep the Dodgers in, or at least near, Brooklyn. O'Malley, of course, first began to think seriously about moving the Dodgers after watching the newly-transplanted Milwaukee Braves shatter the National League single-season attendance record in 1953.

2. **2004 Montreal Expos - 749,550.** The 1994 players strike and its financial consequences ruined the Expos, who finished that abbreviated season with the best record in baseball. The Expos also failed to gain the support of the Quebec provincial government for a new ballpark, and were operated by the NL during their final three years in Montreal before they became the Washington Nationals in 2005. (The move to Washington for the 2005 season was not final when the Expos opened their last season, but it was generally taken for granted that the NL's operation of the franchise in Montreal would end with the completion of the 2004 schedule.) The Expos had drawn 1,497,609 as recently as 1997, and in 2016, after the Toronto Blue Jays had played several exhibition games before capacity crowds at Olympic Stadium, it was widely believed that major league baseball would be returned to Montreal if a new park could be built. The moribund Oakland and Tampa Bay franchises were considered possible targets.

3. **1960 Washington Senators I - 743,404.** This total actually was the franchise's largest since 1949, and when the team's move to Minnesota was announced a few days after the season, Congress brought pressure to bear on the American League to replace the Senators immediately. This was done within weeks, with the promise of a new ballpark to replace ancient Griffith Stadium, and Washington Senators II (along with the Los Angeles Angels) began play in 1961. This fast-tracking flew in the face of contentions by NL president Warren Giles and commissioner Ford Frick throughout the 1965 season that the Braves could not

be replaced in Milwaukee by an expansion team in time for the 1966 season.

4. **1967 Kansas City Athletics - 726,639.** Unlike Milwaukee - and perhaps *because* of Milwaukee - Kansas City after the 1967 season was promised an expansion team to begin play in 1969 in exchange for the city's commitment to replace Kansas City Municipal Stadium, a converted minor league park. MLB owners thought Kansas City had been underserved by Charles O. Finley and deserved a second chance to prove it could support major league baseball. They were proved correct. Kauffman Stadium, opened in 1973 as Royals Stadium, has been in use ever since (and is still considered state-of-the-art as a major league baseball plant).

5. **1969 Seattle Pilots - 677,944.** The Pilots, of course, lasted only one season in Seattle before becoming the Milwaukee Brewers in 1970. As with Kansas City, the expansion franchise was granted in 1967 with the understanding that Seattle would build a stadium for the team, but the Kingdome wasn't completed until 1976. In the meantime, the franchise went into financial default in early 1970, and Bud Selig bought it from the bankruptcy court that had seized it.

6. **1971 Washington Senators II - 655,156.** Like O'Malley in 1957, Senators owner Bob Short throughout most of the 1971 season duped his team's fans into believing that their presence at RFK Stadium might enhance the team's chances of staying in Washington. Short didn't reveal his true plans until late in the season, and like Walter O'Malley and Bill Bartholomay, Short became a symbol of chicanery and deceit. During and after the Senators'

last home game at RFK, fans burned Short in effigy, tore seats out of their moorings, and finally stormed the field, forcing a forfeit. Aside from Milwaukee, this was the only case where the age and condition of a home ballpark - RFK had opened only nine years earlier - wasn't an issue in a team's move. Short had run his franchise into the ground - just as he had done as owner of the NBA's first dynasty, the Minneapolis Lakers, in the late 1950s. He needed the rescue money provided by Texas investors in 1972 when the team moved to the Dallas-Fort Worth Metroplex and became the Texas Rangers.

7. **1957 New York Giants - 653,923.** Owner Horace Stoneham in July confirmed the long-standing rumors of the team's move to San Francisco. He had originally planned to move the team to Minneapolis-St. Paul, where Metropolitan Stadium had been built in 1956 and where the Giants had the territorial rights because they were the parent club of the American Association's Minneapolis Millers. But O'Malley convinced Stoneham that their teams' rivalry would continue to profit both if it were to be resumed in California, and Stoneham signed on after being promised a new ballpark in San Francisco.

8. **1965 Milwaukee Braves - 555,584.** As indicated throughout this book, the Braves' situation in 1965 was unique in that they were held in place against their will by a court injunction, and in that the team's fans knew beyond even an unreasonable doubt that the franchise would leave at the end of the season, if not before. While the bulk of the Braves' former fan base either was angry with them or ignored them altogether, the fact the Braves drew the total they did was considered a testimonial to

the loyalty of Milwaukee's baseball constituency, not an indictment of it.

9. **1954 Philadelphia Athletics - 304,666.** The A's usually had been Philadelphia's preferred franchise during the 54 seasons that they shared the city with the Phillies, and the A's owned Connie Mack Stadium (formerly Shibe Park) and had rented it to the Phillies since the National League club was forced to leave its former base, Baker Bowl, in 1938. But the combination of the Phillies' "Whiz Kids" pennant in 1950 and the bickering between members of Connie Mack's family over control of the A's enabled the Phillies to outlast the A's. At around the same time, the wealthy Carpenter family had bought the Phillies, and made much-needed ballpark repairs that the A's couldn't have accomplished with their limited financial means.

10. **1953 St. Louis Browns - 297,238.** As in Philadelphia, the wealthier club was a tenant of the poorer franchise in a city that could support only one team, and as described in an earlier chapter, Bill Veeck bought the Browns in 1951 with the intent of pushing the Cardinals out of St. Louis. But the purchase of the Cardinals by the Anheuser-Busch brewery late in 1952 was the end of that idea, and of the Browns, who moved to Baltimore for the 1954 season.

11. **1952 Boston Braves - 281,278.** As recently as 1948, when they won the NL pennant, the Braves had drawn 1,455,439, and owner Lou Perini, a Bostonian, had the financial means with which to compete with the Red Sox for the Boston market. But one of baseball's worst-ever trades had sent Eddie Stanky and Alvin Dark to the Giants after the 1949 season, and the Braves plummeted

in the standings and at the turnstiles, enabling the Red Sox to win the battle for Boston more or less by default.

• • •

The day after the Braves played their final game in Milwaukee, the group that had been Teams Inc formally was introduced in its new incarnation: Milwaukee Brewers Baseball Club, Inc. Seven men paid $150,000 each to buy capital stock in the task-force corporation, which had no other assets other than the copyright of the Milwaukee Brewers name. The seven investors were Bud Selig, Edmund Fitzgerald, clothing manufacturer Jack Winter, Schlitz Brewing Company president Robert Uihlein, food- and department-store executive (and future U.S. Senator and Milwaukee Bucks owner) Herb Kohl, Gateway Transportation Company president John Murphy, and Oscar Meyer Company chairman Oscar G. Meyer. Other than convincing the White Sox to play a total of 20 "home" games at County Stadium in 1968 and 1969, the new corporation could do little except gauge opportunities, attempt to take advantage of the fact other franchises (including the White Sox) were contemplating moves, and try to sell owners on Milwaukee as a logical location for an expansion franchise. The latter objective, Selig and his partners knew, was remote at best because of the tumult and the litigation that had accompanied the Braves' exit from Milwaukee. The only thing that was certain in October 1965 was that County Stadium would not house baseball in 1966; as soon as the Braves' last season in Milwaukee was over, stadium manager William Anderson gave the go-ahead to begin the sand-blasting of the stadium's outer framework. This work was completed in early 1966, after the Packers' NFL season ended.

Yet even though the antitrust legislation had soured baseball's leadership on Milwaukee as a site for a new or transplanted franchise, hope remained that baseball might return to Milwaukee at some point. Bill Bartholomay had attended the Braves' final home game in Milwaukee, and said he would not object to Milwaukee obtaining another team. Assistant general manager Jim Fanning also denied that baseball would invoke a "freeze-out" of Milwaukee, as sportswriter Jim Enright had asserted in a column in the *Chicago American*. "That's ridiculous, the idea of freezing out a state," Fanning said. "I don't know who (Enright) was quoting, but it wasn't me."

Nevertheless, MLB in 1968 allowed the Kansas City Athletics to move to Oakland, thereby compromising the financial stability of the San Francisco Giants and creating another two-team confrontation in a market that quickly showed it would only support one team unless both the teams were of championship caliber. Baseball also granted 1969 expansion franchises to Seattle, Montreal, Kansas City and San Diego even though only the latter city had a permanent ballpark in place or even under construction.

• • •

Within a month of the Braves' last home game at County Stadium, more pressing events had taken precedence over the ongoing legal maneuverings over Milwaukee's baseball future. As head of MUSIC (the Milwaukee United School Integration Committee), Milwaukee attorney and state Assemblyman Lloyd Barbee had seen little integrational progress by the Milwaukee Public Schools administration or governing board, and had called for Milwaukee parents and children to boycott classes for at least a week starting October 18. (The previous year, a one-day boycott had been observed by as many as 15,000 students, depending on the source of figures quoted.) The district maintained it had made a commitment to better schools for black children by funding 127 new rooms and nine interior renovations within 15 inner-core schools since 1958. The district had built 50 new schools since 1950 and was in the process of building 13 more. But a *Journal* investigative team that was exploring what would come to be called "hypersegregation" in Milwaukee schools and housing pointed to the example of 12th Street School, which in 1959 had undergone a thorough renovation that included a new wing. Of the 757 students at the school, all except three were black, and all five stories of the school had broken windows. Segregation, *de facto* or otherwise, remained fact in Milwaukee.

Another story questioned the veracity of the board's assertion that children in predominantly black schools were getting the same educational opportunities and support as their counterparts in predominantly white schools. North Division High, which was almost exclusively black in 1965, had only two foreign-language offerings - Spanish and Latin - while Pulaski High, which served the south side and was 99.9 percent white, offered French, Polish, German, Latin and Spanish. Marilyn Morhouser, a civil rights leader in the city, said she had visited Roosevelt Junior High, a predominantly black school. In a classroom, she said, she had found a world globe that showed the Ottoman and Austro-Hungarian empires, both of which had ceased to exist in 1918 at the end of World War I. Music and arts programs were minimal at inner-core schools, if they existed at all; in contrast,

Greendale High - built in 1953 to serve the federally financed and planned city that had been built on the southwest edge of the county in the late 1930s - had 700 students, 400 of whom were enrolled in music classes.

In announcing the boycott, Barbee said MUSIC's aim was to create a sense among all parties that the racial imbalance in Milwaukee's public schools was morally, educationally and constitutionally wrong. "I'm for gerrymandering for integration," he said, referring to artificial stimuli such as mandatory busing to address racial imbalance in public schools. "This may be unpopular, but it's the price we have to pay to correct this situation." Barbee's remarks got him into a war of words with school board president John Foley and superintendent Harold Vincent, among other MPS officials, with Foley saying: "We will not be coerced into establishing board policy by threat of any kind and particularly by an illegal act (the proposed boycott)." Mayor Henry Maier called the boycott "Ku Klux Klanism in reverse" - whereupon Barbee called Maier "bankrupt" on civil rights, saying that Maier's record "ranges from a mere whisper to a whining whimper." Foley said the boycott would be "a cruel act (and) an illegal act per se. It breeds disrespect and contempt for lawful authority in the minds of innocent children."

The boycott went off as scheduled on October 18, but lasted only three days instead of a week or more, as MUSIC had intended. About 16,000 student absences were reported during the three days, with children instead attending "freedom schools" set up hastily by MUSIC and other integrationist organizations. No problems were reported at either the conventional or "freedom" schools, but the conflict came close to turning violent on the night of October 19, when Father James Groppi, who was white, emerged as a leading civil-rights activist by leading a mostly black procession into an almost-all-white south side neighborhood. They were met with signs, profanity-laced tirades and some thrown projectiles, but nobody was injured. The federal anti-discrimination lawsuit that Barbee had filed in 1965 ended with a judgment in favor of the plaintiffs in 1976, but it mattered little by then because the *de facto* segregation that Barbee and MUSIC had opposed was too deeply entrenched to be undone by judicial or legislative means.

Eventually, that *de facto* segregation would spread to other parts of Milwaukee as the "white flight" to the suburbs accelerated in Milwaukee and many other large cities throughout the country. Milwaukee's long-standing manufacturing base was still in place, and despite the educational and demographic imbalances, the unemployment rate held steady at 2.7 percent (compared to the national average of 4.4 percent, and the lowest in Milwaukee since 1956) at the end of October 1965. Some neighborhoods, such as the one adjoining Sherman Park in the north-by-northwest part of the city, maintained their equilibrium into the 1970s because jobs were so readily available and many homebuyers stayed there over lengthy periods and collectively built a true sense of neighborhood. But that changed with the erosion of Milwaukee's industrial base in the 1970s and 1980s.

The Menomonee River, Milwaukee's industrial lifeline, because an ecological calamity by the end of the 1970s, and that contributed to the decline of the heavy industry that adjoined the river. The closure of Allis-Chalmers, once an employer of 25,000, in 1987 after more than a decade of hermorraging jobs, was one of the final blows as once-comfortable neighborhoods became enclaves of poverty, desolation and despair. The A.O. Smith plant that once had employed 15,000, and had been the nation's largest manufacturer of car and truck frames, had downsized to 6,000 workers by 1983. (By 2016 A.O. Smith, which was founded in 1874, had switched direction entirely, having become the world's largest manufacturer of water heaters, and although it was providing 13,000 jobs, many of those were outside Wisconsin.) The Milwaukee Road Shops, which had made train cars and locomotives since 1928, shut down in 1985. Three of the city's primary breweries - Pabst, Schlitz and Blatz - ceased operations. And despite the start in 1976 of court-ordered busing intended to alleviate segregation in Milwaukee's schools, the black-white separation became hypersegregation. Nowhere in the country in 2016 was there a greater disparity between the graduation rates and academic-achievement levels of black and white students. The same was true of the disparity between the unemployment rates of white and black adults.

In August 2016, a fatal shooting of a local man by a Milwaukee police officer touched off two nights of violence in the Sherman Park neighborhood that injured 16 law-enforcement officers, resulted in the burning of six of the few businesses still operating in the area, and prompted state and local law-enforcement officials to activate the National Guard. The National Guard was not deployed, and the disorder was not on a level with the 1967 riot that started a few miles from the 2016 flashpoint, but like the '67 unrest, it bluntly illustrated the degree to which Milwaukee was divided along racial lines.

• • •

Meanwhile, the Vietnam War continued to escalate in the final months of 1965. By the end of September, six Wisconsinites, including four from Milwaukee, had been killed since President Johnson had escalated a containment action into a full-scale war. One of those killed was Sgt. Thaddeus Zajac, 21, whose family lived on South 15th Street. Zajac, 29, had less than a month to go on his tour of combat. The day he died, his family received a letter from him indicating that he was in good health and was not in immediate danger. Opposition to the war, scattered at the beginning of the year, by October was mobilizing, and the American involvement and particularly the leadership of LBJ, Secretary of Defense Robert McNamara and commander of Vietnam forces William Westmoreland were being questioned on a far broader scale than had been the case at the beginning of the year. "The war in Vietnam is a farce," one letter to the *Journal* from reader Al Rothmann declared. "It is a war that will rank with the worst acts against mankind, and we as a nation will have lost all Asia as friends after this filthy war is over ... Vietnam will be remembered as the American atrocity war, mark my words." By the start of October, 140,000 U.S. troops would be stationed in Southeast Asia, and a "combat-ready" backup force of 145,000 was in training. In all, 1,161 Wisconsin service personnel died in the war before the last U.S. forces evacuated Saigon in 1975.

• • •

With the expiration of their lease at County Stadium, the Braves at last were freed to complete their move to Atlanta, where they already had transferred most of their employees and operations. But their organizational torpor during their final years in Milwaukee continued to manifest itself in earnest in Atlanta, where the team's new fan base saw essentially the same club that had wallowed in mediocrity during its final years in Milwaukee. Of the Braves' nine starters in their debut at Atlanta-Fulton County Stadium on April 12, 1966, only one - first baseman Lee Thomas, a 30-year-old itinerant who had been obtained from the Red Sox for Dan Osinski and Bob Sadowski in an off-season trade - had not been a Milwaukee Brave. The Braves' Opening Day lineup in 1966 read: Felipe Alou, center field; Eddie Mathews, third base; Hank Aaron, right field; Rico Carty, left field; Joe Torre, catcher; Denis Menke, shortstop; Thomas, first base; Frank Bolling, second base; and Tony Cloninger, pitcher.

Bartholomay and his group had claimed they lost $1.5 million in 1965 because the courts had forced them to honor the final year of their County Stadium lease. Whether or not that loss was in actual cash or in paper-ledger debits and tax write-offs, the fact was that the Braves in 1966 were no more active in terms of improving the team than they had been during their decline in Milwaukee. The Braves did make more changes during their first year in Atlanta than they had in 1965, using 44 players - 19 of whom were new to the organization and/or to the major leagues. Of those 19 newcomers, only four players, all rookies, had any significant impact on the franchise. Second baseman Felix Millan became a three-time All-Star and two-time Gold Glove winner. Starting pitcher Ron Reed, who came up for two games at the end of the 1966 season, won 18 games in 1969 as the Braves won the National League West. Pat Jarvis, who didn't make his major league debut until age 25, notched 83 wins for the Braves over seven seasons. Cecil Upshaw, who pitched three innings in his only game with the Braves in 1966, had 70 saves over four seasons as the Braves' closer in the late 1960s and early 1970s.

Otherwise, fans at Atlanta-Fulton County Stadium found themselves watching the likes of John Herrnstein, George Kopacz, Arnold Umbach, Lee Bales, Jay Ritchie, and Joey Jay (the onetime Braves bonus baby who ended his major league career by making nine starts for the '66 Braves, going 0-4 with a 7.89 ERA). The Braves led the NL in home runs for the second straight year, with 207, including 44 by Aaron, 36 by Torre and 31 by Alou. But they were no more diversified offensively in their first year in Atlanta than they had been in their last year in Milwaukee, and it didn't take long for Bartholomay and his partners to realize that Atlanta would not be the epiphany for which they had longed for more than three years. They soon found that Southern sports fans cared far more about the Southeastern Conference and NASCAR than they did about the National League. Moreover, the team itself was in full-scale decline in 1966, and that decline would become precipitous. On June 3, the Braves were in ninth place with a 20-30 record, and Bobby Bragan was fired on August with his 52-59 team in seventh place, 12 1/2 games out of first. Frank Bolling retired at the end of the season, and John McHale resigned as general manager on January 11, 1967. Eddie Mathews, at age 34, had career lows of 16 homers, 50 RBI and 134 games played while batting .250 in 1966, and was traded to Houston in December for Bob Bruce and Dave Nicholson. He moved on to Detroit later in 1967, and in 1968, his final major league season, he earned his second World Series ring, although he batted only .212 for the Tigers while hitting the last three of his 512 home runs.

The Braves drew 50,671 for their Atlanta debut, and 12,721 - only a handful more than had attended the Milwaukee Braves' last home game - for their game the next night. Their attendance for the season was 1,539,801, good only for sixth in the 10-team NL, and almost 300,000 fewer than the Braves had attracted in 1953 during their first season in Milwaukee. And it would be their highest turnstile count in Atlanta until 1982, the year the team won only its second division title since arriving in Atlanta. (The first had come in 1969, when the Braves won the NL West but were swept in the inaugural National League Championship Series by the New York Mets.) In 1975, the year before Bartholomay sold the team to television mogul Ted Turner, only 534,672 customers trudged into the ballpark - fewer than the Braves had drawn in Milwaukee in 1965. It wasn't until Turner bought the team and nationalized it with his WTBS "Super Station" in the early 1980s that the Bartholomay group's vision of a cable-TV monopoly in (and beyond) the Deep South finally became reality.

Atlanta-Fulton County Stadium, which loomed as a revenue stream and an attraction unto itself at the time the Braves moved in, hosted major league baseball only until 1996, after which the Braves moved into the main 1996 Olympics stadium, which was reconfigured for baseball and named Turner Field. Atlanta-Fulton County Stadium was torn down in 1997, while Milwaukee County Stadium, the venue that the Atlanta park was supposed to render obsolete, stayed in use until it was demolished after the 2000 season to make way for Miller Park. The Braves were set to move *again* in 2017, this time to a suburban ballpark more than a half-hour's drive from downtown Atlanta. And while their 14 straight division titles from 1991-2005 (excluding the strike-shortened 1994 season) represented a sustained run that superseded even those of the mighty Yankees teams from 1921-64, the total of World Series championships that the Braves won in Atlanta at the end of the 2016 season remained exactly what it had been during their 13 seasons in Milwaukee - one.

In Milwaukee, some Braves fans switched their allegiance to other teams, especially after the White Sox moved a total of 20 "home" games to Milwaukee in 1968 and 1969, and indicated they might be interested in moving into County Stadium on a fulltime basis. The Cubs, of course, had thought they would benefit from the Braves' departure, and some fans began following the Cubs more closely after they became contenders under Leo Durocher in the late 1960s. Said Bill Streicher in 2016: "I never went to Wrigley Field for a baseball game ... haven't gone to this day and I really don't have any desire to. But what did happen was that after the Braves left, people started listening to the Cubs. They played only day games then, of course, and you could pick up WGN radio very easily. You could pick up a fuzzy picture on WGN TV here too if you were on the south side and wriggled the rabbit ears on your TV just right." But most Wisconsin fans understandably found it difficult to form even a minimal attachment to any Chicago team. They either yearned for the return of major league baseball to Milwaukee, or swore off the sport altogether.

• • •

If Bartholomay and Atlanta thought that their move to Atlanta would enable them to sidestep the litigation - and particularly the antitrust suits - that had dogged them throughout their final year in Milwaukee, they were very much mistaken. Led by Milwaukee County, Wisconsin jurisdictions pressed their fight to nullify baseball's antitrust exemption even after the Milwaukee Braves ceased to exist. They came closer - one judicial vote - to doing so than any antitrust plaintiff since the U.S. Supreme Court's original landmark ruling in 1922 had declared that baseball was not interstate commerce and therefore wasn't subject to the Sherman Antitrust Act.

J. Gordon Hylton, the former Marquette law professor who has researched and written extensively about the case, offered this synopsis on a blog post in 2012:

Forty-six years ago, the baseball world trained its attention on the Wisconsin Supreme Court and its impending decision in the case of Wisconsin v. Milwaukee Braves, Inc., soon to be reported at 31 Wis. 2d 699, 144 N.W.2d 1 (1966). At issue was whether a Milwaukee trial judge, acting on behalf of the State of Wisconsin, could prevent the Milwaukee Braves Major League Baseball team from relocating to Atlanta, Georgia. After the team's Chicago-based owners had announced their plans to move to Atlanta for the 1966 season, a criminal action was filed in Milwaukee County Circuit Court. It alleged that the Braves and the other nine teams in the National League had conspired to deprive the City of Milwaukee of Major League Baseball and, moreover, had agreed that no replacement team would be permitted for the city. Thus, the complaint alleged, the defendants were in violation of the Wisconsin antitrust law. The defendants initially removed the lawsuit to the United States District Court for the Eastern District of Wisconsin, but on December 9, 1965, District Judge Robert Tehan remanded the case to the state court. There trial was conducted before Judge (and former Marquette Law School professor) Elmer W. Roller.

On April 12, 1966, only hours before the Braves were to open the season with a game against the Pittsburgh Pirates in Atlanta, Judge Roller ruled that the owners of the Braves and the other National League teams had acted in "restraint of trade" and thus were in violation of the Wisconsin antitrust law. Roller fined the defendants $55,000, plus costs, and enjoined the Braves from playing their 1966 home games anywhere other than Milwaukee unless the National League agreed to place a new team in Milwaukee in 1967. To give the National League time to make arrangements for an expansion team for 1967, Roller stayed his judgment until mid-June, an act that allowed the Braves to continue playing in Atlanta. The Braves' owners immediately appealed Roller's decision to the Wisconsin Supreme Court, which agreed to hear the case on an expedited basis. On June 9, 1966, the appeal was argued - a day on which the Braves, who never had a losing season while in Milwaukee, sat in sixth place in the National League with a record of 25-30. With the stay extended, the Braves continued to play in Atlanta, and six weeks later, on July 27, a day that would see the Braves slumping all the way down to eighth place, the Wisconsin Supreme Court overturned Roller's lower court ruling by a narrow vote of 4-3. (Justice E. Harold Hallows, also formerly a law professor at Marquette, was one of the three dissenters who would have sustained Roller's injunction against the move to Atlanta.)

The Court's majority opinion was based on two different rationales, and the Court explained that one was embraced by two justices and the second by two others. The first rationale was that organized baseball's exemption from the federal antitrust laws, most recently upheld by the U.S. Supreme Court in Toolson v. New York Yankees (1953), extended to state antitrust rules as well. The alternative theory concluded that even if organized baseball was not exempt from state antitrust regulation generally, the portion of the remedy imposed by Judge

Roller that ordered the National League either to return the Braves to Milwaukee or else to give the city a new team ran afoul of the United States Constitution's Commerce Clause and constituted an unenforceable interference with interstate commerce.

The majority did not dispute Roller's findings of fact concerning the monopolization of baseball in Milwaukee. The three dissenters disagreed with both of the theories in the majority opinion and concluded instead that Congress should be presumed to have left the regulation of baseball to the states until it explicitly exercised its own regulatory authority. They also maintained that the legitimate interests of the State of Wisconsin in this case took priority over the "restrictive effect on interstate commerce that might result from the enforcement of Wisconsin's laws." Not willing to concede defeat after such a narrow loss, the State of Wisconsin sought review in the United States Supreme Court. However, while the state's petition for a writ of certiorari was pending, Judge Roller's lower court order was dissolved, and the Braves were free to play out the season in their new southern home. Although the Braves lost again on July 28, to fall into ninth place, the Wisconsin Supreme Court decision seemed to clear away the cloud of bad play that had hung over the team all season. The Braves played inspired baseball the rest of the season, and ended up with a record of 85-77, good for fifth place in the 10-team league and within 10 games of the pennant-winning Los Angeles Dodgers.

Milwaukeeans had to wait until December 12 to learn that the United States Supreme Court had denied the state's petition for certiorari. However, in an uncharacteristic move, the Court revealed that it was badly divided on whether to hear the case. Justices William O. Douglas, Hugo Black, and William J. Brennan, Jr., were in favor of hearing the case, but certiorari was opposed by Chief Justice Earl

Warren and Justices Tom C. Clark, John Marshall Harlan II, Potter Stewart, and Byron White. Although he had taken the oath of office as a Supreme Court justice on October 4, Justice Abe Fortas, according to the Court's announcement, "took no part in the consideration or decision of this petition." In any event, the attempt to involve the nation's highest court died as a result of the failure of a fourth justice to support the petition.

In another unusual development, Wisconsin filed a petition requesting that the Court rehear the petition for certiorari, perhaps in hopes that Fortas might be now willing to support the petition, but rehearing also was denied. On January 23, 1967, the litigation over the Braves' departure finally came to an end when the Court simply announced that the rehearing petition had been denied and that Justice Fortas had not participated in the review. Thus, by late January, it was clear that the city of Milwaukee would be without major league baseball for 1967. When the National League announced in November 1967 that it would be adding two additional teams for the 1969 season, Milwaukee applied for one of the franchises, as did groups from Dallas-Fort Worth, Denver, Buffalo, San Diego, Toronto, and Montreal. However, when the two new franchises were awarded in May 1968, the National League ignored Milwaukee and awarded teams to San Diego and Montreal. As a result, except for a total of 20 Chicago White Sox games played in County Stadium in 1968-1969, Milwaukee remained without Major League Baseball until 1970. That, of course, is when Bud Selig and his associates bought the bankrupt Seattle Pilots shortly before Opening Day and moved the one-year-old American League team to Milwaukee, where they were renamed the Brewers.

Was there anything that could have been done to prevent the situation that resulted in the Braves' departure? The real aberration in

Milwaukee baseball history was the attendance figures of 1953–1959, not those for 1960–1965. Given its population, Major League Baseball attendance in Milwaukee in the early 1960s, at least through 1964, was actually pretty good. Selling the team to owners with no commitment to Milwaukee in 1962 probably made it inevitable that the team would soon be relocated to a larger, more lucrative market.

Baseball's antitrust exemption would come under attack again in the early 1970s, when Cardinals star Curt Flood sued to become a free agent after the Cardinals traded him to the Philadelphia Phillies following the 1969 season. Players then were subject to the so-called reserve clause, which bound them indefinitely to the team to which they were under contract unless they were sold, traded or released. Flood lost that case, though it opened the way for an arbitrator's ruling in the mid-1970s that eliminated the reserve clause and soon led to relatively unfettered free agency.

• • •

Of course, by the time the Milwaukee Braves were officially and legally consigned to memories and court files in 1967, there was little if any interest in Milwaukee in actually bringing them back, and only lukewarm interest in Milwaukee regaining major league baseball at any time in the immediate future. By the time Bud Selig and Milwaukee Brewers Baseball Club, Inc., brought the Seattle Pilots to Milwaukee in 1970, the city and the region already had undergone upheaval on the political, demographic and economic fronts, and would undergo many more changes in the decades to follow. None of those changes had much, if anything, to do with baseball, and while the early Milwaukee

Braves had thrived on the field and broken MLB attendance records, the nascent Brewers struggled to build a support base of
their own. They didn't reach the 1 million mark in attendance
until 1973, their fourth American League season, and they didn't
record a winning season until 1978, the franchise's ninth year in
Milwaukee. As of the end of the 2016 season, they had won only
one pennant (in the American League in 1982) and had reached
the postseason only four times in 47 seasons in Milwaukee.

Yet in 1983, with a fifth-place, 87-75 team, the Brewers surpassed the highest-ever Milwaukee Braves attendance total, with
2,397,131 paid admissions, and after the opening of Miller Park
(on what had been the County Stadium parking lot) in 2001, their
attendance counts had surpassed the 2 million mark every year
since 2004 even though they were playing in the smallest media
market in major league baseball (and in a city that lost more than
100,000 in population from 1960-2010), and had registered only
five winning records in 16 seasons at Miller Park at the end of
2016. In 2008, 2009 and 2011, the Brewers played before more
than 3 million fans at home.

The fact the Braves ever called Milwaukee home is known
faintly at best to one generation of Wisconsin baseball fans, and
remembered only through a mist by most members of the generation before. The Brewers in 2016 completed their 47th season
in Milwaukee, while the Braves were there for only 13 seasons.
The Milwaukee Braves' final season, 1965, is little more than a
postscript in virtually all that has been written and said about
the Milwaukee Braves team that, with 12 more victories over
three seasons, could have become the only team other than the
Yankees to win four straight World Series.

The year 1965 marked the end of a team - and, for many, a way of life - that turned out to be only temporary. Yet in many ways, it also represented a more permanent beginning.

Made in the USA
Lexington, KY
27 March 2017